A refreshing new look at autonomy regimes as a possible response to secessionist and irredentist claims around the world.

Donald Rothchild, University of California, Davis

Weller and Wolff provide a comprehensive collection on autonomy arrangements, covering a rich range of institutional variations, as well as several different parts of the globe. The importance of their subject can hardly be exaggerated, as autonomy often remains the only choice between the unwanted incorporation of minorities on the one hand, and the disintegration of states on the other.

Professor John McGarry, Canada Research Chair in Nationalism and Democracy, Queen's University, Canada

Autonomy, Self-governance and Conflict Resolution

This book compares and contrasts recent cases from Europe, Africa, Asia and Latin America in which new forms of autonomy regimes have been implemented in ethnically diverse societies.

Acknowledging the significance of recent developments in the design of complex and innovative autonomy regimes and focusing on different options that are available for their design, this book makes an important contribution to, and moves forward, the current debate among scholars and practitioners on institutional design in ethnically diverse societies by:

- Establishing the role of institutional design in ethnically diverse societies;
- Analysing in-depth a key approach to state construction in ethnically diverse societies – the creation of autonomy regimes – and assessing its applicability from the perspective of viable political institutions;
- Examining recent cases from Europe, Asia and Latin America in which new forms of autonomy regimes have contributed to peace and stability in ethnically diverse societies;
- Comparing and contrasting, on the basis of in-depth case studies, the features that characterise successful institutional design of autonomy regimes in ethnically diverse societies;
- Assessing the current state of the theory and practice of institutional design in ethnically diverse societies.

Autonomy, Self-governance and Conflict Resolution will interest students and researchers of governance, ethnic conflict and nationalism.

Marc Weller is the Director of the European Centre for Minority Issues, in Flensburg, Germany, and both a fellow and lecturer in international law and relations at the University of Cambridge. **Stefan Wolff** is Professor of Political Science at the University of Bath.

Routledge advances in international relations and global politics

Autonomy, Self-governance and Conflict Resolution

Innovative approaches to institutional design in divided societies

Edited by Marc Weller and Stefan Wolff

Routledge
Taylor & Francis Group

LONDON AND NEW YORK

First published 2005
by Routledge
2 Park Square, Milton Park, Abingdon, Oxon, OX14 4RN

Simultaneously published in the USA and Canada
by Routledge
270 Madison Ave, New York NY 10016

Routledge is an imprint of the Taylor & Francis Group

Transferred to Digital Printing 2008

Typeset in Baskerville by Wearset Ltd, Boldon, Tyne and Wear

British Library Cataloguing in Publication Data
A catalogue record for this book is available from the British Library

Library of Congress Cataloging in Publication Data
Autonomy, self-governance, and conflict resolution : innovative
approaches to institutional design in divided societies / edited by
Marc Weller and Stefan Wolff.
        p. cm.
    Includes bibliographical references and index.
    1. Autonomy. 2. Self-determination, National. 3. Ethnic
conflict–Political aspects. 4. Conflict management. I. Weller, M.
(Marc) II. Wolff, Stefan, 1969–
    JC327.A893 2005
    320.1′5–dc22

                                                    2004020261

ISBN 0-415-33986-3

Publisher's Note
The publisher has gone to great lengths to ensure the quality of this
reprint but points out that some imperfections in the original
may be apparent

Contents

Illustrations

Figures

Tables

Contributors

Willem Assies is Research Professor at the Colegio de Michoacán, Mexico.

Bill Bowring, a practising English barrister, is Professor of Human Rights and International Law at London Metropolitan University, where he also directs the University's Human Rights and Social Justice Research Institute.

Wolfgang F. Danspeckgruber is the founding director of the Liechtenstein Institute on Self-Determination at Princeton University and teaches international relations at Princeton's Woodrow Wilson School of Public and International Affairs. He is also founder and chairman of the Liechtenstein Colloquium on European and International Affairs, Vaduz, a private diplomacy forum.

Erik Friberg is a Research Fellow at the Centre for Strategic and International Studies in Jakarta, Indonesia.

Elisabeth Nauclér is the Head of Administration in the Government of the Åland Islands, Finland.

Mark Turner is Professor of Development Policy and Management at the University of Canberra, Australia.

Marc Weller is a Lecturer in the Centre of International Studies in the University of Cambridge, a Fellow of the Lauterpacht Research Centre for International Law and of Hughes Hall and the Director of the European Centre for Minority Issues.

Stefan Wolff is Professor of Political Science at the University of Bath in England and Senior Nonresident Research Associate at the European Centre for Minority Issues in Flensburg, Germany.

1 Self-determination and autonomy

A conceptual introduction

Stefan Wolff and Marc Weller

Introduction

Autonomy is neither a new phenomenon, nor has it been understudied. However, up to the period of time when the post-Cold War transitions in Central, Eastern and South Eastern Europe were beginning, it appeared to be at best a highly unusual tool of state construction, or at worst a highly dangerous one. It was seen to be unusual, inasmuch as autonomy generally seemed to be attached to fairly obscure, historical examples, born out of very distinctive historical settings. Often autonomy regimes operated in remote or otherwise geographically unique locations, such as islands (for example, the Åland autonomy) or enclaves (for example, Klaipeda). These types of cases, it was widely believed, could not offer a great deal by way of guidance in less unique circumstances. Even the few new autonomies that were established after World War II, such as South Tyrol, were until recently taken to be too dependent on the special local conditions to be of wider interest. Similarly, the Soviet and other socialist autonomies were taken to be too deeply rooted in ideology, rather than genuine practice, to be of wider applicability.

Autonomy was also not given a great deal of consideration because the concept was, rightly or wrongly, associated with self-determination struggles. Outside of the colonial context, any self-determination discourse was viewed with great suspicion by governments, seeing it as a first step onto that slippery slope that inevitably leads towards irredentist or secessionist claims. Thus, autonomy was widely regarded as a somewhat dangerous concept that a state would only employ at its own peril.

Since the end of the Cold War, this climate has changed somewhat. In the transitional states of Central and Eastern Europe, the almost simultaneous breakdown of mechanisms of external (through the Warsaw Pact Organisation) and internal control (through dictatorial forms of government) led to the re-emergence of the so-called national minority question. In Georgia, Moldova, the new Russian Federation, and in relations between Armenia and Azerbaijan, the doctrine of territorial integrity was undermined by intense armed conflict. These conflicts, framed in the rhetoric of self-determination, and the prospect (and subsequently the reality) of the dissolution of Yugoslavia added to the perceived threat to the principle of territorial integrity.

In response, autonomy was re-discovered as a potential remedy to self-determination claims. It was now no longer seen as the secessionists' stepping stone towards independence, but instead, in a 180-degree reversal of the previous position, autonomy was now considered as a possible tool in accommodating separatist movements without endangering the continued territorial integrity of an existing state. In 1990, the member states of the Conference on Security and Cooperation in Europe (CSCE), as it then was, were still cautious when noting

> the efforts undertaken to protect and create conditions for the promotion of the ethnic, cultural, linguistic and religious identity of certain national minorities by establishing, as one of the possible means to achieve these aims, appropriate local or autonomous administrations corresponding to the specific historical and territorial circumstances of such minorities and in accordance with the policies of the State concerned.
>
> (Article 35 (2), 1990 Copenhagen Document of the Conference on the Human Dimension of the CSCE)

But by 1991, the governments of the member states of the European Community (EC) went further in endorsing autonomy as a means of addressing minority issues and ethnic conflict when establishing conditions for recognition of the new states of Central and Eastern Europe emerging from the dissolution of the Soviet Union, the separation of Czechoslovakia and the disintegration of Yugoslavia. In two declarations on European Political Cooperation, one addressing all of Central and Eastern Europe, the other pertaining to Yugoslavia, minority rights and, to a certain extent, autonomy for national minority groups was prescribed as part of the price that the states of that region might have to pay for diplomatic relations with the member states and institutions of the EC. This demand built upon the work of the EC Peace Conference on Yugoslavia. Through that conference, the EC member states attempted to achieve an agreed dissolution of the Socialist Federal Republic of Yugoslavia. Serbia was the only republic vigorously opposed to this approach. In an effort to address Serb concerns, two successive peace plans provided by Lord Carrington, the Chair of the Conference, offered autonomy arrangements for Serb communities living outside the boundaries of the Serbian Republic within the crumbling Socialist Federal Republic of Yugoslavia.

In the meantime, autonomy as a tool of state construction was of course being applied, discussed and analysed outside the context of the former Yugoslavia as well. Some states in Western Europe have embraced autonomy (or devolution) as a means of maintaining their territorial integrity.

In addition to the more established case of Belgium, Spain and the United Kingdom have also made startling progress in this direction. Even central-ist France has attempted to move towards autonomy as a means of address-ing the Corsica conflict. A number of innovative settlements have been adopted in relation to other areas of conflict or ethnic tension, some of which are principally autonomy-based, such as Gagauzia in the Republic of Moldova or Crimea in Ukraine. Autonomy structures also play a part in several new models of more complex forms of power-sharing that can be found in Northern Ireland, and further afield, in the framework agree-ment for Sudan and in Bougainville and Mindanao.

More widespread implementation of autonomy regimes as mechanisms to address self-determination conflicts have been complemented by an increased scholarly interest and output in this respect, with several significant scholarly works on autonomy published over the past decade.[1] In terms of standard-setting, the Organisation on Security and Coopera-tion in Europe (OSCE, the successor organisation of the CSCE) has also maintained an interest in the issue. Its *Lund Recommendations* provide perhaps the most comprehensive reference to autonomy as a means of good governance and state construction in an authoritative international document thus far. Moreover, the United Nations General Assembly has addressed itself to this – previously altogether too delicate – topic in the shape of the *Liechtenstein Initiative on Self-determination through Self-administration,* which seeks to offer autonomy as an alternative to seces-sionist self-determination claims. The United Nations Working Group on Minorities has also been cautiously addressing the issue of autonomy.

Thus, developments over the past decade and a half seem to indicate that there is renewed interest among scholars and practitioners to engage with the thorny issue of autonomy alongside an apparently increasing willingness among major actors in the international community to recommend, and where necessary impose, autonomy regimes on states that might otherwise collapse under the pressure of self-determination conflicts. Increasingly, autonomy is also made available in situations where a self-determination conflict has not yet fully developed. While self-determination conflicts are characterised by a claim to a unilateral change in status, in other instances, ethnic groups may merely be seeking a greater expression of their identity within the state. This can take the form of a claim to enhanced regional or local self-governance.

Taken together, these two trends make it now possible to consider auto-nomy as a means of state construction that does not always, and of neces-sity, have to raise the spectre of self-determination struggles and ultimate secession. Instead, autonomy is just seen as one element of state construc-tion addressing the needs of diverse communities.

Accordingly, this book attempts to test the proposition that autonomy, including territorial autonomy, can substitute for self-determination dis-course within states. Of course, we do not proceed from the simple assumption that autonomy in itself will be a simple substitute for secessionist tendencies. Instead, autonomy needs to be an element of well-balanced constitutional design that matches the sense of regional self-administration and identity with the strengthening of an interest within the autonomous entity in the success of the overall state.

This introductory chapter outlines our core assumptions about the nature and determinants of self-determination conflicts and campaigns for enhanced self-governance. These are then linked to the different models of state designs that are principally built around autonomy solutions. The introduction first examines ethnicity and territory – two of the key determinants of many self-determination conflicts or campaigns for enhanced self-governance. While we are aware that not all such conflicts are per se ethnic in their nature, most of them are, in one way or another, conflicts between communities that distinguish themselves from one another by 'ethnic' criteria, such as language, religion, culture, etc. Self-determination conflicts and campaigns for enhanced self-governance will, by definition, appear to focus on a struggle for control over territory. In the more extreme manifestations, these can take the form of secessionist and irredentist conflicts; they can also manifest themselves as, or be combined with, a struggle for territorial control and/or 'ethnic purity', leading to policies of ethnic cleansing. Thus, tensions or conflicts, and their potential solutions covered in this volume, are characterised by the politicisation of ethnicity and territory.

Ethnicity

An ethnic group is 'a type of cultural collectivity, one that emphasises the role of myths of descent and historical memories, and that is recognised by one or more cultural differences like religion, customs, language, or institutions' (Smith 1991: 20). As a self-defined community, ethnic groups are distinguishable by a collective name, a myth of common ancestry, shared historical memories, one or more differentiating elements of common culture, the association with a specific homeland, and a sense of solidarity for significant sectors of the population (Smith 1991: 21).

Key to understanding the political implications of ethnic identity and of the formation of conflict groups based on ethnicity is the link between the tangible and intangible aspects of ethnic identity. Connor (1994: 104) has noted that tangible characteristics are only important inasmuch as they 'contribute to this notion or sense of a group's self-identity and uniqueness'. In turn, then, a threat to, or opportunity for, these tangibles, real or perceived, is considered as a threat to, or opportunity for, self-identity and uniqueness. Confronting this threat or taking this opportunity leads to ethnicity being politicised, that is, to the ethnic group becoming a political actor by virtue of its shared ethnic identity. As such, ethnic identity 'can be located on a spectrum between primordial historic continuities and instrumental opportunistic adaptations' (Esman 1994: 15). However, it would be simplistic to regard ethnic groups per se as collectivities seeking to use their distinctiveness to enhance their status. Where an ethnic group is in a non-dominant position, such a desire primarily results from state pressure to assimilate an ethnic group, exploit its non-dominant role or perpetuate a status quo that is advantageous to a favoured group.

Viewed against this background, ethnic minorities make demands that reflect both the historic continuities and perceived contemporary opportunities (or necessities) (see Table 1.1). These claims are generally related to one or more of four closely intertwined areas (nature of the ethnic claim) – self-determination; linguistic, religious, and cultural rights; access to resources/equality of opportunity, and/or material and political aid in support of these other three claims. Ethnic minorities make these claims vis-à-vis their host-state or their host-nation, and/or, where applicable, their kin-state or kin-nation (addressee of the ethnic claim). In the absence of a kin-state willing or able to support an external minority, kin-groups in countries other than the kin-state or other external actors (international organisations, individual states) may be sought out and lobbied to assume this patron role.

Territory

Europe has one of the longest traditions of state-building and with it of the institutionalised definition of state territories. For states, territory possesses certain values in and of itself. These include natural resources, such as water, iron, coal, oil, or gas, they extend to the goods and services

Table 1.1 The nature and addressees of ethnic claims[2]

Nature of the ethnic claim	Addressee of the ethnic claim
Self-determination Internal External	*Host-state* Russians in Crimea Republicans and nationalists in Northern Ireland
Linguistic, religious, and/or cultural rights	*Host-state/Host-nation* Indigenous peoples in Latin America
Access to resources/equality of opportunity	*Host-state/Host-nation* Ethnic minorities in China
Material and/or political aid/support	*Kin-state* Serbs in Croatia and Bosnia *Kin-nation/other kin-group* Albanians in Macedonia *International actors* Kosovo Albanians

produced by the population living in this territory and the tax revenue generated from them, and they can comprise military or strategic advantages in terms of natural boundaries, access to the open sea, and control over transport routes and waterways. Even where there is no tangible value to be extracted from a given territory, most governments will nevertheless feel a historic duty to ensure the continued territorial integrity of the state they represent.[3]

Ethnic groups, too, may be connected to territory in intangible ways. Their territorial appurtenance may be a constitutive element of their identity. Territory is then conceptualised more appropriately as 'place', bearing significance in relation to the group's history, collective memories, and 'character'. The deep emotional attachment to territory that ethnic groups can develop and maintain can lead to intense conflict. Nevertheless, for ethnic groups, too, territory is, or can become, a valuable commodity as it provides resources and a potential power base in their bid to change an unacceptable status quo. In the case of minorities with a kin-state, a relationship is also established between host-state and kin-state, which shapes, and is in turn shaped by, the relationship each of the states has with the minority. In many cases, this state-state relationship is not so much one determined by the concepts of 'ethnicity' and 'nation', but rather one that is founded on the notion of 'territory', precisely because of the value territory has for states.

Disputed territories are, thus, a phenomenon of inter-state relations as well as of inter-ethnic relations, and similarly to ethnic claims, it is possible to distinguish between the nature and the level of the territorial claim (see Table 1.2).

Table 1.2 The nature and level of territorial claims

Nature of the territorial claim	Level of the territorial claim
Irredentist/secessionist	*Kin-state vs. host-state and minority vs. host-state* Northern Ireland pre-1998
Irredentist/non-secessionist/autonomist	*Kin-state vs. host-state and minority vs. host-state* Germanic-speaking Alsatians in France, 1919–1939
Non-irredentist/secessionist	*Minority vs. host-state* Albanians in Kosovo
Non-irredentist/non-secessionist/autonomist	*Minority vs. host-state* Germans in South Tyrol

Conflict and patronage: the role of state actors

In their attempts to preserve, express, and develop their distinct identities, ethnic groups may at times be mobilised in ways that make them perceive threats and opportunities and then devise their responses to them in a particular way. The more deeply felt these perceptions are, the more they will be linked to the very survival of the group and the more intense will be the conflict that they can potentially generate. This links the issue of ethnicity to the notion of political power. The political implication of this connection between ethnicity and power is that any ethnic group that is conscious of its uniqueness, and wishes to preserve it, is involved in a struggle for political power – either retaining the measure of political power it possesses or striving to acquire the amount of power that it deems necessary to preserve its identity as a distinct ethnic group, that is, to defeat the threats and seize the opportunities it faces. This desire to gain political power for an ethnic group is expressed in the concept of (ethno)nationalism; according to Smith (1991: 20) 'an ideological movement aiming to attain or maintain autonomy, unity and identity for a social group which is deemed to constitute a nation'.

When incompatible ethno-nationalist doctrines are at the centre of the relationship between minority and host-state, opportunity and threat acquire various, yet concretely identifiable, meanings, being either positively or negatively related to the preservation, expression, and development of a group's ethnic identity and to the ability of the host-state to preserve the integrity of the territorial or civic nation. For a minority, opportunities will manifest themselves, for example, in rights of self-administration or self-government, and they can be realised in local, regional, or federal frameworks within the host-state; alternatively, opportunities may also arise in the separation from the host-state, leading either to independent statehood or, where applicable, to unification with the kin-state. Threats generally occur when state institutions deny an ethnic group access to the resources that are essential for the preservation, expression, and development of a group's identity – access to linguistic, educational, or religious facilities as well as to positions of power in the institutions of the state. Threats can also become manifest in policies of unwanted assimilation, in discrimination, and in deprivation. At their most extreme, they take the form of ethnic cleansing and genocide.

It is in these most extreme cases that the relationship between minority and host-*state* coincides with that between minority and host-*nation*, that is, the titular or dominant ethnic group has monopolised all institutions of the state. Although recent European history has provided a number of examples of this kind, this is, nevertheless, not the rule. Yet, even in its less extreme forms, the relationship between minority and host-nation is often characterised by inter-ethnic tension, resulting from the politicisation and radicalisation of different ethnic identities and claims for the establishment of conditions conducive to their preservation, expression, and development. Responses to such claims made by the respectively other ethnic group are then perceived as threats (which often, but not exclusively, result from resource competition) and/or opportunities (which often, but not exclusively, result from policies of accommodation).

Thus, ethnopolitical conflicts are best described as a form of conflict in which at least one of the parties involved interprets the conflict, its causes, and potential settlements along an existing or perceived discriminating ethnic divide and pursues policies related to one or more of the ethnic and territorial claims outlined above (either seeking to counter or to realise such claims). Such conflicts can thus either occur as group-state conflict, i.e., conflict between an ethnic group and the institutions of its host-state, or as inter-ethnic conflict, i.e., between different ethnic communities within the same state, e.g., between an ethnic minority and the titular nation of its host-state (or parts thereof). The two may, but need not, occur simultaneously or coincide. In addition, as ethnic conflicts are rooted in the perception of threats and the policies formulated to counter them, ethnic conflicts may also give rise to other forms of conflict within a country, for example, between host-nation and host-state – as a result of an actual or perceived 'over-accommodation' of the interests of an ethnic minority, which (sections of) the host-nation may regard as being detrimental to their own interests. This is very often, but not necessarily, the case where accommodation of minority interests is pursued territorially, yet the territory contains a significant portion of members of the host-nation as well.

The simultaneous occurrence of inter-ethnic and group-state conflict is another potential reason for conflict between host-state and host-nation. As inter-ethnic conflict threatens the social integrity of the host-state, actions of the host-nation may be perceived as one source of this threat and be countered accordingly by the host-state. This, in turn, can be perceived by the host-nation, or at least by some sections within it, as denying an opportunity to defend, or establish, conditions conducive to the preservation, expression, and development of its own ethnic identity.[4] Table 1.3 gives an overview of the different types of threat (perceptions) that can become sources of ethnically based self-determination conflicts.

A somewhat different pattern of relationships emerges in cases where a minority has a kin-state. Here, the relationship between the two is based on common ethnicity and a territorially divided ethnic nation, and is, therefore, normally not one of ethnic conflict, but rather one of patronage. Patronage results from one of two aspects, and often from a combination of both – national sentiment and national interest. Popular sentiment concerning the fate of members of the nation living in another state and the desire to unite the national territory and bring together in it all the members of the ethnic nation finds its expression in irredentist or pan-nationalism (Smith 1991: 83). Yet, as national sentiment is not always

Table 1.3 Perceived threats as sources of ethnopolitical conflicts in the host-state

Threats allegedly originating from	*Threats perceived by*		
	Minority	*Host-state*	*Host-nation*
Minority	–	Territorial integrity Societal integrity	Competition for resources deemed essential for the preservation, expression, and development of ethnic identity[5]
Host-state	Unwanted assimilation Discrimination Deprivation	–	'Over-accommodation' of minority interests
Host-nation	Competition for resources deemed essential for the preservation, expression, and development of ethnic identity[5]	Societal integrity	–

expressed in irredentist nationalism, so is the relationship between minority and kin-state not always about the secession of the territory inhabited by the kin-group and its subsequent unification with the kin-state. Informed by domestic and foreign national interests, territorial unification may not be considered desirable for either kin-state or minority, or it may not be possible given geo-political or regional interest and opportunity structures.[6] Alternatively then, the relationship between minority and kin-state can be one of 'repatriation', as with the Federal Republic of Germany and German minorities in Central and Eastern Europe in the post-1950, and especially the post-1989, period, or it can be one of facilitating the establishment of conditions in the host-state conducive to the preservation, expression, and development of the ethnic identity of the kin-groups in this state. With varying degrees of success, the numerous bilateral treaties concluded between the states of Central and Eastern Europe after 1989 testify to this.

A conflictual relationship between minority and kin-state is then likely to develop when their respective political agendas are mutually incompatible. This can be the case if the irredentist nationalism of the kin-state is not reciprocated by the minority, or by sections within it. Conflict is also possible between the minority and its kin-nation, for example in cases where certain interest groups or political parties pursue an agenda that threatens the status and security of the minority in the host-state.[7] Vice versa, a conflictual relationship develops if the 'secessionism' of the kin-group is not welcomed by the kin-state, or when some of its manifestations are perceived as a threat to the kin-state's security and relationship with the host-state. Here the classic examples are the cases of South Tyrol, whose secessionism throughout most of the inter-war period was 'inconvenient' for both Austria and Nazi Germany, and of Northern Ireland, where, despite a formal constitutional commitment to 'irredentism' that existed in the form of Articles 2 and 3 of the Irish Constitution before 1998, violent Republicanism has always been perceived as a threat to the Republic of Ireland. Yet these two cases also show that, given a responsive host-state, a non-irredentist kin-state can have a significant effect of moderation on the policies pursued by its ethnic kin-group abroad (cf. Wolff 2002).

In the absence of kin-states or in cases where they are unwilling or unable to support a self-determination movement among a kin-group abroad, minority communities have increasingly taken recourse to appealing to other actors in the international arena, including states and coalitions of states, international governmental and non-governmental organisations and ethnically akin diaspora groups in third countries. Enabled by powerful transnational networks, media interest and coverage, as well as by an increasingly global and globalised discourse on human and minority rights, self-determination movements among disadvantaged and suppressed minority groups have often, but by no means always, managed to attract international attention and support. While states will generally join together in opposing secession anywhere, humanitarian suffering and regional instability that has resulted from secessionist conflicts have generated international involvement and pressure for a settlement, although generally within previously existing state boundaries. Exceptions are cases where secession had occurred and could no longer be reversed, as happened when the Socialist Federal Republic of Yugoslavia imploded. At times, external actors have chosen to involve themselves in particular self-determination conflicts due to their own geostrategic considerations. Hence, while vigorously opposing Chechnya's secession, Russia has at the same time offered support to separatist campaigns in South Ossetia and Abkhazia and in Transdnistria. While international responses have been varied, international involvement in such conflicts certainly introduces an additional layer of complexity. International actors' interests, combined with the resources and skills they have at their disposal, can easily overwhelm the more immediate parties to any self-determination conflict. Temporarily suspending their full ability to act through strategic and tactical incentives and pressures can produce settlements, but if these are unable to command significant support among local elites and their constituencies, they can only be sustained through long-term international involvement (such as currently in the Balkans and Afghanistan) or will sooner or later face collapse (such as in Cyprus in the 1960s). This, too, is an important lesson to be borne in mind when discussing the viability of autonomy regimes for the settlement of self-determination conflicts.

In summary, then, through the multiple connections between territory and ethnicity, ethnic and territorial claims are often closely linked. Moreover, through the various ethnic and territorial claims, minority/self-determination movements, kin-state/nation (where they exist), host-state, and host-nation are likewise connected. As the character and intensity of these claims change over time, so does the relationship between all of these potential conflict parties. In the current international environment they are also more likely than not to find themselves acting within a context in which third-party external actors become involved in their particular self-determination conflict, bringing with them an additional and very specific agenda of their own and often fundamentally altering the opportunity structures for the more immediate conflict parties.

Defining autonomy

In a recent book on conflict in the Caucasus, Tim Potier (2001: 54) has noted that

> international lawyers have failed to come to any agreement on a 'stable' workable definition for autonomy ... it escapes definition because it is impossible to concretise its scope. It is a loose and disparate concept that contains many threads, but no single strand.

In political science, too, the difficulty to pin down and conceptualise autonomy has been recognised: two of the most eminent scholars in the field, Brendan O'Leary and John McGarry, observed in 1993:

> Overlapping cantonisation and federalisation there exists a grey area of territorial management of ethnic differences which is often found in conjunction with external arbitration. International agreements between states can entrench the territorial autonomy of certain ethnic communities, even though the 'host state' does not generally organise itself along either cantonist or federalist principles.
> (McGarry and O'Leary 1993: 32)

Despite this appreciation of the difficulty to define clearly what autonomy is, political scientists and international lawyers have not hesitated to propose a variety of definitions. Michael Hechter (2000: 114) describes 'political autonomy' as 'a state of affairs falling short of sovereignty'. In Ted Robert Gurr's (1993: 292) understanding 'autonomy means that a minority has a collective power base, usually a regional one, in a plural society'. Hurst Hannum and Richard Lillich (1980: 859) state in their influential essay on 'The Concept of Autonomy in International Law' that autonomy is understood to refer to independence of action on the internal or domestic level, as foreign affairs and defence normally are in the hands of the central or national government, but occasionally power to conclude international agreements concerning cultural or economic matters also may reside with the autonomous entity.

In similar terms, Tim Potier (2001: 54) makes the point that autonomy

should be understood as the means whereby an authority, subject to another superior authority, has the opportunity to determine, separately from that authority, specific functions entrusted upon it, by that authority, for the general welfare of those to whom it is responsible.

In her extensive study on autonomy, Ruth Lapidoth draws a clear distinction between 'territorial political autonomy' and 'personal autonomy'.[8] To her,

[t]erritorial autonomy is an arrangement aimed at granting a certain degree of self-identification to a group that differs from the majority of the population in the state, and yet constitutes the majority in a specific region. Autonomy involves a division of powers between the central authorities and the autonomous entity.

(Lapidoth 1997: 174–175)

In contrast to this territorial conception,

[p]ersonal autonomy applies to all members of a certain group within the state, irrespective of their place of residence. It is the right to preserve and promote the religious, linguistic, and cultural character of the group through institutions established by itself.

(Lapidoth 1997: 175)

Regardless of the scope and detail of the above definitions, the one feature they all share, directly or indirectly, is the transfer of certain powers from a central government to that of the (thereby created) autonomous entity. In practice, autonomy arrangements incorporate executive, legislative, and judicial powers to varying degrees. In cases where it is used as an instrument for ethnic conflict prevention and settlement, autonomy ideally includes such a mix of the three that enables the ethnic group in question to regulate independently the affairs central to the concerns of its members, which are normally easily identifiable as they manifest themselves in concrete claims. However, as autonomy falls short of full sovereignty, this normally happens within the broader constitutional and legislative framework of the minority's host country and under the supervision of a central government or similar agencies ensuring the compliance of all actions of the autonomous institutions with the regulations set up for the execution of the autonomy. However, as Daftary (2000: 5) rightly asserts, autonomy means that

> powers are not merely delegated but transferred; they may thus not be revoked without consulting with the autonomous entity ... the central government may only interfere with the acts of the autonomous entity in extreme cases (for example when national security is threatened or its powers have been exceeded).

Thus, for the purpose of this volume, we define autonomy as the legally entrenched power of ethnic or territorial communities to exercise public policy functions (legislative, executive and adjudicative) independently of other sources of authority in the state, but subject to the overall legal order of the state. Autonomy as a strategy of preventing and settling ethnic conflict, thus, is based on the recognition of group-specific concerns[9] alongside and on par with concerns of individuals (independent of their ethnic identity) and the state. It is equally based on accepting that, for whatever reasons, to endow an ethnic group with legislative, executive, and judicial powers to address these concerns effectively will contribute to individual, group, and state security, and thus to preventing the disruption of the territorial and/or social integrity of a given country.

Depending on settlement patterns of ethnic groups, it is necessary to clarify what the territorial dimensions of the autonomy regulations are in the framework of which these group-specific concerns are to be addressed. The more compact the ethnic group and the more 'its' territory is exclusively populated by its members, the less problematic is a territorial administration of autonomy. On the other hand, an ethnic group which lives dispersed across the territory of its host-state and which does not have a particular area of settlement (in a historical and/or contemporary sense) represents an ideal case for a non-territorial autonomy arrangement. Although these ideal types are only rarely to be found, we use them initially to explore the concepts of territorial and non-territorial autonomy.

Territorial autonomy

The basic idea underlying this particular concept of autonomy is that the autonomous entity is defined in territorial terms. Thus, a population living in a certain territory is granted an autonomous status regardless of whether the individuals living on this territory belong to one or another ethnic group.

Territorial autonomy can be implemented to various degrees, from so-called administrative autonomy to full self-government. Administrative autonomy most commonly describes an arrangement of executive independence within the framework of central legislation, thus, the autonomous territory does not have its own legislature or judicial system. Full self-government, on the other hand, incorporates the right for the population of the designated autonomous territory to elect its own legislature, it endows them with the authority to take charge of all executive and administrative functions usually provided by central state institutions except in the areas of foreign and defence policy and in relation to the broad framework of economic and monetary policy, and also grants significant judicial powers to the autonomous entity. While various forms of administrative territorial autonomy can be found in connection with decentralised (or regionalised) forms of the institutional organisation of a state along the principle of subsidiarity, such as, for example, in Italy, full self-government resembles more closely federal arrangements, such as in Germany. Regardless of the degree of autonomy granted to the specific territory, the country's overall constitutional framework will be preserved, and the autonomous territory will remain an integral part of that country.

However, this continued integration cannot be assured through legislative measures alone. The population of the autonomous territory and their representatives must be incentivised to want to remain part of the larger polity. This can be assured, for example, by adequate representation of the autonomous entity at the central level, constitutionally guaranteed procedures for the resolution of disputes between autonomous entity and central government, and mechanisms that ensure the protection of the human rights of all residents in the autonomous territory, regardless of their ethnic identity, including a right to appeal to judicial institutions at the central level.

Likewise, access to education, particularly specialised and higher education, should be guaranteed for residents of the autonomous area in other parts of the country and abroad. Especially if the autonomous territory is relatively small, without its own colleges or universities, the provision of education in other parts of the country can play a vital role in fostering a sense of social integrity of the country as a whole despite the autonomous status of a particular part of its territory.

Equally important in this context is the nature and intensity of economic and financial ties between autonomous territory and other parts of the whole country. This includes a proper structure of the autonomous area's public finances, consisting of central government grants for the provision of all services in relation to devolved powers and independent sources of revenue. In addition, the autonomous territory should receive a fair share of central government investment in public services and infrastructure. Through a combination of political, social, and economic ties, relationships can be solidified between the autonomous area and the rest of the country which are mutually beneficial and the preservation of which is therefore desirable from the perspective of all entities involved.

As a specific arrangement for clearly demarcated parts of a state's territory, territorial autonomy need not affect the general institutional organi-sation of a state. Depending on the respective state's ethnic composition, special autonomy status can, for example, be granted to one or more areas within a framework of regionalisation in an otherwise unitary state, such as in South Tyrol (Italy) or Corsica (France).

Non-territorial autonomy

Non-territorial autonomy means that the autonomous entity is defined in 'personal' terms, that is, a particular (ethnic) group is granted autonomy rights and all its members can enjoy these rights, regardless of where they live on the territory of their host-state.

Early implementations of non-territorial autonomy related primarily to cultural and/or religious affairs of distinct groups. In the Middle Ages and in early modern times, Jews were granted, by some European rulers, the right to administer their community affairs according to their own laws and traditions. Similarly, the Ottoman Empire adopted the so-called millet system, according to which non-Muslim communities enjoyed some degree of religious and cultural autonomy. In this century, the Baltic states of Latvia, Lithuania, and Estonia ensured a certain degree of cul-tural, and in particular educational, autonomy for national minorities in their post-1919 constitutions. After the collapse of the eastern bloc, some of these provisions were re-enacted, and Hungary's legal framework pro-vides for a far-reaching protection of ethnic minorities on the basis of non-territorial autonomy regulations. A very complex consociational arrangement including a form of cultural non-territorial autonomy has been in place in South Tyrol since 1972.

The concept of non-territorial autonomy itself has been developed systematically in political theory since the mid-nineteenth century, espe-cially in Austria.[10] Later on, in the early twentieth century, it was taken up again by the Austro-Marxists Karl Renner (1902 and 1918) and Otto Bauer (1923 and 1924). After World War II, it has played a significant role in consociational theory, which is primarily associated with the work of Arend Lijphart (especially 1968 and 1977). Throughout the post-Cold War period, too, constitutional theorists (Lijphart 1995) and practitioners[11] have seen non-territorial autonomy as an instrument to deal with the cultural dimension of ethnic conflict, that is with matters of education, language, and religion.

Despite this narrowing down of the concept of non-territorial auto-nomy, there is no need to conceive of it as being in principle confined to cultural and educational matters only. Especially in mixed areas with high levels of inter-ethnic tension, the transfer to the ethnic groups of powers outside these two areas can facilitate the easing of tensions because groups can administer their affairs more independently of one another and power differentials, real or perceived, will have a lesser impact.

Autonomy in combination with other tools of state construction

As was noted above, autonomy solutions to ethnopolitical tensions need to offer sufficient space to non-dominant groups to experience genuine self-governance, without jeopardising the integrity of the state. With respect to the diverse ethnic and territorial claims that occur in ethnic conflicts, this means that autonomy and self-governance regimes can only make a positive contribution to peace and stability where alternatives to preserving the territorial integrity of a given state do not exist. In other words, there must not be an external territorial claim (e.g., by a neighbouring or kin-state) and host-state and minority (or minorities) must be able to compromise on their various ethnic and territorial claims in such a way that territorial autonomy and/or self-governance provide both the space for genuine self-governance and the framework within which the overall state's territorial integrity can be preserved.

These two purposes of autonomy regimes, then, need to be accommodated within the autonomy regulations from both an institutional and a procedural point of view. Autonomy regulations need to provide for social-structural conditions that ensure the necessary degree of political homogeneity – an institutional consensus about the political process in the autonomous area in which all ethnic groups living there have a stake – while at the same time affording each ethnic group enough independence to address the specific concerns of its own members within an overall framework that includes mechanisms for dispute resolution in cases where accommodating one group's concerns has the potential to disadvantage unduly another group. Territorial autonomy regulations alone are very unlikely to achieve this. If the ethnic minority at the centre of the (potential or actual) conflict is in an absolute minority position, i.e., even in a minority within the autonomous area, it will see few if any of its concerns addressed by a devolution of powers to an entity which somehow just replicates its (numerically and otherwise) disadvantageous position. If this particular ethnic minority, however, is in the position of a local majority, territorial autonomy arrangements will inevitably raise fears among other ethnic groups in the autonomous territory about their future status. Hence, additional mechanisms, such as human rights provisions and local power-sharing tools, need to be employed in such circumstances. Where such provisions are not sufficient, territorial autonomy may not be the solution of choice and instead other means of giving expression to the collective identity of the relevant group may need to be considered.

Before competences in specific policy areas can be devolved to non-territorial authorities with any chance of success, a more general framework of inter-ethnic relations needs to be established within which autonomy regulations can be negotiated and administered, and possible disputes settled. Three essential pre-conditions for such a framework in which territorial and non-territorial autonomy institutions can co-exist are:

- The preparedness of all ethnic groups to grant the respective other(s) the same degree of non-territorial autonomy as they desire for themselves;
- The acceptance of such a framework as a mutually beneficial and conflict-preventing set-up;
- The willingness to make concessions and to settle for compromises in the process of negotiating and administering the institutional arrangement of autonomy. Since the setting of most ethnic conflicts is a minority-majority situation, this must include an acceptance that simple democratic procedures of majority decision-making will not be sufficient as safeguards to prevent (a renewed) escalation of the conflict.

In a case of the ethnic minority at the centre of the conflict constituting a local majority, a classical consociational arrangement based on the four principles developed by Lijphart (1977) – grand coalition, (cultural) segmental (or non-territorial) autonomy, proportionality, and minority veto – is feasible. An absolute minority, however, will hardly be satisfied with such an arrangement. Similarly unsatisfying in such cases will be integrative solutions, as suggested by Horowitz (1985), which rely on incentives for cooperation across ethnic cleavages, in particular through voting systems that encourage pre-election inter-ethnic coalitions. Potential areas of conflict would then become de-ethnicised prior to their handling by traditional democratic institutions. The implication of this, however, is that issues that cannot be de-ethnicised, and these are usually the crucial ones, would then be decided on a majority-minority basis, which is not desirable from the point of view of the minority ethnic group in any given case.

By maintaining the ethnic alignment of society and combining it with certain consociational techniques, the consociational model stands a better chance to address the issue of distributing political power between the ethnic groups in the autonomous area. However, the functioning of this model depends very much on the homogeneity of each ethnic group, its political discipline, the degree of control respective elites exercise over their groups, and the numerical balance between them. Ideally, ethnic groups would have to have a highly homogeneous interest structure, be politically disciplined, and of similar numerical strength (Lijphart 1977).

In less ideal cases, much depends on the extent of non-territorial political powers, that is, on the degree of group autonomy. Non-territorial competences, in practice as well as in consociational theory, usually encompass only cultural matters. Because the ethnic minority at the centre of the conflict would exercise a greater degree of legislative political power on the basis of its numerical superiority at the territorial level of autonomy, cultural non-territorial autonomy is normally sufficient as an instrument to address the conflict at the level of non-territorial autonomy.

However, this is not the case in mixed areas which include an absolute minority. Here, non-territorial competences must extend to more political issues as well.[12] This would serve the following purposes: each ethnic group would achieve greater political control over its own fate; the limitation of traditional democratic principles owed to consociational techniques at the territorial level could be compensated at non-territorial level; the whole system would be less dependent on group homogeneity and discipline; elite dominance of their respective groups could be minimised; intra-ethnic elite competition could exist at non-territorial level and would not endanger the functioning of the consociational model at territorial level; the possible dominance of one ethnic group would have limited effects, and de-ethnicisation of critical issues would not be necessary.

Additional arrangements would have to be made in cases of kin-state involvement. Here, it might be useful to equip the minority group and/or the autonomous territory as a whole with a limited amount of 'foreign policy' powers in order to establish and maintain meaningful relationships with its kin-state and nation.[13] If, as presumed earlier, this happens on the pretext that territorial claims at the international level have been settled, i.e., withdrawn by the kin-state, there will be no danger of abusing such an arrangement in order to undermine the territorial and social integrity of the host-state.

However, there are two criticisms which can be levelled against such a model: first, that it would, even more than the traditional consociational concept with only cultural non-territorial autonomy, reinforce the ethnic divide between the groups, and, second, that it does not include a guarantee for inter-ethnic cooperation at territorial level, which would still remain an essential condition for the overall successful execution of the autonomy, and thus for the prevention or settlement of the ethnic conflict in question.

Our answer to the first criticism is that continued ethnic segmentation does not necessarily imply an increased likelihood of conflict. A clear (functional, as opposed to enforced physical) separation between groups that does not have any discriminating aspects to it might, in cases of deeply divided yet mixed areas, rather facilitate de-escalation and prevention and/or settlement of a conflict as it would decrease the number of potentially conflictual issues handled by both groups together.

A possible solution for the second criticism – missing guarantees for inter-ethnic cooperation at territorial level – may be found in the adoption of specific parliamentary election (various types of proportional or preferential election systems) and voting (qualified majority voting and/or parallel consent mechanisms) procedures.

Institutional designs for the settlement of self-determination conflicts: theory and practice

The contributions in this volume seek to identify innovative and complex autonomy designs, reflecting the increased interest in autonomy as a possible solution to ethnopolitical conflict.

'Self-Governance plus Regional Integration: A Possible Solution to Self-determination Claims' is the title of Wolfgang Danspeckgruber's chapter, in which he argues that in order to surmount the insistence, on the part of a community seeking self-determination, on full sovereignty and independence (with its negative consequences for conflict development and settlement), the community and its leadership should be offered maximum autonomy and the largest possible freedom to participate in the global marketplace. In practice, this would encompass independence in all internal matters, encompassing religious, cultural, educational, even fiscal, local security, and judicial autonomy. Parallel to this extensive self-governance, an incentive for trans-border inter-regional cooperation and integration should be launched. Over time such integration on a regional as well as international scale, and among self-governing communities in sovereign entities with their traditional boundaries intact, would most certainly enhance local, cross-border cooperation and eventually erode the hardness of the separating international boundaries – both in practice and in perception.

Marc Weller considers recent constitutional settlements in the former Yugoslavia and assesses the relative role assigned to autonomy in them. He establishes an analytical framework to classify different approaches to territorially based self-government and concludes that autonomy elements are less pronounced in the more advanced settlements that followed the Dayton Accords. Weller also emphasises that a far more subtle approach to autonomy is adopted in the more recent settlements and identifies the ways in which autonomy arrangements are balanced by other elements of state construction. In this way, he makes an attempt at resolving the purported tension between autonomy-based and consociational solutions and instead proposes an integrated approach which also covers human and minority rights and elements of international involvement in self-determination settlements.

Using the conceptual framework developed by the editors in Chapter 1, Bill Bowring explores the many legal and political problems which beset the Autonomous Republic of Crimea. As he points out, apart from the constitutional anomaly of being an autonomous area located within a unitary state, it also contains a double, or even triple, minority problem of textbook complexity: the majority population of the peninsula are ethnic Russians, who are a minority in Ukraine; the Ukrainian titular nation are a small, almost invisible minority in the Crimea; and the Crimean Tatars, who claim Crimea as their homeland, are, although highly visible and asserting their status as indigenous people, a minority in the Crimea as well. Despite the need to resolve these problems, which were at times exacerbated by Russian irredentism, no realistic or lasting solutions have been put in place. Employing legal concepts such as the right of peoples to self-determination, minority and language rights regimes as proposed by the Council of Europe and the OSCE, and the rights of indigenous peoples, and drawing on the theory of nationalism, Bowring offers a thorough and compelling examination of the merits of proposals for multicultural citizenship, as well as non-territorial autonomy for Crimea.

Elisabeth Nauclér then explores the experiences of the three Nordic autonomous territories (Åland, Greenland and the Faroe Islands) in two areas of international cooperation, Nordic and continental European. The Nordic Council and Nordic Council of Ministers are forerunners in international cooperation regarding the representation of autonomous territories, while the European Union shows no signs of preparedness for accepting members that are not sovereign states. All three territories have the same representation in the framework of Nordic cooperation, but have experienced very different treatments in the European Union. This raises important issues on a conceptual and practical level for the design and operation of autonomy regimes within and beyond the European context, in particular with regard to new challenges and opportunities for autonomy to live up to its promise to resolve ethnopolitical conflicts or tensions.

One distinctive feature of many recent applications of autonomy regimes to resolve complex self-determination conflicts has been their combination with various other forms of conflict management. In Western Europe, the predominant trend in this context has been the creation of power-sharing institutions within a territorially autonomous region to ensure that devolved powers are not abused by local majorities to the detriment of local minorities, thus providing a double mechanism of conflict resolution and minority protection. Examining the cases of Brussels, Northern Ireland and South Tyrol, Stefan Wolff in his chapter focuses on the factors that make such an approach viable and assesses which conditions need to be in place to ensure the long-term stability of such arrangements.

While a major humanitarian crisis evolved in the western Sudanese region of Darfur in the summer of 2004, the government in Khartoum and a southern-based rebel group concluded a two-year negotiation process that began with the signing of the Machakos Protocol on 20 July 2002 and ended with the signing of a comprehensive peace agreement on 9 January 2005. Hailed as a major breakthrough in a civil war that had been ongoing since the late 1950s, the conflict parties had negotiated a comprehensive, albeit in many parts still vague, framework for an interim settlement. As Marc Weller points out in his analysis, this framework is the best opportunity to date to allow the conflict parties to test whether autonomy is a viable institutional modus vivendi in which they can settle their differences by political and peaceful means. Weller draws particular attention to the fact that, rather than being arrangements for a mere transitional period on the way towards independent statehood for the South, the settlement commits both parties to use their best efforts to make the agreement work and autonomy an attractive and long-term option to the people in the South on which they will be able to decide in a referendum at the end of the interim period.

The case of Sudan indicates that autonomy arrangements are not the exclusive provenance on European conflict settlements. Beyond Europe, they also extend into other parts of the world, as the remaining chapters on Latin America, Indonesia, and China of our volume show. In his comparative analysis of autonomy regimes in Latin America, Willem Assies examines how, and with what consequences, indigenous peoples' movements have become important social and political actors in a significant number of Latin American countries over the past decades. The dialectics between the identity politics practiced by the movements and the politics of recognition that have been adopted by the states have contributed to the dynamism of what has been called the 'ethnic emergence'. The subsequent recognition of indigenous peoples' rights has prompted a number of states to acknowledge collective rights and implement autonomy regimes that combine territoriality with proper forms of self-governance. The success of indigenous peoples' movements has also prompted them to go beyond their initial demands for compensation for historical grievances to forge new alliances and to articulate new visions of the state and the nation. In this way indigenous peoples' demands and responses to these demands have become important elements in the ongoing processes of transformation of the Latin American states that got under way in the context of the democratisation processes and the processes of structural adjustment and adaptation to, or insertion into, the globalised world. These processes have opened up new opportunities and posed new threats. Democratisation and adjustment often go together with decentralisation policies that open up or broaden sub-national political arenas, which offer new opportunities for political participation. At the same time, the insertion into the globalised economy often involves the intensification of national and transnational economic activity in hitherto 'marginal' regions, where indigenous peoples until now found refuge. As the implementation of autonomy does not imply separatism or isolationism but is conceived as a basic condition for participating in the wider polity, the emergence of autonomy regimes has consequently involved a strengthening of subnational processes as well as of supranational integration. The emergence of so-called 'network states' thus has profound implications for the current model of the 'nation-state' and the concepts of self-determination, citizenship, democracy, human rights and development predicated upon it.

Decentralisation, devolution and regional autonomy in Indonesia are the topic of Mark Turner's comparative analysis. Indonesia, the most populous Muslim state on earth, has engaged in what could be called the devolutionary form of decentralisation, but which is officially referred to in Indonesia as 'otonomi daerah' (regional autonomy). As a particular form of state construction based in the vertical layering of authority, it has no primary basis in ethnicity – the autonomous regions (districts and provinces) are simply those territorial divisions which already existed – and there have only been very few modifications since the autonomy laws were implemented, i.e., a large number of functions were devolved to the regions. However, there are two provinces for which special autonomy provisions are being applied – Aceh and West Papua. Focusing its analysis on these regions in particular, and comparing them with the rest of the country, this chapter examines the contribution that autonomy can make to the settlement of violent secessionist conflict while at the same time providing a broader view on the Indonesian experience with decentralisation, devolution and autonomy.

Mainly from a legal perspective, Eric Friberg assesses autonomy arrangements in China, considering the 2001 amendments to the 1984 Law on Regional Ethnic Autonomy and recent local institutional developments. He argues that the constitutionally protected, yet limited and ambiguous, powers granted under this law continue to be inadequately safeguarded in the current institutional landscape: weak legal language in the statutory texts, the lack of adequate dispute resolution mechanisms and the existence of multiple horizontal and vertical 'ladder of approval' procedures contribute to the limited differences in the degree of local self-governance enjoyed by autonomous and non-autonomous areas. Recent trends in local institutional developments in China, including increasing, yet limited, downwards accountability through the strengthening of local representative 'legislative' bodies, and experiments of multi-candidate elections at local levels, however, can encourage local agency to put real content in the existing autonomy provisions, particularly at the county level. In this context, the author stresses the necessity for institutional structures in order to achieve any effective autonomy arrangement in China and emphasises that with a central government that has begun to allow more divergence in local practices, this trend could, over time, demonstrate to the Chinese leadership that enhanced local self-government *promotes* rather than *challenges* national unity and could go some way to meeting the increasingly 'internal' self-determination demands in China.

Finally, Marc Weller and Stefan Wolff re-examine current theory and practice of the resolution of self-determination conflicts through autonomy and thereby offer a comprehensive assessment of the present and future of institutional design approaches to resolving self-determination conflicts. They summarise the findings on complex autonomy regimes and their different components, such as international mediation and monitoring, cross-border institutions, supranational integration and power-sharing, as well as the way in which these are linked. Drawing on the volume's individual contributions, Weller and Wolff compare and evaluate the origins, morphology and prospects of stability of autonomy regimes for resolving self-determination conflicts.

Notes

1 This was led by the groundbreaking survey by Hannum (1990) and accompanying documents (1993).
2 Examples in this or any of the following tables are neither exhaustive, nor does the mentioning of a particular case in one category mean that it could not also be used as an example in another one.
3 In a recent article, Barbara Walter (2003) provided evidence that reputation building in the face of a potential multitude of territorial claims vis-à-vis a beleaguered central state may be a decisive factor determining a state's response to territorial demands by one group.
4 A good western European example for this is the marching season in Northern Ireland: Some of the most contentious parades have been banned or re-routed over the past several years to avoid violent clashes between the two communities; yet this often resulted in violent protests by Loyalists not only against the Nationalist/Republican community, but also against the British authorities.
5 Threats perceived by minorities comprise all of the features in both boxes. Depending on the specificity of the situation it is not always possible for the minority (or the outside observer) to determine the source of the threat with absolute accuracy. In particular, in situations where the host-nation has complete control over the institutions of the state and uses them against the minority, distinctions between host-state and host-nation are blurred, and to some extent even irrelevant.
6 On various occasions, Horowitz has emphasised the variety of factors that make successful, or even desirable, irredentas very unlikely. Cf. especially, Horowitz (1985: 229–288), and shorter, Horowitz (1991).
7 Political representatives of ethnic German expellees from Poland and Czechoslovakia have frequently demanded restitution of properties and the right to return to their former homelands. These demands have been rejected by the German minorities in the two countries (as well as the Polish, Czech and German governments) as counter-productive to reconciliation and the demands of the minorities for cultural and linguistic rights.
8 This distinction is made by a number of scholars, including Heintze (1997: 37–46), Hechter (2000: 72ff.) and Potier (2001: 55f. and 59f.)
9 Heintze (1997: 34) notes in this context (my translation): 'The legal subject of autonomy always has to be a group. The granting of autonomy thus requires both the recognition of the group as a minority or ethnic group and the acceptance of collective rights.'
10 To my knowledge, the first comprehensive analysis in this context is Frischhof (1869).
11 Estonia's and Hungary's constitutions and specific minority legislation provide good examples.
12 This should include tax raising and collecting powers for the autonomous institutions of each group from within its own community in order to secure a higher degree of financial independence as compared to a situation in which

central institutions at territorial or national level have exclusive tax authority
and fund non-territorial autonomy bodies through fund allocation. The
allocation of state grants would have to remain a source of income for both
territorial and non-territorial autonomy institutions in the framework of decentralisation.

13 In recent years, developments within the European Union have led to regions
being entitled to sign cross-border agreements with other regions in member-
states of the European Union. Also, the 1993 constitution of Belgium has transferred significant foreign policy powers to the parliaments and governments of
the country's three constituent national groups (Flemings, Walloons, and
Germans). This indicates that there are ways in which autonomous entities can
exercise a certain degree of foreign policy competence falling just short of a
full confederal arrangement.

References

Bauer, Otto (1923) *Die österreichische Revolution.* Leipzig.
Bauer, Otto (1924) *Die Nationalitätenfrage und die Sozialdemokratie.* Leipzig.
Connor, Walker (1994) *Ethnonationalism. The Quest for Understanding.* Princeton,
NJ: Princeton University Press.
Daftary, Farimah (2000) *Insular Autonomy: A Framework for Conflict Settlement. A Com-
parative Study of Corsica and the Åland Islands.* Flensburg: European Centre for
Minority Issues.
Esman, Milton J. (1994) *Ethnic Politics.* Ithaca: Cornell University Press.
Frischhof, Adolf (1869) *Österreich und die Bürgerschaften seines Bestandes.* Vienna.
Gurr, Ted Robert (1993) *Minorities at Risk.* Washington, DC: United States Insti-
tute of Peace Press.
Hannum, Hurst (1990) *Autonomy, Sovereignty, and Self-Determination. The Accommoda-
tion of Conflicting Rights.* Philadelphia: University of Pennsylvania Press.
Hannum, Hurst (1993) *Documents on Autonomy and Minority Rights.* Leider: Marti-
nus Nijhoff.
Hannum, Hurst and Lillich, Richard B. (1980) 'The Concept of Autonomy in
International Law', in *American Journal of International Law* 74, 858–889.
Hechter, Michael (2000) *Containing Nationalism.* Oxford: Oxford University
Press.
Heintze, Hans-Joachim (1997) 'Wege zur Verwirklichung des Selbstbestim-
mungsrechts der Völker innerhalb bestehender Staaten', in Heintze, Hans-
Joachim, ed., *Selbstbestimmungsrecht der Völker – Herausforderung der Staatenwelt.*
Bonn: Dietz, 16–59.
Horowitz, Donald L. (1985) *Ethnic Groups in Conflict.* Berkeley: University of Cali-
fornia Press.
Horowitz, Donald L. (1991) 'Irredentas and Secessions: Adjacent Phenomena,
Neglected Connections' in Chazan, Naomi, ed., *Irredentism and International Poli-
tics.* Boulder, CO: Lynne Rienner, 9–22.
Lapidoth, Ruth (1997) *Autonomy. Flexible Solutions to Ethnic Conflicts.* Washington,
DC: United States Institute of Peace Press.
Lijphart, Arend (1968) *The Politics of Accommodation: Pluralism and Democracy in the
Netherlands.* Berkeley: University of California Press.
Lijphart, Arend (1977) *Democracy in Plural Societies.* New Haven, CT and London:
Yale University Press.

Lijphart, Arend (1995) 'Self-Determination versus Pre-Determination of Ethnic Minorities in Power Sharing Systems', in Kymlicka, Will, ed., *The Rights of Cultural Minorities.* Oxford: Oxford University Press, 275–287.

McGarry, John and O'Leary, Brendan (1993) 'Introduction. The Macro-Political Regulation of Ethnic Conflict', in McGarry, John and O'Leary, Brendan, eds, *The Politics of Ethnic Conflict Regulation.* London: Routledge, 1–40.

Potier, Tim (2001) *Conflict in Nagorno-Karabakh, Abkhazia and South Ossetia. A Legal Appraisal.* The Hague: Kluwer International Law.

Renner, Karl (1902) *Der Kampf der österreichischen Nationen um den Staat.* Vienna (published under the pseudonym of Rudolf Springer).

Renner, Karl (1918) *Das Selbstbestimmungsrecht der Nationen in besonderer Anwendung auf Österreich.* Leipzig.

Smith, Anthony D. (1991) *National Identity.* London: Penguin.

Walter, Barbara F. (2003) 'Explaining the Intractability of Territorial Conflict', *International Studies Review*, vol. 5, no. 4, 137–153.

Wolff, Stefan (2002) *Disputed Territories: The Transnational Dynamics of Ethnic Conflict Settlement.* New York and Oxford: Berghahn.

2 Self-governance plus regional integration

A possible solution to self-determination claims

Wolfgang F. Danspeckgruber

Introduction

The problem of self-determination, namely the search for greater autonomy and even secession, has become important anew – though in a more
restrictive dimension. In the international system emerging since September 2001 issues of the State, protection of the suppressed, possible humanitarian intervention, and readiness to redraw external boundaries have
given way to immediate concerns of security, terrorism, international
terror networks and problems of economic security. Arguably, the world
has entered a much more uncertain, unpredictable and indeed insecure
period than during the Cold War with its mutually assured destruction
and super power hegemony. Besides the fear of terror attacks and prolifer-
ation of weapons of mass destruction, recent secession crises have also
shed light on the influence of organized crime in the realm of activists for
self-determination, thus providing incentive for central authorities to
embark on more restrictive – some would say repressive – policies against
activists for independence. While the independence of East Timor was the
high point of the search for sovereignty and independence in recent
times, sovereignty issues in Kosovo, Chechnya, and Kashmir remain unresolved to this day.

It appears increasingly unlikely that the international community would
easily recognize a new state, especially if such state formation would imply
rearranging boundaries of presumably more than just one state and hence
would cause change and potential instability in a region, in addition to
setting a potentially dangerous precedent. No creation of a new state is
possible without international recognition, and approval by the five
permanent members of the United Nations Security Council. Nevertheless, to simply deny a community the right to greater independence as a
matter of principle will continue to have limited success in light of general
awareness of human and group rights in today's international environment and the increasing importance of individual empowerment. On the
other hand, sustained avoidance or suppression of such demands by
central authority will over time only exacerbate the explosive potential of

such problems.¹ But experience with self-determination crises has also proven that in most cases where one specific community is looking for greater independence from the center, at least one other community exists within the same sovereign territory, frequently more. This community/ies will also be affected by the outcome of the search for greater autonomy of the first community. Hence the struggle for self-determination is rarely a zero-sum game between one community and the center, but has repercussions for other communities within the same state, and in neighboring states as well. In light of the decreased readiness to recognize new states in the emerging international system it is thus important to offer new concepts that can address the search of a community for greater independence as well as fulfill their dream of relatively independent outside (international) presence and wide-ranging autonomy in interaction with other sub-states, states, international, and supranational organizations. In the emerging international system it is important to try to achieve this, but avoid triggering new state formation and the redrawing of existing boundaries.

This chapter tries to develop a solution – self-governance plus regional integration – to this conundrum between communal desire and reality. It is divided into five parts. The first defines the problem, the second outlines the major conceptual dimensions, the third offers potential solutions and describes the new notion of self-governance plus integration, the fourth considers possible applications, and the fifth offers conclusions and recommendations.

The problem of self-determination

Generally, one can think of five scenarios or outcomes if a community seeks to obtain greater autonomy:

1   Secession followed by independent statehood;
2   Secession followed by accession to another state;
3   Partition and partial secession followed by either independent statehood or accession to another state;
4   Continuation of the status quo;
5   Self-governance plus regional integration.

Solution 1 leads to the formation of a *new* independent actor in the international system, with new territory, boundaries and international recognition. Presumably it changes the situation in the region and raises questions regarding economic viability, stability, and security (combined with prolonged international involvement). It also addresses the future international status of that actor, such as issues of alliance membership or neutrality, and membership in supra or international organizations. Solutions 2 and 3 in turn presuppose the (active) involvement of a third – the to-be-accessed – state in the region and causes a change in boundaries. This may affect the communities within that state and certainly its geostrategic role and weight, and that of the other actors within it, though it does not lead to a new independent state.

Solutions 1 to 3 comprise the redrawing of external boundaries, as well as the re-arrangement of internal administrative ones. Only solutions 4 and 5 help avoid such alterations and thus may prove to be more supportive of regional stability. However, from the point of view of the community concerned option 4 will presumably prove to be unacceptable and become a cause for further problems if not conflict. On the other hand, options 1 to 3 will most likely prove unacceptable both to the central government of the state in question and to the neighboring states and their governments since they may fear negative impact on their own national situation, as well as on communities which are related or elsewhere.

In order to offer a community enough incentive to ignore the strong inclination to become independent and secede from a given state, this new notion has to carry attraction and conviction. Three elements are critical: 1) the credible engagement of capable outside powers, 2) the attractiveness of the plan and the offer to fulfill some of the aspirations of the community's longing for freedom, and 3) the feasibility of the initiative.

With respect to the first requirement, the onus is on the international representatives to convince the community of the plan's attractiveness. The notion of 'self-governance plus regional integration' however has to offer more than the traditional 'freedom' and 'autonomy' that the community has 'enjoyed' previously.[2] It also has to address two concerns of the community: the future and security of the younger generation, and minimal interference with direct contacts with the outside world, the region, and the global market place. 'Internal sovereignty' should hence be accompanied by wide-ranging 'external competencies' – both form an integral part of 'self-governance *plus* regional integration.' On the other hand, the outside world should help in fostering stronger intra-regional interactions, both economic and cultural, and assisting with provisions of the appropriate regional security arrangements.

A key condition, however, rests in the acceptance of multiple identities and a flexible political culture. The members of the community in question ought to accept that their community membership represents just one of perhaps several identities. For example being a Kashmiri may also mean holding Indian or Pakistani citizenship, just as a South Tyrolian may also be an Italian citizen. This multiple identity will include efforts in education and the implementation of transparency and justice. This will also encourage trans-border activities and thus regional integration, which in turn will alleviate the external boundaries.

Self-governance plus regional integration will thus help avoid redrawing existing external boundaries. Through increased regional interaction,

Table 2.1 Characteristics of different self-determination regimes

		Self-determination regime			
		Status quo (none)	Secession (statehood)	Autonomy	Self-governance plus regional integration
Boundaries	Internal	Old	New	Old	Old
	External	Old	New	Old	May alter over time
International recognition		None	Yes	None	None
Internal sovereignty	Local governance	Probable	Independent	Autonomous	Independent
External competencies	Foreign treaty-making powers	None	Independent	Dependent	Limited independence
	Foreign representation	None	Independent	Dependent	Possible
	International organization membership	No	Yes	No	Possible
	Regional foreign policy and organization membership	No	Yes	No	Possible

Note
* The author is grateful to Tyler Felgenhauer for assistance.

the widened authorities of the community, and eventual regional integration the boundaries will change over time in character and meaning. Such a solution will help minimize instability and challenges to regional peace.

The community should perceive such a solution as a credible option facilitating the enjoyment of its linguistic, ethnic, and religious identity. This option should also offer a maximum degree of socio-cultural development, democratic and transparent policy, and the capability to participate as independently as possible in regional integration and the global market place. This should offer hope for its young people and counteract the dangerous 'brain drain.' It is critical that the community perceives a gain in safety, an enhancement of its status and rights, that its cultural identity is not threatened, and that it discerns a viable future for its children. This has to be combined with the guarantee of sustained and credible international assistance and involvement in the region. Only under such conditions will any community accept a lasting solution short of full sovereignty and creation of new external boundaries.

Major conceptual dimensions

The most important dimensions can be summarized as follows:

- Community
- The influence of diaspora and irredenta;
- Self-determination;
- Sovereignty versus autonomy;
- Boundaries and international recognition;
- Communal leadership;
- The role of gender and generational dimensions;
- The role and influence of the media;
- Security and the potential interactions with terrorism and organized crime;
- The danger of access to weapons of mass destruction;
- Regionalization and integration;
- Technological progress as it influences the national and regional setting as well as global real-time information and mobility.

Due to space considerations, only selected dimensions will be dealt with here.

Community

Community is clearly the key concept for any struggle linked to self-determination. Traditionally 'community' has been defined as a group which derives its identity from blood, religion, language, race, common history or any other defining special feature. The Liechtenstein Draft Convention on Self-Determination Through Self-Administration' (section 1, article 1) defines community as 'the members of a distinct group which inhabits a limited area within a State and possesses a sufficient degree of organization as such a group.'[3]

This means there should be a 'group of people' – not necessarily but possibly linked to a certain territory which it has inhabited during a certain time – that defines itself clearly by distinctive characteristics. These typically comprise cultural, religious, or ethnic qualities, or other aspects of identity. That group of people must also have a common solidarity or the sense of preserving the group's heritage and traditions (Watts 2002: 369). Its concerns typically include equality and justice, safety, cultural freedom from repression, a viable future for the young, economic opportunities, etc.[4]

A community can be a majority, minority or sub-group within the same state. For those remaining outside the state's or community's territory, it can also be irredenta (separated by borders) or diaspora (leaving abroad, elsewhere) (see below). A community can have another community – a minority – within its territory.

Minority

One of the most important dimensions in any discussion related to self-determination concerns the role of minorities, their protection, their relative situation in the state with regard to other (also related) communities, as well as their possible development. A discrepancy seems to exist in the awareness of established legal instruments and international treaties concerning the protection of national minorities. The following enumerates certain basics (cf. Danspeckgruber 2002b).

The issue of a 'minority' has always consisted of four major dimensions:

- The 'we-they'-problem (with antagonism);
- The *other* community – frequently the majority, but also 'just' another minority;
- Boundary (inter-state or intra-state): potentially dividing an ethnic group into a majority on one side and a minority on the other, as an international issue – when it is a question of irredenta – or as a domestic issue, i.e., when the boundary is administrative, within a sovereign territory, where it becomes an issue of national governance;
- International recognition: the ability to be recognized as a minority by the central authorities – and, if necessary, also by outside states and organizations – and the role of a minority in world policy as a function of increasing global interdependence and the resulting challenge to state and sovereignty (cf. Krasner 2001).

From very early on the concept of the nation-state *could not accept* those who were not part of the same community as the majority – with regard to race, language, religion, culture, etc. – within the same sovereign boundaries. So whoever was within that same border but was a member of *another group* was seen as an *outsider or de facto a foreigner*. Thomas Musgrave argues in his book *Self-Determination and National Minorities* that 'minorities were anomalies within the nation state ... and were perceived as elements which weakened and divided it' (Musgrave 1998: 10). Since it was not possible for these 'outsiders' to contribute to nation-building, they were frequently seen as alien, thus setting the stage for tensions to rise.

In discussions of self-governance, i.e. maximum autonomy, or traditional self-determination, the right of minorities to self-determination, i.e. declaration/recognition of a new state in the international system, is still widely rejected. This is due to the threat perceived by the international community to the existence of states as such, the danger of tempting minorities elsewhere, and the overall stability of areas concerned. There is however a caveat: in case there is a clear case of repression, other rules apply (International Kosovo Commission 2000).

Irredenta

This is a national minority created from a redrawing of boundaries that places it outside the main territory of the nation state. Revanchism can be a form of expression of dissatisfaction with an irredenta. It has been argued by nationalists that the irredenta could not be satisfied without joining the nation state to whose community it belongs. It is important to accept that in rigid internal structures with serious internal – albeit soft – administrative boundaries, and irredenta can also cause problems if it reflects parts of an ethnic community in one administrative unit and the majority of the other. Such a situation can be further complicated in case an irredenta is found in areas with mixed populations (Musgrave 1998: 11).

Diaspora

Diaspora ('dispersed' in Greek) implies a permanent separation from the state where the community presently resides, and is in conflict with the need to demonstrate loyalty. Members of a diaspora are outsiders, i.e. live in another state, but retain strong bindings – frequently via friends and relatives – in the (old) home country. The impact of the diaspora on (and support for) any issue in the former home country can be matched by the impact of the diaspora on the formation of policies in its new state of residence. Diasporas have a particular relevance for Russia, as the break-up of the USSR left some 25 million Russians outside sovereign Russian borders.[5] Equally there is a significant Chinese diaspora abroad, e.g. in the United States, as well as a large Indian diaspora.

Self-determination

Self-determination has been one of the most prevalent causes of international and inter-state crises since the middle of the nineteenth and beginning of the twentieth centuries, and has been of renewed importance following the fall of the Berlin Wall in 1989, the subsequent unification of Germany and the end of the Cold War (cf. Halperin et al. 1992, Tomuschat 1994). Struggles for autonomy and secession have been the source of tremendous human suffering and destruction in Africa, Europe, and Asia.

Since September 11 2001 however the 'war on terrorism' has hampered the possibilities for self-determination, since most central authorities have become more resistant to movements for autonomy and independence. This clearly reduces the parameters for those who work for such ideals and intentions of a community – namely for greater autonomy and freedom from the center. Too many times have actors been considered in 'the bad light' between legal and illegal operation and accordingly accused by other parties in a given state which object to their aims. What was in the past a 'freedom fighter' and 'patriot' is now easily labeled a 'terrorist.'[6] Notwithstanding the fact that the final entry into the history books will be determined by the victorious' power's emergence from the struggle.

What has changed in the immediate aftermath of September 11 concerns the fundamental attitude of many governments and leaders, which in the past worried that the United States would oppose their suppressive treatment of autonomy movements (for example Belgrade, Indonesia, and East Timor), which obviously influences the struggle for self-determination or autonomy. Now, in the post-9/11 international environment central authorities resisting such movements either find encouragement for that hardened attitude in Washington, or sell their suppression of liberation movements as their own direct contribution to the U.S.' 'war on terrorism.' A situation which assists the blurring of the distinction between those searching for greater autonomy in earnest, and those fighting central authority with terrorist intentions. Indeed it might itself contribute to the difficulty to identify and bring to justice those who really are engaged in terrorist activities. The current environment clearly favors those governments that enforce restrictive and defensive positions and unleash the full force of national police and security apparata.[7] This includes tightened controls of borders, trans-border activities, the media, and even 'profiling.' Whether this hardened and uncompromising attitude improves chances to find peaceful solutions in situations tense due to self-determination or whether increased suppression contributes to radicalization and adds an escalatory dimension as it strengthens the resolve of those searching for greater freedom, remains to be seen.

Classical self-determination, in the Wilsonian sense, includes two dimensions:[8] the search for full independence and sovereignty by a community at the expense of the existing state, and the right to form a government and administration according the community's wishes.[9] The redrawing of new international boundaries and international recognition offer the quintessential test of the 'slippery slope' potentially entered in the implementation of classical self-determination towards possible full scale independence. Interestingly, over the course of history communal and ethnic empires gave way to larger, multi-ethnic empires, which in turn were again destroyed by nationalism and re-introduced self-determination. During the Cold War self-determination was seen primarily in the context of decolonization, influencing the movement of the non-aligned states. In the 1980s and particularly the 1990s regionalization, trans-border contacts, and empowerment of communities with global real-time technologies and the Internet has begun to challenge the traditional position of the nation state and national central authorities.

There exists a dichotomy between the traditional perspective of state, state authority and state formation in the Westphalian System and the ultimate freedoms and empowerment of communities reflecting such elements as heightened access to information and knowledge of and access to the global market place. It seems as though in the international system one would deny to the community what the state takes for granted – to integrate and to permit its citizen intensified interaction with all other states and organizations (as long as they are not illegal). Self-determination is thus a notion very much in vogue in today's situation, but the continuing tendency of states to protect their interests, institutions, and their territory, as well as current global security concerns, hamper effective translation of a community's self-determination desires. Hence it seems important to try to find a solution which addresses that dilemma while accepting the national interest of the powers concerned.

Regionalization

Regionalization reflects the intention to preserve some degree of self-governance on the local or communal level that is independent of external national boundaries. If subsidiarity means 'government by the lowest possible level,' 'regionalization' means the closest possible interaction between communities and peoples who like to cooperate, under circumstances favored by inter-communal relations, geography, and tradition. Several 'regionalist waves' took place in the 1960s and 70s.[10] Since the enlargement process of the EU and NATO in the 1990s regionalization obtained yet another meaning, as it did also by the forming of economic and financial regions in Europe, Asia, and Latin America. Communities are torn between the attraction to participate in integration, economic advance, technological progress, and the global market place, while preserving some of their 'old certainties, structures,' and traditional ethnic-cultural values.[11]

The underpinnings of regionalization may comprise geography, social and cultural affinities, traditional ethnic relations, trade and infrastructure, and even internal and external security.[12] Regionalization furthers decentralization and democratization by encouraging responsibility and autonomy from below, which ought to inspire the regions to develop their own appropriate capabilities to compete with other regions.

It is predictable that the ongoing economic and strategic developments will contribute to the formation of other mega regions elsewhere. The North American Free Trade Agreement (NAFTA) fosters free trade and economic-industrial cooperation between Canada, Mexico, and the United States, and similar initiatives such as the Black Sea Economic Cooperation Pact (BSEC)[13] and now the Indian Ocean Rim States Organization (IOR-ARC)[14] are cases in point. The (gradual) integration of several states in a larger region offers the most effective answer to modern economic challenges and the intention to trade and cooperate beyond established borders, while permitting the continued enjoyment of communal identity, cultural and religious values, and traditions if the boundaries of the existing states become too narrow, and since it seems inconceivable to alter them for each case where such desires prevail. In 1997 former U.S. Federal Reserve Chairman Paul Volcker suggested that three global currency regions may develop: The Dollar in the Americas, the Euro in the EU and neighboring states, and the Yen in Asia. Taking one of the strongest regional currencies and pegging the others in the same region to it seems an effective way to foster regional trade and integration and thus cohesion between regional entities.

In Eastern Europe and the Former Soviet Union (Bosniaks, Montenegrines, Kosovars, and Chechens) leaders of many communities have frequently expressed their desire to become internationally recognized as independent sovereign entities, while at the same time stressing their interest in joining the European Union. Interestingly there has been ignorance concerning the implicit tension between these two objectives. The EU is a supranational organization with the right – granted by its member states – to limit sovereignty and infringe upon the rights and competencies typically performed by central governments. It can impose EU regulations in such critical areas as taxation, fiscal policies, home affairs (visa, citizenship), minimum human- and socio-economic rights, technical standards and safety, and increasingly even education and certain foreign and security issues. Thanks to the powers of the European Court of Justice, the European Commission even has the capability to enforce its decisions and levy penalties from member governments.

It is important to recognize that in a region with increased integration, like *Euroland*, sovereignty and independence – and thus self-determination – are of decreasing relevance, though 'subsidiarity' offers communities maximum autonomy in cultural, educative, and other dimensions important for identity.[15] The key to a functioning supranational society is the flexibility and openness for other cultures and the readiness to accept multiple identities. In turn, maximum possible and direct contact between the community and those beyond the international boundaries of its state is critical to alleviate constant demands for independence. This concerns the level and extent of treaty-making powers, permission for various foreign affairs agenda – independent from the central administration – the quest for participation in customs and border protection, even certain dimensions of participation in defense agenda.

Regional integration in combination with maximum parallel self-governance will be an effective, albeit longer-term, recipe for satisfying the aspirations to freedom of ethnic communities. It would appeal to the reasoning of the community and the responsibility of state, neighborhood, region, and international community. It would also bring about greater prosperity and stability while slowly alleviating the relevance of the respective hard international boundaries in a time of global interdependence.

Potential solutions to self-determination crises

In order to offer communities an acceptable and predictable way towards their dream of greater freedom and to achieve feasible standards both for the central government and the other communities concerned it is possible to: 1) clearly delineate self-governance and secession modes and mechanisms in the constitution of a state in order to also demonstrate to the national and international community the various thresholds imposed. 2) to try to find a feasible and acceptable alternative to full classical self-determination (i.e. secession and independence) which is in line with the emerging, globalized international system and which helps avoid the continuing separation being accompanied by bloodshed and destruction. At the same time, this process provides for a peaceful and lasting solution, namely the proposed self-governance plus regional integration.

The institutionalization of self-determination

In light of a more general trend to introduce meaningful democratic principles into daily life, several states have recently tried to offer provisions permitting classical self-determination, that is, secession, to their communities. Two constitutions can be seen as examples for specifically enumerating the right of self-determination: the constitution of Ethiopia and the constitution of South Africa. Article 39(1) of the Ethiopian constitution reads, 'Every Nation, Nationality and people in Ethiopia has an unconditional right to self-determination, including the right to secession.' Chapter XIV, section 235, of the constitution of South Africa offers self-determination as well.[16] In the Principality of Liechtenstein, in Central Europe, an amendment to the constitution of 1921 introduced the right to self-determination in its new Article 4 in order to offer communities the possibility to search for new legal arrangements:[17]

1. The change in the boundaries of the territory of the state can be accomplished only by law. Changes of boundaries between communities require a majority vote of the Liechtenstein citizens in the communities in question.

Each community has the right to secede. Secession is to be regulated by law or on a case-by-case basis by contract. Secession must be approved by a majority of Liechtenstein citizens resident in the community in question. In the case a majority approves secession the reigning prince shall have the right to order within thirty days a vote of reconsideration six months later.

Self-governance plus regional integration

Self-governance is a concept more positive, extensive, humane, and forward looking than classical self-determination. It avoids the slippery slope to secession and independence, i.e. state shattering, and contains less emotionally loaded connotation of past ethnic-historical experiences. The notion of self-governance is 'progressive,' leading to increased gender equality and non-discriminatory politics, cultural flexibility, and environmental awareness, i.e. the readiness to accept multiple identities (Falk 1997). To the extent that self-governance plus regional integration affects international borders at all, it will do so gradually, through enhanced economic, cultural, and person-to-person contacts, greater independence, and effective international and regional assistance.

Self-governance and regional integration can be defined as a combination of maximum autonomy, i.e. 'internal sovereignty,' and wide-ranging 'external competencies.' Internal sovereignty would encompass concern for the areas of culture, education, language, religion, finance, judicial administration, and public safety, as well as certain industrial, energy, and infrastructure projects, while external competencies should include as many dimensions as possible for permitting a community maximum freedom to interact with its neighbors, in the region, and with other states and international organizations.[18] Internal Sovereignty can be understood as 'partial' or 'limited' sovereignty, but the term sheds light on the will by the community to have certain sovereign rights for certain agenda, and the readiness of the central government to grant these rights. This should consider the attractions and constraints of modern day (global) interdependence and should also be seen within the – eventual – greater regional integration. Self-governance should allow for the local administration of daily communal or regional affairs and offer more freedom for creativity to adapt local institutions, organs, laws, and regulations to the specific needs of the community, though it remains bound by the constitution of its sovereign state. Such enhanced rights and authority oblige the community to recognize and respect the rights of minorities within its territory. Thus self-governance is inherently democratic – whatever 'democracy' may mean in view of the tradition and political culture of the community. However, self-governance plus regional integration ought to ascertain the cultural independence and human rights of any minority within that community.[19]

In practice 'self-governance plus regional integration' ought to include substantial independence if not sole competence for such agenda as: local administration; religious, cultural, educational, judicial, and even fiscal authority; and local security, even adequate communal contribution to external security. It is important that the community perceives equality both in comparison to the other communities in the state and in the just order of a transparent and decentralized national structure. Competencies within self-governance ought also to consist of certain international treaty-making powers and representation, as long as they do not challenge national (federal) objectives as laid forth in the constitution. Such 'external competencies' could comprise cultural, educational, scientific, and technical contacts with other regions and sub-states, or even states and international organizations.[20] In certain regions of the world there already exists exchange in experience and information regarding security mechanisms, crime prevention, and catastrophe and humanitarian assistance between regions and sub-states.[21]

But effective self-governance and regional integration can only be achieved by introducing the readiness to identify with multiple identities – being a Catalan, a Spaniard, and a European; or being a Kashmiri as well as an Indian or Pakistani citizen.[22] Stringent efforts in education and representation and special emphasis on the media, presumably under some sort of neutral supervision, are a critical condition for such a readiness to accept multiple identities.

The examples of the German State of Bavaria, the Austrian Bundesland Oberösterreich, the Spanish Region of Catalunya, and the Italian Region Bolzano-Südtirol offer a significant level of internal sovereignty for the respective communities, and demonstrate also considerable external competencies and the ability to conduct 'regional foreign policy' (particularly for Bavaria and Oberösterreich).[23]

Often federalism or confederalism are seen as a possible solution. Federalism is a potential solution for devolution from the center to the federal states. It is based on a strong constitution which delineates the various competencies as separated between *Länder* and the Federal government. The Federal Republic of Germany and the Republic of Austria are good examples of federal states that have extensive rights but are still held accountable by the Central government. In the case of Switzerland, the Helvetic Confederation, the Cantons wield maximum rights, including distinctly separate cultural and education policies, taxation, and defense and security arrangements. Switzerland represents perhaps the most elaborate model of Federalism or 'confederalism' as the name suggests, grown over five centuries and combined with the outmost of direct democracy. The federal structure of Germany though is more restrictive, as is the Austrian. Both have a parliamentary democracy and are federal republics. In the case of Germany fiscal control and taxation rank amongst the critical controls which the federal government has over the *Länder* – besides federal legal and executive regulations.

Self-governance in its optimum form may however function more like the confederal model. Daniel Elazar defines confederalism as 'several existing polities joined together to form a common government for strictly limited purposes . . . that remains dependent upon its constituent polities . . . and must work through them' (cf. Elazar n.d.). Anthony D. Smith (1995: 119–120) sees new relevance in regional or pan-continental associations or federations. Such 'pan-nationalisms' on the basis of culture or accepted basic norms – such as for instance the acquis communitair – could offer a 'supersession of existing national states in the interest of much larger super states' or supranational entities.

Parallel to establishing structures and institutions for such extensive self-governance, an immediate incentive has to be launched for trans-border inter-regional cooperation and integration in conjunction with 'outside' (either international or by the central authorities) economic, industrial, and infrastructural assistance programs, and the (inter-national) guarantee of security and the borders. This parallel initiative is critical to provide credibility to the offers of maximum self-governance and for the community to trust in international efforts for an appropriate and equal, fair, and effective new status. Resulting increase in people-to-people contact, mobility, trade, regional income, and openness to mutual interaction will influence the regional setting and possibly ameliorate inter-communal frictions while reducing the desire for separa-tion and full independence. Over time such regional development and integration within and beyond the state (including the other communities there) will relax the hardness of the external boundaries and will change their character to softer administrative boundaries, permitting the free movement of people, goods, services, and capital. Much like the four European Economic Area (EEA) freedoms of movement (goods, services, capital, and citizens)[24] such softened boundaries will permit regional eco-nomic development, integration, and participation in the global market. There ought to be effective engagement of the governments of all the neighboring states concerned, since effective regionalization is only possible thanks to their engagement. All this changes the borders both in practice and perception while avoiding their redrawing. It offers the community in question maximum independence from the central authority while avoiding the problems associated with obtaining full independence.

Self-governance requires stability, predictability, transparency, and, most important, communal security. The experiences during the conference on security and cooperation in Europe (CSCE) in the early 1970s may be of relevance in this case. Then critical dimensions concerning regional security, both internal and external, as well as the plight of minorities, etc. were separated into military strategic, socio-economic, and humanitarian 'baskets.' In order to establish a benevolent and encouraging framework for a viable region such considerations are also relevant today and elsewhere.

Military security is of obvious relevance; para-military organizations can hinder effective self-governance by the existence of arms and armed forces or groupings as well as criminal elements, organized locally or regionally. Demilitarization and decriminalization (including disarmament) of the region are a conditio sine qua non for the successful introduction of self-governance and a peaceful decentralization process. Detraumatization and specific education and employment programs for the young are of importance as well.[25] In the post-9/11 discussions and emphasis on the 'war against terrorism' this has obtained an urgent and more complex meaning. The process of stabilization of a region may well be taken one step further by introducing neutralization; thus denying foreign actors the right to use the territory as a staging ground for any armed or military operations and therewith reducing the danger of armed clashes. An international guarantee of the inviolability of the rights and territory of the community in question may bring added stability and reduce the urge for armed forces to secure borders.

Most importantly, the leadership in the community, region, state, and abroad must have the will and farsightedness to concern itself with the real interest and fate of individual citizens, the young and the old, the rich and the poor, instead of concentrating on personal interests and advantages. Too many times, issues of self-determination have been employed to serve leadership interests rather than the true interest at the very core of self-determination – the safety, economic and political possibilities and rights of individual men, women, and children. It is for them we ought to implement feasible and acceptable solutions that will provide in the long run for their peace, justice, and prosperity.

Possible applications

In the Balkans

On many occasions it has been suggested to create an integrated zone in the Balkans among all successor-states of the old Federal Republic of Yugoslavia and the newcomers in the EU with Hungary, Austria, and Slovenia in the north, Romania and (eventually) Bulgaria in the east, and Greece in the south, including the need to speed up the admission process of Turkey (cf. Danspeckgruber 1999). This integration process, with a special internal security framework being established in parallel, would permit to leave the final status of Kosovo (UN Res 1244) open while maximizing Pristina's self-governance and participation in the integration process, i.e. offering also wide-ranging external competencies, independent from Belgrade. Currently Kosovo is an international protectorate, under UNMIK, though it seems plausible that this status could be at one point transferred under EU auspices. Obviously security, migration, and relations with neighboring countries would fall under stringent EU/NATO regulations. Swedish emissary Carl Bildt detailed the institutional forging of closer links between the EU and the Balkan states. He suggested that 'The EU should provide clear blueprints for reforms that would pave the way [for closer cooperation and integration] . . . if not full-blown [EU] membership . . . [including] the possibility of making them part of a broader Euro-zone.' (Bildt 1999, cf. also Steil and Woodward 1999, and United States Institute of Peace 2002).

Chechnya

The (legal) basis for the Chechens' claim to independence lies in their refusal to sign the Russian Federation Treaty of 1992, as well as the claim that because the dissolution of the Soviet Union was illegal then legal arguments based upon the Soviet Constitution have become invalid.[26]

It still appears that President Aslan Maskhadov and his government are not insisting on full sovereignty and unconditional independence. Some of his representatives even refer to the example of Puerto Rico within the United States as a potential model to build upon. This conforms to the idea of 'self-governance plus regionalization,' namely that borders should not be changed, rather self-governance should be maximized and cooperation and integration among states and sub-states in the region enhanced.[27]

Kashmir

The introduction of multiple identities as part of 'self-governance plus regional integration' could offer a possible solution for the traditional Kashmir problem. Instead of making a decision on the territory and searching for a solution for redrawing external boundaries, self governance plus regionalization could be introduced to permit the Kashmiris and those on either side of the Line of Control (LoC) to keep their sovereign territories and could spare India from giving up completely what it considers to be within its borders. Sir John Thomson suggests offering the Kashmiris south of the LoC both Kashmiri ID cards and Indian Passports, and those on the Pakistani side, hence north of the LoC, both Kashmiri ID cards and Pakistani Passports. This solution would help to avoid a redrawing of international boundaries and neither India nor Pakistan would lose Kashmir (or Jammu and Kashmir for India). No territorial change would take place and international assistance could be arranged to monitor borders or help prevent influx on either side of criminal elements.

Conclusion

It has been demonstrated that self-governance plus parallel regional integration can be a model for offering a community most of the sought-after freedoms, while also assisting other neighboring communities and avoiding the difficult path of redrawing international boundaries. The protection of minorities, the provision of communal and regional security, and the introduction of stability and reduction of criminality in the region are, however, critical conditions for an eventual introduction of self-governance in the region. But several other important conditions have to be fulfilled as well in order to enable it to work.

First, any solution of a new status for a community ought to include the idea of respect for multiple identities accepted throughout the region. This appreciation of diversity allows for increasing flexibility in defining the relationship between geographical living space and local, state, and regional hierarchies. An important condition is significant tolerance in education and culture towards the complex intricacies of ethnic and religious identities. Once multiple identities are accepted, the influence of militant nationalism may wane, and tolerance for other identities will increase. As we have seen in successful cases of self-governance, a person can 'hold several identities' – e.g., be proud to be a Catalan, as well as a Spaniard, a Mediterranean, and a European. Interestingly, research has shed light on the relationship between significant wealth and heightened readiness to accept multiple identities. This suggests the immediate need to address the socio-economic situation in a community searching for greater independence.

This evolution is a question of understanding, education, and time, and most importantly is linked to a new generation of leaders. The role of the diaspora – all those living outside the national territory – may influence the readiness for such heightened flexibility as in 'multiple identities.' Typically, diasporas wield negative influence in the critical phases and can contribute to antagonism. It will be for the communal and national authorities to limit the negative influence of those who live abroad.

Second, the involved parties must develop a flexible and forgiving (political) culture based, ideally, on democratic values and notions such as tolerance, flexibility, forgiveness, and compromise. Such a culture allows minorities – even within the community that searches for greater independence from the center – to contribute and play a role. Democratization offers a just and appropriate way to ascertain a community's will and to ensure international acceptance and continued support. This includes the very important aspect of equality of communities and offering equal rights in a transparent and just way, so that the community and its leadership gains trust in the just, fair, and equal treatment of any of its demands, not only by other communities and majorities, but also by the central authorities. This in turn will take away the base for radicalization, and deprive extremism of its attraction, especially if combined with better economic conditions.

Third, organized crime and all kinds of semi-legal actions need to be eliminated. In most cases this works only with a concomitant major investment in micro and macro aspects of economic development, industrialization and availability of training and jobs for the young, and – at least in the start-up phase – significant international assistance. It is also relevant to address the need for a regional framework based on binding agreements between the governments concerned. This presumably includes some form of international guarantee or, at least, involvement. Experience has proven that frequently communities in search of greater autonomy are those who need economic assistance most.[28] Indeed their economic hardship and frustration is often part of the cause for their search for self-determination. Effective and imminent international assistance has such critical meaning for many important dimensions – from decriminalization to effectively assisting the development of livelihoods.

Fourth, it is indispensable to create immediate efforts on neutral and objective education, teaching materials and information, and general economic programs with real effects for the community – in other words, to create possibilities and hope for the young. This should offer enhanced possibilities for employment and create positions and opportunities for all, especially also the young. This will help fulfill the aspirations of the younger generation, hinder the dangerous brain drain, and keep the young off the streets and away from illegal activities. This also concerns education, cultural performances, and the dissemination of reliable information in order to minimize negative interference and exaggeration and create a realistic picture of the environment and the other communities concerned, while diminishing idealization and romantic images. Education serves also to introduce the notion of multiple identities and a forgiving, flexible political culture.

Fifth, in a globalized world the international media has to recognize its responsibility in terms of 'de-emotionalizing' reporting, reducing hype and not lending itself to cheap, albeit publicity-effective, reporting which ignores the truth and puts news reports into a local and timely context. Real-time media 'life' is by definition more powerful than those reports which one knows stem from 'prior-to yesterday.'

This has particular influence on diasporas, which can most effectively mobilize human, financial, and material support for those involved in a self-determination or secession crisis and which have to be curtailed or brought to reason in order to avoid escalatory rhetoric or other influence.

Traditionally, diasporas have proven to be more radical and nationalist than those actually living in the area.

Sixth, there has to be a sustained effort to educate political leaders about the many-fold possibilities to address self-determination conflicts by mechanisms short of secession from an existing state. This relates obviously to the willingness of the international community to participate in such endeavors and credibly demonstrate longer-term commitment and involvement, both active and in terms of concrete support.

Finally, it is imperative that the central authority offers a community the prospect of trust, transparency, justice, and serious commitment to legal, administrative and economic development, and that the community can count on equality in national and regional life. For the sake of stability and peace, any attempt to suppress communal striving for autonomy cannot and will not function in the long run – certainly not in a world where access to information has become global and immediate.

On the international scale it is thus imperative to create a mechanism with anticipatory capabilities to permit the community searching for greater independence from the center to engage in a transparent, predictable, and fair process. This requires three simultaneous developments: 1) to engage in negotiations for autonomy, 2) to commence regional cooperation and enhance a trans-border process, and 3) to draw on international attention and assistance so as to ascertain security and economic assistance in order to avoid escalation or crises in the region. In the end, however, it is the individual man and woman, child and elder, who have to bear the consequences. It is for them that peace, justice, and prosperity ought to reign – it is their interests that government must serve.

In times of heightened international tensions – as is the case during the 'war on terror' and in a situation comprising change and the appearance of new rules – self-determination and related matters thus once again experience challenges and the need for adaptation. As stated earlier, international readiness for humanitarian intervention or recognition of new, seceded territories is low. So why not search for new concepts which may offer the parties concerned a solution that address their needs and desires? Offer more freedom but retain the geopolitical status quo, at least for the near future. Self-governance and regionalization may do so – less dramatic, less costly and more effective, certainly than drawn-out political and legal battles, or worse, conflicts and wars which destroy dreams and togetherness.

Notes

1 See Kohli's (2001) arguments on the 'bell curve' of self-determination.
2 Typically the community will insist that this 'autonomy' really has become increasingly limited and that the situation now is unbearable, and that its members find themselves always at a disadvantage, particularly compared to the other communities of the state. In turn the central government will argue

that the community enjoys all freedoms as guaranteed in the national legal framework (constitution) and that it, the central authority, has to uphold law and order in the state, and justice towards the other communities.

3 See Danspeckgruber (1997: 38).
4 We need to determine which entity can justifiably argue for self-determination and perhaps classical independence: a 'community,' a region, a (suppressed) people, a former colony? For an excellent discussion of this issue see Anderson (1983) and Horowitz (1985).
5 See the excellent collection by Michael Mandelbaum (2000), as well as his earlier edited work (1998).
6 However, one has to keep in mind then-Yugoslav President Slobodan Milosevic's assertion in the mid-1990s that any Kosovo Albanian opposing central government (Serbian) is a 'terrorist.' The West and then even Russia saw them as 'fighters for Kosovo's equal status' and Kosovo-Albanian patriots. Eventually the harsh Serbian repression of Kosovo Albanians and the beginning of ethnic cleansing led to NATO intervention in 1999 – though not with agreement by the UN SC. Also, the Moscow leadership has, after the Moscow gas explosions of 1998, consistently and predominantly referred to Chechen fighters as 'terrorists' or 'criminals' – very much like Milosevic. Today there might be no assistance whatsoever, and President Putin has received the green light in his 'fight against terrorism' by U.S. President George Bush (allegedly also for other reasons than the United States' engagement in its defense against terrorism).
7 It is interesting to observe the increased frequency of the use of the terms 'terrorist' and 'terrorist activities' in international media reporting from South Asia or other areas since 9/11.
8 Woodrow Wilson and originally distinguished external internal self-determination: external being the right of a nation/community to exert freedom in choosing its allies; internal bestowing the right of freely choosing one's government. See Cassese (1995).
9 Continued analysis sees the critical seven 'S's': state, sovereignty, self-determination, security, subsidiarity, supranational, and symbolism in cases dealing with self-determination.
10 For an excellent volume on regionalization see Fawcett and Hurrell (1995); on regionalism and self-determination, see Alexander and Friedlander (1980) and Moore (1998).
11 Kirchner and Christiansen (1999: 4).
12 Regionalization understood as the emergence of subregions, of several smaller states or parts of states according to infrastructural needs, is based upon similarities in ethnicity, history, geography, and even climate.
13 http://www.photius.com/bsec/bsec.html.
14 http://www.ficci.com/ficci/International/ior.html.
15 For a discussion of regionalization and subsidiarity in Europe see Danspeckgruber (2002b).
16 The right of the South African people as a whole to self-determination, as manifested in this Constitution, does not preclude, within the framework of this right, recognition of the notion of the right to self-determination of any community sharing a common cultural and language heritage, within a territorial entity in the Republic or in any other way, determined by national legislation.
17 Available online at: http://www.fuerstenhaus.li/uploads/media/Verfassung_2003_02.pdf.
18 'Internal sovereignty' should contain all those rights and obligations as set forth by the respective constitutions, the practice of the relevant governments

and possible regional and international organizations. There exists an extensive literature dealing with sovereignty in the contemporary international
system: see Hashmi (1997), Krasner (2001), Philpott (2001), and Spruyt
(1994).
19 Regarding the rules of democracy embedded within the concept of self-
governance see also Prince Hans Adam II. of Liechtenstein (2002).
20 'External competencies' are like those under 'internal sovereignty' to facilitate
a community's interaction with other regions outside the sovereign state territory. They are also regulated by the constitution and administrative laws of the
state. However there may be a discrepancy between legal competencies and
material actions, including direct contacts with regions, cooperations in
science and technology, security, environment, etc.
21 The author is grateful for an interview granted by Dr. Erich Haager, Presidency
of the Upper Austrian Government, Linz, July 25 2002.
22 The introduction of multiple identities as part of 'self-governance plus regional
integration' could offer a possible solution for the Kashmir Conflict – see
below.
23 They would, however, exclude national defense, currency, or an independent
foreign service.
24 For excellent studies of the Province of Südtirol see Magliana (2000) and Wolff
(Chapter 6).
25 These obligations for immediate action in a region to assist and reconstruct
can be summarized in the seven 'Ds': De-militarization; De-mobilization; Decriminalization;   De-traumatization;   De-radicalization;   De-centralization;
Democratization, as well as the seven 'Rs': Re-construction; Re-patriation; Reconciliation; Re-legitimization; Re-integration; Regionalization; Re-education;
see Danspeckgruber (2002a).
26 Most importantly, the Khasavyurt Agreement (October 30 1996), signed by
both the Chechens and the Russians, explicitly refers to the right of self-
determination and stipulates that relations between the Chechen Republic and
the Russian Federation be governed by the universally accepted principles and
norms of international law.
27 http://www.princeton.edu/~lisd/caucasus.html.
28 Though, interestingly, Slovenia and the Czech Republic are the exceptions
which prove that rule. Both were looking for independence because they
found that union with the rest of their respective states has proven over time to
be economically and politically disadvantageous for them.

References

Alexander, Yonah and Friedlander, Robert A. (1980) *Self-Determination: National,
Regional, and Global Dimensions.* Westport, CT: Westview Press.
Anderson, Benedict (1983) *Imagined Communities: Reflections on the Origin and
Spread of Nationalism.* London: Verso.
Bildt, Carl (1999) 'Embracing the Balkans,' *Financial Times* 19 February, 14.
Cassese, Antonio (1995) *Self-Determination of Peoples: A Legal Reappraisal.* Cam-
bridge: Cambridge University Press.
Danspeckgruber, Wolfgang (1999) 'Subregional Crisis and Potential Lessons for
Future Self-Determination Conflicts: The Case of Kosovo,' in Laurent Goetschel,
ed., *Security in a Globalized World: Risks and Opportunities.* Baden-Baden: Nomos
Verlagsgesellschaft, 119–136.
Danspeckgruber, Wolfgang (2002a) 'Final Assessment,' in Wolfgang Danspeckgru-

ber, ed., *The Self-Determination of Peoples: Community, Nation, and State in an Interdependent World*. Boulder, CO: Lynne Rienner Publishers, 335–357.

Danspeckgruber, Wolfgang (2002b) 'Self-determination and Regionalization in Contemporary Europe,' in Wolfgang Danspeckgruber, ed., *The Self-Determination of Peoples: Community, Nation, and State in an Interdependent World*. Boulder, CO: Lynne Rienner Publishers, 165–199.

Elazar, Daniel J. (n.d.) *Federal Systems of the World: A Handbook of Federal, Confederal, and Autonomy Arrangements*. Available online at: http://www.jcpa.org/dje/books/fedsysworld-intro.htm.

Falk, Richard (1997) *On Humane Governance*. Philadelphia: Pennsylvania State University Press.

Fawcett, Louise and Hurrell, Andrew (1995) *Regionalism in World Politics*. Oxford: Oxford University Press.

Halperin, Morton H. and Scheffer David J. with Small, Patricia L. (1992) *Self-Determination in the New World Order*. New York: Carnegie Endowment for International Peace.

Hashmi, Sohail H., ed. (1997) *State Sovereignty*. Philadelphia: Pennsylvania State University Press.

Horowitz, Donald L. (1985) *Ethnic Groups in Conflict*. Berkeley: University of California Press.

International Kosovo Commission (2000) *Report*. Oxford: Oxford University Press.

Kirchner, Emil J. and Christiansen, Thomas (1999) 'The Importance of Local and Regional Reform', in Emil J. Kirchner, ed., *Decentralization and Transition in Visegrad*. New York: St. Martin's Press, 1–18.

Kohli, Atul (2001) 'Can Democracies Accommodate Ethnic Nationalism?,' in Wolfgang Danspeckgruber, ed., *The Self-Determination of Peoples: Community, Nation, and State in an Interdependent World*. Boulder, CO: Lynne Rienner Publishers, 287–314.

Krasner, Stephen, ed. (2001) *Problematic Sovereignty: Contested Rules and Political Possibilities*. New York: Columbia University Press.

Magliana, Melissa (2000) *The Autonomous Province of Bolzano-Südtirol – A Model of Self-Governance?* Bolzano: European Academy.

Mandelbaum, Michael, ed. (1998) *The New Russian Foreign Policy*. New York: Council on Foreign Relations.

Mandelbaum, Michael, ed. (2000) *The New European Diasporas: National Minorities and Conflict in Eastern Europe*. New York: Council on Foreign Relations Press.

Moore, Margaret (1998) 'The Territorial Dimension of Self-Determination,' in Margaret Moore, ed., *National Self-Determination and Secession*. Oxford: Oxford University Press, 134–157.

Musgrave, Thomas D. (1998) *Self-Determination and National Minorities*. Oxford: Oxford University Press.

Philpott, Daniel (2001) *Revolutions in Sovereignty*. Princeton: Princeton University Press.

Prince Hans Adam II. of Liechtenstein (2002) *Democracy and Self-Determination*. London: IISS.

Smith, Anthony D. (1995) *Nations and Nationalisms in a Global Era*. Cambridge: Polity Press.

Spruyt, Henrik (1994) *The Sovereign State and Its Competitors*. Princeton: Princeton University Press.

Steil, Benn and Woodward, Susan L. (1999) 'A European "New Deal" for the Balkans,' *Foreign Affairs*, vol. 78, November/December 99–105.

Tomuschat, Christian (1994) 'Self-Determination in a Post-colonial World,' in Christian Tomuschat, ed., *Modern Law of Self-Determination*. The Hague, Boston and London: Martinus Nijhoff Publishers, 7–15.

United States Institute of Peace (2002) 'Kosovo Final Status – Options and Cross-Border Requirements,' *Special Report 91*. Washington, DC: United States Institute of Peace.

Watts, Arthur (2002) 'The Liechtenstein Draft Convention on Self-Determination Through Self-Administration – A Commentary,' in Danspeckgruber, Wolfgang ed. (2002), *The Self-Determination of Peoples: Community, Nation, and State in an Independent World*. Boulder, CO: Lynne Rienner Publishers, 365–381.

3 Enforced autonomy and self-governance

The post-Yugoslav experience

Marc Weller

Introduction

The former Yugoslavia furnishes the clearest examples of the application of autonomy and self-governance for the purpose of retaining the territorial unity of the state. As was noted in the introduction, the EU Carrington Peace conference on Yugoslavia attempted to use autonomy to buy off Serbia's territorial ambitions with respect to areas inhabited by ethnic Serbs located outside of the Republic of Serbia. Croatia, in particular, was pressed hard to offer full autonomy in relation to the Krajina area. Bosnia and Herzegovina was kept together through the Dayton accords, but only under the condition of very wide-ranging self-governance for its constituent units. Kosovo was placed under an internationalized, progressively more wide-ranging regime of self-governance. The Macedonia settlement, negotiated under significant international pressure, established what was called enhanced local self-governance, or autonomy by another name. Finally, Serbia and Montenegro, the latter being a reluctant bride, were pressed into a State Union of two self-governing entities, at least for a standstill period of three years.

In the analysis that follows, an attempt will be made to consider the contribution made by this experience to our wider understanding of autonomy as a means of state construction. Only cases where there has been international involvement in generating a settlement are considered.[1] When undertaking this review, it is important to bear in mind that the attempts of state construction in the former Yugoslavia have had to be conducted against the background of an extraordinarily dramatic recent history. It is still too early to form a view as to the success or failure of these attempts. Instead, it must suffice for the moment to see to what extent autonomy has remained a remedy aimed at reconciling competing ethnic identities with the wish to retain the territorial unity of the former constituent republics of socialist Yugoslavia.

For the purpose of this book, we have adopted a fairly broad working definition of autonomy, supplemented by a similarly broad view of the related concept of self-government, which is of special relevance in relation to Kosovo.[2] We use the term autonomy to describe the legally entrenched power of ethnic or territorial communities to take public decisions and execute public policy independently of other sources of authority in the state, but subject to the overall legal order of the state. While autonomy would be typically focused on exercising public powers of relevance to the identity of the community in question (for instance, in relation to schools), self-governance encompasses all aspects of public power other than those which the unit of self-government cannot effectively perform on its own.

Background factors

Yash Ghai (2001: 1–24) has identified a number of factors that must be present if autonomy is to have a chance of success, including:

- Autonomy should be introduced concurrently with a regime change. International community involvement is helpful, but the introduction of the autonomy arrangement needs to be achieved with widespread public support;
- Need for an established tradition of democracy and the rule of law;
- Need for uncontested sovereignty of the state; autonomy in itself does not promote secessionism;
- Preference for more than two principal ethnic groups in the state;
- Need for mechanisms to manage relations between the autonomous unit and the overall state (credible dispute settlement mechanism);
- Need for careful design.

Regime change and international and public support. In none of the cases to be considered here did a regime change occur in parallel with the introduction of the new state structures, including whatever autonomy elements may have been provided for. In Croatia, the nationalist Tudjman government remained in power throughout the period of the introduction of special provisions for Eastern Slavonia. When a new, more moderate government came to power some years later, new provisions for autonomy were generated, but not with specific reference to this territory. In Bosnia and Herzegovina, the 'war-time' political structures remained in place for most of the constituent entities and their units. While there was some exchange of personnel in the Republika Srpska, including the departure of Radovan Karadzic and Radko Mladic, the political structures they had generated remained and their party continued to attract support. Subsequent attempts by the international implementation agencies to assist in generating an electoral outcome in that entity that would bring to power a more moderate leadership were not fully successful in the early phases.

In Kosovo, a 'regime change' of sorts did occur when Serb/Yugoslav authorities were forcibly displaced in June 1999. However, at least in terms of the ethnic Albanian side, the end of the conflict did not result in a change of its own leadership. The LDK, led by Ibrahim Rugova, and the former KLA, which transformed itself into two political parties, the PDK and AAK, continued to operate, with much the same personnel in place. These groups had already represented Kosovo at the Rambouillet talks, where an attempt had been made to agree an interim settlement providing for wide-ranging autonomy or self-governance of Kosovo.

At the time of the negotiations leading to the Ohrid accords, no change of government took place in Maceondia. Instead, the ethnic Macedonian/ethnic Albanian coalition government remained in power until the next elections, with its ethnic Macedonian majority element rapidly distancing itself from the agreement. The implementation of the agreement was therefore delayed for more than a year, until elections resulted in a new coalition government of the former ethnic Macedonian and ethnic Albanian opposition parties.

In Belgrade, the transition from Milosevic had taken place by the time of the Serbia/Montenegro agreement. However, there was not the kind of sea-change of political reform one would ordinarily associate with regime change. Instead, a conservative presidency under Vojislav Kostunica was struggling against divided government headed by Zoran Djindjic, making progress very difficult.

In all five instances, however, there was a considerable element of international involvement. In Kosovo, a new constitutional framework was drafted in 2001 by the international administration of the territory. While there was genuine discussion involving ethnic Albanian experts nominated by the main local political parties, the basic features of the arrangement were not subject to negotiation. The design of the document was therefore essentially an international one, which also had to take account of the interests of ethnic Serbs living in the area whose representatives generally boycotted the discussion process.

At Dayton, the international negotiators played a very significant role in shaping the constitutional documents for post-war Bosnia and Herzegovina. Similarly, the Macedonia Framework Agreement of 13 August 2001 was obtained only through quite determined, and, from the perspective of the majority parties, rather rough, negotiating techniques of the international mediators, this time the EU acting in tandem with a US representative and backed by then NATO Secretary General, Lord George Robertson.

With the latest settlement in the region, the *Accord on Principles in Relations between Serbia and Montenegro* of March 2002, also being the result of EU mediation conducted under high pressure, only Croatia remains somewhat exceptional. Zagreb had settled with the UN for temporary autonomy for Eastern Slavonia under international administration as a means of peacefully reintegrating that territory. However, it refused international pressure to establish a permanent autonomy regime for that territory, or indeed, to offer genuine autonomy for the even more sensitive Krajina region, where a significant exodus of the Serb community had taken place in the wake of the forcible re-incorporation of the area into Croatia.

In none of the above instances did the settlement engender a significant element of popular support. The Bosnian Serb and Croat communities were not even represented at Dayton. Instead, they were bound by the consent given by the (then) FRY and Croatian presidents, Milosevic and Tudjman, respectively. In two other cases, Macedonia and Serbia/Montenegro, provision was made for an element of ratification through parliamentary action. In the former case, this took the form of the adoption of constitutional amendments and legislative changes; in the latter, provisions were made for a process of drafting a new Constitutional Charter and seeking its approval through all three relevant parliaments, i.e., the republican Montenegrin and Serbian parliaments and the federal parliament.

Democratic tradition and rule of law. Socialist Yugoslavia had been one of the more enlightened states constructed according to the Marxist Leninist model. Nevertheless, it could not boast a democratic tradition in a Western liberal sense. Neither was it possible to speak of a tradition of the rule of law. In fact, the attempt to transform Yugoslavia into a multi-party democracy led to the assumption of power by the Milosevic regime in Serbia. The abuse of the federal state structure, and the political role played by the highest judicial bodies of the Federation in this context, greatly contributed to the impetus that led initially Croatia and then Slovenia to leave the state altogether. The reign of what may be described as 'ethnic democracy' in most of the target states for internationalized settlement also did not contribute to the establishment of a genuine democratic tradition. In Bosnia and Herzegovina, the violent nature of conflict polarized the population segments to an extraordinary yet understandable extent. Electoral decisions continue to be taken according to ethnic appurtenance, rather than specific, non-ethnic subject interests. Contrary to the best efforts of the international agencies involved in the process, and even their alleged attempts to engage in electoral engineering in the early phases of international involvement in governance there, radical nationalist parties have continued to perform well. In fact, at times they appear unchallengeable among 'their' ethnic community. In Kosovo, too, the political scene is not one that can be described as interest-based. Instead, party loyalty among the ethnic Albanian community has remained strangely constant, attaching itself to the perceived 'war-time' performance of individual charismatic leaders. While change has occurred in Serbia and Montenegro, the radical, nationalist parties have continued to attract very significant support, constantly threatening to undermine, if not reverse, the reform process. Finally Macedonia has seen a fluctuation of voter preferences. However, the democratic system has not really been strengthened in consequence. Instead, a deep disillusionment has set in amongst the voters. There is a sense that electoral choices are not real, as government will not discharge its functions properly, whatever coalition is in charge.

Overall, therefore, there has neither been a democratic tradition to build on, nor has the post-settlement period generated such a tradition, at least in the ideal-typical Western liberal sense. Moreover, all settlements were achieved under strong international pressure and they have generally not been legitimized by popular consent.

No secessionist aims of the protagonists. In at least four of the five instances under consideration, the dispute that was to be addressed through the new constitutional setup was precisely one about secession. The representatives of the Serb-occupied areas of Croatia had proclaimed either statehood or declared themselves in favour of merger with a Greater Serbia while they held control over Krajina and Eastern Slavonia. Both the Serb and the Croat entities within Bosnia and Herzegovina had declared statehood by the time the Dayton agreement was concluded. Kosovo had considered itself an independent state since 1991. And the Montenegro-Serbia agreement was concluded precisely to suspend for some time the issue of the dissolution of the new Yugoslav Federation under its 1992 constitution. The only possible exception may be Macedonia, as the ethnic Albanian groups that had taken up arms did not generally agitate for independence, but instead for self-government and equal rights within Macedonia. There was, however, a considerable element of distrust on this point held by the ethnic majority population and also by elements of the organized international community engaged in this crisis.

No bi-ethnic conflict. In all five cases, there existed more than one majority and one minority population. However, in all cases, the essential dispute was nevertheless one between two principal ethnic groups. In Krajina and Eastern Slavonia, it was ethnic Croats against ethnic Serbs. In Bosnia and Herzegovina, there were of course three groups in conflict, but it was not a trilateral conflict. Instead, the actual dispute was conducted in two parallel pairs: ethnic Croats against what became known as the Bosniak community in areas with a significant ethnic Croat population, and ethnic Serbs against Bosniaks in most other areas. In Kosovo, the principal struggle was of course one pitting ethnic Albanians against ethnic Serbs, although other groups, such as Roma and Bosniaks, also suffered after the expulsion of the Serb authorities. In Macedonia, the dispute polarized ethnic Albanians and ethnic Macedonians.

Need for careful construction. Four out of the five instances of constitutional reform were the result of an emergency operation, rather than of a careful and well thought through attempt at societal construction. The fifth, addressing Serbia and Montenegro, initially only provided the roughest outline for a settlement requiring considerable further negotiations.

The Dayton settlement did not really provide for a balanced constitutional negotiation. Instead, the greatest issue of contention was the territorial division of the entities. This territorial settlement, based on war-time occupation of territory, was the price of peace. Once that had been achieved, two of the three parties (the Bosnian Serb and Croat communities represented by Serbia and Croatia respectively) were mainly focused on retaining as much control as possible for the mainly Serb entities, or the mainly Croat cantons within the Bosniak-Croat Federation. It was known both to the international mediators and the representatives of the parties that the constitutional settlement in itself was unlikely to function in the longer term.

During the Rambouillet negotiations on Kosovo, a very complex and possibly unworkable system of governance was proposed, mainly aimed at reassuring Belgrade in relation to ethnic Serbs who could continue to live in the territory. Once again, the focus was not really on constitutional design, but instead on conflict termination. This was replaced, however, by a simpler design generated by the UN administrators for Kosovo. However, that design left many questions unanswered as well. This is not altogether surprising, given the provisional nature of the constitutional framework and the dynamics of a gradual transfer of power to Kosovo authorities foreseen by it. The constitutional framework was not, however, an abstract drafting effort by international officials aimed at generating the best possible interim constitution. Instead, the document was subject to very substantive political battles, going beyond attempts to engage Belgrade in the process of drafting it. First, there was the so-called Quint, composed of the US, Britain, France, Germany and Italy—NATO states that had taken a special interest in the Kosovo conflict and the subsequent international administration of the territory. The Quint was what had been left over after Russia departed from the so-called Contact Group that had fulfilled this role, along with the UN, at the time of the outbreak of hostilities against Yugoslavia in 1999. Russia, and the restoration of the Contact Group through its renewed inclusion, formed the second line of battle in seeking a consensus on an interim constitution. Finally, the Security Council would need to approve any constitutional instrument, which meant not only a veto power for Russia, but also implied a need to bring China, another critic of NATO's use of force against Yugoslavia, back on board. Kosovo, too, therefore, does not provide an example of expert constitutional drafting, but there was a considerable element of international politics involved.

The Ohrid settlement was also the result of intense international pressure and engagement. However, the settlement negotiations were more focused, at least on the international side. The EU and the US interlocutors cooperated closely, and there were no overwhelming external and political interests other than the consensus that the territorial integrity of Macedonia would have to be preserved. Moreover, the actual negotiators had learnt the lessons of Bosnia and Kosovo. Hence, their proposals avoided some of the pitfalls of those two settlements that had already become evident in their implementation and the result was far more realistic and workable.

The Serbia and Montenegro settlement that was mediated and insisted upon by the EU was so brief as to be meaningless in terms of offering substantive guidance as to the future constitutional relations between both entities. This was supplemented later by a Constitutional Charter generated principally by the local parties. Finally, there is the case of Croatia, where pressure was unsuccessfully brought to bear in favour of an autonomy settlement for Krajina.

Hence, when considering the criteria put forward by Yash Ghai for the success or failure of autonomy agreements, a rather depressing result transpires in relation to the former Yugoslavia. It appears that not a single one of the conditions for successful autonomy settlements were fulfilled. Perhaps uniquely, almost every one of the five cases under review constitutes a veritable antithesis to these conditions. The conflicts were essentially bi-ethnic in nature and secessionist in character. There was no genuine political transition, no democratic tradition, no local ownership or acceptance of the settlements, and often no real focus on drafting workable constitutional arrangements.

The role of autonomy in the settlement

In all five instances, the extent of provision for autonomy or self-governance differs. This section seeks to locate the elements of autonomy and self-governance that are established, to classify them and to relate them to other elements of the settlement that may have been arrived at. Before turning to this task, it may be useful to address the issue of non-territorial autonomy. It is possible to do this briefly, as non-territorial, or cultural autonomy has not been widely employed in any of the five cases, irrespective of the expectations one might have had.

Non-territorial autonomy

In relation to Bosnia and Herzegovina, the Dayton accords promise the restoration of a multi-ethnic state. Non-territorial autonomy would ordinarily be expected to be emphasized in order to facilitate the re-establishment of multi-ethnicity. However, the actual settlement does not go down this route. It imposes very pronounced territorial divisions at the level of entities, and, within the Bosniak-Croat entity, at the level of cantons. These hard territorial divisions, which place almost unfettered public power at the disposal of the local majority in the respective unit, are not counter-balanced by non-territorial autonomy that would generate space for the preservation of non-dominant identities. This lack of provision is also not compensated for by strong central powers that could challenge discriminatory practices in the entities. Instead of granting non-territorial autonomy, there was insistence on compliance with human rights standards more generally. However, without an effective dispute settlement and enforcement mechanism that could reach into the respective territorial units, this often proved illusory.

With respect to Kosovo, the initial international attempt at imposing a settlement, the Rambouillet accords, provided for localized autonomy, often focused on local communes, at the expense of full self-governance for Kosovo as an overall unit. To this there were added unprecedented powers of non-territorial self-governance for 'communities', in particular the ethnic Serb population, complete with an institutional and even electoral structure. This design was however entirely abandoned in the constitutional framework generated by the UN administration of Kosovo. Instead of significant provision for non-territorial autonomy, there is, once again, insistence on the application of human rights equally for all throughout the territory. It has been possible to enforce this requirement to some extent in areas where the UN administration is in a position to control the agencies of provisional self-government. However, as the Kosovo Human Rights Ombudsperson has repeatedly confirmed, significant and widespread discriminatory practices have nevertheless occurred. Moreover, the UN has failed to insist on extending its reach into areas occupied by a 'parallel', exclusively Serb, administration in northern Kosovo.

Territorial autonomy

Bosnia and Herzegovina

The Dayton settlement, or General Framework Agreement for Peace in Bosnia and Herzegovina, of November/December 1995, is notoriously complex. It has been variously analyzed as an example of power-sharing or as an example of extreme autonomy, or rather different autonomies (Bieber 2003). The principal constitutional provisions are contained in Annex 4 (Constitution of Bosnia and Herzegovina) and Annex 6 (Human Rights). An integral part of the agreement, however, is also the Washington Framework Agreement of 1 March 1994, establishing a Federation of Bosniaks and Croats covering a little more than half of the country's territory. The agreement is reflected in Federation constitutional law.

The Constitution of Bosnia and Herzegovina determines that the overall state enjoys legal continuity and legal personality in terms of international law. It is composed of two entities, the Federation and the Republika Srpska. The Federation, in turn, is composed of cantons and municipalities. The cantons can form joint structures, essentially establishing a further sub-division of governance into a *de facto* ethnic Bosniak and a *de facto* ethnic Croat entity.

The provisions for autonomy are so extensive that it is preferable to speak of self-government within overall legal structures established in the Framework agreement. In fact, the overall state only enjoys competences in relation to a narrowly defined set of areas, including foreign policy, foreign trade, customs and monetary institutions. The entities even retain competence in relation to their own defence force. Article 3(a) accordingly provides expressly that '[a]ll governmental functions and powers not expressly assigned in this Constitution to the institutions of Bosnia and Herzegovina shall be those of the entities.'

Republika Srpska is sub-divided into communes (municipalities). This feature notwithstanding, Srpska features in fact a highly centralized state structure without any significant provision for autonomy for minority populations through local self-government. This is consistent with the establishment of that entity as an ethnic state, but less consistent with the aim established in the Framework agreement to reverse the results of demographic manipulation through ethnic cleansing.

The Federation, on the other hand, is not only divided into local communes but also into regional cantons. The government of the Federation exercises competence over defence, citizenship, economic policy, energy and financial policy. Human rights, health, environmental policy, communication and transport, social welfare policy, natural resources, etc., are subject to parallel jurisdiction of the federation and the cantons. According to Article II (3) of the Washington Agreement, the cantons enjoy authority over 'all responsibility not expressly granted to the central government'. This includes policing, education, culture, housing, public services, regional financing, etc.

The rights of communities (i.e., minorities representing one of the three constituent peoples, ethnic Serbs, Croats, Bosniaks) are assured in two ways. On the one hand, there are extensive power-sharing and veto mechanisms, protecting the entities from state-wide decisions that might affect vital national interests of the communities. Such provisions also exist within the Federation. Otherwise, it is up to the entities to provide a safe and secure environment for all persons in their respective jurisdictions. Attached to this requirement is the second level of protection which is provided through human rights. These apply throughout the state and also cover the so-called smaller minorities. The European Convention on Human Rights and its Protocol are directly applicable.

In summary, the Serb entity enjoys nearly undiluted self-government, which is organized in a fairly centralized way. The Federation, on the other hand, is fractionated into highly autonomous cantons. These have, in practice, joined together to form a Bosniak and an ethnic Croat sub-entity. The latter even attempted in 2001 to remove itself from the Federation altogether.

Croatia

On 12 November 1995, a US/UN mediated Basic Agreement on the region of Eastern Slavonia, Baranja and Western Sirmium was concluded by Serb and Croat government representatives.[3] The agreement provided for the modalities of the restoration of Croat governmental control over these areas, which had been hitherto occupied by Serb forces. In addition to provisions for troop withdrawals, there were guarantees for the return of refugees to their homes, policing and human rights standards. A UN-led Transitional Administration was to be established for a period of up to two years to administer this process. At the end of that period, Croatia resumed full authority over the territory.

As opposed to other settlements, this agreement did not establish a permanent special status for the area in question.[4] The area as a whole is therefore not autonomous or self-governing. Instead, it is merely being returned to the application of Croatian legislation, including the Croatian Constitution and the *Constitutional Law on Human Rights and Freedoms and the Rights of Ethnic and National Communities or Minorities in the Republic of Croatia*. The only additional feature is contained in Article 12 of the agreement, which provides for local elections at all levels, including municipalities, districts and counties and adds that the Serb community is entitled to appoint a Joint Council of Municipalities.

The agreement was, however, supplemented by a letter dated 13 January 1997 from the Republic of Croatia to the President of the UN Security Council.[5] In that letter, pledges are made for the representation of ethnic Serbs from the area under administration in senior posts in certain governmental departments of Croatia, as well as in legislative bodies. The letter also guarantees to those members of the Serb minority, in accordance with the existing Croatian laws and statutes and internationally accepted standards, 'full rights with respect to educational and cultural autonomy'. The letter continues:

> 7. With respect to education, the members of the Serb minority, and the members of other minorities within the area under the Transitional Administration, shall be entitled to prepare and implement a curriculum that fosters cultural identity, history and heritage insofar as it does not prejudicially affect any right or privilege with respect to international educational standards and Croatian laws.

> 8. With the cultural identity of the members of the Serb minority or any other member of other minorities within the above-mentioned area, they shall, under the law, have full rights to preserve and foster individual cultural identity provided that it does not affect any right or privilege with respect to the Croatian members.

9. The members of the Serb ethnic community may establish a Council of the Serb Ethnic Community. The Council may apply to the President of the Republic and the Croatian government, proposing and promoting the solution of issues of common interest for the national minority.

Elements of local territorial autonomy that were foreseen in the general Constitutional Law for 'local self-government and administration units' also apply. However, such territorial autonomy was very limited indeed, relating to the use of national signs and symbols and local holidays. Other competences, for instance in relation to education and religion, are not expressly granted, but may be provided in the Law on Local Self-government.[6] Otherwise there are the usual guarantees of cultural autonomy that apply elsewhere in Croatia (Constitution, Article 15). Article 11 of the *Constitutional Law on Human Rights and Freedoms and the Rights of National and Ethnic Communities in the Republic of Croatia* adds:

> Members of national and ethnic communities or minorities are free to found cultural and other societies aimed at preserving their national and cultural identity. These societies are autonomous and the Republic of Croatia and local self-governing bodies provide financial support in accordance with their financial resources.

Hence, rather than meaningful territorial autonomy, there are references to non-territorial autonomy. However, even these have not become particularly active.

On 13 December 2002, a further Constitutional Act on the Rights of National Minorities in the Republic of Croatia was adopted. That Act provides for local minority self-governance, guaranteed representation of minority communities in Parliament, and the creation of national minority consultative bodies. The Act was adopted a significant period after the period of conflict settlement that is under review here, without significant international involvement. However, one may note that it has, thus far, remained largely unimplemented, although most recently some steps have been taken to address this failure.

Kosovo

The international, UN-led administration of Kosovo has progressed significantly on the road to fulfilling its mandate of establishing the 'development of provisional democratic self-governing institutions', as is provided in its mandate contained in Security Council Resolution 1244 (1999). The resolution also refers to the establishment of 'substantial autonomy and self-government' taking full account of the Rambouillet accords, pending the transfer of authority from Kosovo's provisional institutions to those established under a final political settlement.

The UN administration of Kosovo assumed principal and original authority over the territory under this Chapter VII Security Council mandate of 10 June 1999 and has been exercising legislative, executive and to some extent adjudicative powers. After having governed through a significant number of decrees (Regulations promulgated by the Special Representative of the UN Secretary General), a Constitutional Framework for Provisional Self-Government was adopted on 15 May 2001. This Framework itself takes the form of a UN regulation (UNMIK/REG/2001/9). In addressing its principal features, it is useful to contrast it with the agreement that had been put forward at Rambouillet before the armed conflict involving NATO and the Federal Republic of Yugoslavia.

The Rambouillet agreement sought to establish an interim structure of government for a period of three years or possibly longer. It provided for an extraordinarily complex layering of authority, from the local communes in Kosovo, to the national communities, to Kosovo-bodies, Serb authorities and Federal Yugoslav structures. The agreement provided for 'self-government' (autonomy, given the previous experience, not being an acceptable term to the ethnic Albanian majority population). The authority for self-government was to be based on the commitment to the territorial integrity of the FRY and perhaps also in the sovereignty of that state. However, principal authority in Kosovo was to be located at the level of local communes, which would enjoy public powers in relation to all areas not allocated elsewhere in the agreement. In this way, the legal personality of Kosovo as an entity was hollowed out. Instead, the communes, which were presumed to be inhabited mainly by one or other ethnic community, would be the principal mechanisms of autonomous governance, enjoying a significant range of powers. In addition, the national communities (in particular the Serb community) were accorded a novel form of institutionalized cultural autonomy. That is to say, in addition to territorial autonomy, the Serb community would, through democratically elected institutions, take action to preserve their culture, provide for the use of language and education, protect national traditions through the application of their own family and inheritance law, maintain a separate health service, etc., throughout Kosovo.

The Kosovo institutions (President, Parliamentary Assembly, Government, Courts) enjoyed competence in strictly defined areas. They were precluded from interfering with, or circumscribing, the territorial or institutionalized cultural autonomy. The federal and Serbian governments in Belgrade would retain certain competences. Individuals could choose to participate in the political structure of those two additional layers of governance and could use these institutions, including, under certain circumstances, courts and public services.

The arrangements under the Constitutional Framework are rather different. There are only three layers of authority: the municipalities, the Kosovo-wide institutions and the UN administration. The UN administration retains general residual authority, and direct authority in relation to a number of issue areas (including approval and audit of the budget, monetary policy, customs, judicial appointments, law enforcement and control over the Kosovo Protection Corps). However, principal authority is bestowed upon the Kosovo-wide institutions. These powers are specifically enumerated and can be expanded upon subsequently. The municipalities remain the basic territorial units of self-government. They retain autonomous powers, but within guidelines established by, and under the control of, the Kosovo-wide institutions. Their powers are established through Regulations issued by the SRSG, rather than in the constitutional framework, and they are no longer the holders of all authority not assigned elsewhere.

There is also no provision for federal or Serb authority. The notion of 'communities' is retained and they are placed under the special protection of the SRSG. However, the communities now merely enjoy the usual elements of cultural autonomy, without the institutional structure that was assigned to them in the Rambouillet document. In addition, a wide range of international human rights instruments has been made part of the applicable law.

Macedonia

The Macedonia Framework Agreement of 13 August 2001 was reached with intensive EU and US mediation. The agreement was concluded by the principal ethnic Macedonian and Albanian parties then in government. While the former considered it the outcome of unjustified intervention by the organized international community, the latter supported its adoption wholeheartedly.

In its basic principles, the agreement confirms that Macedonia's sovereignty and territorial integrity and 'the unitary character' of the state are inviolable and must be preserved. At the same time, the multi-ethnic character of Macedonia's society is to be preserved as well. The development of local self-government is emphasized.

To this end, a revised Law of Self-government was to be drafted. This law was to establish 'enhanced local competencies', or 'additional independent competencies of the units of local self-government'. The former term is part of the basic principles at the head of the agreement, the latter phrase, which signals a move from local self-governance to autonomy, is hidden in an annex. In fact, it took some three years to generate such a law and its implementation is, at the time of writing, leading to a renewed rise in inter-ethnic tension.

The areas of enhanced local self-government are listed in the main agreement:

- public services;
- urban and rural planning;
- environmental protection;
- local economic development;
- culture;
- local finances;
- education, social welfare;
- health care;
- local authorities are free to use emblems marking the identity of the majority of the community in the municipality.

This listing is probably not exclusive. In addition, the Annex contains another somewhat hidden clause, providing that the state shall henceforth only legislate in relation to these areas where the exercise of independent local competences cannot achieve the intended aim equally as effectively. Where that is the case, such legislation shall further promote the municipalities' independent exercise of their competencies. In other words, through a strict subsidiarity requirement, parallel competence of the state is very significantly reduced. Where parallel competence is exercised, this very act of exercising it will in future increase local competence.

In this instance, local self-governance is very much the same as autonomy as defined above, given the fact that most of the local units of government at issue are mainly ethnic Albanian. This factor is to be strengthened by realignment of municipal boundaries after a census—an issue that has also proven to be very controversial.

In addition to these competencies, a process of joint appointment of local heads of police by the central government and municipal councils is provided for. Equal opportunities and equitable representation for all communities in public service and in the private economy are to be provided for. There are also procedures for minority representation on the Supreme Court and certain other bodies.

The agreement also provides a legislative programme to enhance education and the use of the languages of all communities. Special treatment is given to communities representing at least 20 per cent of the population, including provision of university-level education and the recognition of their language as an official state language.

The very sophisticated settlement is not only to be translated into action through ordinary legislation on these issues. Instead, the first annex to the agreement contains the actual wording of constitutional changes that are to be effected within a specific time-frame. While the time-frame was somewhat stretched, this aim was achieved after a very controversial debate in Macedonia. Throughout, these amendments avoid the impression that Macedonia is being transformed from an ethnic Macedonian state into a bi-national state (the declared aim of the ethnic Albanian leadership). Instead, the state is de-ethnicized as a matter of principle, being turned into a state of equal citizens. Then, certain 'soft' power-sharing elements are added, such as weighted voting procedures in the parliament on issues of special concern to non-dominant groups (but not necessarily easily available veto mechanisms) and provision for representation of all communities in high public office and in the civil service.

Serbia and Montenegro

On 14 March 2002, after an all-night negotiating session, the governments of Serbia, of Montenegro and of the Yugoslav Federation reached an *Accord on Principles in Relations between Serbia and Montenegro*. The agreement had been brokered by the High Representative for Common Foreign and Security Policy of the EU, Javier Solana. Great pressure had been brought to bear to achieve this settlement in advance of an upcoming EU summit.

The agreement is a very short and a very odd one. On its two-and-a-half pages it is agreed that the parties would settle on a constitutional charter before the end of 2002. This charter was to be mindful of the independent personality of Serbia and Montenegro respectively, while transforming the Federation into the common state of Serbia and Montenegro. After the expiry of a three year period, either entity is entitled to leave the common state. If such an act is affected by just one of the two, then the other remains the universal successor, it seems, although this provision is not entirely clear.

The charter that was eventually adopted provides for a State Union of Serbia and Montenegro, each considered an equal 'member state'. The Union enjoys single legal personality at the international level, although the member states may also engage in foreign relations to the extent that is compatible with the competence of the State Union whose competences are restricted to defence, foreign relations, domestic implementation of international obligations, border issues, standardization, immigration, visas and asylum, and maintenance and financing of Union institutions. A member state may 'break away' from the state union after a period of three years and after the holding of a referendum. Given the very limited powers of the central institutions, all other powers and residual authority lie with the 'member states'.

Powers and institutions

The powers of devolved institutions determine the extent of autonomy that has been granted. An analysis of the layering and assignment of competences is therefore crucial to understand a particular autonomy settlement.

Bosnia and Herzegovina

The state-wide institutions are organized according to power-sharing considerations. There is a three-member collective presidency and the few other positions of central government are apportioned according to ethnic/territorial quotas. The Parliamentary Assembly is divided into a House of Peoples, representing the three principal ethnic/territorial constituencies in equal proportion. The House of Representatives is also composed of two thirds representatives of the Federation and of one third representatives from the Republika Srpska. Complicated blocking mechanisms at present make it virtually impossible to arrive at decisions that are not supported by all three communities. The state-wide institutions are naturally constrained in their authority for the limited areas of state competence.

The only mechanism to ensure coherence in policy and compliance of the entities or other units with the state constitution is the Constitutional Court, which included international members on its bench. The court deals with disputes between entities and institutions of the state and it exercises supreme appellate jurisdiction. The Constitutional Court can also adjudge at the request of a lower court on the compatibility of laws on which that Court's decision may depend with constitutional law, the European Convention for Human Rights and Fundamental Freedoms and its Protocols and public international law.

A Commission on Human Rights, consisting of an Ombudsperson and a Human Rights Chamber with a majority of international members, was available to address violations of human rights, including apparent discrimination on the ground of association with a national minority. The Human Rights Chamber can issue binding decisions and can order specific performance by governmental agents or agencies throughout the territory. There is, however, no firm enforcement mechanism in relation to entities, mirroring a defect also apparent in relation to the Constitutional Court.

Croatia

Beyond the proposal to establish a Council of the Serb Minority, no institutional provisions were made at the time of the transition from international administration of Eastern Slavonia, or upon the re-incorporation of Krajina, that go beyond the general provisions for the establishment of cultural or educational associations for minorities in other areas of Croatia. As was noted above, a more sophisticated system was introduced in December 2002, although it has not yet been implemented.

Kosovo

The institutions of provisional self-governance generated in the Constitutional Framework are the Assembly, the President, the Government, the Courts and other bodies. They exercise responsibilities in relation to a long list of areas of responsibilities, although subject to the limitations outlined above. In addition to exclusive powers, there are the powers of supervision of municipal government and powers that may be exercised in consultation with the SRSG. Over time, the UN administration has transferred all so-called non-reserved powers and accepted a gradual increase of the role of local institutions in the exercise of reserved functions.

The Assembly, the government and the executive are arranged according to power-sharing principles. There is guaranteed representation for minority communities, although, in contrast to the Rambouillet draft, not disproportionately so. The absolute veto mechanism of Rambouillet was replaced by a somewhat less vigorous system of co-decision that can delay decisions claimed to affect the vital interests of a community.

There is provision for a Supreme Court, District Courts, Municipal Courts and Minor Offences Courts. A special chamber of the Supreme Court can address challenges to the constitutionality of legislation, including human rights issues.

Macedonia

In principle the institutional structure of Macedonia remains unchanged. However, the confirmation of 'independent' local authority emphasizes a change in the weight of some institutions. The procedures for filling top positions in government, the executive and the judiciary is also noteworthy. The only additional institution that is being created is a Committee for Inter-community Relations. Rather than institutionalizing ethnic politics by establishing a second chamber of parliament to achieve ethnic representation, this body exercises an advisory function in relation to legislative ventures. The Committee does however enjoy the authority of deciding by majority vote upon the application of the qualified voting mechanism in the Assembly. The composition of the Committee does not offer an option of veto for any single community.

Serbia and Montenegro

The Constitutional Charter provides for the establishment of certain institutions of the state union. These are the Parliament, President, Council of Ministers and the Court. As was noted, the competence of these bodies (or at least the executive) is limited to the areas of foreign affairs, defence, international economic affairs and the protection of human and minority rights. Even where these bodies enjoy competence, there are very rigorous

consociational mechanisms in operation, for instance relating to Ministerial representation, decision-making in the Assembly, rotation of
representation in international bodies, the composition of the Supreme
Court and the exercise of command responsibility over the armed forces.

Dispute settlement

A crucial element of state construction involving autonomy relates to the
management of relations between the autonomous entity or entities and
the centre. This function is ordinarily exercised by constitutional courts.
In some of the settlements under review, there is also provision for international intervention to resolve disputes. While this was not originally
intended to be the case, the High Representative in Bosnia and Herzegovina has taken on such a function. Given the extensive nature of self-
government provided by the Dayton and the Federation structure, there
are very few local mechanisms that can effectively govern conflicts of competences. The Constitutional Court is the principal body provided for this
purpose, but it lacks enforcement powers. Hence, the High Representative has over the years taken an ever greater role in deciding upon issues
of this kind, in removing officials, even elected officials, from office if
they appear to violate the Dayton framework, and in imposing legislation
or decisions where the state organs have been unable to come to a
conclusion.

In Croatia there were no autonomous layers of authority established.
Hence, there were also no special mechanisms to address conflicts
of authority between layers. However, the new Act of 2002 does provide
for access to judicial dispute settlement for minority representative
institutions.

In Kosovo, a Special Chamber of the Constitutional Court is charged
with addressing issues of hierarchy and competence. The SRSG also exercises supervisory functions that include the power of veto of legislation
adopted by the Assembly.

As there are no new structures of governance introduced in the Ohrid
settlement, no new issues of hierarchy of powers apply. However, if there
is a weakness in the framework agreement, it is the absence of a formal
mechanism to assist in overcoming disputes during the implementation
phase. At an informal level, international involvement and drafting
support for the parliament has played such a role.

Relations between the states of the Union of Serbia and Montenegro
are mediated through the means of a Court of Serbia and Montenegro,
composed of an equal number of judges from both states.

Conclusion

This brief survey reveals the application of five or six distinct models of autonomy or self-government as a means of internationalized state construction in the Balkans.

At the most modest level, one finds international involvement in the transfer of a territory to the governmental authority of its sovereign after a period of occupation. This is the case in Croatia and Eastern Slavonia. During the stabilization phase, international action contributed to confidence-building among the respective communities. However, the end state that had been established from the beginning did not foresee the establishment of permanent territorial autonomy of the territory in question. Instead, the application of the law of local government applicable throughout the central state was re-established, with cultural autonomy for minority populations. It was only some years after the transition that a new Act was generated, providing for the possibility of some elements of territorial autonomy through local minority self-governance. This process of normalization by applying structures for local self-governance in a way that fosters territorial autonomy was generated within Croatia, although pressure for change in view of potential EU membership may have helped to generate this impetus. Still, there remains a difference in the adoption of such provisions and their implementation.

The next example is of the significant increase of cultural autonomy through a broad programme of minority legislation in Macedonia. In addition, there is the establishment of virtual local territorial autonomy through the guise of enhanced local self-administration. This is coupled with soft power-sharing mechanisms at the central level and pro-active steps to increase the stake of underrepresented groups in the state and in its development. The Ohrid model can be seen as the most advanced amongst those reviewed here. It carefully balances enhanced self-governance with a number of other tools for power-sharing.

A third model, proposed but not implemented, was the Rambouillet draft. There, the territorial unity of the FRY and the appurtenance of Kosovo to Serbia was to be maintained. However, at the same time, the vision of self-government was to be realized for Kosovo. While the entity was granted institutions of self-governance, including a President, a Parliamentary Assembly, an Executive and a Judiciary, its legal personality was highly diluted. This was to be principally located in the constituent units of local governance, providing for very broad territorial autonomy for mainly Serb-inhabited areas. In addition, there was provision for the use of Yugoslav and even Serb institutions by members of the Serb communities, including Courts. Finally, a very extensive standard of minority right protection was to be complemented by highly institutionalized cultural autonomy. This was to be coupled with power-sharing and veto mechanisms at the Kosovo-wide level.

The Constitutional Framework that was established instead of the Rambouillet design devolves significant authority to Kosovo as an entity of self-government. However, significant residual powers are maintained by the international administration. There are fewer hard power-sharing mechanisms, such as veto mechanisms for minorities, than might have been expected. Instead, human and minority rights apply and are (or should be) enforced, internationally if necessary. There is provision for local self-government, but limited to specified areas and subject to centralized guidance and control.

The example of Bosnia and Herzegovina is one of formal self-government for Republika Srpska, and virtual self-government for the Bosniak and Croat communities with the Federation entity. Excessive power-sharing mechanisms often render the weak structures of the central state ineffective. There is also no territorial autonomy for minority communities within the Srpska entity or the cantons of the Federation. Instead, there is provision for extensive human rights protection that is supposed to reach into the entities, but has not been fully effective.

Finally, there is the case of Serbia and Montenegro. This is an example of the most extensive form of self-government, establishing in effect merely a loose union of two states, each of which is essentially already a sovereign entity.

In four of the five cases under review, the settlements were internationally imposed in the hope that autonomy or self-governance would help to terminate secessionist campaigns threatening the territorial unity of the state in question. In relation to Serbia and Montenegro, virtual independence was meant to replace actual independence. The continued existence of the State Union for a period of three years, it was hoped, would allow secessionist tempers to cool. By the end of that period, the magic of the integrative power of self-governance or autonomy would have made the state union viable in the longer term, having made irrelevant the previous desire to obtain independence.

In Kosovo, too, the prolonged delay of the organized elements of the international community in grappling with the status issue was only in part motivated by the inability to forge an international consensus on what to do. Many of the actors, in particular many foreign ministries in Western Europe, were convinced that Kosovo, too, would lose its appetite for independence, if only the process of provisional self-governance could be spun out for long enough. Once persuaded of the benefits of self-governance, the Kosovars would no longer have reason to oppose a return to Serbia.

In Bosnia and Herzegovina, self-governance of the entities, or within the entities, was designed extraordinarily widely. There the hope was that the overall state of Bosnia and Herzegovina would be sufficiently diminished to make its continued existence acceptable to the ethnic Serb and ethnic Croat communities within it. Again, the hope was and is that the continued existence of the state as a whole, initially enforced militarily, would gradually become self-sustaining once the integrative force of self-governance took hold and consolidated the overall polity.

In Macedonia, there could be a trade-off between autonomy (disguised as enhanced local self-governance) and a confirmation of the continued territorial integrity of the state, given that the ethnic Albanian community had not actually demanded full independence. It was hoped that the practice of autonomous life would remove entirely the future prospect of a campaign for territorial change among the ethnic Albanian communities.

In Croatia, no autonomy settlement could be imposed, as Zagreb had won back control over the Krajina region through force of arms. Croatia did not have to settle for a solution that would have traded self-governance for certain territory. Given this precedent, and the demonstrated efficiency of its armed forces, Croatia only needed to accept temporary autonomy during the transitional period preceding the hand-over of Eastern Slavonia. There was, however, a hope on the part of the international community that Croatia would extend autonomy provisions to areas mainly inhabited by ethnic Serb communities of its own volition.

What of the results of this experimentation with quite a broad range of solutions and designs across the former Yugoslavia? Of course, it is too early to tell. But perhaps some initial trends can be detected. One does, of course, need to bear in mind when considering this experience that there have been some unique features at play in this region. In the first place, this relates to the interrelationship of most of the cases considered here. The pressure for a Serbia and Montenegro settlement, for instance, originated in a fear on the part of international actors that a dissolution would threaten stability in relation to Kosovo. A settlement for Kosovo has in part been avoided, due to the fear that independence for that entity might enhance pressure for the removal of Republika Srpska from Bosnia and Herzegovina. And events in Kosovo have had a significant impact on developments in Macedonia and the insistence of the US and the EU on a settlement, however reluctant the parties may have been at the time.

Another unique feature has been the long-term interest of international actors. As the Balkans crisis has occurred within Europe, it is not surprising that European institutions have focused on its various phases of development. Given the initial inability of the European actors to exhibit effectiveness in this venture, they tended to be gradually displaced by the US. Both, the EU and the US, were able to mobilize very significant resources through the UN system in relation to the Balkans. More recently, with the creation of a more efficient EU machinery for conflict management, Europe has been able to assert itself again, and in the instance of Macedonia, with some success.

While international action has not always been effective, it has nevertheless been quite sustained over what is now a decade and a half. Hence, whatever stability or instability has been generated, the very strong influence of these actors must be borne in mind.

Furthermore, there has been the additional tool of addressing the conflicts of South Eastern Europe in the context of EU accession. The promise of integration into the EU has had quite a significant effect on the calculations of political actors within the region. This prospect has helped to demonstrate that domestic stability may pay dividends in the longer term, by making EU accession a realistic prospect.

Seen against this background, was the faith placed in the integrative power of autonomy and self-governance by the organized international community engaged in the attempt to 'manage' the dissolution of Socialist Federal Yugoslavia justified? Until Kosovo's status is addressed in a definite way, the provisional system of self-governance will remain unstable. That status is unlikely to remain one of autonomy or wide-ranging self-governance, leaving the territorial integrity of Serbia untouched. Hence, the hope that interim self-governance would diminish the thirst for independence within that territory if only it is prolonged as much as possible may well be disappointed. While it is not possible to predict the future, the continuance of the State Union of Serbia and Montenegro beyond the minimum period of three years is also subject to some doubt. The experience of virtual statehood may not be enough to prevent a drive towards formal statehood. Bosnia and Herzegovina, on the other hand, has stabilized to a greater extent than could have been expected. True, given the imperfect way of constitutional drafting, there will remain great pressure for constitutional change. But there does appear to be a chance to keep Bosnia together as a state. Given the depth of the conflict and the magnitude of human suffering it brought with it, that would be a very impressive testimony to the strangely integrative function of self-government and autonomy solutions that was noted at the outset of this book. Macedonia, too, appears to come to terms with the Ohrid agreement, even if the actual process of decentralization still poses enormous challenges. Barring an importing of instability from Kosovo, it may be possible to move from a situation of conflict termination to one of state transformation. The lure of EU accession is now starting to take effect in relation to Croatia, which had been resistant to attempts to impose a permanent, as opposed to a transitional, autonomy settlement upon it. However, the emergence of the possibility of genuine local minority self-government now exists on the statute books, and that prospect may generate some implementation before too long.

How can one explain the fact that autonomy and self-governance appears to have an integrative effect in three cases, and no such effect in the two others? Autonomy does appear to be supporting efforts to maintain the territorial integrity of Croatia, Macedonia and perhaps even of Bosnia and Herzegovina. Quite extensive self-governance of Kosovo and of Montenegro, on the other hand, does not seem to have inhibited the drive towards independence of both entities. Part of the answer lies in the availability of independence as an alternative to autonomy. It is clear that Montenegro, as one of the six former Yugoslav republics, always had the legal right and the effective option of secession. The State Union agreement, achieved under heavy EU pressure, does not dilute this entitlement in any way. If the experience of life together under the loose roof of the Union does not satisfy secessionist groups, secession will be the answer.

One might say that Kosovo, too, should have been treated in the way of the other constituent republics at the time of the dissolution of the Socialist Federal Republic of Yugoslavia. However, given its dual status as a Federal entity and a province of Serbia, it was not awarded the option of independence by the international agencies involved in attempts to manage the Yugoslav crisis. Nevertheless, there is a widespread belief that the extent of suppression under Serbia's rule, and the outcome of NATO's intervention, have made eventual independence for Kosovo a fact of life that cannot be ignored. Thus, there is little or no incentive for the majority ethnic Albanian population to embrace and develop self-governance or autonomy, however wide-ranging, in any genuine way. Instead, these concepts are seen as part of an imposed, transitionary phase towards independence. No integrative effect emerges from the experience of self-governance. Moreover, the present experience is an artificial one. Provisional self-governance is exercised under the authority of the UN administration of the territory, not of Serbia. Were this authority to be replaced by that of Serbia, conflict would immediately erupt again. Hence, even if self-governance under the present regime were actually in some sense stable, this stability would not translate itself into a definite settlement that would mean self-governance within Serbia, or Serbia and Montenegro. Given this artificial state, the hope of several EU governments that an extension of the present situation will remove the pressure for independence cannot be fulfilled.

Based on the limited experience of the cases surveyed here, self-governance and autonomy do, therefore, only appear to offer a prospect for the maintenance of the territorial integrity of the state where no alternative, such as independence, exists. In Croatia, Bosnia and Herzegovina and Macedonia, the organized international community has vigorously insisted on the maintenance of the structural principle of territorial integrity and territorial unity. Moreover, the attempted secessions were actually defeated in the former two. In relation to Macedonia, this experience may have lead to a toning down of demands from the outset. Hence, the 'liberation' fighters of the NLA engaged in a campaign for autonomy and equal rights, independence (or rather a merger with a neighbouring territory) not being an option, even as a result of an armed struggle.

In such circumstances, it seems that even violent secessionists can be persuaded to buy into an autonomy settlement. Where there has been no decisive victory by the central government, and where external agencies have not made it absolutely clear that secession will not be countenanced, even if a secessionist struggle succeeds, we tend to find so-called frozen conflicts. In the cases of Abkhasia and South Ossetia in relation to Georgia, and of Trandiestria in relation to Moldova, Russia's informal support for the secessionist entities has permitted them to benefit from a prolonged period of de facto independence from Georgia and Moldova respectively (coupled with a partial dependence on Russia). A maintenance of this status quo, or even the hope of eventually consolidating de facto independence into statehood, fostered by external actors with a controlling stake in the international system charged with administering self-determination crises, are inhibiting the move towards a settlement based on self-governance.

Of course, this is not to say that autonomy can only ever work if the possibility of secession has been excluded. There are many cases where autonomy or federal-type self-governance functions well, despite the fact of secession being formally on the menu. Hence, Quebec has been able to function successfully within Canada, notwithstanding the fact that referenda on independence have been available. Scotland has had a similar experience. However, there are two differences between these two examples, and the instances of opposed unilateral secession that have been considered here. First of all, the right to secede is not contested, but instead constitutionally established. Hence, internally, it is nothing that must be fought for, and internationally, there is no reason to resist it. After all, the doctrine of territorial unity does not in any way preclude secession by agreement between the centre and a departing entity, or the consensual dissolution of the state. The former occurred in relation to Ethiopia and Eritrea, the latter in the cases of the USSR and Czechoslovakia. The second difference lies in the absence of prolonged and violent conflict that makes eventual accommodation within the state far less palatable.[7]

On the other hand, where there has been an attempted unilateral secession, together with the attendant deep violent conflict, the Balkan experience appears to indicate that autonomy or self-governance settlements will only take root if independence has been firmly precluded as a potential option. One may venture to speculate that this lesson will be confirmed in those cases outside Europe, where self-governance has been made available for a prolonged interim period, at the end of which there is a promise of a referendum on independence. For instance, the settlements on Bougainville and on Southern Sudan provide for such a solution. The secessionist groups clearly see the prolonged interim period of self-governance as a preparation for independence that will inevitably come. The central governments, on the other hand, appear to believe that the experience of self-governance within the continued territorial unit of the state will remove the desire for independence altogether.

Having pointed to the limitations of the integration-pull exercised by autonomy or self-government settlement, one may turn to consider some of the more down-to-earth lessons concerning the crafting of such settlements.

Among the three potentially successful autonomies, one may also observe a certain evolution. The model of very wide-ranging self-governance exhibited by the Dayton construction, coupled with the application of extensive consociational power-sharing mechanisms, has been abandoned. This is most strikingly evident in the approach to self-governance within Kosovo, where limited autonomy is balanced with a sensible apportionment of central authority, at present still subjected to considerable residual international authority. There is power-sharing, but generally no direct veto mechanism.

This more balanced approach has been refined further in the Macedonian framework agreement. In that case, the temptation to create an ethnic polity has been avoided. Instead, there is an unobtrusive local autonomy coupled with soft power-sharing and with mechanisms aiming to achieve full equality for members of all communities. This includes the smaller minorities that are so often entirely overlooked in the arrangements that were previously considered.

The most advanced settlement—applied in Macedonia—is, however, in some way incomplete. Given the reluctance of the political parties representing the majority community, no sufficiently strong dispute settlement mechanism could be deployed. This could also not be balanced by a formal international role in implementation, and in resolving the inevitable deadlocks in the implementation process. Instead, there has been a persistent need for soft international intervention, supporting and at times pressuring the government and the majority parties into complying with the Ohrid commitments. This process has been a draining one, and one that has started to undermine the credibility of the settlement in the eyes of the minority representatives. Hence, if the Macedonia settlement were to fail in the end after all, this would be less due to its state design elements, and more due to the absence of an effective implementation support mechanism.

Overall, the learning curve of those involved in state design and conflict transformation activities in the Balkans has been fairly steep. While one might forgive the people and politicians from the region for feeling as if they have been experimented upon in some measure, there is a notable progression in the sophistication of the design of autonomy-based settlement. This sophistication manifests itself in the realization that autonomy is not enough. It is only one element in the entire armoury of state construction tools that can be applied. And any autonomy-based settlement needs to be backed up by a comprehensive array of implementation support measures, based on a sustained international interest in its success.

As has already been noted, here exist a number of instances of so-called frozen conflict in the wider Europe that will need addressing over the next decade, and that might finally be addressed, if all external actors adopt a clear line on which outcomes are acceptable and which are not. There certainly now exists a pool of useful experience that can be employed towards the development of realistic autonomy and self-government settlements for these conflicts.

Notes

1 Hence, autonomy arrangements in Slovenia, or the attempt to restore autonomy in Vojvodina, are not addressed.
2 See Chapter 1.
3 S/1995/951, Annex.
4 Originally, Croatian law provided for the establishment of special status territories. This provision was, however, never implemented and was subsequently removed.
5 S/1997/27.
6 See *Opinion on the Constitutional Laws on the Rights of National Minorities in Croatia, adopted by the Venice Commission*, 47th Plenary Meeting, 6–7 July 2001.
7 It might be said that self-governance has been the solution of choice after a period of prolonged violent conflict. While the success of that settlement is not yet fully established, Northern Ireland represents a different type of case. In the territory, the majority of the population is not, in fact, secessionist, or in favour of territorial change. In fact, the majority remains structurally disposed towards territorial unity. Hence, it is a different kind of struggle—a struggle within the entity seeking secession, as opposed to a struggle between the entity and the centre. In all the other instances of secession, a territory attempts to leave the central state, given that its population is structurally disposed in favour of independence.

References

Bieber, Florian (2003) 'Institutionalizing Ethnicity in Former Yugoslavia: Domestic vs. Internationally Driven Processes of Institutional (Re-)Design', *The Global Review of Ethnopolitics*, vol. 2, no. 2, 3–16.
Ghai, Yash (2001) *Autonomy and Ethnicity*, Cambridge: Cambridge University Press.

4 The Crimean autonomy
Innovation or anomaly?

Bill Bowring[1]

Introduction

Crimea with all its complexities can serve as a case-study for lack of institutional design, or at any rate an example of precarious adaptation of such design to historical reality. Three radically dissonant self-determination movements intersect in this small territory, almost an island, which happens to be one of the very few (perhaps the only?) examples of an Autonomous Republic situated in a unitary State.

First, there is Ukrainian nationalism, which has at last achieved independent statehood in Ukraine, although in Crimea the Ukrainians are a small minority, and those who live in Crimea are much Russified. Second, Ukraine has been beset by Russian separatism or irredentism, since ethnic or at any rate linguistic Russians are the great majority of the population of Crimea, and a substantial part of the population of Ukraine. Third, there are the Crimean Tatars, whose official aspirations are for the status of indigenous people, despite their having at most some 12 per cent of the population of Crimea.

Moreover, Crimea is full of deeply rooted symbolic, literary and historical memories that are fundamental for Russian, Crimean Tatar and Ukrainian national identities. As Gwendolyn Sasse points out, 'it was one of the few territories in the Former Soviet Union that had multiple "ethnic" claims to it, all of which were plausibly historically grounded' (Sasse, 2002: 3). Andrew Wilson notes that:

> Crimea ... occupies very different places in different national mythologies. To the Ukrainians it was the Cossacks' outlet to the sea; to the Russians it was the jewel in the crown of empire and a site of military glory – or at least glorious defeat, the most emotive symbol in all of the former soviet territory that Moscow lost in 1991. To the Crimean Tatars, it is their historical homeland.
>
> (Wilson, 2002: 151)

All three groups are most certainly 'peoples' for the purpose of exercising the right in international law to self-determination. The saving grace is that neither the Russians nor the Crimean Tatars is presently seeking or even envisaging secession as the means of exercising that right. The other modalities for 'internal' self-determination have by no means yet been decided. Therein lies the great interest of this topic.

To add to the complexity, no less than four international organisations have influenced or in some cases intervened in the evolving situation: the United Nations, through its UNDP sponsored *Crimea Integration and Development Programme* (CIDP);[2] the OSCE, through its mission based in Kyiv and in Simferopol, and more significantly through the work of the High Commissioner on National Minorities (HCNM); the Council of Europe, especially through the *Framework Convention for Protection of National Minorities* and its *European Charter for Regional or Minority Languages*,[3] as well as Resolution No. 1455 of the Parliamentary Assembly of the Council of Europe of 5 April 2001;[4] and finally the European Union, through its relations with Ukraine. For example, on 9 February 1994 the European Parliament adopted a 'Resolution on linguistic and cultural minorities in the European Community'.[5] I will touch in particular on the influence of the HCNM on the development of the specific model of Crimean autonomy which is now being tested.

Several of the editors' categories and cross-cutting issues are exemplified in Crimea. There is only one kin state able to influence or disrupt the course of events, but a very large one: the Russian Federation. The Russians in Crimea have at various stages made irredentist/secessionist claims at the levels of kin-state against host-state and minority against host state – Ukraine of course. More frequently and to the present day they make irredentist/non-secessionist/autonomist claims against Ukraine (it is notable that official Russian foreign policy has not actively pursued any policy with respect to Crimea, except as noted below). In these claims the Crimean Russians can be said to have largely succeeded, for the time being. Wilson notes, more controversially, that 'The Russian minority is likely to contest its immigrant status, arguing that, outside western Ukraine, they too are indigenes with a long history of continuous settlement' (Wilson, 1997: 154). Many Ukrainians would accept that the Russians of Ukraine are – classically – a national minority with a kin-state.

The Crimean Tatars, as they frequently point out, have no kin-state. The existence of Tatarstan, as a radically autonomous subject of the Russian Federation, provides no real support to them, although some Crimean Tatars go to study in Kazan, its capital.[6] The Volga Tatars, like the Siberian Tatars, are different peoples with different histories. Nor does the existence of the very large Crimean Tatar diaspora help very much – at least five million people of Crimean Tatar descent in Turkey,[7] and others all over the world.

Some Crimean Tatars, in more emotional moments, can make non-irredentist/secessionist claims, where the notorious though – in too many ways – similar example is that of Abkhazia in relation to Georgia. It cannot be forgotten around the Black Sea that the Abkhazian population, no more than 20% of their autonomous republic in Georgia, drove the majority of the Georgians out in a successful example of mass ethnic cleansing which has resulted in a self-proclaimed state recognised by no other state in the world, even Russia which has often been accused of fomenting Abkhaz separatism.

The Crimean Tatar claim for indigenous status could be subsumed under the rubric non-irredentist/non-secessionist/autonomist. The treaty whose ratification by Ukraine they seek, with the support of some Ukrainian politicians, especially those of nationalist outlook, is the ILO Convention No.169 of 27 June 1989 *Concerning Indigenous Peoples and Tribal Peoples in Independent Countries.*[8] This is the only international treaty recognising the right of a people as a collective right, rather than a right to be exercised by each individual, perhaps in community with other members of their group. A further specific feature of the Crimean dilemma is the fact that the Crimean Tatars fear assimilation, not by Ukrainians, but by Russians. Mustafa Dzhemilev, leader and symbol of the Crimean Tatars, has recently stated that at present only 10 per cent of Crimean Tatar children can study in their native language. The remaining 90 per cent must go to Russian schools.[9]

Ukrainians express a wide range of views. Wilson has identified one end of the spectrum:

> Ukrainian nationalists, however, tend to deny that Ukraine is a multinational state at all. Moreover, their arguments draw on three of the same concepts that underlie Baltic and other forms of ethno-nationalism: namely the idea of 'homeland' and the special rights of the indigenous people, the right to cultural self-preservation and (to a much lesser extent) the notion of forcible integration into the Soviet Union and the consequent illegitimacy of subsequent changes to national demography or patterns of language use.
>
> (Wilson, 1997: 149)[10]

For them only one people has lived on the territory since time immemorial – the Ukrainian people (in Crimea – Ukrainian and Crimean Tatar). Nevertheless, it is the Ukrainian language which is in need of protection. Even though Ukraine is one of the larger states of Europe, by territory and population, Russia is of course several times larger. President Kuchma himself has noted that Russia publishes per head of the population 2.3 times more books than Ukraine.[11]

Contrary, perhaps, to expectation, a study, cited by Hans van Zon (2001) has shown that people more often identify themselves with their religion (that is, *Ukrainian Orthodox* – Moscow Patriarchate, *Ukrainian Orthodox* – Kiev Patriarchate, *Ukrainian* Autocephalous *Orthodox, Ukrainian Catholic* (Uniate), *Protestant, Jewish*) than with the Ukrainian state or

Ukrainian or Russian ethnos. The great majority of Russians in Ukraine support Ukrainian statehood. Even in Crimea, irredentist movements by Russians have been short-lived and sparsely supported. Most important, van Zon points out that 'ethnicity usually ranks low among other forms of social identity. A 1999 study shows that only 8 per cent of secondary school students attach significant meaning to their ethnicity (Filippova, 1999: 3). There is a high degree of tolerance between Russians and Ukrainians.'[12]

I therefore adopt the following strategy for exploring the issues. First, I present some key issues of the demography of Ukraine as a whole and Crimea in particular. Second, I outline the reasons for the relatively long period of gestation between the declaration(s) of independence and adoption of a Constitution for Ukraine, with its Chapter on the Autonomous Republic of Crimea, taking into account Crimea's complex history. Third, I analyse the Constitution of Ukraine and fourth, that of the Autonomous Republic of Crimea.

The demography of Ukraine

The shifting demography of Ukraine is a crucial factor underlying the form of autonomy now being tested in Crimea. The results of the census which took place in December 2001[13] pointed not only to an inexorable decline in the population of Ukraine as a whole (a 6.1 per cent decline, or 3 million people, from 51,706,700 in 1989, the last census, to 48,457,100) but a sharp fall – a drop of 5 per cent – in the numbers describing themselves as Russians.[14] There was a corresponding rise in the numbers describing themselves as Ukrainian and speaking the Ukrainian language. Taras Kuzio points out that today's Ukrainian (77.9 per cent) and Russian (17.3 per cent) ethnic shares have reversed the trend of the Soviet period, and returned Ukraine to the position recorded in the 1959 census. The fact that 70 per cent of education is now delivered in Ukrainian returns schools to the levels of the 1950s prior to the mass 'russification' campaigns of Nikita Khrushchev and Leonid Brezhnev (Kuzio, 2003). The number of ethnic Russians has declined by 3 million: a 5 per cent fall in their share of the population, but a 27 per cent decline in their absolute numbers.

The position of Crimea is once again in the spotlight. Many Russians have left Crimea, and the Crimean Tatar population has grown. Thus, the share of ethnic Russians in the Crimean population has declined from 65.6 per cent in 1989 to 58.3 per cent in the latest census. The overall population of Crimea has declined slightly, by 1 per cent, from 2,063,600 in 1989 to 2,033,700. Of these, 1,180,400 are Russians, 492,200 are Ukrainians (a decline from 26.7 per cent in 1989 to 24.3 per cent today), and 243,400 are Crimean Tatars – a dramatic increase from 1.9 per cent in 1989 to 12 per cent now.[15] It should be noted that the numbers of returning Crimean Tatars peaked, at 41,400 in 1991, and have been rapidly falling in each year since.[16] Nevertheless, Kuzio notes that if these trends continue, by the next census in 2011 Crimea will have lost its position as the only Ukrainian region with an ethnic Russian majority. The existence of the Russian majority was the only substantial reason an exception was made when the status of Crimea was upgraded from an oblast to 'Autonomous Republic' (see below). It should also be remembered that the lease of part of the port of Sevastopol to the Russian Black Sea Fleet will come to an end in 2017.

A very large number of Crimean Tatars were excluded from the voting population for the parliamentary elections of 1998 and the presidential elections of 1999 by virtue of the fact either that they were not citizens, or that they have not yet been able to return to Crimea. According to research carried out in 1997 by the Uzbek Centre for Sociological and Marketing Research 'Expert', there were still 188,722 Crimean Tatars living in Uzbekistan, at least 73 per cent of whom intended to move to Crimea. There are a number of reasons why they have not yet done so. As many as 57 per cent of those intending to return cite the absence of anywhere to live in Crimea, while 18 per cent fear unemployment. As many as 92 per cent of them declare that their main problem in life is the impossibility of returning to their homeland, to rejoin their family and their people.

About 44 per cent of those who have returned to Crimea do not have their own home (128,700 people, 40,000 families), of whom 58,000 are in the process of constructing their own homes, and the rest are on housing waiting lists. In 70 per cent of the approximately 300 existing 'compact settlements' of returnees there is no running water, while 25 per cent have no electricity, and none of them have any drainage at all. Unemployment among the Crimean Tatars in Crimea stands at 49.6 per cent.[17] The largest concentrations of Crimean Tatars are to be found in Belogorskii Raion (32 per cent), Sovetskii Raion (26 per cent), and Simferopol (22.2 per cent), while the smallest is that of the predominantly Russian resort city of Yalta (0.9 per cent).

Ukraine's constitution(s) and the problem of Crimea

Ukraine had no pre-history of independent statehood. In the nineteenth century Russians comprised the overwhelming majority of the population of Kyiv. The present day source of the most radical Ukrainian nationalism is Galicia, historically part of the Austro-Hungarian Empire. Lviv was a Polish city. It should therefore be no surprise that the legal fact of Ukrainian statehood was established over several years.

Thus, on 22 July 1990, while the USSR was still very much in existence, the Verkhovna Rada (Supreme Soviet) of the Ukrainian SSR proclaimed the Declaration on State Sovereignty of Ukraine.[18] This had the following key aims:

expressing the will of the people of Ukraine; striving to create a democratic society; acting on the need for all-encompassing guarantees of
the rights and freedoms of man; respecting the national rights of all
nations ... having as a goal the affirmation of the sovereignty and self-
rule of the people of Ukraine.

This Declaration was firmly based on the declared right of the 'Ukrainian
nation' to self-determination, notwithstanding the fact that it was not at all
clear what this nation actually comprised. It stated that:

The Ukrainian SSR, as a sovereign national state, develops within
existing boundaries on the basis of the realisation of the Ukrainian
nation's inalienable right to self-determination. The Ukrainian SSR
effectuates the protection and defence of the national statehood of
the Ukrainian people.

There was no mention of Crimea, although the Declaration stated that:
'Citizens of the republic of all nationalities comprise the people of
Ukraine.' But the declaration could not be consummated: the USSR con-
tinued in existence until December 1991.

The abortive Moscow 'putsch' of August 1991 forced the issue for advocates of Ukrainian independence, and on 24 August 1991 the Verkhovna
Rada proclaimed independence. This date is now celebrated as Ukrainian
Independence Day. On 1 September 1991 the Verkhovna Rada more formally declared 'the independence of Ukraine, and the creation of an
independent Ukrainian State – Ukraine'. According to the preamble, this
was done

in view of the mortal danger surrounding Ukraine in connection with
the state coup in the USSR on August 19, 1991, continuing the thou-
sand-year tradition of state building in Ukraine, based on the right of
a nation to self-determination in accordance with the Charter of the
United Nations and other international legal documents, and realis-
ing the Declaration on State Sovereignty of Ukraine.[19]

It has been widely recognised that Ukraine's declaration of independence
in 1991 was a direct cause of the collapse of the USSR in December of that
year. Nevertheless, Ukraine only managed to adopt a Constitution after
five years, on 28 June 1996.[20] Part of the reason for this long delay was the
fact that the declaration of Ukrainian independence in August 1991 and
the collapse of the USSR in December 1991 were answered by a series of
attempts by the Crimean Russians to assert their own interests.[21]

It has already been noted that Crimea is now the only region of
Ukraine where Russians are in a majority. This is because Crimea has a distinctive history: until the twentieth century it was not part of Ukraine at

all. The Crimean Tatars declare that they are the indigenous people of Crimea, as mentioned above. However, in contrast to many other indigenous peoples, they do not have a primordial or 'immemorial' origin. Their myths of origin and ethnic history are complex. Accounts vary, but it seems clear that Tatar invaders, who swept across Russia as the 'Golden Horde', invaded Crimea in the 1230s. They then mixed with populations which had settled in Eastern Europe, including Crimea since the seventh century: Tatars, but also Mongols and other Turkic groups (Khazars, Petchenegs, and Kipchacks), as well as the ancient – and perhaps truly – indigenous populations, the Kumans.[22] Brian Williams concludes that the Crimean Tatars should be seen as a heterogeneous ethnic group having its roots in the deepest Crimean antiquity and claiming descent from a vast array of earlier ethno-religious groups who occupied the diverse terrains of the Crimean peninsula (Williams, 2001).

From about 1475, following the capture of the Genoese ports on the Crimean coast by Ottoman naval forces, the Crimean Khanate came, from time to time and to varying degrees, under the control of the Ottoman Empire. Crimea was annexed by the Russian Empire under Catherine the Great in 1783 (see Fisher, 1978). Russification of the peninsula proceeded rapidly, and Crimean Tatars in large numbers fled from their homeland. Emigrations to the Ottoman Empire, especially Turkey, accelerated after the Crimean War (1853–1856) which was fought over the question of Russian expansion and threat to the Ottomans. The Brest-Litovsk Treaty of 1918, ending Russia's involvement in the First World War, awarded Crimea to Ukraine, but the Bolsheviks, on regaining control, created a Crimean Autonomous Soviet Socialist Republic (ASSR) in October 1921, within the Russian Socialist Federation of Soviet Republics (RSFSR). For a time until the late 1920s Soviet nationalities policy resulted in the appointment of a relatively large number of Crimean Tatars to government positions, together with intensive development of their language and culture (Stewart, 2001: 117). This policy, seen by some as generating a short-lived 'golden age' for the Crimean Tatars, was brutally reversed once Stalin consolidated his power in the late 1920s to early 1930s.

The Crimean Tatars were deported en masse in the early morning of 18 May 1944, by order of Stalin, for alleged collaboration as a people with the Nazis. In all, 191,044 men, women and children were taken to Central Asia. In the first three years following deportation, according to conservative NKVD estimates, approximately 22 per cent of the Crimean Tatar population perished from infectious diseases, malnutrition, and dehydration. According to Crimean Tatar accounts, however, the losses are much higher, consisting of 46 per cent, or approximately half the then population. In addition to residing in Crimea and places of former exile such as Uzbekistan, there are still large populations of Crimean Tatars in Turkey where they number over five million, Bulgaria (10,000), Romania (40,000), the United States (6,000) and Germany (an unknown number) (Uehling, 1989).

In 1945 the 'Autonomy' was abolished, and Crimea became just another Oblast (region occupied by ethnic Russians) in the Russian Socialist Federation of Soviet Republics (RSFSR). All traces of Tatar history including monuments and place names were obliterated, and the peninsula was settled increasingly by ethnic Russians, many of them military personnel and workers in the tourist industry. The homes and farms of Crimean Tatars were· almost without exception occupied by the newcomers, a source of continuing bitterness for those returning.

Crimea remained part of Russia until 1954, when it was transferred from the RSFSR to the Ukrainian Soviet Socialist Republic. This 'gift' by Nikita Khrushchev[23] marked the 300th anniversary of the Pereyaslav Treaty of 8 January 1654, by which the Ruthenian/Ukrainian (actually Cossack-Orthodox) polity of Hetman Bohdan Khmelnytsky had sworn an oath of allegiance to Russia/Moskovy in exchange for military support in his battles with the Kingdom of Poland. It should be noted that on the 400th anniversary of Khmelnytsky's birth in 1995, the President of independent Ukraine Leonid Kuchma defined the Pereyaslav Treaty as giving birth to a new state, Ukraine, which was independent of the Polish-Lithuanian Commonwealth. In other words, not submission to, or 'reunion' with Russia as the treaty was traditionally understood.[24]

The leaders of the ethnic Russian majority of Crimea seized the opportunity presented by the collapse of the USSR in 1991 to declare a 'Crimean Autonomous SSR'. As Wilson points out (1998: 291), the Communist-dominated Crimean leadership presented this as a restoration of the inter-war Crimean ASSR. '[I]ronically, many Crimean Tatars looked back on the period of the original Crimean ASSR as an era of relative freedom and Tatar pre-eminence ... in historical fact, the Crimean ASSR was not an ethnic republic as such' – and certainly not for the Russians. The proposal received the support of 93 per cent of an 81 per cent turnout in a referendum held on 20 January 1991, and on 12 February 1991 the Ukrainian Supreme Soviet adopted a law providing autonomous status for Crimea within the borders of Ukraine. Meanwhile, in June 1991, the Second Kurultay (Congress) of the Crimean Tatar people met for the first time since the deportation in 1944, and elected the Mejlis, consisting of 33 members, which has continued to be the main representative body of the Crimean Tatar people (Belitser, 2003: 3).

The ASSR was 'upgraded' by the Russian majority in the Crimean Supreme Soviet to a 'Crimean Republic' in February 1992, with a Constitution providing for the right to secede from Ukraine. Some senior Russian politicians sought to inflame the situation of Crimea. In May 1992, a resolution of the Russian State Duma declared the transfer of Crimea to Ukraine to have been illegal. In July 1993 the Duma resolved that Crimea was a part of Russia, and in April 1995 invited the separatist Speaker of the Crimean parliament, Sergei Tsekov, and a delegation, to discuss the situation. Indeed, in January 1994, with just such promises of secession, Yurii Meshkov was elected President of Crimea, and his 'Russia' bloc won 54 of 94 seats in the then Supreme Soviet in March 1994. The Mayor of Moscow Yuri Luzhkov raised the temperature by making widely reported statements in 1995 claiming that Sevastopol was and always would be a Russian city.

It took the supposedly Russophile President Leonid Kuchma, elected in June and July 1994, to bring Crimea into line. He was helped by Russia. The Russian Federation made it clear that as a state it opposed irredentist tendencies, namely Crimea's separation from Ukraine and (re)unification with Russia. President Yeltsin repeatedly made statements recognising Ukraine's territorial integrity and that Crimea was part of Ukraine. The Russian Foreign Minister stated to the Ukrainian Foreign Minister that 'Russia will not interfere in the Crimean situation.' As Natalie Mychajlyszyn points out, this removed a 'potentially explosive factor from the situation' (2001: 213).

Russia's recognition of Ukraine's territorial integrity was included in the January 1994 Tripartite Agreement between Russia, Ukraine and the United States. Russia influenced the situation by making the signing of a Treaty of Friendship and Co-operation with Ukraine conditional upon the settlement of the status of Crimea. This was a treaty Ukraine strongly desired in order to normalise relations with Russia. The Ukrainian Verkhovna Rada made this possible by enacting a law of 17 March 1995 'On the Status of Crimea', which abolished not only the Crimean Constitution of 1992 and all laws and decrees contradicting those of Ukraine, but also the office of the Crimean Presidency.

Furthermore, appointments to the Crimean government were made subject to President Kuchma's approval (Wilson, 1997: 167). Ukraine imposed its own choice of Prime Minister, Anatolii Franchuk, and of Speaker of the Supreme Soviet (Verkhovna Rada) of Crimea, Yevgenii Supruniuk. In Autumn 1995 a new Crimean constitution was adopted. The Treaty of Friendship was finally signed in May 1997 after Crimea's autonomous status was recognised in the June 1996 Constitution. A preliminary Crimean constitution was ratified in part by the Ukrainian parliament in April 1996, before the national constitution, but the final version of the Crimean constitution was only approved by the Ukrainian parliament on 23 December 1998 (Sasse, 2002: 5).

The OSCE's HCNM also played a key role – a part of his 'quiet diplomacy' (Packer, 1998; Kemp, 2001; Kulyk, 2002). He first visited Ukraine at the invitation of the Ukrainian government in February 1994, and began actively to promote political solutions based on implementation of OSCE principles as contained in its documents, especially the Copenhagen document of 1990.[25] His strategy was to see inclusion of provisions within the new Ukrainian and Crimean constitutions which would adequately reflect the peninsula's autonomy within Ukraine (Mychajlyszyn, 2001: 201). Thus, he recommended that the reference in the Crimean Constitution to

'Republic of Crimea' should be changed to 'Autonomous Republic of Crimea', and – for the sake of legal correctness – that 'citizens of Crimea' should become 'citizens of Ukraine residing in Crimea'. Further, he recommended that the Crimean Constitution should recognise Ukrainian as the state language and Russian and Crimean Tatar as official languages on a par with Ukrainian. He wanted Ukrainian flags and symbols to be used alongside those of Crimea. Most importantly, he recommended that Crimea should end its pursuit of a separate Crimean citizenship.[26] Some but by no means all of these proposals are to be found in the Constitutions of Ukraine and the ARC.

His interventions on the issue of Ukrainian citizenship for Crimean Tatars, too, were judicious and effective. In 1991 Ukraine adopted an admirable 'zero option' with regard to its new citizenship. According to the Law of 8 October 1991 *On the Citizenship of Ukraine*, all those resident in Ukraine on 13 November 1991, when the law came into force, who were not citizens of another state, and did not declare themselves against receiving citizenship, became citizens of Ukraine automatically, regardless of origin or any other distinction. However, many Crimean Tatars arrived after this date, and many of them had been granted – without their consent – citizenship of Uzbekistan in 1992. There were therefore many Crimean Tatar residents of Ukraine without citizenship, many stateless, still more had become citizens of another state. Ukraine prohibited dual citizenship, and to lose Uzbek citizenship was complex and expensive. Non-citizens are excluded from not only the right to vote in elections, but many civil and political rights, and – of crucial importance to Crimean Tatars – participation in land privatisation (Bowring, 1999). This problem was in part resolved in August 1998, as a direct result of the HCNM's recommendation, by the Agreement on the Prevention of Dual Citizenship signed by the Ukraine and Uzbek governments, which allowed for an accelerated and simplified procedure for renouncing Uzbek citizenship and acquiring Ukrainian citizenship.[27] As Belitser has pointed out,

> the two successive new versions of law on Ukrainian citizenship of 1997 and then of 18 January 2001 provided a simplified procedure for gaining Ukrainian citizenship by affiliation for those persons and their first- and second-degree descendants, who were forcibly displaced from Ukraine by the Soviets. As a result, and due to generous financial and organisational support from the UNHCR, this difficult problem was solved successfully by the time of the elections of 31 March 2002.
>
> (Belitser, 2003: 7)

Whatever the reasons for delay, the new state constitution of Ukraine was finally adopted at the Fifth Session of the Verkhovna Rada (Supreme Council) of Ukraine on 28 June 1996. Wolczuk argues that this constitution 'like all previous drafts, was an outgrowth of the temporary configuration of forces at that time.' She adds:

> Apart from having an organising function (establishing the basis for the institutional delineation of authority), a constitution also performs legitimising and integrating functions in a new state. However, in Ukraine the heterogeneity of the society was projected onto politics through the lack of fundamental agreement on government according to a common set of rules.
>
> (Wolczuk, 1998: 118–119)

According to its Preamble, this Constitution was expressed to have been made by the Verkhovna Rada 'on behalf of the Ukrainian people – citizens of Ukraine of all nationalities'. This was a great improvement on the 'Ukrainian nation' of 1990.

One of the most contentious articles of the Constitution for Ukraine, including Crimea, has proved to be Article 10, on the State Language. This provides:

> The state language of Ukraine is the Ukrainian language. The State ensures the comprehensive development and functioning of the Ukrainian language in all spheres of social life throughout the entire territory of Ukraine. In Ukraine, the free development, use and protection of Russian, other languages of national minorities of Ukraine, is guaranteed. The State promotes the learning of languages of international communication. The use of languages in Ukraine is guaranteed by the Constitution of Ukraine and is determined by law.

Wilson describes the many hours during which deputies argued over this Article, even the comma in the phrase 'Russian, other languages of national minorities'.

> Bracketing Russian together with Bulgarian or Greek represented a huge diminution of its past status. Ukrainian nationalists were even concerned to omit an 'and' after 'Russian' – hence the rather ungrammatical sentence ... Significantly, the state 'guarantees' the use of Ukrainian, but only 'promotes' languages of international communication ... It was also important to Ukrainophone nationalists that the state language function 'in all spheres of social life' ... and on 'all the territory of Ukraine'.
>
> (Wilson, 2002: 208–209)

That is, in Crimea as well.[28]

The weakness and ambiguity of the Article was demonstrated by the advisory decision on 14 December 1999 of the Ukrainian Constitutional

Court, which, with one strong dissent, gave an interpretation to Article 10 which delighted some Ukrainian nationalists but strayed far beyond the actual words of the Article. It concluded that the Ukrainian language was the only 'compulsory means of communication for officials of local government bodies and local self-government structures, and in all spheres of public life' including education. Consequently, according to a circular sent out by the Government, officials must use only Ukrainian, lack of knowledge of the language could lead to dismissal, and higher education must be in Ukrainian only. The Court appeared not to pay much attention to a highly important sentence of Article 10: 'In Ukraine, the free development, use and protection of Russian, and other languages of national minorities of Ukraine, is guaranteed'.

The result of successful lobbying by the Crimean Tatars and their allies is to be found in Article 11, with its express reference to 'indigenous peoples'. It states: 'The State promotes the consolidation and development of the Ukrainian nation, of its historical consciousness, traditions and culture, and also the development of the ethnic, cultural, linguistic and religious identity of all indigenous peoples and national minorities of Ukraine'.

Indigenous peoples and national minorities also find a reference in Articles 92 (exclusive jurisdiction of the laws of Ukraine) and 119, which provides:

> Local state administrations on their respective territory ensure: ... 3) the implementation of national and regional programmes for socio-economic and cultural development, programmes for environmental protection, and also – in places of compact residence of indigenous peoples and national minorities – programmes for their national and cultural development.

These references were placed in the Constitution for a purpose – they were intended to lead to laws of Ukraine on indigenous peoples, which would have special reference to Crimea. During 1996 the Ukrainian government established an Expert Group to develop a Draft Concept of National Policy of Ukraine in Relation to Indigenous Peoples, and relevant draft laws. The then Minister of Justice of Ukraine, Serhiy Holovaty, circulated the Concept to local and international experts for discussion.[29] This contained a highly controversial proposal: 'an objective criterion for determination of ethnic groups in Ukraine which belong to indigenous peoples'. This was:

> (a) descent from the populations which from time immemorial inhabited certain geographical regions of Ukraine in its present state boundaries; (b) preserving cultural, linguistic, religious group identity different both from the identity of the dominant nation and national minorities in Ukraine, and desire to maintain and develop such iden-

tity; (c) existence of own historical traditions, social institutions, self-government systems and bodies; (d) non-existence of ethnically con-gener national state or homeland (kin-state) beyond Ukraine's boundaries.

This definition was carefully crafted to include Crimean Tatars and exclude Russians. Acts consequent on adoption of the Concept were to include a new Law of Ukraine on the status of the Crimean Tatar people regulating the status of the Medjlis (the representative body of the Crimean Tatars); representation in local legislative and executive bodies and in the Ukrainian parliament; ratification of the ILO convention (see above); taking measures for restoration of the rights of deported peoples. These provisions were anathema for the Communist and Russian elements in both the Ukrainian and Crimean Verkhovna Radas. The Concept has disappeared practically without trace, and very little has been done in legal terms either to protect the rights of indigenous peoples, or to recognise the Crimean Tatars.

Despite the long years of gestation, the Constitution of Ukraine has inde-terminacy and ambiguity at the heart of some of the most important provi-sions of the Constitution – not the most solid foundation for the provisions establishing the Autonomous Republic of Crimea. Wilson comments:

> Not surprisingly, the constitution was a compromise text: the right got most of what it wanted in terms of the constitutional expression of the 'national idea', Kuchma got most of what he wanted in terms of state structures and the balance of constitutional powers . . . On paper, the constitution reflects Ukraine's 'European' tradition by enshrining key principles of the rule of law and the separation of powers. In practice, power is concentrated in the hands of the presidency, the state bureaucracy is still highly politicised, judicial independence is as yet unestablished and significant hangovers from the Soviet era persist.
>
> (1998: 197)

Crimean autonomy in the constitutions of Ukraine and Crimea

Chapter X of the Constitution provides for the Autonomous Republic of Crimea. It contains no reference to the Crimean Tatars, or indeed to indigenous peoples. Article 134 makes it clear that there is no question of secession: 'The Autonomous Republic of Crimea is an inseparable con-stituent part of Ukraine and decides on the issues ascribed to its compe-tence within the limits of authority determined by the Constitution of Ukraine.' Nevertheless, as Wolczuk points out: 'The status quo of Crimea was confirmed, as evidenced by its title . . . although Ukraine was desig-nated a unitary country' (Wolczuk, 1998: 134).

The ARC's constitutional powers are limited by Article 135. Its constitution must be approved by the Ukrainian parliament, and its normative acts must not contradict the Ukrainian Constitution or laws. The scope of those normative acts is severely circumscribed. By Article 137:

> The Autonomous Republic of Crimea exercises normative regulation on the following issues: 1) agriculture and forestry; 2) land reclamation and mining; 3) public works, crafts and trades; charity; 4) city construction and housing management; 5) tourism, hotel business, fairs; 6) museums, libraries, theatres, other cultural establishments, historical and cultural preserves; 7) public transportation, roadways, water supply; 8) hunting and fishing; 9) sanitary and hospital services.

The last sentence of this Article is especially significant, giving the President of Ukraine draconian powers of intervention:

> For reasons of nonconformity of normative legal acts of the Verkhovna Rada of the Autonomous Republic of Crimea with the Constitution of Ukraine and the laws of Ukraine, the President of Ukraine may suspend these normative legal acts … with a simultaneous appeal to the Constitutional Court of Ukraine in regard to their constitutionality.

The competence of the ARC is detailed in Article 138. It includes holding of local elections and referendums, managing property belonging to the ARC, formulating the budget of the ARC 'on the basis of the uniform tax and budget policy of Ukraine', developing programmes for socio-economic and cultural development and environmental protection in accordance with national programmes, and 'ensuring the operation and development of the state language and national languages and cultures in the Autonomous Republic of Crimea' as well as 'participating in the development and realisation of state programmes for the return of deported peoples'.

These Articles cumulatively thus appear to give the ARC no greater powers than any regional authority in Ukraine – compare these provisions with those of Article 119 on 'local state administrations', which have specific powers and duties with respect to national minorities and indigenous peoples. While the Constitution stipulates that Crimea will have its own constitution, parliament and government, the Ukrainian president can prevent any Crimean legislative or executive act from entering into force, at least temporarily, until there has been determination by the Ukrainian Constitutional Court. The Constitution also retains the institution of the representative of the President of Ukraine in Crimea, a very powerful figure who exercises powers of presidential monitoring and control. Susan Stewart outlines the political background to the compromise reflected in this Chapter. She describes it as '[t]his skeletal definition' (2001: 123–124). Nordberg is more positive:

> Since independence [Crimea] has been the only autonomous region in Ukraine, with its own constitution and greater local economic control ... Although its constitution must be approved by the Verkhovna Rada in Kyiv, Crimea is allowed its own prime minister and parliament along with greater regulatory and budgetary freedoms.
>
> (1998: 46)

Furthermore, all of the powers listed above are entirely consistent with a Russian-dominated population and government in the ARC. There is no mention of the Crimean Tatars or of indigenous peoples, although there are three references to indigenous peoples elsewhere in the Constitution. The sole gesture in the direction of the Crimean Tatars – without naming them – is that the ninth competence is: 'participation' in the development and realisation of state (presumably Ukraine and the ARC) programmes for the return of deported peoples. The most numerous deported people is – the Crimean Tatar people.

The Constitution of the Autonomous Republic of Crimea[30] was adopted at the Second Session of the Verkhovna Rada of the ARC on 21 October 1998, two years after the Ukrainian Constitution. It was approved by Order of the Verkhovna Rada of Ukraine, and signed by President Kuchma, on 23 December 1998. Article 1 of the Constitution declares that the ARC is 'an inalienable component part of Ukraine and within the limits of the competence, defined by the Constitution of Ukraine [and] decides questions under its jurisdiction', while Article 2 states that the legal foundation for the status and competence of the ARC, its Verkhovna Rada and Council of Ministers is 'the Constitution of Ukraine, the laws of Ukraine, and the Constitution of the ARC'. By Article 3, its 'basic principles' include 'the coincidence of the interests of the ARC and the general state interests of Ukraine'.

The autonomy of Crimea is established by a formulation that imposes clear limits. The 'basic guarantees' of the ARC are 'legal, organisational, financial, property and resource independence (autonomy) within the limits established by the Constitution of Ukraine, guaranteeing the existence of the competence of the ARC' and the duty on the part of the Ukrainian government to take into account 'the specificities of the ARC as foreseen by the Constitution of Ukraine, when taking decisions relating to the ARC'. It is noteworthy that the Russian text uses the Russian word *samostoyaltelnost* rather than *nezavisimost* – both are usually translated into English as 'independence', but the former has the connotation of personal autonomy, while the latter is used for state independence. This is another clear sign of the determination of Ukraine not to compromise its sovereign integrity.

The Crimean Tatars will have noted with disquiet the fact that Article 6 restricts to citizens the right to participate in elections and referenda, as well as the right to complain to court 'as to acts and actions or failure to act of organs of power of the ARC, as well as institutions, organisations or responsible persons violating their rights'. This provision therefore excludes those who have recently arrived in Crimea – especially deported persons.

Chapter 3 of the Constitution of the ARC sets out the 'Guarantees of the rights and freedoms of citizens of Ukraine, and the rights of nationalities in the ARC'. It is no surprise, given the controversy surrounding Article 10 of the Ukrainian Constitution on the state language of Ukraine, that a number of crucial provisions deal with the question of language. Thus, Article 10 is entitled 'Guarantees for the functioning and development of the state language, Russian, Crimean Tatar, and other national languages in the ARC', and continues that 'In the ARC the Russian language as the language of the majority of the population and a language admissible for inter-ethnic communication is used in all spheres of social life'. The right of education in their mother tongue in pre-school educational institutions is guaranteed, as well as education in the Russian language in public educational institutions. Article 11 provides for 'the language of documents defining the status of a citizen of the ARC'. These are to be completed in Ukrainian and Russian 'and, at the request of the citizen – also in the Crimean Tatar language'. By Article 12, the language of court proceedings and legal advice and assistance is to be Ukrainian, except where a party to proceedings requests Russian 'as the language of the majority of the population of the ARC'. Thus, the Crimean Tatar language may be used for the state documents described in Article 11, but not in a wide range of court and other proceedings. Russian is privileged in a way which is in doubtful accord with Article 10 of the Ukrainian Constitution.

This tendency is further exemplified in Article 13, which provides that post and telegraph communications are to be accepted for transmission in the Ukrainian or Russian languages. In all spheres of service to the citizen (communal services, public transport, the health service and others) and in the enterprises, institutions and organisations connected with them, the Ukrainian or Russian languages, or another language accepted by the parties, will be used ... Again, Russian is privileged as against Crimean Tatar or other languages.

Article 18 provides for the competences of the ARC. Its language is significant. Point 17 includes:

> Taking into account the specificities of the ARC defined in the Constitution of Ukraine, and in accordance with the Constitution of the ARC, the preparation, definition and realisation of programmes and the resolution of questions of guarantees for the functioning and

development of Ukrainian as the state language, and the Russian, Crimean Tatar and other national languages, the organisation and development of education, science and culture, the protection and use of monuments of history and culture.

Point 21 moreover specifies 'participation in the preparation and realisation of the state programme of Ukraine for the return of citizens deported from Crimea'. This last provision again fails to take account of the fact that most of the Crimean Tatars and others deported from Crimea have had to apply for Ukrainian citizenship.

The Supreme Soviet (Verkhovna Rada in Ukrainian) of the ARC is, by Article 22, to be composed of 100 deputies elected for four-year terms. By Article 23 they must be citizens of Ukraine, with the right to vote, over 18 years old, and living in Ukraine for not less than five years. The competences of the Verkhovna Rada, by Article 26, include (point 14) 'the decision of questions on the guaranteeing of the functioning and development of the state, Russian, Crimean Tatar and other national languages and cultures in the ARC'. Chapter IV deals with local self-government in the ARC. The deputies of the Verkhovna Rada of Crimea are predominantly heads of enterprises and institutions – this includes the six (plus one communist) elected Crimean Tatars. The most recent elections to the Crimean Verkhovna Rada took place on 31 March 2002. Remzi Illyasov, Deputy Chairman of the Medjlis of the Crimean Tatar people, complained that 'without a legal mechanism of guaranteed representation of the Crimean Tatar people in the parliament of the autonomy we cannot receive the number of seats proportionate to the number of Crimean Tatars in the population of the peninsula ... only six Crimean Tatars out of 13 possible [seats].'[31] The background to this disappointment was the fact that in 1994, following mass protest actions of Crimean Tatars in the peninsula, 14 seats were reserved in the Crimean parliament for representatives of the Crimean Tatars, and one seat for each of the other former forcibly displaced peoples – ethnic Armenians, Bulgarians, Greeks and Germans, also deported from the Crimea in 1994. This 'quota' was lost in the 1998 elections. From 1994 to 1998 there were indeed 14 Crimean Tatar deputies in the Crimean parliament.

However, according to Refat Chubarov, who is one of two Crimean Tatar deputies in the Ukrainian Verkhovna Rada, the results of the election were generally positive, as a result of in-fighting between the major political forces in Crimea. All in all, 933 Crimean Tatars were elected to councils of all levels: equivalent to 14% of all elected members. Seven Crimean Tatars from the Medjlis were elected to the Crimean parliament, and the deputy chairman of the Medjlis, Ilmi Umerov, became the Vice Speaker of the Crimean parliament. Three Crimean Tatars became members of the Crimean government. Edip Gafarov became the Vice Prime Minister of the Crimea and was one of only seven out of 23 ministers who remained from the previous government. Aziz Abdullayev became the Minister of the Industry, Transport and Communications of the Crimea, and Server Saliyev was appointed to the position of head of the Crimean Committee for Nationalities and Former Deportees.

The major change for the Russian majority was that the Russian Communists lost their position of power. The notorious Leonid Grach lost the position of Speaker of the Verkhovna Rada, being replaced by Boris Deich. Sergei Kunitsyn became Chairman of the Cabinet of Ministers. The Crimean Tatars voted for both of them.

Conclusion

Uncharitable commentators have wondered whether Ukraine is viable in the long term as an independent state. Political deadlock and corruption in the Ukrainian polity have led some scholars to refer to 'virtual politics' and even a 'blackmail state'.[32] This is compounded by tendencies to disintegration. Lurid paranoid fantasies every so often erupt among the Russian irredentists of Crimea and Eastern Ukraine and the Ukrainian nationalists of Western Ukraine – slogans including words such as 'apartheid' and 'cultural genocide' are heard too often. It is to the credit of the young Ukrainian state that there has – so far – been little or no violence in Crimea, despite the potentially explosive tendencies at work in the expression of Russian and Crimean Tatar interests. The key question is whether and to what extent the constitutional arrangements for Crimean autonomy have played a role in conflict prevention. Gwendolyn Sasse points out that:

> Given the legal ambiguity of the constitutional settlement, the budget disputes, the continuing wrangling between the regional organs of power, the population's alienation from the Crimean constitution and the exclusion of the Crimean Tatars from the autonomy arrangement, Crimea's autonomy status is politically weak.
>
> (2002: 11)

She concludes by emphasising 'the political process of constitution-*making* at the regional and national level as a key determinant of conflict-prevention rather than the actual institutional outcome – Crimea's autonomy status, which is symbolically significant, but politically weak' (Sasse, 2002: 22).

Nevertheless, since she wrote her comments, one important development appears to strengthen the foundations – the institutional design – of Crimean autonomy. In 2002 a number of right-wing factions – 50 deputies in all – applied to the Constitutional Court of Ukraine for declarations of unconstitutionality of a number of provisions of the Constitution of Crimea, in order to cut down or extinguish the rights of the ARC. On 22

January 2003 the Court ruled (with one strong dissent by Judge Viktor Skomorokha) that several articles, including that relating to the territory of the ARC, were constitutional. Both the Prime Minister and the Chairman of the Supreme Court of Crimea welcomed this decision as an important contribution to stabilisation of the situation in Crimea.[33] The Permanent Representative of the President of Ukraine in Crimea, Aleksandr Didenko, described the decision as a 'triumph of justice'. According to him, the Constitutional Court had brought a halt to political discussions calling the status of the ARC into question, and clearly confirmed Crimea's authority, by recognising its administrative-territorial integrity, its economic rights to collect taxes and duties on its territory, the possibility of conducting experiments in the sphere of taxation, and its rights to an emblem, flag and anthem.[34] Writing in *Zerkalo Nedeli (Mirror of the Week)*, Nikolai Semena quoted Boris Deich as being of the opinion that now, many declarative competences of the autonomy included in the Constitution of the ARC, which earlier were not exercised, begin to work. The decision of the Constitutional Court gives the Crimean authorities 'the right not to persuade and request, but to demand'. In Semena's view – that is correct.[35]

This chapter has shown that the (re)creation of the Crimean autonomy, a multinational quasi-state (if this is not too strong a term in the circumstances) within the unitary state of Ukraine, was primarily a response to the threat of irredentism by the – still now – preponderant Russian majority. These arrangements are and will continue to be unique in Ukraine. No other region of Ukraine has manifested similar demands for greater autonomy, even Galicia. Evidence has been provided that the Russian state had no interest in fostering irredentism, and that the interventions of the OSCE's High Commissioner on National Minorities and membership of the Council of Europe have helped to produce a form of autonomy which is, perhaps, an anomaly, but is nevertheless firmly situated within the Ukrainian state. The latest decision of the Ukrainian Constitutional Court has further entrenched the autonomy. However, as I have also shown, the constitutional settlement now established in Crimea takes practically no account of the aspirations or even the presence of the Crimean Tatars, so many of whom have now returned to their homeland. Thus, the 'wild card' which has increasingly manifested itself in Crimea is the presence of the well-organised Medjlis of the Crimean Tatar people. This is now exerting its influence not only in Crimea itself, but also – successfully playing the Ukrainian political game – in Kyiv, as well as at the Council of Europe and in the relevant bodies, on rights of indigenous peoples, in the United Nations.[36] The latest census has shown that demographic trends may reverse the current situation. This will be the real test for the autonomy now established.

Ukraine's unusual experiment in autonomy within a unitary state may have helped to prevent conflict or may simply have coincided with a period of civic calm. But it is now sufficiently established, after nearly five years, for a provisional judgement to be made. It has not failed; it may even succeed, if it can take greater account of the vociferous presence of the Crimean Tatars. In sum, Ukraine's experiment has proved much more durable than at first expected, despite its weak institutional design and many ambiguities, born of political compromise.

Notes

1 I am very grateful to the editors of this volume for their incisive and helpful advice on earlier drafts of this chapter, to Natalie Belitser for her own invaluable comments, and to Andrew Wilson and others for their guidance and assistance on previous occasions. Any errors are mine alone.
2 The author's first visits to Crimea, in 1993–1994, were as an expert for CIDP.
3 The author's most recent work in Ukraine was acting as Council of Europe expert at a conference, attended by Russians, Ukrainians and Crimean Tatars, on ratification of the Languages Charter, in November 2002.
4 This resolution, which the author helped to draft, sought to address the particular problems of the Crimean Tatars, including their exclusion from the possibility to participate in the privatisation of agricultural land.
5 Official Journal of the European Communities, No C 61, 29.2.1994, pp. 110–113, A3-0042/94.
6 More Crimean Tatars go to study in Turkey, with Turkish government support, or in the USA.
7 Turkey is, however, generally supportive of the Crimean Tatars.
8 Available online at http://193.194.138.190/html/menu3/b/62.htm.
9 See the interview with Mustafa Dzhemilev, Chairman of the Mejlis of the Crimean Tatar People and member of the Ukrainian Verkhovna Rada on 4 June 2003, at http://aspects.crimeastar.net/english/press/interview/int.php.
10 It should be noted that Wilson's use of the term 'nationalist' is controversial, and that Ukrainian politics are complex and dynamic, especially as concerns those most anxious to preserve Ukrainian statehood.
11 *Kyiv Post*, 10 November 2000.
12 Nevertheless, the noisy events of November 2003 concerning Russian construction works at Tuzla Island in the Kerch bay (Azov Sea), were accompanied by evidence that a stronger Ukrainian civic – or even ethnic – consciousness is emerging. See, for example, http://www.unian.net/eng/news/news-45691.html.
13 See Oleh Wolowyna '2001 Census results reveal information on nationalities and language in Ukraine', *Ukrainian Weekly*, at www.ukrweekly.com/Archive/2003/020302.shtml.
14 See also Askold Krushelnycky 'Ukraine: first Post-Soviet Census Results Sparking Controversy' (14 January 2003), at www.referl.org/nca/features/2003/01/140120033155934.asp.
15 Ministry of the Interior figures show that the numbers of Crimean Tatars may well be larger: 262,600 persons returned, of whom 259,600 were Crimean Tatars.
16 The figures are 1989 – 28,200; 1990 – 38,800; 1991 – 41,400; 1992 – 27,600; 1993 – 19,300; 1994 – 10,800; 1995 – 9,200; 1996 – 8,100; 1997 – about 5,000. See I Pribytkova (1997) *Vliyaniye Instituta Grazhdanstva po Protsessi Vozvrashcheniya I Obustroistva Raneye Deportirovannikh v Krymu (The Influence of Citizenship on the Processes of Return and Settlement of Previously Deported People in Crimea)* Kiev; also in *Grazhdanin* No 1(7) 1998, p. 23.

17 All these figures are taken from Budzhurova (1998).
18 English translation at http://www.ukrweekly.com/Archive/1990/299002.shtml.
19 See http://snake76.by.ru/texts/doi_ua.html.
20 For a translation into English, see http://www.rada.kiev.ua/const/conengl.htm.
21 It should be noted that this long delay gave all interested parties and groups the maximum opportunity to debate the new constitutional order.
22 See http://members.fortunecity.com/timurberk/kirim/ttrbg/origins.html, and http://www.euronet.nl/users/sota/krimwho.html.
23 Natalya Belitser (2003, p. 2) has pointed out that the transfer from Russia to Ukraine was prompted as much by economic failure in Crimea despite Russian settlement, and the hope that closer ties to Ukraine would improve the situation.
24 See http://www.rferl.org/pbureport/2002/05/18-070502.html.
25 To be found at http://www.osce.org/docs/english/1990-1999/hd/cope90e.htm.
26 Letters from the HCNM to the Minister for Foreign Affairs of Ukraine, 12 October 1995, 5 April 1996.
27 UNHCR Press Release 22 June 1999, http://www.unhcr.ch/news/pr/pr990622.htm.
28 Although the Ukrainian government, wisely, did not push this issue in Crimea.
29 Copy, dated 25 November 1996, in the possession of the author.
30 See the Russian text at http://www.rada.crimea.ua/konstit/.
31 See 'Research Update: Crimean Tatar Issue and Recent Election Results', at http://old.ucipr.kiev.ua/english/rupdate/2002/05/27052002.html. It should be noted that the final result was '7 + 1' – seven representatives of the Medjlis plus the Communist Crimean Tatar Lentul Bezaziuev.
32 See Domique Arel 'Kuchmagate and the Demise of Ukraine's "Geopolitical Bluff"'? (pp. 54–59), Andrew Wilson 'Ukraine's New Virtual Politics' (pp. 60–66), and Keith Darden 'Blackmail as a Tool of State Domination: Ukraine under Kuchma' (pp. 67–71), all in (2001) Vol. 10, Nos. 2–3 *East European Constitutional Review*
33 See http://www.analytik.org.ua/eng/current-comment-eng/2003-01-25/pagedoc1986_2/.
34 See http://aspects.crimeastar.net/english/news.php?action=240103.
35 Mykola Semena '*Konstitutsiya Kryma konstituttsionn. Pochti ... (The Constitution of Crimea is constitutional. Almost...)*' 1–7 February 2003 No. 4 (429) Saturday *Zerkalo Nedeli*, at www.zerkalo-nedeli.com/ie/print/37503/.
36 At the Council of Europe conference celebrating five years of the Framework Convention for the Protection of National Minorities which took place in Strasbourg at the end of October 2003, the Medjlis of the Crimean Tatars was represented by Nadir Bekirov, who made a lengthy and effective intervention – the Crimean Tatars participate in Council of Europe mechanisms effectively, despite the fact that they deny that they are a 'national minority'.

References

Allworth, E. A. (ed.) (1998) *The Tatars of Crimea: Return to the Homeland* Durham: Duke University Press
Arel, Domique (2001) 'Kuchmagate and the Demise of Ukraine's "Geopolitical Bluff"' *East European Constitutional Review*, v. 10, n. 2–3, pp. 54–59
Belitser, N. (2003) 'Crimean Autonomy: Positive and Negative Aspects in Terms of

Ethnic Conflict', paper delivered at the International Conference on Regional Autonomy of Ethnic Minorities, Uppsala University, Sweden, 12–17 June (in possession of the author)

Bowring, B. (1999) 'New Nations and National Minorities: Ukraine and the Question of Citizenship', pp. 233–250 in Cumper, Peter and Wheatley, Steven *Minority Rights in the 'New' Europe* Leiden: Martinus Nijhoff

Budzhurova, Lilya (1998) 'Citizenship is a fundamental human right, since it is nothing other than the right to have a right' *Politika*, a journal published in Evpatoria, 8–15 September, p. 4

Darden, Keith (2001) 'Blackmail as a Tool of State Domination: Ukraine under Kuchma' *East European Constitutional Review*, v. 10, n. 2–3, pp. 67–71

Filippova, O. (1999) 'Ukrainians and Russians in Eastern Ukraine; Ethnic Identity and Citizenship in the light of Ukrainian Nation-Building', paper prepared for the conference 'Nationalism, Identity and Minority Rights' (Bristol: September)

Fisher, A. (1978) *The Crimean Tatars* Stanford: Hoover Institution Press

Kemp, W. A. (2001) *Quiet Diplomacy in Action: The OSCE High Commissioner on National Minorities* The Hague: Kluwer Law International

Krushelnycky, Askold (2003) 'Ukraine: First Post-Soviet Census Results Sparking Controversy' Radio Free Europe, Radio Liberty 14 January at www.referl.org/nca/features/2003/01/140120033155934.asp

Kulyk, V. (2002) 'Revisiting a Success Story: Implementation of the Recommendations of the OSCE High Commissioner on National Minorities to Ukraine, 1994–2001' pp. 1–146 in Zellner W., Oberschmidt R., Neukirch C. (eds) *Comparative Case Studies on the Effectiveness of the OSCE High Commissioner on National Minorities* Hamburg: CORE (CORE Working Paper No. 6)

Kuzio, T. (2003) 'Census: Ukraine, More Ukrainian' v. 2, issue 3 (4 February) *Russian and Eurasia Review* at http://russia.jamestownorg/pubs/view/rer_002_003_003.htm

Mychajlyszyn, N. (2001) 'The OSCE and Regional Conflicts in the Former Soviet Union' *Regional and Federal Studies*, v. 11, n. 3, pp. 194–219

Nordberg, M. (1998) 'State and Institution Building in Ukraine', pp. 41–55 in Kuzio, T. (ed.) (1998) *Contemporary Ukraine: Dynamics of Post-Soviet Transformation* Armonk, NY: M. E. Sharpe

Official Journal of the European Communities, No C 61, 29.2.1994, pp. 110–113, A3-0042/94

Packer, J. (1998) 'Autonomy within the OSCE: the case of Crimea', p. 302 in Suksi, M. (ed.) *Autonomy: Applications and Implications* Dordrecht: Kluwer Law International

Pribitkova, I. (1998) 'Vliyaniye Instituta Grazhdanstva po Protsessi Vozvrashcheniya i Obustroistva Raneye Deportirovannikh v Krymu (The Influence of Citizenship on the Processes of Return and Settlement of Previously Deported People in Crimea)' Kiev: UNHCR; also in *Grazhdanin*, Publication of the Foundation for Naturalisation and Human Rights 'Sodeistviye (Cooperation)', Simferopol v. 1, n. 7, pp. 23–49

Sasse, G. (2002) 'Conflict-Prevention in a Transition State: The Crimean Issue in Post-Soviet Ukraine' *Nationalism and Ethnic Politics*, v. 8, n. 2, pp. 1–26

Semena, Mykola (2003) 'Konstitutsiya Kryma konstituttsionn. Pochti. (The Constitution of Crimea is constitutional Almost.)' *Saturday Zerkalo Nedeli* 1–7 February, n. 4 (429) at www.zerkalo-nedeli.com/ie/print/37503/

Stewart, S. (2001) 'Autonomy as a Mechanism for Conflict Regulation? The Case of Crimea' *Nationalism and Ethnic Politics*, v. 7, n. 4, pp. 113–141

Taras, R. (1997) *Postcommunist Presidents* Cambridge: Cambridge University Press

Uehling, G. L. (1989) *The Crimean Tatars* at http://www.iccrimea.org/krimtatars.html

van Zon, Hans (2001) 'Ethnic Conflict and Conflict Resolution in Ukraine' *Perspectives on European Politics and Society* 2: 2 pp. 221–240

Williams, B. (2001) *The Crimean Tatars: The Diaspora Experience and the Forging of a Nation* Leiden: Brill Academic Publishers (Brill's Inner Asian Library, v. 2)

Wilson, A. (1997) *Ukrainian nationalism in the 1990s: A minority faith* Cambridge: Cambridge University Press

Wilson, A. (1998) 'Politics in and around Crimea: A Difficult Homecoming' pp. 281–322 in Allworth, E. A. (ed.) (1998) *The Tatars of Crimea: Return to the Homeland* Durham: Duke University Press

Wilson, Andrew (2001) 'Ukraine's New Virtual Politics' *East European Constitutional Review*, v. 10, n. 2–3, pp. 60–66

Wilson, A. (2002) *The Ukrainians: Unexpected Nation* New Haven: Yale Nota Bene

Wolczuk, K. (1998) 'The Politics of Constitution Making in Ukraine', pp. 118–138 in Kuzio, T. (ed.) (1998) *Contemporary Ukraine: Dynamics of Post-Soviet Transformation* Armonk, NY: M. E. Sharpe

Wolowyna, Oleh (2003) '2001 Census results reveal information on nationalities and language in Ukraine' *Ukrainian Weekly*, at www.ukrweekly.com/Archive/2003/020302.shtml

5 Autonomy and multilevel governance

Experiences in Nordic and Continental European cooperation

Elisabeth Nauclér

Introduction

Intuitively, the concepts of autonomy and multilevel governance not only seem not mutually exclusive but almost as two sides of the same coin. Autonomy—the exercise of exclusive jurisdiction in distinct policy areas—and multilevel governance—the distribution of power and competences through the vertical layering of public authority from the supra-state to local government level—appear to originate from the same concern for subsidiarity. In theory, the principle of devolving the decision-making process to the lowest possible level in order to make democratic governance locally more relevant, accountable and transparent, as well as more effective and efficient underlies both regimes of autonomy and of multilevel governance. However, in practice, when multilevel governance extends beyond the boundaries of the traditional Westphalian nation-state and involves supra-state layers of authority, such as in the European Union and its forerunner institutions or the Nordic Council, matters become more complicated. State-internal arrangements of divided and shared sovereignty cannot be easily accounted for in emerging supra-state regimes, which by their very nature have their origins in the cooperation of states and their governments, even if they may over time develop into more institutionalised forms of cooperation from their inter-governmental roots.

This phenomenon is of particular interest for the discussion of autonomy as a conflict settlement mechanism. The editors of this volume define autonomy as the legally established power of ethnic or territorial communities to take public decisions and execute public policy independently of other sources of authority in the state, but subject to the overall legal order of the state (see Wolff and Weller, Ch. 1). In the context of multilevel governance it is particularly important to bear in mind that autonomy as a strategy of preventing and settling ethnic conflict is based on the recognition of individual, group-specific and state concerns, and on accepting that to endow an ethnic group with legislative, executive, and judicial powers to address these concerns effectively will contribute to individual, group, and state security, and thus to preventing the disruption of the territorial and/or social integrity of a given country. From this perspective, preserving existing autonomy regimes and/or enhancing their status is a key requirement in the process of supra-state cooperation and integration, both for stability and security within the individual state concerned as well as of the larger supra-state entity. While it would be difficult and unreasonable to argue for a static approach to this question, the dynamics of autonomy regimes usually allow for a degree of flexibility that makes it possible to make use of new opportunities that emerge in the context of regional integration (see Danspeckgruber, Ch. 2). On the other hand, the primary European example of regional, supra-state integration, the European Union, requires that member states surrender elements of their sovereignty to supra-state institutions and comply with, and implement decisions taken at this level. This means that supra-state integration can potentially also bring with it constraints on the capacity of autonomous entities within member states to exercise their autonomous powers fully, constraints that go beyond those identified in Wolff and Weller's definition as 'the overall legal order of the state'.

Taking three autonomous territories as examples—the Faeroe Islands, Greenland, and the Åland Islands—this chapter examines the paradox of autonomy regimes within the institutional structures of supra-state arrangements. Looking at the way in which these three autonomous territories have fared in the context of the Nordic Council and the European Union, different institutional arrangements and their shortcomings are explored from the perspective of whether regional integration preserves and enhances the status of autonomous territories within member states. As the outcome of this inquiry leads to very different findings in relation to the Nordic Council and the European Union, an underlying concern of this chapter is to establish what mechanisms and institutional arrangements need to be adopted in order to avoid the erosion of autonomy regimes as a consequence of regional integration. This is of particular concern for the Åland Islands, whose status as an autonomous territory derives from an international treaty meant to settle a conflict, rather than from a central government's decision to devolve authority to sub-state units, as in the case of the Faeroe Islands and Greenland.

The chapter is divided into three main parts. Part one gives a brief overview of the three autonomous territories; part two examines the evolution of Nordic cooperation and the institutional arrangements adopted to account for the specific status of the three territories within the two states concerned (Denmark and Finland); while part three analyses some of the key aspects that distinguish Nordic cooperation from the institutional and inter-governmental integration processes of the European Union and its forerunner organisations where these are relevant for the status of the three autonomous areas concerned. In a concluding section some important trends and lessons from these case studies are outlined and their broader importance for the impact of regional and supra-state integration on the stability of autonomy regimes identified.

The Nordic region and the autonomous territories of the Faeroe Islands, Greenland and the Åland Islands

The Nordic region consists of five independent states and three autonomous territories. The region has a total population of about 24 million but my presentation will focus on the three autonomous territories. They are not three islands, but several thousand islands with a total population of 130,000. These three small jurisdictions are very far from each other and have little in common. Their economies differ greatly. The Faeroe Islands and Greenland are almost totally dependent on fisheries. The main emphasis of economic development in the Åland Islands has traditionally been on shipping, agriculture and fishing. Today, the Åland Islands form a typical service economy with more than a million tourists visiting the islands every year and a transport sector that accounts for 45.5 per cent of the gross domestic product. The economy of the Åland Islands relies heavily on neighbouring areas (the Stockholm and Turku regions) and on contacts with them, whereas the Faeroes and Greenland are far from the Nordic mainland. This explains why one of them decided to remain outside the European Union, one seceded from it and one decided to join it but remain outside the tax union. They may be very different but they do have one thing in common; they are autonomous territories with home rule and legislative powers. They are members of the Nordic Council and the Nordic Council of Ministers, fly their own flags, and exercise certain other independent rights.

The Faeroe or Sheep Islands, so called because when the ancestors of the present inhabitants first arrived they found an abundance of sheep— the only survivors of an earlier settlement—have a population of 46,000 spread across a total land area of 1,399 sq. km. Despite long periods during which the written language was abandoned in favour of Danish for educational and official use, the Faeroese maintained a distinctive spoken language. In the 19th century, a new written language was created, but Faeroese was not permitted in education until 1937 nor recognised as a legal language until 1948 (Isherwood 1997).

In 1380, the Faeroe Islands came under the rule of the joint Norwegian and Danish crown, and when the union was dissolved in 1814, the Faeroe Islands, along with Iceland and Greenland, came under the Danish crown. Home rule has its origins in the aftermath of World War II. When German forces invaded and occupied Denmark in 1940, British forces landed on the Faeroes, because they are strategically placed between Scotland and Iceland. During the war, when they were cut off from Denmark, they were obliged to govern themselves. They flew their own flag on their ships and it was recognised by the Allies. At the end of the war, the Faeroese were unwilling to return to their previous status and in 1948 the autonomy of the Faeroe Islands was established by regular Danish statutes. These expressly reserve foreign affairs as the remit of the Danish government. However, this does not mean that the Faeroe Islands are necessarily included in treaties concluded by Denmark, nor has it prevented Denmark from concluding treaties concerning the Faeroes separately. The Faeroe Islands have themselves been allowed to conclude agreements with foreign powers concerning matters within their autonomy, such as fishing rights in the respective economic zones (Grahl-Madsen 1985: 6f.). The government of the Faeroe Islands now decides on practically all areas of policy apart from justice, monetary affairs, defence and foreign policy. In 1992, Denmark ceded to the Faeroes the management of natural resources, including what may be major oil deposits on the Faeroese continental shelf (Isherwood 1997).

Greenland or Kalaallit Nunaatt—the land of the people—is, like the Faeroe Islands, part of the 'Realm of Denmark'. It has a population of 56,000 and a land area totalling 2,166,086 sq. km., some eight times the size of the British Isles. The indigenous people—the Inuit—are ethnically very different from the Scandinavians; their kinfolk inhabit Alaska and the northern territories of Canada (Grahl-Madsen 1985: 7). In 1397, Greenland came under the rule of the Danish monarch at the time of the union that joined together Denmark, Sweden and Norway. The issue of national sovereignty was settled in 1933 when the International Court ruled in favour of Denmark and against Norway, which had occupied parts of eastern Greenland two years earlier. During World War II, the United States recognised Danish sovereignty and agreed to defend it until the end of the war. American bases were built to safeguard allied shipping and this defence relationship has continued under the bilateral Treaty on the Protection of Greenland (Isherwood 1997). When the war was over the Greenlanders were no longer willing to accept the low level of investment and restrictive monopoly of the Royal Greenland Company. Under the new constitution approved by Denmark in 1953, Greenland ceased to be a colony, but it was not until the 1970s that the movement for home rule took off, and it was not achieved until 1979. Under the Home Rule Act, Greenland now decides on all areas of policy apart from nationality, justice, monetary affairs, defence and foreign policy. Accordingly, responsibility for Greenland's vast raw material potential, and for environmental protection, also rests with the autonomous institutions (Isherwood 1997).

The Åland Islands are a demilitarised, neutralised and autonomous area of Finland. Their population is 26,000, and the land area totals 1,552 sq. km. The Åland Islands are an archipelago consisting of more than 6,500 islands (Isherwood 1997). The Ålanders have always been Swedish-speaking and are, therefore, part of the Swedish cultural heritage. Since Åland is a group of islands, its autonomy is considered to be

territorial, even though it would also fit into the notion of cultural autonomy, as the Swedish language and culture constitute the foundations of it.

Åland was a very old region of Sweden and had a Swedish population
long before Finland was incorporated into the Swedish realm in the thir-
teenth century. The Ålanders, therefore, in addition to economic and
geographic links, developed close social contacts with Stockholm, and the
nearby coastal area of Sweden. The Åland Islands, together with Finland,
belonged to Sweden until 1809, at which time Sweden, after losing a war
with Russia, was forced to relinquish Finland, together with Åland, to the
victor. When the Russian Empire started to disintegrate, but before
Finland declared independence in December 1917, the Ålanders started
to struggle for reunion with their traditional mother country, Sweden. A
petition in favour of reunion was signed by 96 per cent of the resident
Ålanders of legally competent age and conveyed to the King of Sweden.
But the new-born state of Finland, which had been proclaimed by virtue of
the principle of national self-determination, was not prepared to give up a
part of its territory and was not concerned that a section of the population
did not feel at home with their new-found statehood. After a dispute
between Finland and Sweden, the Åland issue became international and,
on a British initiative, was brought before the League of Nations in
Geneva. In 1921, the League decided that the Åland Islands should
belong to Finland but have autonomy that would guarantee their Swedish
language and heritage. Ten states guaranteed Åland's demilitarisation and
neutralisation. In other words, Åland's autonomy is of international standing, and has been used as an exemplar for solving minority conflicts
throughout the world. Like the two other aforementioned autonomous
territories, Åland has legislative competence in areas such as social and
health care, the environment, trade and industry, culture and education,
transportation, postal services, policing, radio and TV broadcasting and
local government, but relatively little authority to levy taxes compared
with the other two.

Nordic cooperation

Only a few years after World War II, in 1952, the Nordic Council was
created as a forum where representatives of the four members (Denmark,
Norway, Iceland and Sweden) could exchange opinions and compare
experiences. Finland joined in 1955. The Nordic Council was founded as
a parliamentary forum for cooperation among the five independent
Nordic countries. It should be noted that the Nordic Council is not a parliament in the orthodox sense of a deliberative organ with powers, i.e.
with the formal power to enact laws that are binding and other preroga-
tives. Nevertheless, it is considered one of the key players in the process of
developing cooperation on legislation. It cannot demand that its recommendations be implemented, nor is it directly elected by the people,

unlike the European Parliament, but it has still achieved many of its goals (Arter 1983).

The Nordic Council has been a precursor for other international organisations in the context of autonomous territories. The autonomous territories are not observers. Instead, their parliaments choose members of the Council on the same terms as the sovereign states, but this was not the case in 1952. Initially, Nordic cooperation was not based on any international treaty but on national decisions taken by the five participating states. The need for a formal agreement did not arise until 1962, when the Treaty of Cooperation embracing Denmark, Finland, Iceland, Norway and Sweden (the Helsinki Treaty) came into force. The autonomous territories did not participate in the work in either a formal or informal capacity at that time, but thanks to Danish generosity the Faeroe Islands were brought in as part of the Danish delegation, a precedent which later helped the Åland Islands. It was a Danish government proposal which in 1967 raised the issue of formal representation for Åland and the Faeroes. The proposal resulted in a report from a committee (known as the Kling committee) suggesting an amendment to the Helsinki Treaty. Before that, the Faeroe Islands already had a representative through the Danish delegation, whereas Greenland had not yet obtained autonomy. Eventually, in 1970, the Helsinki Agreement was modified and the Faeroese Lögting could from then on elect two representatives who became part of the Danish delegation. Correspondingly, Åland's Landsting could elect one representative who became a member of the Finnish delegation. The number of Council members was increased from 73 to 78. The governments of the respective states were also represented in the delegations. The government representatives have the right to speak in the Council's plenary assembly, but have no vote. From 1971, one representative of Åland's Landskapsstyrelse was included in the Finnish delegation and one representing the Faeroese Landsstyre was included in the Danish delegation (Wendt 1981: 658).

The Nordic Council of Ministers was established in 1971 to implement cooperation at governmental level. The autonomous areas were not formally included in this cooperation but continued their struggle, and in 1976, as a result of a joint preliminary request, the governments of the Faeroes and the Åland Islands were given the right to send representatives with observer status to meetings of the Council of Ministers when questions relating to the Faeroes and the Åland Islands were being discussed. Later, the Faeroe Islands raised the question of equal representation several times. In 1980, the Danish Government submitted a proposal suggesting that Greenland (which had in 1979 attained self-government), the Faeroe Islands and the Åland Islands should have independent representation in the Nordic Council. To study the matter, a committee (known as the Petri committee) was appointed. It consisted of the executive body of the Nordic Council and the Ministers of Justice of the Nordic countries. The report established that the status of the autonomies in Nordic cooperation should be consolidated (Lindholm 1985: 79–84). The Report culminated in 1983 in extended rights for the three autonomous territories, including participation in the work of the Nordic Council of Ministers.

The parliaments of the three autonomous areas now had the right to elect two members each to the Nordic Council. Just like in the case of the state members of the Council (Denmark, Finland, Iceland, Norway, Sweden), the governments of the three autonomous areas can send as many government representatives as they wish to the meetings of the Nordic Council of Ministers. In order to ensure the continued participation of government representatives in the plenary session of the Nordic Council, parliamentary and governmental delegates from states and autonomous territories were combined into 'national' delegations on a per-state basis. In the case of Denmark and Sweden, these delegations, therefore, consist of the delegations of the central government and parliament and of the autonomous territories.

As the autonomous territories were given only two seats, they could not have seats in all the different Committees of the Council. Article 27 of The Rules and Procedures of the Nordic Council was, therefore, changed in a generous way that made it possible for their representatives to attend and speak at the meetings of the Committees in which they did not have members.

The most important change was that the autonomous areas were granted the right to participate in the work of the Council of Ministers. This unique arrangement came about through another change in the Helsinki agreement (Article 60).

Decisions in the Nordic Council of Ministers are based on consensus but only require the acceptance of those countries that are covered by the decision. Eventually, the question was raised whether all eight governments had to agree on a certain issue. After long deliberation, it was decided that the consent of the autonomous areas was not required. On the other hand, decisions would not be binding on the autonomous areas if the issue fell under their areas of legislative competence and the Home Rule Government in question had not given its consent. This procedure is usually labelled 'the right of consent' (Article 63). All three autonomous areas have frequently exercised this right. The governments of the autonomous regions have also obtained the right to make governmental proposals under the same conditions as the governments of the sovereign states (Article 55). Subsequently, the work of the Nordic Council has changed and been restructured, but the fundamental principles are still valid. The prime ministers have acquired a greater role and hold regular meetings in conjunction with Nordic Council sessions, to which the heads of governments of the autonomous territories are also invited.

In comparison with other international intergovernmental organisations, the Nordic Council is therefore regarded as something of a model for the equal participation of entities below the level of sovereign nation-states. Whether at the Council of Europe or under the Treaty of Rome, the Treaty of Paris or the Statute of the Interparliamentary Union, non-sovereign territories or national minority groups do not formally and equally participate in these bodies and their representatives have, at best, been able to obtain some form of observer status. The general structure of Nordic cooperation must therefore be viewed as a good example of what international cooperation can accomplish. Primarily, it serves as a good example for cooperation between other sovereign states with minorities, autonomous areas or regions with cross-border links.

The future of Nordic cooperation

For a number of years, the Faeroese government has discussed alternatives to their present status within Denmark. After internal disputes, and little interest in the Danish capital, a mutual understanding seems to have been reached on transferring more areas of responsibility to the Faeroese authorities, except, so far, for foreign policy, defence and citizenship. However, at the initiative of the Danish Prime Minister, a new law is being prepared with the aim of enabling the Faeroese authorities to act internationally in areas under their legal competence. The government of the Faeroe Islands has, in accordance with the purpose of this new law, also asked for their competence to be enlarged in the Nordic Council and Council of Ministers. The matter was discussed with the government of the Åland Islands and Greenland in their preparatory talks for the meeting of the Nordic Prime Ministers in 2002. The Faeroese representative thereafter informed the Prime Ministers that the Faeroe government had decided to ask to become a contracting party to the Helsinki Agreement.

In February 2003, the Faeroese government asked the Parliament to agree to present a request to the Nordic Council, and the Nordic Council of Ministers. After discussions in the Faeroese parliament, the government submitted a letter to the Nordic Council and the Council of Ministers referring to the meeting in Helsinki asking to obtain status as contracting party to the Helsinki Agreement, and other agreements based on the Helsinki agreement.[1] A letter was also sent to the Danish Prime Minister to inform him of the initiative. The matter has so far not been discussed in the Nordic Council or Council of Ministers. As it is considered to be a Danish question, and not a Faeroese, the Nordic secretariat is waiting for a letter from the Danish Prime Minister.

The government of Greenland decided in 2002 to set up a committee to produce a report on the Autonomy of Greenland and its future relation to Denmark. The extensive (630-page) report was presented in March 2003, and resulted in a proposal for a 'Mutual Agreement on Cooperation'. The report does not suggest any measures to be taken in this respect, but makes reference to the initiative set forward in the debate at the plenary session of the Nordic Council in 1999 aiming at revising the Helsinki Agreement so that Greenland could become an independent member.

If this is to be a future trend with the Faeroe Islands and potentially Greenland as frontrunners in attempts of all the autonomous territories within the Nordic Council to seek membership in the organisation independent of their 'home-state' (except in economic matters), the multi-level governance model of the Nordic Council would gain another dimension to its institutional structure, the significance of which is not clear yet, but which could be potentially quite far-reaching, both in terms of setting precedents for other regional organisations and for the status of autonomous territories and the competences that the governments of autonomous territories would enjoy outside and beyond traditional domestic self-governance.

The Nordic autonomous territories in a European context

The experience of Nordic cooperation meant that inhabitants of the autonomous territories in the Nordic countries grew used to direct representation in regional organisations which were able to decide directly on matters affecting them. Members of their Parliaments were members of the Nordic Council and their governments had to consent to decisions made by the Council of Ministers, otherwise they were not bound by the decisions.

The situation in the European Union, often seen as a model of multi-level governance and the implementation of the subsidiarity principle, is very different for that in the Nordic Council. Crucially, the EU so far lacks any clear provision comparable to the treatment of the autonomous territories in the Nordic Council, i.e., the EU of today does not recognise any other members than independent states. The reason why the current EU system has so far not been more seriously questioned is that those Nordic autonomies that could have challenged it, in accordance with their constitutions, chose to remain outside the organisation when their 'home-states' joined, except for one, namely the Åland Islands. In addition, when the organisation was formed several decades ago, sub-state autonomy was, on the whole, an exception in the six founding countries. Only in the Federal Republic of Germany ten *Länder*, and in Italy four regions with special autonomy statutes, at the time constituted sub-state autonomies. However, these statistics have changed dramatically: there are now also three autonomous regions in Belgium (one of the original founder members), the accession of Spain and Portugal added a further seventeen autonomous communities and two autonomous regions, German unification and Austria's membership raised the number of *Länder* in 1990 and 1995, respectively, while devolution in the UK and federalisation in Italy now means that sub-state autonomies are, although perhaps not yet the norm, certainly no longer an exotic exception (Bullain 1998). With the exception of the Isle of Man and the Channel Islands, all these autonomous entities had one thing in common: they could not remain outside the EU when their mother states joined. This distinguishes them sharply from the situation of the autonomous territories in the Nordic countries, whose status allowed them exactly that: the option to 'opt out' of EU membership. Examining their reasons for doing so and the consequences of their actions will shed further light on the structure and implications of multi-level governance in the EU and the impact it has on autonomous territories.

Greenland

Denmark, including Greenland, which had not yet obtained autonomy, joined the EEC in 1972 following a referendum in which 70 per cent of Greenland's electorate voted against EEC membership, but were obliged to comply with the Danish decision. For Greenland, the decision meant that its waters became part of EEC waters and foreign fishing fleets would have the right to fish in them. After having obtained home rule, Greenland organised a new referendum and the 'no' result was repeated. In 1985, Greenland left the EEC but retained links with the organisation through an Overseas Countries and Territories Agreement. The basis for accepting the secession of an autonomous territory was the fact that Greenland did not enjoy home rule when Denmark joined the EEC, and therefore at that time did not have the option of joining or staying outside.

The Faeroe Islands

Under the Danish Accession Treaty with the EEC, the Faeroe Islands were given the option of deciding whether or not to join the EU. In addition to this option, the Act of Accession also provided the Danish government with the opportunity to delay the application of specific treaties and agreements to the Faeroe Islands for as long as three years, primarily because the Faeroe Islands' economy was entirely dependent on fishing and there were major uncertainties regarding the future direction of the EEC's Common Fisheries Policy. In any case, two years after Denmark's accession, the Faeroese decided in a referendum to reject membership of the EC (Fagerlund 1997).

The Åland Islands

Brussels—Helsinki—Mariehamn: Consequences of new multilevel governance structures

In 1994, the time came for the Åland Islands to decide upon their fate as Finland was in the process of joining the EU. In accordance with the Act on Autonomy of Åland, the Ålanders had the option to remain outside, by not giving their consent when the Accession Treaty was to be passed. Not only had the Åland Islands the possibility to remain outside, they also had the right to be informed of the course of the membership negotiations.

A solution that left the Åland Islands on the outside would certainly not have appeared attractive to Finland. Hence, the Åland Islands had an advantageous negotiating position and Finland chose to assist the islands in negotiating a solution that would convince the islanders that membership was acceptable. After long discussions and having carefully scrutinised the different possibilities, the outcome was that the Åland Islands were given the same choice as the Faeroe Islands, i.e., the opt-in/opt-out option. Two referenda were held; the first concerning the question whether Finland should join or not, and the second whether the Åland Islands should join or not. In both referenda, a majority of Ålanders voted yes.

The specific solution negotiated between Finland, the EU and the Åland Islands takes the shape of a separate protocol for the Åland Islands, making it a member of the EU's customs union, but not of the tax union. In addition, rights pertaining to the Right of Domicile (an indigenous right) remain in force even in cases where they infringe community rules. Among other provisions, the protocol determines that, with reference to Åland's special position under international law, the islands enjoy certain exemptions from treaties that are fundamental to the European Union. This means that the articles of the Treaty of Rome shall not infringe on Åland's continued right to limit—on a non-discriminatory basis—the rights of physical persons who do not have the Right of Domicile as well as the rights of juridical persons to acquire real property without permission. Åland may also limit the rights of physical persons or juridical persons who do not enjoy the Right of Domicile to set up a business enterprise or to offer services without permission from the Åland authorities.

The aim of the derogation was to maintain a viable local economy in the islands, and so the huge ferries operating between Finland and Sweden were allowed to retain their duty-free regime and also provide the islands with a necessary transportation system. The legal construction, with the Åland Islands considered as a third territory outside the EU's tax union, was not obtained on an Åland request but rather as a result of the effort within the EU to reach an acceptable solution, because leaving outside the community an island group as dependent on contacts and communications with their surrounding areas as the Åland Islands are would not have been viable.

At that time, within political circles, it was expected that autonomy would be strengthened through cooperation with the various agencies of the Union. Among other things, it was imagined that due to its special position within Finland, Åland would be able to negotiate directly with Brussels on matters relating to Åland and over which the Government has authority, enabling the islands to act more or less independently of Helsinki (Jansson 2002).

By joining the European Union, the Åland Islands surrendered competences to Brussels accorded to them in the original autonomy statute and in subsequent amendments. As the EU only knows and recognises sovereign states as members, all mechanisms of compensation for the loss of power also apply only to member *states*, i.e., they obtain seats in the European Parliament and they can appoint a Commissioner(s). In the case of a jurisdiction such as the Åland Islands, not being an independent state, there is no such mechanism. The Åland Islands received just one seat in the Committee of Regions, a body consisting of a variety of local authorities, some with and some without legislative authority. The Committee exercises purely advisory powers and does not constitute an EU institution in the formal-structural, decision-making sense. Even though access to information and contacts with other legislative regions should not be underestimated in its value and potential lobbying leverage, they do not constitute any form of compensation for the delegation of legislative competence from Mariehamn to Brussels.

In order to compensate for the loss of legislative competence and influence on matters within the sphere of autonomy, the Act on the Autonomy of Åland was amended in connection with the accession. The new chapter 9a provides that the Government of Åland shall be notified of matters under preparation in the institutions of the European Union, if the matters are within the legislative power of Åland or may for other reasons be especially important to it. However, the relevant clause does not deal with the problem of the member state and the autonomous region disagreeing on the national position. Yet the solution in cases of disagreement is quite obvious: the EU only knows independent states as members and consequently has no satisfactory way of resolving an issue concerning a dispute between a state and an autonomous area within it. Furthermore, the Åland Government shall formulate Finland's national position on those parts of an initiative that fall under the legislative power of Åland when the EU's common policies are being applied to Åland.

As a result, the Autonomy Act has over time proven unable to provide sufficient compensation for the loss of sovereignty. The autonomy of the Åland Islands is considered to have been eroded to some extent following the implementation of Finland's EU accession. In other words, multilevel governance in this particular case has meant the delegation of competences *upwards* without adequate compensation measures for the sub-state autonomous area.

Another amendment to the Autonomy Act came into force on 1 June 2004, with the aim of rectifying the shortcomings of the system. The purpose of this amendment is to strengthen the influence of the Åland government in the preparation of the Finnish position on decisions made by the European Union. As it is not a question of devolution of power, but a division between Finland and Åland, the Finnish position could not replace or overturn the opinion of the Åland government in cases where the two jurisdictions could not agree. The new provision therefore outlines the possibility of passing on two different, and even contradictory opinions to the European Union in matters where Finland and Åland disagree. Finland as the member of the European Union would always give the opinion of the member state, but at the request of the Åland government their opinion would be submitted alongside the Finnish position— with yet unknown consequences regarding the relevant EU decision.

The amendment also includes a new provision aimed at ameliorating the possibility of being represented in the Finnish delegation to the European Union in the preparation of different matters. The Åland government should be informed of matters pertaining to their legislative competence, and their representatives should, if so requested, be included in the delegation. The way the procedure is described in the amendment shows that, despite all the good will of a member state to accommodate the specific rights of the Åland Islands, it is in fact not possible for a member state to come to terms with the fact that only an independent state could be a member of the European Union. In contrast to arrangements in the Nordic Council, the Åland representative remains a member of the Finnish delegation and does not have an independent right to deliver his opinion or even cast an independent vote on the relevant issue. However, because of the complex domestic legal situation, deriving from the particular status of the Åland Islands under the international treaty that guarantees their autonomous status and regulates relations and competences between Mariehamn and Helsinki, the actual wording of the amendment to the Autonomy Act has tried to introduce a degree of 'constructive ambiguity' to accommodate the problems arising from this.

Another paragraph aims at solving the problem when the Åland government and the Finnish government do not agree. The principle rule is that the division of legal competence between the Åland parliament and the Finnish parliament is laid down in the Act on the Autonomy of Åland, and can not be circumvented in any way. However, there is no clear mechanism for how to deal with situations in which only one decision can be communicated to the European Union, especially in terms of a possible disagreement between the Finnish and Åland governments. All that is said is that the 'decision should be made after consultation between two parties with the goal to obtain concord and the view of the Åland Government should as far as possible be observed'. Thus the key issue that has (and probably could) not be addressed at this level within the multilevel governance structures of the EU that comprise the Åland-Finland relationship is this: How does a separate jurisdiction, which is not an independent member of the European Union, cooperate with another jurisdiction that is an independent member of the European Union if they are of different opinion if they have a formal legal relationship constituted under international law that assigns clear competences to them in different areas?

The most disputed issue so far has been how to deal with the fact that the European Court of Justice only recognises independent states when determining the penalty to be paid when a jurisdiction has failed to fulfil an obligation under the EC Treaty. According to Article 228 in the EC Treaty the Court of Justice can specify a penalty to be paid by a Member State. When determining the sum the Court should consider it to be appropriate in the circumstances. The sum should be paid by the Member State and be appropriate for a state. So far this has not been a problem, but what if the Åland government refused to fulfil an obligation under the Treaty in its exclusive jurisdiction, i.e., beyond the competence of the Finnish government? How would the penalty be specified? What would be appropriate? A sum reflecting the number of inhabitants of Finland as is current court practice? On the other hand, should Finland pay for the refusal of the Åland government to fulfil an obligation that the Finnish government could not possibly have enforced because the Åland government has exclusive jurisdiction in the relevant area? While the question so far remains in the realm of the theoretical, the less satisfied the Ålanders are with the influence on different decisions taken by the European Union, the more likely is it that such an issue could become reality.

So far, neither the Åland government nor the Finnish government have been able to find a satisfactory solution; thus the recent amendment to the Åland Autonomy Act does not include a provision on this matter. The Constitutional Commission in the Finnish parliament would however not agree to leave this problem unsolved, and introduced a paragraph aiming at resolving the problem. According to the proposal, the Åland authorities should always carry the responsibility for any payment that Finland should make if the Åland authorities had failed to comply with the obligations. The cumbersome procedure outlined in the amendment offers the possibility of an adjustment of the sum after negotiations between the Finnish and the Åland government. In case there is no agreement between the two, the issue could be taken to the court, and the court specified in this case is the Administrative Court in Mariehamn. This, however, runs counter to the traditional way of resolving disputes between Helsinki and Mariehamn. So far all questions implying potential disputes between Finland and the Åland Islands have been referred to the Åland Delegation, an arbitration body composed of members representing the Finnish State and the Åland Islands, who could avail themselves of the possibility to approach the Supreme Court of Finland. Excluding this issue from the competence of the Åland Delegation and to give the first Administrative Court in Mariehamn, with neither previous experience of mediation between the two parties nor of European Union matters, this new duty is not only surprising but raises some concerns for the ability of Mariehamn and Helsinki to address disputes between them constructively in the future. From this prospective, European integration, thus, seems to have a potentially detrimental effect as it imposes modifications on a tried and tested conflict resolution mechanism with uncertain outcomes.

The fact that the question of payment of penalty has been so difficult, and that no agreement was found at an earlier stage, leads to two conclusions. The first is that the problems evolving from the fact that the European Union does not accept autonomous territories to become members of the EU could not be accommodated in the internal legislation in a satisfactory way. The second conclusion is that the way in which the European Union approaches a country with two separate jurisdictions will have profound and potentially unintended negative consequences for the relations between central government and autonomous government.

The independent states becoming members of the European Union obtain seats in the European Parliament. This could be seen as a compensation for the loss of competence transferred to the European Union, or rather a way of participating in the decision-making process. The Åland islands were not given any such compensation when becoming a member of the EU. This makes Åland the only jurisdiction with no representation in the European Parliament. All other territories with legislative power have a seat, some because they have enough inhabitants to form a constituency, others because they are granted a seat by their mother countries. The German minority in Belgium has a seat despite their small numbers. Greenland had one seat before it left the EU.

The work carried out by the members of the European Convention has naturally directed the work of the Committee of Regions towards reinforcing the role of the regions, and of the Committee itself. The most interesting initiative from an Åland point of view has been the effort to give the regions with legislative authority a special role on the European scene. The question raised has been how to recognise the regions in general and Regions with Legislative Authority in particular within the European treaties. Some of the answers suggested are: by reinforcing the Committee of Regions role and powers by creating an institution with advisory capacity, and even making it compulsory to abide by its opinion; by enshrining the Regions with Legislative Authority and the Committee of the Regions right of recourse before the European courts; by increasing participation and boosting dialogue between the Commission and the Regions with Legislative Competence. Some of the initiatives taken are interesting from an Åland point of view, others are not as they try to ameliorate the situation within the national framework, which is either already in place in the relation between Finland and Åland, or would not be sufficient. It is also obvious that the widespread range of competence among the members is resulting in some conclusions more in favour of keeping the present system so as not to endanger the process of European integration. It is obvious that there is no common final objective among the different members. Some regions have therefore favoured the idea of giving the Regions with Legislative Authority a special role as they are perceived as having at least one common denominator that would lead the thoughts to a second Chamber based on the Regions. These regions are a minority of the members of the regions in the Committee, and the result will therefore most likely only be the creation of a specialised body Committee of the Regions to present the interest of the Regions with Legislative Authority.

One of the key questions has been the principle of subsidiarity, along with the question of proportionality. Some regions would like to safeguard the principle of subsidiarity, saying that the Regions should be involved in monitoring the principle, but there is not enough consensus for a joint initiative that would result in effective results. Besides all this the question is whether the extensive discussion on the question of subsidiarity among regions is at all applicable to the Åland islands. In the case of the regions it is the question of devolution of power, and decision-making in this context. Is this applicable in the Åland case where the legislative power is not distributed through devolution, but division of power, and could accordingly not be withdrawn, altered or abolished, except with mutual agreement?

Conclusion: the two faces of multilevel governance

It will be up to Ålanders to choose whether to insist on the path of European integration or defend their autonomy and Swedish character. So far they have succeeded in combining both possibilities. In the near future other stringent choices might emerge. But the real success of a form of autonomy rests on its ability to renew itself in harmony with external developments.

(Scarpulla 1999: 91)

Is it possible for a member state to remedy shortcomings in the procedural system of an international organisation? The answer is no. It is not possible as long as the system remains unable to comply with the undertakings and obligations concluded by the member states under national constitutional law or, as in the case of the Åland Islands, under international law. At present, the EU is unprepared to accommodate autonomous members.

The complicated wording in the Amendments to the Act on the Autonomy of Åland shows that even if a member state has the good will to improve the situation for an autonomy as extensive as that of the Åland

Islands the European Union does not give the space for an adequate arrangement within their framework for decision-making.

In contrast, the Nordic Council and Nordic Council of Ministers are said to be forerunners regarding the participation of the autonomous areas. Why is that so? It is important for central governments to understand that foreign relations are not a sacrosanct and inalienable attribute of sovereignty but can be devolved to local or autonomous governments (Hannum 1988: 273). Could the reason be that the work of the Nordic Council and Council of Ministers is of little importance and can therefore be shared with the autonomous regimes, while the European Union is preoccupied with important matters? That could of course be the answer, but on the other hand one recalls that the members of the United Arab Emirates were, according to article 123 of their constitution, permitted to retain their individual memberships in the Organisation of Petroleum Exporting Countries (Hannum 1988: 278–279), most probably because the organisation is of such vital interest to them.

The three autonomous territories in question are considered as subjects according to international law in the context of the Helsinki Agreement, but not in a European Union context. This resulted in one autonomous area joining the EU, one withdrawing from it and one joining with certain derogations. Yet they are all members of the Nordic Council and the Nordic Council of Ministers on an equal footing.

Is there a future for the autonomous territories within the European Union, or should they try to distance themselves from it? The European Union is a supra-state organisation that does not recognise the construction of sub-state autonomy among its members. The autonomous territories do not have the right of participation on an equal footing with the independent states, or to be represented in a decision-making process. The Treaty of Rome makes no mention of autonomy and the question of division of power between a state and an autonomous area is an internal issue for each state to resolve under its domestic regulations.

The European Court stated in a case against Italy that, '[w]hile each Member State may be free to allocate areas of internal legal competence as it sees fit, the fact still remains that it alone is responsible towards the Community under Article 169 for compliance with obligations under Community law.'[2] The concern of the Court in this case was to stress that although Member States might devolve matters of transposition and enforcement of European law to the regional level of government, it is the state itself and not the region that is legally bound to uphold Community law (Burrows 1999). The enabling of regional-level governments to bring an action for annulment under Article 230 on the same terms as those recognised for Member States has been widely discussed, and a proposal on the matter has been put forward. This example shows the attitude of the European Union towards autonomous areas. Recognition of autonomy in the same way as within the Nordic Council and the associated

Helsinki agreement is, however, not practicable under the existing treaties.

The passport carried by Åland inhabitants is the only passport carried by EU citizens, apart from Gibraltar, reflecting the three identities they consider themselves to have by including the European Union, Finland and the Åland Islands on the front page. However, are there really three adequate layers within the European Union? Is there a modus vivendi for the autonomous territory, or has there to be created a new concept for them? Or will they have to either accept to fade away or remain outside as is the case with the Faroe Islands and Greenland? When the Åland Islands joined the EU a British journalist wrote, 'The Ålanders have to carve out a place for themselves on the map of Europe.' Unfortunately, however, such an endeavour would be unproductive as long as the structure of the EU and its political approach to autonomous areas remain unchanged.

Notes

1 There have been previous initiatives in the Nordic Council to obtain individual/independent membership, most notably a 1980 Danish proposal that resulted in the report of the Petri committee in 1982, which ruled out independent membership for non-independent territories arguing that the Nordic Council consists of independent states as contracting parties. However, the World Trade Organisation, also a body in which the original contracting parties were sovereign states, has intermittently accepted Hong Kong, Macau and China as independent members, even though Hong Kong and Macau are parts of China.
2 Cf. Case C-33/90 Re Toxic Waste: Commission v Italy (1991) I ECR 5987.

References

Arter, David (1983) *The Nordic Parliaments: A comparative analysis*. London: Routledge.
Bullain, Iñigo (1998) 'Autonomy and the European Union', pp. 343–356 in *Autonomy: Applications and Implications*, ed. Markku Suksi. The Hague: Kluwer Law International.
Burrows, Noreen (1999) 'Nemo me impune lacessit: The Scottish Right of Access to the European Court(s)', unpublished manuscript, Glasgow.
Fagerlund, Niklas (1997) 'The Special Status of the Åland Islands in the European Union', pp. 189–256 in *Autonomy and Demilitarisation in International Law: The Åland Islands in a Changing Europe*, eds Lauri Hannikainen and Frank Horn. The Hague/London/Boston: Martinus Nijhoff.
Grahl-Madsen, Atle (1985) 'The Evolution of the Nordic Autonomies', *Nordic Journal of International Law* 4–9.
Hannum, Hurst (1988) 'The Foreign Affairs Powers of Autonomous Regions', *Nordic Journal of International Law* 273–288.
Isherwood, Julian (1997) *The Nordic Autonomous Areas: The Nordic Council of Ministers*, Copenhagen.
Jansson, Christer (2002) 'Åland's Prospects for Development in the European Union', pp. 201–212 in *The Second Åland Islands Question: Autonomy or Independence?*,

eds Harry Jansson and Johannes Salminen. Mariehamn: The Åland Islands Peace Institute.

Lindholm, Göran (1985) 'The Right of Autonomous Regions to Participate in Nordic Cooperation', *Nordic Journal for International Law* 79–84.

Scarpulla, Claudio (1999) 'The Constitutional Framework for the Autonomy of Åland: A Survey of the Status of an Autonomous Region in the throes of European Integration', *Meddeland från Ålands högskola*, no. 10.

Wendt, Frantz (1981) 'Nordic Cooperation', *Nordic Democracy*.

6 Complex autonomy arrangements in Western Europe

A comparative analysis of regional consociationalism in Brussels, Northern Ireland and South Tyrol[1]

Stefan Wolff

Introduction: consociation and autonomy

Institutional designs in multiethnic societies are infinitely varied. Given the variety of contexts that constitutional engineers encounter, this is hardly surprising. At the same time, however, variation is often a question of detail and there are far fewer principal mechanisms of conflict settlement than settlements as such. Very prominent among such principal mechanisms are consociational power-sharing and territorial autonomy. As the latter has been extensively dealt with in the introduction to this volume, I will focus my attention at the beginning of this chapter on the nature of consociations.

The term 'consociational democracy'[2] is most closely associated with the work of Arend Lijphart, and more recently that of John McGarry and Brendan O'Leary. Lijphart examined consociations as a type of democratic system in greater detail for the first time in the late 1960s, when making reference to the political systems of Scandinavian countries and of the Netherlands and Belgium (Lijphart 1968a, b). He followed up with further studies of political stability in cases of severely socially fragmented societies, eventually leading to his fundamental work *Democracy in Plural Societies* (Lijphart 1977).

The phenomenon Lijphart was describing, however, was not new. As a pattern of social and political organisation, characterising a territory fragmented by religious, linguistic, ideological or cultural segmentation, it had existed long before the 1960s. These structural aspects, studied, among others, by Lorwin (1971), were not the primary concern of Lijphart, who was more interested in why, despite their fragmentation, such societies maintained a stable political process, and recognised its main source in the agency of political elites. Furthermore, Lijphart (1977: 25–52) identified four structural features shared by consociational systems – a grand coalition government (between parties from different segments of society), segmental autonomy (in the cultural sector), proportionality (in the voting system and in public sector employment) and minority veto.

These characteristics, more or less prominently, were exhibited by all the classic examples of consociationalism: Lebanon, Cyprus, Switzerland, Austria, the Netherlands, Belgium, Fiji and Malaysia. Schneckener (2002: 241) adds to that the need for an arbitration mechanism as a means to overcome impasses resulting from the exercise of veto powers.[3]

With some of these consociations having successfully functioned over long periods of time, such as in Switzerland, Austria, the Netherlands and Belgium, and others having failed, like Lebanon, Cyprus, Fiji and Malaysia, Lijphart tried to establish conditions conducive to consociational democracy. These included overarching, i.e., territorial, loyalties, a small number of political parties in each segment, about equal size of the different segments, and the existence of some cross-cutting cleavages with otherwise segmental isolation. The small size of the territory to which a consociational structure is applied and its direct and indirect internal and external effects, as well as a tradition of compromise among political elites, are also emphasised by Lijphart as conditions enhancing the stability of a consociational settlement (Lijphart 1977: 53–103). In addition, McGarry and O'Leary (1993: 36f.) have emphasised that, for consociational settlements to provide stable long-term solutions for ethnic conflicts, three fundamental conditions are required. Integration or assimilation of the respective other group must not be on the agenda of either of the ethnic groups in conflict with each other in the short or medium term. Successive elites must be motivated to work for the preservation of the consociational settlement, and they must enjoy a sufficient degree of autonomy within their communities, enabling them to make compromises and concessions without having to fear outbidding and outflanking by ethno-centric radicals.

Apart from their dependence upon elites and the factors determining their political agency, the history of consociational settlements has shown them also to be particularly vulnerable to outside interference – the Turkish invasion of Northern Cyprus and the involvement of Syria and Israel in the breakdown of the Lebanese consociation are just two examples of this. The reason for this vulnerability is that outside intervention dramatically alters the carefully preserved balances of power within a consociational process – in reality, as in the cases of Cyprus and Lebanon, or in the perception of one of the communities that is part of the consociation, as was the case in the first brief period of Northern Irish consociationalism in 1973/1974. Yet, at the same time, some degree of involvement of an outside agent may in fact prove helpful in persuading specific conflict parties that a consociational settlement is their best bet, as was the case in South Tyrol in the 1960s. Furthermore, a cross-border dimension, i.e., the involvement of its kin-state in the consociational settlement beyond the negotiation stage, might be required by one of the conflict parties for it to accept a settlement along consociational lines at all, especially if its original aspiration was for unification with the kin-state.

Again, South Tyrol and, to some extent, Northern Ireland are cases in point.

This raises the question of the overall suitability of consociationalism to the settlement of ethnic conflicts. At an abstract level, it is initially possible to determine how the ethnic and territorial claims of the conflict parties must be structured to give consociational settlements a decent chance of long-term survival. As they are essentially *internal* settlements, i.e., as they seek accommodation of conflicting ethnic and territorial claims without redrawing state boundaries, external agents such as the kin-state must withdraw or postpone their territorial claims, and domestic conflict parties must moderate their territorial claims such that they can be accommodated within the state's existing international boundaries. In addition, domestic conflict parties will have to find a compromise on their ethnic and (internal) territorial claims. Thus, fundamentally for consociational agreements to be reached there needs to be an absence of irredentist and secessionist claims, or agreed procedures to address such claims at a future point, and preparedness for compromise within, and reform of, an existing territorial and institutional framework.

This does not mean that consociational designs should not be applied to conflicts with irredentist or secessionist dimensions. Rather, it means that:

- Mediators and constitutional designers should leave options open for future institutional reform aimed at overcoming rigid consociational designs in favour of either more integrative models of power-sharing and democracy or with a view to permanent separation of conflict groups, i.e., creating new states;
- Consociational institutional structures should also be regarded more as interim solutions facilitating a transition from violent conflict to a more peaceful political process in which secessionist and irredentist claims can be negotiated with non-violent political means; and
- Strategies need to be crafted and concrete policies formulated that will enable, where necessary, a transition from consociational power-sharing to other institutional arrangements suitable for a particular conflict situation.

While this sets out the pillars for future research, my concern in this chapter is with three more 'routine' cases of regional consociational power-sharing which will provide better insights into institutional designs of consociations where irredentist and secessionist claims either do not exist or have been postponed, as this will also help design transitional consociational regimes whose success is crucial for the peaceful settlement of a given conflict in the long term, regardless of the length of the transition period.

In the existence of claims for wide-ranging segmental autonomy –

territorial as well as non-territorial – many ethnic conflicts resemble patterns in consociational societies even though the nature of claims in the latter is not always related to ethnicity in the strict sense, but can be ideological, as in Austria, or ideological and religious, as in the Netherlands. Switzerland and Belgium, of course, are examples of consociational democracies where ethnic and linguistic claims play a significant role.

Apart from looking at the basis of the consociation (ethnic, ideological, religious), another important distinction has to be made in relation to the territorial scale of the arrangement. In the four classic examples of consociational democracies in Europe, the arrangements extend to the entire territory of each state. In instances of ethnic conflict, this is not always, or necessarily, the case. In fact, the disputed areas often only form a small proportion of the host-states' territories. Thus, as is the case with South Tyrol and Northern Ireland, consociational arrangements may only extend to the disputed territory and the ethnic groups living there, rather than be the organising principle for the state's institutional structures as a whole. This is also true for the example of the Belgian capital of Brussels, which from this perspective also represents a regional consociation,[4] but one that has been established within a sovereign consociation. Generally speaking, depending on the political system of the host-state as a whole such a regional consociation can be established in one federal unit or one region without affecting the political structure of other territorial entities in the host-state.

Regional consociations thus combine two elements of traditional conflict resolution approaches: territorial autonomy[5] and consociational power-sharing. From a conflict-resolution perspective there are three particularly interesting dimensions, namely the factors in relation to structure and agency that make it possible for a regional consociation to be established; their institutional design; and the conditions that are conducive to their stability. My primary interest in this chapter is in the institutional design of regional consociations, but I will preface my analysis with some observations on their origin and otherwise only occasionally touch upon stability conditions in the following comparative institutional study of South Tyrol, Northern Ireland and Brussels.

The choice of these three cases is primarily dictated by the contextual similarities between them. They are comparable in the sense that they are all set within Western Europe and thus within a broader democratic framework. They are also small, contiguous territories with small populations (between 0.5 million in South Tyrol and 1.5 million in Northern Ireland). There are, however, also a number of significant contextual differences. In the cases of Northern Ireland and South Tyrol, kin-states have exercised their influence during crucial negotiation stages, while the regional consociation in Brussels, in some way, came into being within the process of reaching a broad national compromise over state reform in Belgium. While both French- and Dutch-speakers thus have kin-communities within the Belgian polity, the dynamics of their involvement are different from those arising from the existence and engagement of a kin-state.

The structure of this chapter is simple and straightforward. After some initial observations on the origin of regional consociations, I provide a brief background to the three conflicts that I analyse in detail. I then examine the institutions of each regional consociation and subsequently compare and contrast them with respect to the types of institutional structures, the ways in which horizontal and vertical forms of power-sharing are combined, the distribution of powers among and the coordination of policies between different vertical and horizontal centres of authority, and the mechanisms to guarantee the preservation of the agreed structures. On this basis, I will then formulate some conclusions: first, as to the common features that regional consociations exhibit and to what extent these are different from sovereign consociations, and second, as to the place regional consociationalism takes in the conflict resolution tool box.

The origins of regional consociations

In their authoritative taxonomy of macropolitical forms of ethnic conflict regulation, McGarry and O'Leary (1993) identify eight methods to manage or eliminate the differences at the bottom of ethnic conflicts. The methods for eliminating differences are genocide, forced mass-population transfers, partition and/or secession and integration and/or assimilation; those for managing differences are hegemonic control, arbitration, cantonisation and/or federalisation and consociationalism and/or power-sharing (McGarry and O'Leary 1993: 4). Regional consociations, i.e., the application of consociational principles to only one part of an existing state, is thus only one among a broader range of options available to negotiators who seek to resolve a particular self-determination conflict.

McGarry and O'Leary (1993: 35) emphasise that consociational principles 'can operate at the level of an entire state, or within a region of a state characterised by ethnic conflict', i.e., they do not explicitly require the combination of territorial autonomy with consociational power-sharing for a regional consociation as I have defined it above. Practically, however, it is almost impossible to imagine a regional consociation that does not simultaneously imply substantive regional autonomy. For Lijphart's consociational principles to be implemented in any meaningful way, the government of the relevant entity needs to have original authority in a range of policy areas. In addition, the self-determination conflicts that regional consociations seek to address are about substantive issues rather than institutional forms. Regional (or territorial) autonomy as a mechanism to empower a specific group to exercise a greater degree of self-governance over its own affairs naturally requires that powers, as Daftary (2000: 5) rightly asserts, are not merely delegated but transferred; they may thus not be revoked without consulting with the autonomous entity ... the central government may only interfere with the acts of the autonomous entity in extreme cases (for example when national security is threatened or its powers have been exceeded).[6]

Reasons for the emergence of regional consociations as conflict settlements combining territorial autonomy and consociational power-sharing thus must be identifiable in relation to both of these elements.

First, demands of the group seeking to exercise a right to self-determination within a state that does not contemplate secession from, or partition of, its territory can only be accommodated within a territorial framework of autonomy. Falling short of independence, territorial autonomy means the transfer of control over territory, people and assigned legislative and executive competences in a range of policy areas to the population of the given territorial entity who then elect a government to discharge these functions. The right to self-determination is thus exercised 'internally' by the group claiming entitlement to it at several levels: through participation in the election of a regional and central government and through the relative independence of this regional government in legislating and executing policy in assigned areas of competence.

Second, consociational power-sharing within this autonomous territory is then most likely a result of ethnic demography, i.e., several groups living in the same territory which cannot be partitioned further either because the resident groups do not have their own compact settlements or because the territory as a whole is of particular cultural, historical or other significance to the group seeking self-determination which therefore does not accept having its control limited to only a part of this territory. The need for significant segmental autonomy within such consociational structures is then likely to be very strong if the group seeking self-determination is in a numerical minority or if any of the groups fears gradual assimilation and loss of identity. Consociational power-sharing is thus required to address a (potential) ethnic conflict within the autonomous territory.

Yet, because of the fact that it requires significant compromises (relinquishing partial control over part of its territory by the state in question, withdrawing or postponing claims to independence and accepting the need to share power with other groups on the part of the self-determination movement), regional consociationalism is only attractive in the absence of alternatives. I have already noted the reluctance of the international community to accept changes to international boundaries, which serves as a stumbling block for self-determination movements. However, non-democratic or majoritarian democratic states, including some with questionable past records of conflict management, are equally constrained in their pursuit of eliminating differences by means of genocide or ethnic cleansing, or manage them by means of hegemonic control.

Table 6.1 Internal and external factors facilitating the application of regional consociationalism as mechanisms to settle self-determination conflicts

	Factors encouraging territorial autonomy	*Factors encouraging consociational power-sharing*
Internal	Need to find compromise on demands of conflict parties: self-determination vs. territorial integrity	Ethnic demography in autonomous territory and need to avoid perpetual ethnic conflict there
External	Reluctance of international community to accept boundary changes	Human and minority rights norms and preparedness to enforce them

Integration as a mechanism of conflict regulation is unlikely to be acceptable in many cases to those who would be integrated (let alone assimilated) or to the international community in cases where integration means majoritarian democracy and perpetuation of a given self-determination conflict. In other words, emerging international norms on the treatment of minority populations and an increasing willingness to enforce them (such as in Bosnia and Herzegovina, Kosovo, East Timor, etc.) encourage the application of regional consociationalism as a mechanism to resolve self-determination conflicts. This is clearly facilitated by the fact that international mediation in self-determination conflicts is often pre-disposed towards consociational or regional consociational settlements.

Thus, in summary, regional consociations rarely have their roots in grand designs. They are more likely to be the result of compromises reached between the parties to a self-determination conflict whose options are constrained internally by what is feasible as a compromise between their own and their opponents' preferences, and externally by emerging sets of human and minority rights norms and an increasing willingness to enforce them (see Table 6.1).[7]

Background to case studies

Northern Ireland

As a result of the partition of Ireland in 1920, Northern Ireland is constitutionally a part of the United Kingdom, yet geographically it is located on the island of Ireland. Consisting of six counties, its population is just over 1.5 million. For almost 80 years after partition, a conflict has existed between one section of the population in Northern Ireland that aimed at the restoration of a united Ireland, and another section and the British state seeking to secure the union between Northern Ireland and Great Britain. This conflict about fundamentally different political aspirations has been exacerbated by inequalities between the Unionist and

Nationalist communities, by the wounds inflicted through violence, but also by increasing intra-communal diversity. 'Nationalist' and 'Unionist' are terms that refer very broadly to the political divide in Northern Ireland. While this political divide, to some extent, coincides with the religious divide between Catholic and Protestant congregations, the conflict in Northern Ireland is not ethno-religious, but, ethnonational in its nature.

Violence has marked the conflict in Northern Ireland in particular between the late 1960s and mid-1990s. Over 3,000 people were killed, several times as many injured. Since 1997 the major paramilitary organisations have, by and large, abided by their ceasefires, and the number of killings has significantly decreased. Non-deadly, politically motivated violence, however, remains a significant problem and poses a threat to stability and security in Northern Ireland even now, more than five years after the conclusion of the Good Friday (or Belfast) Agreement.

South Tyrol

South Tyrol – a mountainous, trilingual area in northern Italy where speakers of German are in a two-thirds majority over about thirty per cent Italians and four per cent Ladins – had for centuries been part of the Habsburg Empire before it was annexed to Italy in the peace settlement of St. Germain in 1919. Initial promises for far-reaching autonomy made by the Italian government to the sizable German-speaking community in the area were not kept in full, and the fascist takeover in 1922 saw the beginning of a comprehensive campaign of forced assimilation carried out against the German-speakers of South Tyrol. After the Second World War, South Tyrol remained with Italy, and Austria, the kin-state of the German-speaking community, ceded all territorial claims to the province in exchange for Italian promises of substantive autonomy in the so-called Gruber-De Gasperri Agreement, annexed to the Paris Peace Treaty of 1946.

In contrast to the conflict in Northern Ireland, the dispute in and over South Tyrol is no longer about different conceptions of national belonging, but about control over the territory of South Tyrol. It was, and is, primarily a conflict between German-speakers and the central government in Rome, but remained in nature an ethno-national conflict. In an effort to resolve the conflict, which briefly turned violent in the early 1960s, a special autonomy statute of 1972 (and its revised version of 2001) granted wide-ranging legislative and administrative powers to the province, and the influence of the central government has been reduced in some crucial areas compared to an earlier autonomy statute dating back to 1948. The constitutional status of the province is now very similar to that of a state in a federal country (i.e., its relation with the Italian state is that of a federacy, see below), allowing for the free and protected development of all three ethnic groups.

Brussels-Capital Region

When Belgium gained its independence in 1830, it was very much a country dominated linguistically, culturally, economically and politically by a French-speaking minority. Flemish nationalism was a feature of Belgian politics from the middle of the nineteenth century onwards and managed to gain important concessions, initially in the field of language use, by the end of that century. Demands for federalism and greater autonomy of the language communities increased, first on the Flemish side, and subsequently also among the Francophone population. While Flemish nationalism was primarily offensive, and at times militant, Francophone nationalism developed as a defensive movement after the Second World War. Regardless of their direction and agenda, the two converged from the late 1960s onwards in a process that saw several major constitutional reforms in Belgium in 1970, 1980, 1988 and 1993 which created a federal and consociational regime in the country, as embodied in the 1994 constitution.

In contrast to Northern Ireland and South Tyrol, Brussels is thus a regional consociation within the consociational framework of the Belgian federal state. Not only is Brussels the capital of Belgium and seat of major EU and NATO institutions but it is also the largest mixed area within Belgium and highly symbolic for the two predominant linguistic communities in the country – Dutch-speakers and French-speakers. In addition to the symbolic value of Brussels, its status and governance have been, and continue to be, highly sensitive issues in Belgian politics. Although Flemish-speakers are overall in a 60 per cent majority, they are outnumbered in Brussels, thus giving French-speakers a potential 2:1 majority on the level of regional governments. For a long time, the consequent fear of Flemish-speakers that they would become a dominated majority in an increasingly federalised Belgian state prevented a resolution of the Brussels issue. It was only finally dealt with in the latest set of constitutional reforms in 1988 and 1993, while it had been previously avoided or marginalised as an issue in institutional reform processes in 1970 and 1980.

Institutional structures

Northern Ireland

The 1998 Agreement deals with three main issues: (1) democratic institutions in Northern Ireland; (2) the North-South Ministerial Council; and (3) the British-Irish Council, the British-Irish Inter-Governmental Conference, and Rights, Safeguards and Equality of Opportunity.

Concerning democratic institutions, the Agreement provides for the establishment of a 108-member assembly, to be elected by the single transferable vote system (STV) from existing Westminster constituencies. The

Assembly exercises full legislative and executive authority over all the devolved powers previously held by the six Northern Ireland government departments, namely economic development, education, health and social services, agriculture, environment and finance. Subject to later developments, the assembly could take on responsibility for other matters in accordance with the Agreement. That is, currently so-called reserved matters – criminal law, criminal justice and policing – could subsequently also be devolved into the competence of Northern Ireland's power-sharing institutions. A third category of powers is to remain indefinitely with the British government. These excepted matters are foreign and defence policy, the Crown and monetary policy.

To ensure that all sections of the community can participate in the work of the assembly, and to protect them in their rights and identities, the following safeguards were included: specific procedures for the allocation of committee chairs, ministers and committee membership in proportion to party strength in the assembly; the primacy of the European Convention on Human Rights (ECHR) and any future Bill of Rights for Northern Ireland over any legislation passed by the assembly; arrangements to ensure that key decisions are taken on a cross-community basis (parallel consent and weighted majority voting procedures); and the creation of an Equality Commission. Crucial for the operation of the Assembly is that its members register their identity as Nationalist, Unionist or Other, in order to have a measurement of community support for any vote carried out under either the parallel consent or the weighted majority procedures.

According to the Agreement, a committee for each of the main executive functions of the Northern Ireland administration was established. Chairs and deputy chairs of these committees are allocated proportionally according to the d'Hondt system and avoiding a committee chair from the same party as the relevant minister, while membership in the committees is in proportion to party strength in the assembly. The responsibilities of the committees include scrutiny, policy development, consultation and legislation initiation functions with respect to the departments with which they are associated. Their powers include: considering and advising on departmental budgets and annual plans in the context of overall budget allocation; approving relevant secondary legislation and taking the committee stage of relevant primary legislation; and initiating inquiries and making reports. In addition to these permanent committees, the assembly has the right to appoint special committees as required.

Executive authority on behalf of the assembly rests with the First and Deputy First Minister and up to ten ministers with departmental responsibilities. Following the election of the first minister and deputy first minister on a joint ticket, the posts of ministers are allocated to parties according to the d'Hondt system. An executive committee, comprising all ministers (including the first minister and deputy first minister), handles all issues that cut across the responsibilities of two or more ministers in order to formulate a consistent policy on the respective issue. Ministers have full executive authority in their departments within a policy framework agreed by the executive committee and endorsed by the assembly. Ten departments for the Government of Northern Ireland were agreed among the pro-Agreement parties in December 1998: agriculture and rural development; enterprise, trade and investment (including tourism); health, social care and public safety; finance and personnel; education; employment and learning; the environment; regional development; social development; and culture, arts, and leisure.

Legislation can be initiated by an individual member of the assembly, a committee, or a minister. The assembly can pass primary legislation for Northern Ireland in all areas where it has devolved powers. The passing of legislation is subject to decision by a simple majority of members voting (except for decisions that require cross-community support), to detailed scrutiny and approval in the relevant departmental committee and to coordination with Westminster legislation. Any disputes over legislative competence are to be decided by the courts. In its relations with other institutions, the assembly has to ensure cross-community participation.

A North-South Ministerial Council was agreed upon in order to institutionalise formal relationships between the executive organs of Northern Ireland and the Republic of Ireland. Its responsibilities include consultation, cooperation and the implementation of decisions on issues of mutual concern. All decisions of the council have to be by agreement between the two sides, and their implementation is subject to approval by both legislatures. Six so-called implementation bodies for the North-South Ministerial Council were agreed in December 1998: Waterways Ireland; the Food Safety Promotion Board; the Trade and Business Development Board; the Special EU Programmes Body; the North/South Language Body; and the Foyle, Carlingford and Irish Lights Commission. Selected aspects of transport, agriculture, education, health, environment and tourism were additionally agreed as areas of functional cooperation.

Provisions in the third part of the Agreement are only of peripheral consequence for the structure of the power-sharing institutions within Northern Ireland, although arrangements with regard to rights, safeguards, and equality of opportunity have an impact on their operation. The British-Irish Intergovernmental Conference, also dealt with in Strand 3, establishes a mechanism of cooperation between the two sovereign governments of the UK and the Republic of Ireland that plays a significant role in relation to Northern Ireland, especially during periods in which the power-sharing institutions in Northern Ireland are suspended.

As regards the vertical layering of authority in the case of Northern Ireland, the power-sharing institutions established under the 1998 agreement fit in between the central government in Westminster and the 26 local councils within Northern Ireland (see Figure 6.1), and are, as a layer

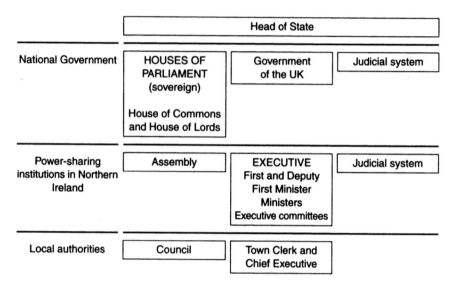

Head of State			
National Government	HOUSES OF PARLIAMENT (sovereign) House of Commons and House of Lords	Government of the UK	Judicial system
Power-sharing institutions in Northern Ireland	Assembly	EXECUTIVE First and Deputy First Minister Ministers Executive committees	Judicial system
Local authorities	Council	Town Clerk and Chief Executive	

Figure 6.1 Vertical layers of public authority in the United Kingom in relation to Northern Ireland.

of public authority, by and large comparable to the institutional structures established in Scotland and Wales since the beginning of devolution in 1997. The national government remains the residual source of all public authority. This includes, contrary to the original agreement of 1998, the power to suspend the power-sharing institutions in Northern Ireland unilaterally. In this respect, Northern Ireland is unique among the cases considered here in that its autonomy can be revoked at any time by the central government. From the point of view of the British government, this is possible because in the Westminster system parliament is the sovereign, and in the absence of a written constitution, no domestic judicial body is able to challenge the government on this point.[8]

An unusual feature of the 1998 agreement is the possibility of a boundary change through a referendum.[9] Should a majority of the people of Northern Ireland express the wish to unite with the Republic of Ireland at some stage in the future, and should a majority in the Republic of Ireland express the same desire, both the British and Irish governments have committed themselves to respect such an expression of the popular will. The British government is to provide for referenda at regular intervals to gauge public opinion on this issue.

The structure of institutions in Northern Ireland mirrors the classical division of powers between legislature, executive and judiciary. The Assembly is directly elected and from it a power-sharing executive is recruited, comprised of a First and Deputy First Minister with coordinating executive functions, Ministers who formulate and execute policy and enact assembly legislation within the remits of their portfolios, and Executive Committees who scrutinise ministerial departments. Legislature and executive are complemented by an extensive judicial system consisting of a High Court, County Courts and Magistrates Courts, an Attorney General, an Advocate General, a Public Prosecution Service, a Chief Inspector of Criminal Justice and a Law Commission. Different from most parliamentary systems of government, however, the legislature cannot, by a simple vote-of-no-confidence, dispose of the executive.

The third layer of public authority relevant in the case of Northern Ireland is that of local authorities. Here, 26 local councils, also referred to as boroughs, have competences in a range of areas including development, tourism, community relations and the environment. Local authorities have a directly elected Council and a Town Clerk and Chief Executive who are responsible for running day-to-day affairs.

Policy coordination is managed through the continued existence of the Northern Ireland Office, as well as through a range of commissions attached to the British-Irish Council, British-Irish Intergovernmental Conference and North-South Ministerial Council. Furthermore, the people of Northern Ireland elect 18 members to the House of Commons (the lower house of the UK Parliament) and a number of politicians from the region have been appointed to the House of Lords as well so that representation of regional interests in the national parliament is guaranteed. There are also a number of UK-wide Joint Ministerial Committees that bring together the relevant politicians from the central and regional governments on general policy issues (heads of government) and on a range of specific issues, such as Europe, health, the knowledge economy and poverty (relevant portfolio ministers). Dispute settlement works primarily through the relevant judicial courts in Northern Ireland and the United Kingdom.

South Tyrol

The autonomy statute, which is the central part of the 1969 Austro-Italian package deal, passed all the parliamentary hurdles in Italy and came into force on 20 January 1972. Its official name – 'Measures in Favour of the Population of South Tyrol' – emphasises that minority protection is only one part within a whole set of measures and regulations, dealing with the distribution of powers between different levels of government and between the two ethnic groups – Germans and Italians. Only 15 articles are specifically and exclusively aimed at the German-speaking population within the province (and thus, by extension, at inter-ethnic relations), while the rest of the articles strengthened provincial autonomy vis-à-vis the region and the central government as a whole and introduced procedures to mediate between all ethnic groups in South Tyrol.

At the heart of the reorganisation of ethnic relations in the province and the region are formalised mechanisms of power-sharing. Going far beyond the original provisions of the 1948 autonomy statute, these mechanisms can be found in relation to three distinct dimensions at both regional and provincial levels: voting procedures in the two assemblies, rotation of high offices between the ethnic groups, and coalition government.

To begin with the latter, the government of South Tyrol has to reflect the ethnic proportions of the provincial assembly. Therefore, a simple majority of votes in the assembly is not sufficient to establish the government unless this majority consists of votes from both Italian and German representatives, i.e., the autonomy statute, in practice, requires a German-Italian coalition government. This 'implicit' coalition requirement is complemented by a more explicit one deriving from the compulsory equitable distribution of the offices of the two vice-presidents of the provincial government between the German and Italian ethnic groups.

Another feature of power-sharing in South Tyrol established by the 1972 autonomy statute is the compulsory rotation of offices in the presidency of the provincial assembly. Elected by the assembly, the presidency consists of one president and one vice-president as well as three deputies, who act as secretaries. In the first half of every five-year legislative period an elected representative of the German-speaking group must be chosen as president, and an Italian as vice-president; in the second half, their roles reverse.

All legislation emanating from the provincial assembly is prepared by legislative commissions. Their members are the president, vice-president and one of the presidency's secretaries, as well as between four and five 'ordinary' members chosen by government and opposition parties in the assembly, thus again reflecting ethnic proportions in the assembly.

At regional level, similar provisions were made to ensure adequate representation of the German and Italian ethnic groups, and thus, by extension, a functioning system of power-sharing. The regional assembly, which is made up of the entire cohort of elected deputies from both provincial assemblies (i.e., South Tyrol and Trentino) operates the same principle of rotating offices between president and vice-president; in addition, it also changes the location of its sessions between Trient/Trento (first half) and Bozen/Bolzano (second half). As for the regional government, the same principles operate that are in force at provincial level.

In order to give each ethnic group additional leverage, and incentives, to make the power-sharing arrangements work, specific voting procedures and other mechanisms for the adoption of provincial laws were established. When any bill is put before parliament that is considered to affect the rights of a particular ethnic group in South Tyrol, a majority of the deputies of this ethnic group may request 'separate voting', i.e., a determination of support for the specific bill among each ethnic group. If this request is denied, or the bill is passed against the vote of two-thirds of representatives of one ethnic group, the group opposing the bill may take the matter to the Italian constitutional court in Rome. Thus, there is no formal veto-power enshrined in the arrangements. While defending democratic decision-making procedures against a blockade of the political process, nevertheless, a mechanism exists that potentially offers legal redress outside the political process. Only in one respect has a more or less formal veto right been established – in relation to the provincial and regional budgets. Here, separate majorities are required from within both the German and Italian ethnic groups. If this is not forthcoming, all chapters of the budget are voted on individually. Those failing to receive the required double majority (parallel consent) are referred to a special commission of the assembly, and if no agreement is reached there either, the administrative court in Bozen/Bolzano makes a final and binding decision.

The focus on the German-Italian dichotomy in respect of power-sharing and in a number of other areas, where the principle of proportional rather than equal representation of all ethnic groups was in force, clearly disadvantaged the Ladin-speaking group. Most of these traditional disadvantages experienced by the Ladins have been formally addressed during the implementation process of the 1972 autonomy statute, and more drastically in its reform in 2001.

The formal settlement of the South Tyrol conflict between Austria and Italy in 1992 according to the procedures set out in the operational calendar did not mean an end to the further development of the autonomy and power-sharing regulations. Led by the South Tyrolese People's Party (the dominant political party among German-speakers), the provincial government sought to improve and extend the regulations of the 1972 statute further in order to increase the province's autonomy and with it to improve the quality of life for all three ethnic groups. From the mid-1990s onwards, the provincial government was granted an extension of its powers in, among others, the sectors of education, employment, transport, finance, privatisation of state-owned properties, energy and European integration.

As part of these and other significant changes, a revised autonomy statute came into effect on 16 February 2001, marking the third autonomy statute for the province since the end of the Second World War. In it, the status and powers of the two provinces Trentino and South Tyrol has been greatly enhanced so that South Tyrol and Trentino no longer constitute subordinate units of the region of Trentino-South Tyrol and have individually more legislative and administrative powers than the region itself. In particular, the following new regulations have increased the degree of autonomy enjoyed by both provinces:

• In contrast to the previous autonomy statute, the revised version of 2001 now explicitly recognises the internationally guaranteed nature of South Tyrol's autonomy. By virtue of its being a constitutional law, the new autonomy statute gives an even firmer guarantee for the inviolability of South Tyrol's autonomous status.

- All legislation in relation to elections is now in the competence of the provinces, allowing them to determine, for example, whether the president of the provincial government should be elected directly or not. Respective legislation no longer requires the approval of the government commissioner.
- Amendments to the autonomy statute can in future also be developed by the two provinces, without involvement of the region.
- If the Italian parliament intends to change or amend the current statute, representatives of the province have now to be consulted, instead of, as was previously the case, those of the region.
- Members of the provincial government can be appointed with a two-thirds majority in the provincial assembly without having to be its members.
- Representation of the Ladins in the presidency of the regional and provincial assemblies and in the regional government is now part of the power-sharing arrangement, and members of the Ladin ethnic group can be co-opted into the South Tyrol provincial government.
- In addition, for the first time ever, the term 'South Tyrol' has been officially incorporated in its German version in the Italian constitution as part of the Constitutional Law on Federalism, which was adopted in March 2001.

From the perspective of vertical layering of authority, the case of South Tyrol represents a four-layered structure: the government in Rome, the Region of Trentino-South Tyrol, the Province of Bozen/Bolzano-South Tyrol and the local communities within the province (see Figure 6.2). This is structurally broadly similar to the rest of Italy, with the exception that the region and its two provinces have traditionally, since 1948, had a so-called special autonomy statute (a feature shared with four other ethnically or geographically distinct regions of Italy) that gave them a set of powers distinct from that of other regions.

The central government is represented in the province by a government commissioner whose job it is to coordinate central government functions (primarily taxation, military and police matters and judicial affairs) within the province, to monitor the exercise of devolved powers by the provincial government, to oversee local government and to appoint commissioners to take over local governments who have been suspended from discharging their duties on grounds of public order and security.

The region, which has been much diminished in status by the 2001 reform of the autonomy statute, is now no longer a body superior to the provinces, but rather the two provinces are considered constituent entities

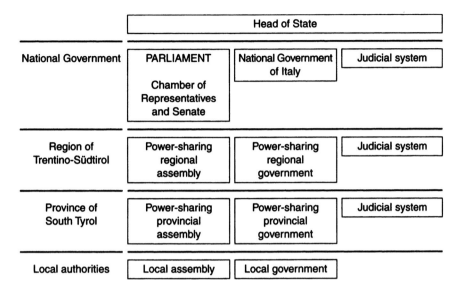

Figure 6.2 Vertical layers of public authority in Italy in relation to South Tyrol.

of the region with their own distinct powers. While the 1948 and 1972 autonomy statutes were essentially meant to devolve powers to the region, from where they were then further devolved to the provinces, the provinces now have original authority in an increased number of areas. Nevertheless, the regional layer of authority remains significant and constitutes its own level of government, comprising a power-sharing executive, the presidency of the executive and a legislative assembly (made up of the representatives of the two provincial diets). Regional competences extend to regional budgetary and financial matters, policy coordination between the provinces, relations with the European Union, language policy, regional administration and social welfare.

At the provincial level, the power-sharing government consists of a directly elected legislature and an executive. The government has primary and secondary competences, the former giving it complete legislative and executive freedom, subject only to the Italian constitution and any international obligations Italy has entered into, while the latter allow the province to legislate and regulate in accordance with existing Italian laws. In all areas of primary competence, the province also has the right to implement relevant EU legislation directly and to conduct its own external relations.

Local governments exercise powers according to the principle of subsidiarity. Even though they do not have original authority, there is a constitutional guarantee of administrative autonomy. Their responsibilities cover all matters of local interest, from social services to planning and economic and cultural development. Local communities also have a limited tax-raising ability in order to ensure that they can raise sufficient funds in addition to grants from the provincial government to discharge all their duties adequately. With the 2001 constitutional reform, the status of local communities has been raised: they are now, alongside the regions, provinces and metropolitan cities, constituent elements of the Italian state and their administrative autonomy has been enshrined in the constitution.

All of the 117 local communities in the province have joined up in so-called *Bezirksgemeinschaften* (district associations). Two provincial laws from 1991 recognised these interest groups as corporate bodies under public law. Member communities have used the opportunity since 1993 to delegate certain of their responsibilities to district associations, especially in the area of social services provision. In addition, district associations have been charged by the provincial government with responsibilities of their own, especially in the area of environmental protection and social, economic and cultural development of the under-developed mountain regions that they represent.

Policy coordination and conflict avoidance and management are ensured relatively effectively through a standing commission at the Office of the Italian Prime Minister, and two standing commissions on regional and provincial affairs that need to be consulted prior to any decision affecting provincial or regional matters. In addition, the heads of the regional and provincial governments have the right to participate in sessions of the Italian government whenever it debates matters relevant to the province or region. There is also an arbitration commission for budgetary disputes at provincial level. People in both region and province elect deputies to the Italian parliament and senate and are thus involved in the national political process as representatives of their electorates as well. Additional institutions of dispute resolution are the administrative courts in Bozen/Bolzano and Rome can adjudicate in disputes between the provincial, regional and national governments.

Brussels-Capital Region[10]

The institutional structure of the Belgian federal state is extremely complex. This is the result of a long process of institutional reforms which sought to accommodate the various social, political, cultural, economic and territorial claims of three linguistic communities living on the territory of Belgium. This institutional complexity is reflected in the structure of the Brussels-Capital Region, the only one of the three regions in Belgium which is bilingual (Flemish and French).

Geographically, Brussels is an enclave of approximately ten square miles within the Flemish region, while, demographically, it is an area of just under one million people, who are in the majority French-speaking, with a large number of foreigners working for one of the many European or international governmental and non-governmental organisations present in the city. The key compromise reached over the course of several constitutional reforms from 1970 onwards turned Belgium into a federal state and made Brussels a constituent component (one of three regions) within it.

As throughout the Belgian polity, the institutions of Brussels can be divided into regional and community institutions. The regional institutions are the council and the government of the Brussels-Capital Region. In addition, there are three community institutions: the Joint, the French and the Flemish Community Commissions. The regional council consists of 75 members, directly elected through separate electoral rolls within each community and according to the linguistic proportions among the city's population (currently 64 French-speaking and 11 Dutch-speaking members). The main function of the council is to legislate and to approve budgets. Seven permanent legislative commissions within the Council, covering different policy areas, exist to scrutinise legislative proposals before they are discussed in the council and a vote is taken. In addition to its legislative function, the council also elects the government and the three regional secretaries of state. The council is also charged to hold the elected government to account and has the right to dismiss it by a constructive vote of no confidence. The power-sharing features of the council are that both linguistic groups, i.e., all members elected on the French and Flemish lists respectively, must be represented in the presidency of the council (president and vice-president), and that each committee must have at least one member from the Flemish linguistic group within the Council. There are no specific voting or veto procedures, but the mandatory presence of at least one member of the minority linguistic community in each of the legislative commissions ensures the functioning of the so-called 'alarm bell procedure' according to Article 54 of the Belgian constitution.[11]

The regional government has executive authority in all areas in which the council has legislative competence, namely urban and regional planning, housing, public infrastructure and utilities, public transport, economic policy and external trade, labour market policy, environment, control of local authorities, scientific research, and international relations in these policy areas. In addition, the government has acquired the authority to execute policy in areas formerly in the competence of the Brussels district, namely fire fighting, medical aid, waste management and taxis.

There are five ministers in the regional government, two from each linguistic group and a President. Only the latter's appointment must be ratified by the monarch. The election process of the government can occur according to two procedures. If there is agreement between the linguistic groups on the composition of the regional government, a single list is presented, signed by a majority of members of each linguistic group. If such a joint list cannot be produced, the council elects the president with a simple majority, and each linguistic group elects its own two ministers. In addition to the five government ministers, there are three regional secretaries of state, one of which must be from the Flemish-speaking group. They are either elected by simple majority in the council following a consensual proposal by the regional government, or, in the absence of such a proposal, the council only determines the distribution of seats among the linguistic groups, and the latter then elect their secretaries of state separately.

Power-sharing procedures are also apparent in the distribution of competences among members of the regional government and in the way in which ministers can be dismissed from office. As for the assignment of portfolios, unless there is consensus among the five government members, the president has the first choice, the ministers representing the numerically stronger linguistic group in the council have the second and fourth choice, and those representing the numerically weaker group have the third and fifth choice of portfolio. The government as a whole can only be dismissed by a constructive vote of no confidence with parallel majorities in both linguistic groups, individual ministers can only be dismissed with the consent of a majority of their own linguistic group, and for the president a simple majority in the council as a whole is required.

Apart from mandatory executive power-sharing, proportionality and minority veto, consociational settlements are also characterised by segmental autonomy for the communities participating in them. In Brussels, this is realised through the presence of separate French and Flemish community commissions. They have competences in a wide range of areas extending far beyond the traditional areas of culture, language and education delegated to community institutions, as for example in South Tyrol and, to a lesser extent, in Northern Ireland. However, because of the overall structure of the Belgian polity, the two commissions do not have original authority of their own, but are dependent in their executive and legislative functions on the degree to which the French and Flemish community (i.e., two of the three constituent communities of the Belgian federal state) delegate and transfer competences to the French and Flemish community commissions in Brussels. Thus far, only the French Community Council (i.e., the parliament of the French community) has transferred significant competences to the French Community Commission in Brussels, enabling the latter to legislate and execute policy in the areas of private facilities for physical education, sports and life in the outdoors, tourism, social advancement, job retraining and continuing professional education, school transportation and health and advisory services. In addition, the French community commission also has the authority, in conjunction with the French community, to establish, finance and control certain institutions in the area of primary and secondary education.

The Flemish and French Community Commissions are each made up of a legislative assembly (i.e., the respective members of the Flemish-speaking and French-speaking linguistic groups in the regional council) and an executive college (the respective Flemish-speaking and French-speaking ministers and state secretaries of the regional government). Independent of the degree of powers transferred to the commissions, they have administrative competences in the areas where powers are assigned to the communities at the federal level, namely culture, education, language use and healthcare and a range of social services (so-called person-related matters).

The Joint Community Commission has a coordinating role between the two communities and that part of the public sector in Brussels which is not part of either of the community sectors. The Joint Community Commission has the same structure as the French and Flemish community commissions, consisting of a legislative assembly (the so-called United Assembly) and an executive college. The membership of the assembly is identical with that of the regional council. Its legislative powers extend to those institutions that do not clearly belong to either one of the two linguistic communities and to personal matters related to healthcare and certain social services. Each decision made by the United Assembly requires parallel consent in both linguistic groups. The legislative process is identical to that in the regional council. However, given the distinct areas of competence which the United Assembly enjoys, it has only three committees (health, social affairs and a united committee on health and social affairs). The executive college of the Joint Community Commission is made up of the four ordinary ministers of the regional government, who have full voting powers, the president of the regional government, who has a consulting vote, and two members each from the French and Flemish community government, who are inhabitants of Brussels and also have a consulting vote only.

A final, but nevertheless important dimension of power-sharing in Brussels is related to the influence that the federal government has retained over laws passed by the regional council or policies implemented by the regional government in the areas of urban development, territorial organisation, public transport and public infrastructure, i.e., in areas relevant to the role of Brussels as the capital city of Belgium and host to a range of international organisations. The federal Council of Ministers may suspend any council law or government regulation within 60 days after its publication. There is then a compulsory consultation procedure in the Committee of Cooperation, a body specifically created for this purpose. If no resolution is agreed, the Council of Ministers may then ask the federal Chamber of Representatives to permanently cancel the relevant law or regulation, which is dependent on parallel consent from both the French and Flemish community groups in the Chamber of Representatives. In addition, if the Council of Ministers is of the opinion that the regional council or government do not fulfil their obligations with respect to the relevant policy areas mentioned above, it can propose measures that it deems suitable to address this situation. Again, a compulsory consultation procedure follows, and failing agreement at the end of it, the Council of Ministers may obtain the relevant power from the Chamber of Representatives to implement itself the policies it deems necessary (again, subject to parallel consent). This not only limits the autonomy of the Brussels-Capital Region, but it also creates an asymmetry between Brussels as a region and the two other regions of Belgium, Flanders and the Walloon region.

In summary, the nature of power-sharing at the level of the regional legislature and executive in Brussels is that of a structurally complete and formalised consociation: cross-community executive power-sharing is mandatory, proportionality in the council and the government is guaranteed, segmental autonomy is far-reaching and provisions for minority veto exist, albeit only in a very limited way and on selected decisions in the regional council (principally the appointment and dismissal of government ministers representing the minority). In addition, the so-called 'alarm bell procedure' serves as a mechanism that can either start a process the result of which is the accommodation of concerns of any of the linguistic communities or that at least delays the implementation of a particular law. The parallel consent requirement for all decisions taken by the legislative assembly of the Joint Community Commission, gives the Flemish minority a further guarantee to exercise veto powers over all matters in the competence of this institution.

The complexity of the consociational structures in Brussels is easily matched by that of the institutions of the Belgian state as a whole. Consequently, power-sharing in Belgium is not only a concept that applies horizontally at different layers of authority (principally the federal and Brussels regional levels), but also vertically by means of a clear division of competences between different layers of authority and different constituent elements of the Belgian federal state. The principal vertical layers of authority are the federal level, the regional level and the community, the provinces and the level of local governments. Leaving aside the largely ceremonial role of the monarch, Belgium thus has a four-layered structure of public authority (see Figure 6.3). The nature of the constitutional compromises leading up to this current institutional framework being one of compromise between two ethnolinguistic groups, the division of powers between these layers is clearly regulated and laid down in the constitution as well as a variety of laws passed with parallel consent in the federal parliament.

Since the 1993 state reform, the main constituent elements of the Belgian state are the three regions (Flanders, Walloon region and Brussels) and the three communities (Flemish, French and German). Regions are geographically defined; communities are defined on the basis of cultural and linguistic markers. Belgium thus incorporates a complex system of territorial and non-territorial autonomies. The distribution of competences reflects the different 'boundaries' of each of these con-

			Head of State		

Federal government

FEDERAL CHAMBERS	Federal Government of Belgium	Judicial system
Chamber of Representatives and Senate		

Regions and communities

JOINT INSTITUTIONS OF THE FLEMISH REGION AND FLEMISH COMMUNITY	WALLOON REGION	BRUSSELS REGION	FRENCH COMMUNITY	GERMAN-SPEAKING COMMUNITY
Flemish Council and Flemish Community Government	Council and government	Power-sharing regional council and government Council and government of the French Community Commission, the Flemish Community Commission, and the power-sharing Joint Community Commission	Council and government	Council and government

Provinces

Provincial council and college	Provincial council and college

Local authorities

Local council and college	Local council and college	Local council and college	Local council and college

Figure 6.3 Vertical layers of public authority in Belgium in relation to Brussels.

stituent components. To begin with, however, the federal level has exclusive legislative and executive competence in the following areas: foreign relations (except where this competence has been devolved in specific areas to the regions), defence, policing, justice, welfare, public health, debt and public services administration. In addition, the federal government also has a variety of reserved competences in those policy areas where powers have been mostly devolved to regions (e.g., environment, utility management, public infrastructure) and communities (education, culture, person-related matters). It also has concurrent competences in the fields of scientific research and export promotion.

Communities, as they are defined in personal terms, have their executive and legislative competences in the fields of education, cultural and language policy and the whole area of personal matters, which include primarily healthcare and other social services. Regional competences include the policy areas of urban and rural planning, environment, economics, agriculture and industry, energy, labour market, public transport and infrastructure, as well as foreign affairs in these areas.

All communities and regions have their own legislature and executive, in the case of the Flemish community/Flanders, regional and community institutions have been merged into one. Thus, there is one Flemish council and government, exercising both communal and regional powers at once. The French community and Walloon region keep separate institutions.

There are ten provinces in Belgium, five in each region, except in Brussels which only has nineteen local government units as further administrative division. Provinces have no original authority of their own and remain under the supervision of their regional council and the federal government, the latter of which is represented by a provincial governor, appointed by the King. Competences of the provinces are minimal and relate primarily to financial management of public infrastructure.

There are a total of 579 local government units in Belgium. As at other layers of authority, power is divided between a council and an executive. Although the self-government of local communities is constitutionally guaranteed, few real powers have remained with them within the Belgian system, only planning, schools administration, local amenities and roads and social services administration.

Unsurprisingly, such a complex system of institutional structures requires significant policy coordination and mechanisms to avoid and manage conflicts. This is formally regulated within the constitution (Chapter V) and a range of specific laws. The principal institutions are the Standing Language Commission, the State Council and the Court of Arbitration. In addition, there are a number of consultative bodies between the federal government and the regional and community institutions, as well as between regions and communities. These take the nature of permanent bodies as well as ad hoc ones. Furthermore, six members of the Flemish-speaking group of the Brussels regional council are also members of the parliament of the Flemish community, and nineteen members of the French-speaking group are members of the council of the French community. As regards the representation of Brussels within the executive bodies of each of the relevant two communities, at least one member of each of the two community executives must be from the region of Brussels. In the case of the French community, this is the president of the Brussels regional council, in the case of the Flemish community, the Brussels member of the executive is not a minister in the Brussels regional council, but is normally responsible, in the Flemish community council, for coordinating the latter's policy towards Brussels and supervising the Flemish Community Commission in the region of Brussels.

Institutional designs in comparison

There are five dimensions to the following comparative analysis. First, the institutional structures themselves can be analysed according to a number of dimensions, primarily the number of vertical layers of authority and the status that the regional consociation has within them, and the structural and functional symmetry and asymmetry of these institutions in relation to the polity as a whole. Second, I will compare how horizontal and vertical forms of power-sharing are combined within each individual institutional structure. This is closely related to the third and fourth areas of comparison, namely the distribution of powers among and policy coordination between different centres of authority. A final structural aspect of the comparative examination of the regional consociations of Northern Ireland, South Tyrol and Brussels is the mechanisms put in place that guarantee the preservation of the agreed structures. This five-dimensional comparison will serve as a tool to establish some key features that are common to the three cases under review here and can serve as a guide for future research.

Types of institutional structures. The first element to consider in this comparative analysis of the institutional structures of regional consociations is the vertical layering of authority, i.e., how and where regional consociations fit into a national polity (see Table 6.2).[12]

Northern Ireland has by far the simplest structure of institutions from the perspective of different vertical layers: a central, regional and local level of government. In the case of South Tyrol, matters are only slightly

Table 6.2 Variation in the vertical layering of authority

Three-layered structures	*Multi-layered structures*
Northern Ireland[13]	Brussels South Tyrol

more complex in that there is an additional provincial level of authority, at which, in the case of South Tyrol, most of the relevant powers are now concentrated. This is a particular and unique phenomenon within the Italian institutional system and is due to a decision made after the Second World War which joined the provinces of South Tyrol (majority German) and Trentino (majority Italian) into one region of Trentino-Alto Adige (majority Italian). Only with the second autonomy statute in 1972, and even more so with the revised third autonomy statute of 2001, did the provinces evolve into sources of real and original authority. South Tyrol, as a layer of authority in a four-tier structure, has thus gained a great deal of substantive autonomy which is also reflected in the guarantees protecting its status and the way in which powers are distributed between the different layers (see below).

The Belgian system of layering public authority is clearly the most complex. However, its complexity arises less from the fact that there are multiple vertical structures, as from the parallelism of different territorial and non-territorial sources of authority. In purely vertical and territorial (i.e., regional) terms, Brussels has one layer of authority above itself (the central government) and one below (local government). It is only because of the way in which the Belgian polity as a whole is structured that things become more complicated: Brussels is not an equal among the three regions (there is potentially a higher degree of influence from the central government on decisions of the regional parliament and executive), and the powers that the two linguistic communities living in the city can claim is highly asymmetric because the Flemish community government, in contrast to the French one, has so far resisted any real transfer of powers to the Flemish linguistic group in the Brussels region. This system has evolved over subsequent constitutional reforms since the 1970s, and it demonstrates the flexibility that institutional structures potentially possess in accommodating competing communal conceptions of autonomy and authority.

The example of Brussels and Belgium in particular suggests another way of looking at structural types of institutions, namely examining the degree to which the three cases represent institutions that are structurally and/or functionally symmetric or asymmetric (see Tables 6.3–6.5).[14]

South Tyrol is a case of structural symmetry because, from a structural point of view, it does not constitute a constitutional anomaly in the Italian state, even though its status is internationally guaranteed.[15] There are 18 other regions, subdivided into provinces and local governments. The symmetry of institutional structures in the case of Brussels is only unambiguous with respect to territorial arrangements – Brussels is a region as are Flanders and the Walloon region. From a non-territorial perspective, i.e., at the community level, the official bilingual nature of the Brussels region sets it apart from the (monolingual) nature of the two other regions, which only have certain areas in which special provisions have been made

Table 6.3 Structural symmetry and asymmetry of institutions

Structural symmetry	Structural asymmetry
Brussels South Tyrol	Northern Ireland

Table 6.4 Functional symmetry and asymmetry of institutions

Functional symmetry	Functional asymmetry
	Brussels Northern Ireland South Tyrol

Table 6.5 Structural and functional symmetry and asymmetry of institutions compared

	Structures		Functions	
	Symmetric	*Asymmetric*	*Symmetric*	*Asymmetric*
Brussels		X		X
Northern Ireland		X		X
South Tyrol	X			X

for intra-regional linguistic minorities (primarily French-speakers in Flanders around Brussels, and German-speakers in the eastern parts of the Walloon region). The structural asymmetry of the case of Northern Ireland is a result of the devolution process that the British state has embarked on since 1997. Institutional structures have been established to accommodate the devolution of powers in three regions – Scotland, Wales and Northern Ireland – while England has remained under the direct control of the Westminster government with no intermediate layer of public authority between the UK government and local communities comparable to that of the three other regions.

From the perspective of functional symmetry, all three cases are in fact part of polities in which powers and functions between different layers of authority are unequally distributed. South Tyrol is a case of above-average powers, accommodating the special situation of the province, historically and within the region to which it belongs, and resolving a very specific self-determination conflict. South Tyrol, thus, is a case of asymmetry from two perspectives: the region to which it belongs has a special autonomy statute which distinguishes it from other regions in Italy, and within the region, South Tyrol enjoys a variety of regulations that give it extra powers in the areas of language use and bilingualism, education, culture and ethnic proportionality in the public sector. Northern Ireland, on the other hand, is, for the time being at least, more limited in its powers than Scotland, but better off than England and Wales. Brussels as a region is subjected to potentially more interference on the part of the central government, and the two linguistic groups living in the region are entirely dependent upon the transfer of powers from the Flemish and French community (of which they are a part given the fact that non-territorial communities are constituent parts of the Belgian state). The asymmetry thereby created results in the French linguistic group in Brussels having substantially more autonomy than its Flemish counterpart. In the case of Northern Ireland, devolution in the United Kingdom has addressed the specific conditions in each of the regions that enjoy devolved authority in such a way that the list of devolved and non-devolved matters varies from one settlement to another.

Comparing structural *and* functional symmetry across the three cases under review here, the only commonality between Brussels, Northern Ireland and South Tyrol is that the polities of which they are part have distributed powers and functions asymmetrically among different entities at the same vertical layer of authority (see Table 6.5). This is independent of the symmetry institutional structures, where we find asymmetric as well as symmetric structures. The possible combinations of asymmetric or symmetric institutional structures with asymmetric allocations of functions and powers adds to the flexibility that constitutional designers have, in particular if one bears in mind the territorial and non-territorial elements of the institutional structures and functions in the case of Brussels.

The combination of vertical and horizontal power-sharing. One element of the complexity of power-sharing as a mechanism to resolve self-determination conflicts results from the fact that constitutional engineers have developed innovative ways to combine traditional structures of horizontal and vertical power-sharing (see Table 6.6). While all cases examined in this chapter are examples of state structures characterised by multiple vertical layers of authority, formal horizontal structures of power-sharing need only, by definition, exist at the regional level (hence the term 'regional consociation').

The fact that in the case of Brussels we find a combination of power-sharing at national and regional level has its reasons in the fact that the self-determination conflict to be addressed was a much wider one,

Table 6.6 Combinations of horizontal and vertical power-sharing

Horizontal power-sharing at regional level only	*Horizontal power-sharing at regional level and above*
Northern Ireland	Brussels South Tyrol

reaching primarily beyond the region of Brussels. In fact, the national compromise in Belgium was established before a compromise over Brussels was found. Furthermore, the demographic distribution of linguistic groups at the national level in Belgium is more balanced (roughly 60:40), whereas in the other two cases, the relevant groups constitute only a tiny part of their host-states' total population. However, the creation of the region of Trentino-Alto Adige in Italy after the Second World War created an analogous situation at regional level, requiring power-sharing institutions to be created there prior to the subsequent provisions in South Tyrol itself. Thus, on the basis of the cases examined here, demography and timing/sequence seem to play the most important part in the decision of whether further power-sharing structures are established beyond the immediate conflict area.[16] Regardless of the factors that lead to the implementation of horizontal power-sharing at different vertical levels of authority, the very fact that such combinations exist between the same conflict parties is an important finding that should caution against assumptions that power-sharing at one level is necessarily sufficient to resolve a particular self-determination conflict. Specific demographic and other factors may require further power-sharing structures to be established, utilising the vertical layering of authority and the territorial division of a given polity it brings with it (region/province in the case of South Tyrol, centre/region in the case of Brussels) as the relevant framework in which they can be implemented.

Distribution of powers. One of the key questions to ask of any vertically layered system of authority is where powers rest, i.e., how different competencies are allocated to different layers of authority and whether they are their exclusive domain or have to be shared between different layers of authority. As with other dimensions in this analysis, there is a certain degree of context-dependent variation across the three cases of regional consociations under examination here. Variation exists primarily with regard to the system according to which powers are allocated and the degree of its flexibility concerning new fields of policy-making not relevant or not included at the time a specific agreement was concluded. The principal mechanism to handle the distribution of powers is the drawing up of lists that enumerate precisely which powers are allocated to which levels of authority and/or which are to be shared between different such levels. These lists can be very specific for each layer of authority or they can be specific for one or more layers and 'open-ended' for other(s). The key difference in the latter case is which layer of authority has an 'open-ended' list, i.e., which layer holds original authority for any partly devolved power or any other policy area not explicitly allocated elsewhere (see Table 6.7).

An unambiguous distribution of powers suggests that the most important issues of the underlying self-determination conflict have either been resolved or postponed (e.g., future referendum on independence) and

Table 6.7 Power allocation in vertically layered systems of public authority

Specific lists	Combination of specific and 'open-ended' lists	
	Open-ended list at centre	Specific list at centre
Northern Ireland	Brussels South Tyrol	

that the potential for conflict re-eruption should be minimal and limited to disputes over emerging new policy areas not covered by the provisions of the original agreement between the conflict parties (provided that the institutions established discharge their functions properly). Where such an unambiguous allocation of powers is missing, in the sense that one layer of authority automatically retains all powers not explicitly allocated elsewhere (and thus implicitly also the competence over all emerging new policy areas in the future), renewed conflict over the distribution of power between different layers of authority is more likely, even though there is no automatism in this. In cases where the central authority retains all not expressly devolved powers, autonomous areas may over time seek renegotiation of past agreements or allocation of additional powers; in the reverse case, central authorities may get continuously weakened, potentially leading to the break-up of the central state.[17] While this is not obviously on the agenda in the near future for any of the three cases under review here, it remains an issue worthy of consideration in the construction of states within complex power-sharing institutional frameworks.

Devolution in Northern Ireland has led to a set of three different lists of powers: devolved, reserved and excepted matters (see above). Subject to the power-sharing institutions functioning (i.e., not being suspended), Northern Ireland has full legislative and executive competence over all devolved matters and could potentially gain the same for all matters on the reserved list. Exercise of these powers is only bound by UK constitutional practice and the country's international obligations, including the European Convention on Human Rights. The drawing-up of these lists has created a situation of mutual exclusiveness of the powers allocated to Northern Ireland and those retained by the UK central government. The same exclusiveness applies to the situation in Brussels and South Tyrol. However, there is one crucial difference: the central governments of Belgium and Italy retained all powers not explicitly devolved to the regional consociations. This means that none of the three cases sees a regional consociation with an open-ended list of powers, i.e., the power to legislate and execute policy in all areas that are not specifically reserved for the central government.[18] One straightforward explanation for this is the fact that all three cases represent instances of centrifugal devolution of powers: the central government is the original source of all authority and has devolved a certain range of powers to lower layers of government.[19]

Types of coordination. Coordination of law and policy-making and implementation is an important issue in the operation of any multi-layered system of government. In the context of self-determination conflicts and power-sharing institutions it assumes additional significance as coordination failures do not only have an impact on the effectiveness of government but also repercussions on the perception of a particular institutional structure designed to resolve a self-determination conflict. The three cases studied in this analysis suggest that, although there is a wide spectrum of individual coordination mechanisms, these can nevertheless be grouped into four distinct categories. Only three of these are relevant for the cases under review: cooptation, joint committees and implementation bodies, and judicial review and arbitration processes (see Table 6.8). The fourth one – direct intervention by the international community – is not applicable in the context of this chapter, but can, for example, be found in the case of Bosnia and Herzegovina.[20]

Table 6.8 indicates that there is a great degree of similarity between the three cases: the main mechanisms for policy coordination are joint committees and implementation bodies and any potential disputes over competences and specific decisions are handled within the judicial system or by interim committees. There is only one exception to this: the parallelism of territorial and non-territorial structures of power-sharing in Belgium made it expedient to use cooptation as an additional measure for policy coordination, tying the two linguistic groups in Brussels more closely into the process of community politics in Belgium.

Entrenchment of institutional structures in international and constitutional law and specific legislation. Guarantees of institutional structures of horizontal and vertical power-sharing are essential to prevent the arbitrary abrogation of devolved powers and thus to ensure conflict parties of the relative permanence of the institutions they agreed upon. Guarantees are particularly important for the relatively weaker party in a self-determination dispute, i.e., a specific minority, to protect it from a state possibly intent on reneging on earlier concessions. However, such guarantees are also valuable for states in that they commit all parties to an agreed structure

Table 6.8 Coordination mechanisms between different layers of public authority in complex power-sharing systems

Cooptation	Joint committees and implementation bodies	Judicial review and arbitration
Brussels	Brussels	Brussels
	Northern Ireland	Northern Ireland
	South Tyrol	South Tyrol

and, in most cases, imply that there can be no unilateral change of recognised international boundaries.

In principle, guarantees can be either international or domestic, in the latter case they can be part of a country's constitution or other legislation (see Table 6.9). Given the complexity of many of today's self-determination conflicts, guarantees often exist on more than one level. In addition, international guarantees can take the form of hard guarantees (international treaties) or of soft guarantees.[21]

The importance of guarantees is clearly recognised in all three settlements that established regional consociations. Thus, we find a variety of domestic guarantees, and in the cases of Northern Ireland and South Tyrol also hard international guarantees. With respect to the latter, the situation in Northern Ireland is such that the hard international guarantee of the 1998 agreement exists in the form of a British-Irish treaty. The crucial difference thus is that for any violation of the treaty (as has arguably occurred on several occasions with the unilateral suspension of the power-sharing institutions by the UK government) to be addressed one of the signatory parties needs to bring a case before a relevant international legal institution (e.g., the International Court of Justice in The Hague). If this does not happen, the protection theoretically afforded by the link between the agreement and an international, bilateral treaty remains an empty shell. In South Tyrol, on the other hand, the internationally guaranteed status of South Tyrol's autonomy is officially recognised.[23]

At the level of domestic guarantees, constitutional guarantees are more entrenched than those which have their source in normal legislation. In practice, the latter have so far proven weakest in Northern Ireland, where, in the absence of a written constitution, another law on the statute books gives the UK government the power to suspend the power-sharing institutions at any time. In Belgium and South Tyrol, on the other hand, interlocked provisions in the countries' constitutions and legislation provide a very strong set of guarantees. In addition, the specific situation of Belgium with power-sharing at national level ensures the adequate representation of both linguistic groups and their interests in the national law-making process.

Table 6.9 International, constitutional and legal guarantees of power-sharing institutions

International guarantees	Domestic guarantees	
	Constitutional guarantees	Guarantees in specific laws
Northern Ireland	Brussels	Brussels
South Tyrol	South Tyrol	Northern Ireland
	Northern Ireland[22]	South Tyrol

Conclusion: complex autonomy designs as part of the conflict resolution tool box

In order to determine the role that complex autonomy regimes such as those analysed here, combining regional territorial autonomy and consociational power-sharing, can potentially play in the future if they are to be applied more widely, it is necessary, first of all, to establish the common features of such regional consociations so as to arrive at an institutional 'core' that appears to be necessary for their functioning. Beyond that, much will be left to the skills and imagination of constitutional designers and their ability to adapt these core features to a particular conflict situation.

As mentioned in the introduction, Lijphart, in his studies on sovereign consociations, identified four structural features all of his case studies had in common – mandatory executive power-sharing between parties from different segments of society, segmental autonomy, proportionality and minority veto. These were also present in all the regional consociations I studied (see Table 6.9). However, the specific study of regional consociations above, although it is only based on three west European cases, suggests two further features. First, Schneckener's arbitration mechanism, while not necessarily an element of sovereign consociations, is clearly present in regional consociations. In addition to these five characteristics, the institutional structures in which regional consociations are embedded also comprise extensive mechanisms for policy coordination (see Table 6.10).

Admittedly, these are not institutions within the framework of the regional consociations themselves. However, from the perspective of regional consociationalism as a recent trend in the resolution of self-determination conflicts, their presence is significant for several reasons. First, policy coordination between different vertical layers of authority (i.e., between regional and central government) can possibly develop into an additional form of power-sharing, independent of, but not unrelated to, the regional consociation that triggered the establishment of these mechanisms in the first place. In this case, policy coordination/power-sharing mechanisms between region and centre also acquire the additional function of providing a further safeguard for the autonomy of regional consociational institutions and the interests of the communities that they bring together. Second, from a more practical point of view, establishing coordination mechanisms is important from the perspective of institutional design and thus has potential implications for the negotiation of a particular settlement. Mediators and negotiators need to be aware of the need for such coordination mechanisms, and that they can potentially amount to additional power-sharing structures. Third, and this remains a hypothesis at this stage, coordination mechanisms, their structure and functioning are likely to play a significant part among conditions

Table 6.10 The features that sovereign and regional consociations share

	Brussels	Northern Ireland	South Tyrol
Mandatory executive power-sharing	Regional Executive	Executive	Landtag
Proportionality	Regional Council and Regional Executive	Assembly and Executive, Offices of First and Deputy First Minister	Landtag, Landesregierung, President and Vice-President/s of the Landtag
Segmental autonomy	Education, culture, and all person-related matters	Primarily education	Primarily education and culture
Minority veto	Executive appointments and dismissals, otherwise only a delaying mechanism	Voting mechanisms (qualified majority and parallel consent) in assembly for appointment of First and Deputy First Minister and if requested by certain number of assembly members	Provincial budget

Table 6.11 The features that distinguish regional from sovereign consociations

	Brussels	Northern Ireland	South Tyrol
Arbitration	Judicial institutions created for this specific purpose	Institutions within the 'regular' framework of the country's judiciary	Institutions within the 'regular' framework of the country's judiciary
Coordination	Standing Language Commission; State Council; various consultative bodies involving region, communities and federal government; cooptation of members of regional council into community councils; mandatory representation of residents of Brussels in community executives	Northern Ireland Office; commissions attached to the British-Irish Council, British-Irish Intergovernmental Conference and North-South Ministerial Council; Joint Ministerial Committees; representation in House of Commons and House of Lords	Provincial governor; three standing commissions; right of head of the regional and provincial governments to participate in sessions of the Italian government; representation in Italian parliament and senate

that account for the success or failure of regional consociations. A well-functioning process of policy coordination can contribute to minimising the potential for conflict between regional and central institutions. This, however, is not unique to polities in which regional consociations exist, but is a common feature of all institutional structures in which authority is vertically layered. Yet, in the context of regional consociations established to resolve a particular self-determination conflict, it acquires extra significance.

A second point to be made about the structural features of regional consociations pertains to their place within the national institutional framework. According to Elazar, (n.d.: 9–10) nine different forms of state with federalist components can be distinguished: confederation, federation, federacy, associated state, consociation, union, league, joint functional authority and condominium. Of these, only two are relevant for the discussion here: federation and federacy (see Table 6.12). For only one of them the decision is straightforward: Belgium is defined as a federal state in its 1994 constitution, i.e., a 'polity compounded of strong constituent entities and a strong general government each possessing powers delegated to it by the people and empowered to deal directly with the citizenry in the exercise of those powers' (Elazar n.d.: 10). As Elazar (ibid.) also mentions consociation as a form of state, Belgium might be classified as a consociational federation.

Elazar's (n.d.: 10) definition of a federacy is that 'a larger power and a smaller power are linked asymmetrically in a federal relationship in which the latter has substantial autonomy and in return has a minimal role in the governance of the larger power' and that 'the relationship between them can be resolved only by mutual agreement'. This is, to some extent, the case for both Northern Ireland and South Tyrol. As for Northern Ireland, the asymmetric link and substantial autonomy are clearly present. Regarding the dissolution of the relationship only by mutual agreement, matters are more complicated. The secession of Northern Ireland from the United Kingdom can only happen as the result of a referendum in the province, which then will require acceptance by the government in Westminster. Suspending the autonomous power-sharing institutions in Northern Ireland also constitutes a case of dissolving this special kind of federalist relationship. Contrary to previous practice, any changes to the Agreement require the consent of the Northern Ireland Assembly, so that,

Table 6.12 Regional consociations and forms of state

	Federation	Federacy
Brussels	X	–
Northern Ireland	–	X
South Tyrol	–	X

if the British government abides by the British-Irish Agreement to which the Agreement was appended, the power-sharing institutions of Northern Ireland cannot be abrogated without their consent.[24] Nevertheless, Northern Ireland has a different position from that of a region in a decentralised unitary state in that it has a full system of governing institutions and original authority in a range of policy fields, neither of which is enjoyed by regions in a decentralised unitary state. Depending on how the criterion of 'a minimal role in the governance of the larger power' is interpreted, the fact that Northern Ireland sends 18 representatives to the House of Commons in Westminster could be seen as such minimal involvement. This is about the same level of involvement South Tyrol is granted. There are no specific provisions in the South Tyrol arrangement as to the dissolution of the relationship by mutual consent. However, it could be argued that nothing would stand in the way of a boundary change if the central government and South Tyrol agreed on the latter's secession. An additional aspect of classifying South Tyrol as a case of a federacy is the fact that South Tyrol, compared to other provinces in Italy, and despite recent moves towards a federalisation of the Italian Republic, enjoys substantially more powers and functions than comparable entities in the Italian polity.

The important point in relation to the institutional design of regional consociations is thus that their establishment either creates a federal relationship with the central government (Northern Ireland and South Tyrol) or exists within an already established federation. However, as this assessment is only based on a small sample of case studies, one should keep an open mind as to the possibility of regional consociations existing within different state structures. One constituent component within a confederation, union or league can be consociational as can an associated state. Yet, there are only a few actual examples of such state structures, and the notion of regional (meaning 'within one state') would at least make it difficult to argue some of these cases. On the other hand, joint functional authority and condominium status may well lend themselves to state forms in which regional consociations could exist. One could, for example, argue that Brussels is a case of joint functional authority (between the two linguistic communities exercising regional powers), and Northern Ireland may well develop into a similar case (involving the UK and the Republic of Ireland, possibly through the already existing institution of the British-Irish Intergovernmental conference).

Clearly, there is no blueprint for the specific design of complex autonomy regimes along the lines of regional consociationalism that could be applied to all self-determination conflicts alike. At the same time, the above case studies also highlight that constitutional designers have a wide range of different options at their disposal for the construction of technically viable regional consociations that are seen as legitimate institutional structures by the conflict parties.

In such designs, six different dimensions are recurring: mandatory cross-communal executive power-sharing, segmental autonomy, proportionality and minority veto, arbitration mechanisms and mechanisms for policy coordination.

The vertical layering of authority is a key component of state structures that incorporate complex autonomy regimes in that it establishes the entity in which power is to be shared consociationally. A second common feature of state construction in such cases is asymmetry in the distribution of powers and functions among different sub-national entities, giving that which is a consociation powers and functions that are distinct from those given to other regions. Third, regional consociations therefore also require a certain structure of the polity overall, which is most likely to take the shape of a (consociational) federation or federacy.

Apart from these common features, the three case studies above indicate that there is a significant degree of variation in the specifics in which these commonalities manifest themselves in each case. This is primarily due to a certain degree of context-dependence, i.e., the fact that each of the three self-determination conflicts examined had features of a very particular nature that required distinct institutional mechanisms for their accommodation. This may be a trivial point, but nevertheless one that is useful to bear in mind if complex autonomies of the regional consociational kind are indeed to become more widespread, and above all stable and durable arrangements for the resolution of self-determination conflicts.

Notes

1 I am drawing extensively on previously published and unpublished research, principally on Wolff (2002a, 2002b, 2003 and 2004). I would like to thank the European Centre for Minority Issues in Flensburg, Germany, for the hospitality and support afforded to me during a four-week residential fellowship in the summer of 2003 during which large sections of this chapter were researched and written. I also owe gratitude to Brendan O'Leary for numerous fruitful discussions on the subject matter and for the opportunity to benefit from several of his yet unpublished papers on consociationalism. Thanks are also due to the Political Studies Association of the UK for funding my participation in the APSA annual conference where an earlier version was presented. The usual disclaimer remains.

2 The phrase itself was actually not coined by Lijphart himself, who makes reference to Althusius's *consociatio* and acknowledges the use of the term 'consociational' by David E. Apter in a study on Uganda. Cf. Lijphart (1969: n. 14).

3 Arbitration is not a required mechanism for consociational democracies in a universal sense. As I will show below, arbitration mechanisms are, however, a defining element in regional (as opposed to sovereign) consociations.

4 I borrow the term 'regional consociation' from McGarry and O'Leary (1993) and O'Leary (2003), as well as its pendant 'sovereign consociation'.

5 I define territorial autonomy as the legally established power of ethnic or territorial communities to take public decisions and execute public policy indepen-

dently of other sources of authority in the state, but subject to the overall legal order of the state (see Chapter 1).

6 Transfer of power from centre to region (i.e., devolution) happens in the case of established states, that is, when the central government is the source of authority. However, one also needs to consider cases in which no such central authority exists or where it is not able to enforce its claim to authority in a credible way. In this case, powers are delegated upwards, and any regional consociation would then have to *retain* a sufficient degree of competences that make the application of consociational principles worthwhile and meaningful in the context of a particular self-determination conflict (as, for example, in the case of the Bosnian-Croat Federation in Bosnia and Herzegovina).

7 In this context, it is important to note that there have been some important changes in the wake of 9/11 and the subsequent reassertion of national and particularly security interests. While the enforcement of human and minority rights has always been selective, i.e., not been applied to cases like Chechnya or Burma, the overriding concern with terrorism has further diminished the opportunities of some self-determination movements to be recognised as such and increased the opportunities of states to crack down hard on them. Yesterday's freedom fighters have, literally, become today's terrorists.

8 However, UK legislation passed in February 2000 to enable the Secretary of State for Northern Ireland to suspend the institutions is in breach of the British-Irish Agreement signed at the time of the conclusion of the Belfast/Good Friday Agreement in 1998, to which the Agreement was appended. The Irish government has made its position on this matter clear by not accepting the suspension formally, but has instead continued paying government officials working on the North-South Ministerial Council as a sign of it considering the institutions still operational. On the other hand, out of political expediency, the Irish government has so far not taken recourse to international courts to challenge the British government's suspension of the institutions.

9 This option of secession by referendum also exists for Quebec.

10 Examples of useful scholarly overviews and analyses of the institutional structures in Belgium and Brussels are Detant (1997), Peeters (1994) and Schneckener (2002).

11 Article 54 of the Belgian constitution states: 'With the exception of budgets and laws requiring a special majority, a justified motion, signed by at least three-quarters of the members of one of the linguistic groups and introduced following the introduction of the report and prior to the final vote in a public session, can declare that the provisions of a draft bill or of a motion are of a nature to gravely damage relations between the communities.

In this case, the parliamentary procedure is suspended and the motion referred to the Council of Ministers which, within thirty days, gives its justified recommendations on the motion and invites the implicated Chamber to express its opinion on these recommendations or on the draft bill or motion that has been revised if need be. This procedure can only be applied once by the members of a linguistic group with regard to the same bill or motion.'

12 As all three cases are from within the European Union, I restrict the analysis to this level of the national polity. Once the empirical basis of the study of regional consociations is broadened beyond the European Union, supranational structures of governance will need to be included in the analysis.

13 This ignores the fact that His/Her Majesty the King/Queen of the United Kingdom of Great Britain and Northern Ireland is the official, albeit largely ceremonial, head of state.

14 I use the terms 'structural' and 'functional' to distinguish between institutions (i.e., the relevant bodies) and their powers (i.e., the functions they exercise).

15 This view might be easily contested by pointing out that the internationally guaranteed autonomous status of South Tyrol does indeed set it apart from any of the other entities in the Italian polity, and we therefore face a case of structural asymmetry. However, I would argue against this (a) that the international guarantees extend specifically to the functional aspects of South Tyrol's autonomy (which would of course be meaningless without its territorial basis) and (b) that there is a larger point here in that regional consociations in general can be part of symmetrical state structures, even though South Tyrol may be only a partial and weak example of this.

16 This is a hypothesis that will require further testing on a larger number of cases.

17 Again, there is no automatism in this. The examples of the United States and Canada suggest another scenario in that the courts in both cases have, over time, allocated additional/new powers to that level of government that has listed powers – in Canada, where the central government has residual authority, to the provinces; and in the United States, where federal states hold residual authority, to the federal government. Clearly, this scenario requires a well-functioning, strong and respected judicial system, which might be absent or only beginning to be established in cases where regional consociations are used as a tool of resolving (violent) ethnic conflict.

18 Northern Ireland could potentially have such an open-ended list of competences, provided that there is agreement in the Assembly to ask for it.

19 This is not necessarily always the case: in Bosnia and Herzegovina, the powers of the central government are strictly limited by the Dayton agreement.

20 The only possible exception in this context is the International Commission on Decommissioning that has been set up for Northern Ireland to monitor and facilitate the decommissioning of paramilitary weapons. While this clearly constitutes an international body, its powers only extend to its own independent judgement without any further powers to act upon it (in contrast, for example, to the powers of the High Representative in Bosnia and Herzegovina).

21 Soft international guarantees are not 'guarantees' in the principal sense of the term. They primarily manifest themselves in the form of the involvement of international organisations in the negotiation, implementation and potentially operation of a particular peace agreement. While not of the same legally binding and thus potentially enforceable status as hard international guarantees, a significant presence of international agents is often instrumental in shaping preference and opportunity structures of the conflict parties. They are not applicable in the three case reviewed here, but can be found in other cases of regional consociations, such as Bougainville and Mindanao.

22 I am grateful to Brendan O'Leary for pointing out to me that the 1998 Agreement on Northern Ireland has guarantees in the Irish constitution and that the House of Lords in the UK also read the 1998 Northern Ireland Act, together with the Agreement, as a constitution.

23 The Paris Treaty of 1946 between Austria and Italy, annexed to the Italian Peace Treaty, called for the granting of autonomous status to South Tyrol. In 1992, the Austrian government deposited a declaration with the United Nations in which it declared that its dispute with Italy over the implementation of the Paris Treaty had been resolved following the implementation of the majority of the measures agreed in the Second Autonomy Statute of 1972. Both countries – Italy and Austria – subsequently agreed that any future dispute between them in this respect would be referred to the International Court of Justice.

24 The British government implicitly accepted this when it declared in the April 2003 Joint Declaration that it would be willing to repeal the powers to suspend the institutions by order.

References

Daftary, Farimah (2000) *Insular Autonomy: A Framework for Conflict Settlement. A Comparative Study of Corsica and the Åland Islands.* Flensburg: European Centre for Minority Issues.

Detant, Anja (1997) *Brussels – Jerusalem: Conflict Management and Conflict Resolution in Divided Cities.* Brussels: Centre for the Interdisciplinary Study of Brussels.

Elazar, Daniel J. (n.d.) 'Introduction', in *Federal Systems of the World: A Handbook of Federal, Confederal and Autonomy Arrangements.* http://jcpa.org/dje/books/fedsysworld-intro.htm (Accessed 17 July 2003).

Joint Declaration by the British and Irish Governments. April 2003. http://www.nio.gov.uk/pdf/joint2003.pdf (Accessed 14 July 2003).

Lijphart, Arend (1968a) *The Politics of Accommodation: Pluralism and Democracy in the Netherlands.* Berkeley: University of California Press.

Lijphart, Arend (1968b) 'Typologies of Democratic Systems', *Comparative Political Studies*, vol. 1, no. 1, 3–44.

Lijphart, Arend (1969) 'Consociational Democracy', *World Politics*, vol. 21, no. 2, 207–225.

Lijphart, Arend (1977) *Democracy in Plural Societies.* New Haven, CT: Yale University Press.

Lorwin, Val R. (1971) 'Segmented Pluralism: Ideological Cleavages and Political Cohesion in the Smaller European Democracies', *Comparative Politics*, vol. 3, no. 2, 141–175.

McGarry, John and O'Leary, Brendan (1993) 'Introduction', in *The Politics of Ethnic Conflict Regulation*, ed. by John McGarry and Brendan O'Leary. London: Routledge.

O'Leary, Brendan (2003) 'Debating Consociational Politics: Normative and Explanatory Arguments', Paper presented at the Annual Meeting of the American Political Science Association, Philadelphia, PA, 27–31 August.

Peeters, Patrick (1994) 'Federalism: A Comparative Perspective – Belgium Transforms from a Unitary to a Federal State', in *Evaluating Federal Systems*, ed. by Bertus de Villiers. Dordrecht: Martinus Nijhoff, 194–207.

Schneckener, Ulrich (2002) *Auswege aus dem Bürgerkrieg.* Frankfurt: Suhrkamp.

Wolff, Stefan (2002a) *Disputed Territories: The Transnational Dynamics of Ethnic Conflict Settlement.* New York and Oxford: Berghahn.

Wolff, Stefan (2002b) 'The Peace Process in Northern Ireland since 1998: Success or Failure of Post-Agreement Reconstruction?', *Civil Wars*, vol. 5, no. 1, 87–116.

Wolff, Stefan (2003) 'Settling an Ethnic Conflict through Power-sharing: South Tyrol', in *Managing and Settling Ethnic Conflicts. Perspectives on Successes and Failures from Africa, Asia, and Europe*, ed. by Ulrich Schneckener and Stefan Wolff. London: Hurst, 57–76.

Wolff, Stefan (2004) 'The Institutional Structures of Regional Consociation in Brussels, Northern Ireland and South Tyrol', *Nationalism and Ethnic Politics*, vol. 10, no. 3, 387–414.

7 Self-governance in interim settlements

The case of Sudan

Marc Weller

The emerging practice of interim settlements

Self-determination conflicts outside the context of decolonisation tend to end simultaneously in triumph and disaster. Generally, it will be a triumph for the central government and a disaster for the secessionists. Very rarely during the period between 1945 and the end of the Cold War have secessionist groups prevailed in self-determination conflicts outside the colonial context and managed to declare a new state.[1] Where new states came about, this occurred with the consent of the central government—it was a divorce by agreement. Hence, it is not appropriate to consider such cases, for instance the independence of Singapore from Malaysia, as a self-determination conflict. Only once did a secession that was opposed by the central government succeed. This was the case of Bangladesh (East Pakistan)—an instance where independence was actually achieved as the result of an armed intervention by neighbouring India. In all the other examples, secessionists were either crushed (Biafra, Katanga), or a protracted asymmetrical conflict emerged, pitting central government forces against self-styled 'national liberation' movements. These conflicts have often lasted for decades, and in many instances for over half a century (e.g., Kashmir, Myanmar/Burma).

At the time of the conclusion of the Cold War, the situation appeared to become more fluid. When the government fell in Ethiopia, the country found itself under the administration of the former armed opposition groups. These felt little hesitation in agreeing to the independence of Eritrea, which had mounted a long-standing secessionist struggle against the former government. After an interim period, the people of the territory were permitted to hold a referendum. It was clear at the outset that this would lead to full independence.[2]

In Somalia, the central government disintegrated as well. This situation permitted Somaliland to establish de facto independence. However, the various coalitions of local leaders that purported to exercise central governmental functions in Somalia under an unending series of UN-sponsored peace accords refused to acknowledge the independence of

Somaliland. As neither the UN nor other agents of the organised inter-national community recognised Somaliland as a sovereign state, it has remained in a position of legal limbo ever since.

More clear-cut results were obtained in Central and Eastern Europe. Czechoslovakia peacefully dissolved into the Czech and Slovak republics, the Baltic Republics regained their independence from the Soviet Union, and all the other constituent republics also achieved independent state-hood when the former USSR was dissolved. Shortly afterwards, the Social-ist Federal Republic of Yugoslavia violently disintegrated into its constituent entities, only Serbia and Montenegro remaining bound together in a rather tenuous relationship that may yet dissolve as well (cf. Weller in Chapter 3).

While these three cases of the complete dissolution of states had to be internationally accepted, the EU and other agencies of the organised international community took a strong view in resisting 'secessions from secessions'. These were instances where an entity at a level below that of constituent republic of a federal-type state sought independence, or where a federal entity sought secession in the absence of an entitlement in a federal constitution to do so. The attachment to the doctrine of territor-ial integrity and territorial unity was simply too strong to allow for any other result. The resistance to any territorial change was reinforced, more-over, due to the fact that several of the secessionist campaigns had been connected with external military intervention and with horrendous viola-tions of humanitarian principles, including ethnic cleansing and quasi-genocidal violence. Hence, the campaigns of South Ossetia and Abkhasia to secede from the former Soviet republic of Georgia were internationally opposed. Similarly, the independence of Transdniestria from Moldova was resisted. Moscow was not seriously inhibited when it forcibly reintegrated Chechnya, despite its commitments under a peace settlement of 1996. Bosnia and Herzegovina was forcibly kept together, notwithstanding the de facto existence of an ethnic Serb and an ethnic Croat entity within the state. The UN committed itself in Resolution 1244 (1999) to the con-tinued territorial integrity of the Federal Republic of Yugoslavia (now Serbia and Montenegro), notwithstanding the fact that a re-integration of Kosovo into Serbia would never be achievable.

Kosovo is in fact the first recent case that pioneered the concept of an interim settlement. An interim settlement is distinguished by a number of features:

- The settlement resolves the self-determination conflict by establishing the secessionist unit as a constitutional self-determination entity. Hence, colonial self-determination conflicts are not covered, as it is clear from the outset that the colonial entity in question is entitled to independence and there is no need for a settlement on that issue. In such instances, there may be a period of interim governance, as was the case in East Timor, before the act of self-determination and almost inevitable independence.[3]

- The secessionist party suspends its claim for independence for a period. That is to say, having won its case for self-determination in principle, the secessionist entity agrees for a freeze on the implementation of that right for a certain period.
- During that period, autonomy or self-governance is developed and applied in good faith, with a view to demonstrating that this solution sufficiently answers the requirements of the secessionist entity. Interim settlements of this kind require that continued territorial unity is 'given a chance'. In this way, they differ from transitional periods that may be agreed in instances when it is clear that secession will take place. For instance, when Ethiopia accepted that Eritrea may secede, provision was made for a transitional period to precede a referendum on independence. There was no expectation that the outcome would be anything other than independence, and the transitional period was not used to establish autonomy or self-governance as an alternative.
- After a fixed period of the application of autonomy or self-governance, there is provision for a referendum on independence, often with international involvement. The fixing of the date for a referendum is a key part of the settlement. It offers the reassurance of a certain automatism to the secessionist party. Other settlements that merely provide for the option of a referendum at some stage in the future (for instance, the Northern Ireland settlement) do not qualify.
- The referendum will be held in the secessionist unit only, and is decisive in itself. There may be a commitment to negotiation in good faith about the terms of the divorce if the referendum is in favour of independence, but the interim settlement can be terminated through a unilateral act by the secessionist entity alone. There is no need to confirm this through a referendum held in the other parts of the state, or through the consent of the central government or of other entities in the case of a federal-type state.

In the case of Kosovo, an attempt was made to apply these principles at the point before a full-scale armed conflict erupted between NATO and the then Federal Republic of Yugoslavia. During the Rambouillet negotiations in early 1999, a last-ditch attempt was made to forestall a military confrontation through an international settlement. The Conference resulted in an Interim Agreement for Peace and Self Governance in Kosovo. The agreement would have provided a complex formula for the self-governance of Kosovo for a period of three years or possibly more. At the conclusion of that period, it was expected that an international meeting would determine a mechanism for a final settlement, *inter alia* on the basis of the will of the people. This was taken (at least by the Kosovo delegation) as a promise for a settlement taking account of a referendum on independence to be held in Kosovo after the three year interim period.[4]

At first sight, the present UN administration of Kosovo might be considered to be an example of an interim settlement. Under the terms of Resolution 1244 (1999), the UN administration is to generate provisional structures of self-governance. This process has been spun out by the UN Security Council for over five years now, in the hope that over time self-governance will become acceptable to the majority of the population and that a solution short of independence can be found. However, given the absence of a time-frame for interim governance, and no clearly established commitment to a referendum at the end of it, it seems preferable to consider this as a separate case—an open ended interim in search of a settlement. Indeed, it may well be that a genuine interim settlement will emerge when the issue of the final status is finally addressed.

The Bougainville peace accords, on the other hand, provide for extensive autonomy, to be exercised over a period of 10 to 15 years. There may then follow a referendum, with independence being available as one of the options. However, this is conditional upon the achievement of benchmarks of good governance during the autonomy period, and the national parliament of Papua New Guinea retains authority to take a final decision on the status of the territory. Hence, given the length of the autonomy period, the conditionality of independence and the assignment of final authority to decide to the centre, this arrangement too may not really qualify as a genuine interim settlement, although it has certainly been perceived as such by most Bougainvillians. Moreover, the agreement is carried by a conviction on the part of the central government that ultimately secession can be avoided if autonomy is made available instead, and if it is given a chance to operate—the decisive factor where interim settlements are concerned. This rationale also applies in the case of Sudan, the most pronounced interim settlement achieved thus far.

Background to the Sudan settlement

Sudan, a vast country, occupying some 2.5 million square kilometres and boasting a population of around 35 million, has been subjected to one of the most devastating of the protracted self-determination conflicts of the world.[5] The population is highly diverse, featuring some 500 tribes and ethnic groups. 70 per cent are Sunni Muslims, 25 per cent follow indigenous beliefs and 5 per cent are Christian. Sudan is divided into 26 states.

The source of the conflict pitting the partly Christian South against the generally Muslim North lies in part in the colonial administration of the territory, and in the circumstances surrounding its independence that came about at the very end of 1955.[6] Sudan had been subjected to a condominium arrangement between Egypt and the United Kingdom in 1899, following upon the 're-conquest' of the territory in the wake of the Mahdi uprising. The agreement was confirmed on 26 August 1936. Egypt's role in the administration of the territory was minimal, although it retained a territorial claim in relation to it.

According to the doctrine of self-determination that consolidated into an international legal requirement with the establishment of the United Nations in 1945, Sudan clearly qualified as a colonial self-determination entity. This status was confirmed in the Anglo-Egyptian agreement of 12 February 1953 which provided for a transitional period of full self-government 'in order to enable the Sudanese people to exercise self-determination in a free and neutral atmosphere'. It was foreseen that the act of self-determination would consist of a popular choice between either integration with Egypt or full independence.

The prospect of self-determination raised the question of the identity of the self-determination entity or entities. On the one hand, Sudan had been administered as one overall colonial unit. Hence, under the legal doctrine of *uti possidetis*, the entire territory would exercise the act of self-determination as one. Should independence result, then the whole state territory would be protected from challenges to its integrity according to the doctrine of territorial unity.

On the other hand, Southern Sudan had in fact been administered quite separately during the latter parts of the colonial area. The British had formed the view that the southern populations would need protection from the North, whose inhabitants had in the past suppressed and exploited those in the South. Accordingly, separate policies were applied in the North and South, and the latter was to some extent removed from Northern influence under the *Closed District Ordinances*. Nevertheless, a view obtained that this distinct form of administration was not such as to render the South into a separate self-determination entity. Moreover, the separate administrative structures were gradually removed as independence loomed, most notably at the 1947 Juba conference.

The act of self-determination did not, however, take place as envisaged. Instead of the referendum that had been foreseen, the Sudan constituent assembly anticipated this event with a declaration of independence, adopted unanimously on 19 December 1955. This was accepted within days by the United Kingdom and Egypt. While the fully representative nature of this decision in relation to genuine southern participation has been the subject of some doubt, the authoritative nature of this decision was internationally accepted.

Southern representatives in the parliamentary assembly understood that their support for independence had been conditional upon a pledge for self-governance for the South. However, this informal reserve was not in the nature of an 'association', safeguarding a separate claim to self-determination for the South and with it a legal right of secession at a later stage. Sudan as a whole therefore enjoyed the protection of the international doctrine of territorial unity.

Relations between North and South deteriorated rapidly upon independence—a period marked by changes between civilian and military rule. A Southern rebellion, commenced around 1958, increased in strength throughout the 1960s. After an abortive attempt to arrange a peace process in 1965, there were a number of attempts to achieve settlements throughout the 1970s. Most notable is the Addis Ababa Agreement of 1972, followed by a changed constitution in 1973. The arrangements confirmed that a 'united Sudan' would continue to exist, but it also promised autonomy for the South. This pledge was not fully implemented and some of the provisions of the deal were later withdrawn. Moreover, Southern pressure for secession increased, as the new constitutional settlement came about in the context of a campaign for the Islamisation of the country. The conflict re-ignited when Islamic law was introduced throughout the country in 1983.

Accordingly, the 1980s were marked by an increasingly bitter military campaign that mainly affected the civilian populations of the South. The Central Government notoriously opposed the rendering of humanitarian assistance to these areas, leading to the establishment of the UN supported operation Life-Line Sudan when severe famine took hold in 1988. The conflict has been pursued by the Government of Sudan (GOS) under General Umar Hasan Ahmad al-Bashir, who had assumed power in a coup of 1989 and was subsequently elected President, and the Southern Peoples Liberation Army/Movement (SPLA/M) led by John Garang. The National Congress Party of al-Bashir claims 355 out of 360 seats in the parliament.

The extent of humanitarian suffering prompted the regional Intergovernmental Authority on Development (IGAD) to pursue a peace settlement. An IGAD Initiative Declaration of Principles adopted in Nairobi on 20 July 1994 referred to the 'right of self-determination of the people of south Sudan to determine their future status through a referendum'. On the other hand, the text also declares that 'maintaining unity of the Sudan must be given priority by all parties', provided certain principles are affirmed. It defined self-determination 'on the basis of federation, autonomy, etc., to the various peoples of the Sudan'. This latter sentence would seem to indicate that the right to self-determination was supposed to be obtained through measures short of independence. Nevertheless, paragraph 4 provides that in case of absence of an agreement on such a settlement, 'the respective people will have the option to determine their future, including independence, through a referendum.'

After further progress had been made in the shape of a *Political Charter* signed in Khartoum on 10 April 1996, a more formal Peace Agreement was signed on 21 April 1997 which specifically assigns to the people of South Sudan, defined as the people inhabiting the former provinces of Bahr el Gal, Equatoria and the Upper Nile, within their boundaries of 1 January 1956, the right to self-determination to be exercised through a referendum. The agreement also expressly specifies the options of unity and secessions for the referendum, which was to be held at the end of an interim period of four years.

While neither of the above agreements were implemented, and the 1997 agreement also did not obtain consent from all of the Southern Sudanese parties, it is noteworthy that the central Sudan government apparently subscribed to them. Hence, at least by 1997, there had been agreement in principle on maintenance of the territorial unity of the Sudan for an interim period, to be followed by a referendum on independence.

A new Sudan constitution that came into force on 1 July 1998, however, adopted a different view on the matter. Article 6 prescribes national unity as one of the aims of the state. The constitution also proclaims that: 'South Sudan is governed by a transitional government that shall strive towards union and coordinate the exercise and termination of the right to self-determination.'

The exercise 'and termination' of the right to self-determination seems to be focused on the aim of strengthening the union, rather than diminishing its powers. There is also a reference to a referendum, although only as a means of amending the constitutional order by an act of will of all of the people of Sudan, rather than the South separately.

A real prospect for a settlement emerged in the second half of 2001, when the US developed a marked interest in the region. In addition to pressure being brought to bear on the GOS to ensure that its territory would not provide a basis for terrorism, there was also an increased interest in stabilising the situation, given that oil had been discovered in some of the disputed regions and that a continuation of the conflict inhibited the development of this resource.

The first signs of progress came when a formal cease-fire was obtained in the Nuba Mountain area, along with a framework for the cessation of attacks against civilians and other measures. IGAD then sponsored a round of peace negotiations between the GOS and the SPLA/M, yielding the ground-breaking Machakos Protocol signed on 20 July 2002 by GOS First Vice President Ali Osman Taha and John Garang. Six further protocols were negotiated over the following two years and approved as the overall framework for a settlement on 5 June 2004. After implementation and ceasefire agreements were signed on 31 December 2004, all the elements of the settlement were tied together in a comprehensive peace agreement of 9 January 2005.

The negotiation process has been a somewhat unusual one. In the background of the talks, the US government, represented by Senator John Danforth, Special Envoy for Peace to Sudan, has played a decisive role in persuading the GOS to settle. However, the negotiation format has been very much arranged by the IGAD, and in particular by Kenya, the host of the talks. The negotiations have been run in a strictly bilateral form, involving only the GOS and the SPLA/M. This exclusivity of representation of the opposition forces through the SPLA/M (which has also survived into the agreements) has given rise to some tensions. While the SPLA/M claims to include among its ranks diverse constituencies from the South, others have objected to this monopolar arrangement of the talks. Moreover, there also exists considerable opposition to the GOS in the North, as the recent conflict in Darfur has demonstrated. These opposition groups have organised themselves in the form of the National Democratic Alliance (NDA). The US took on the role of helping NDA representatives to organise themselves against the government while at the same time persuading them to accept the bipolar format in the negotiations that effectively excluded them from the talks. The SPLA/M, which has gradually also extended its reach into the North, sought to demonstrate that its own structures are fully inclusive also in relation to the North, and that no further representation was required.

Addressing the self-determination issue

The introduction to the Machakos Protocol of 20 July 2002 records that the parties have reached 'specific agreement' on the 'right to self determination of the people of South Sudan'. This preliminary recitation, contained in an instrument negotiated in an internationalised peace process, signed by the parties and witnessed by international mediators, removes any doubts about the legal status of the South. First, the agreement designates the government of the Republic of Sudan and the SPLA/M as co-equal 'parties'. Second, the South is awarded the designation of being composed of a 'people'. While this is not in itself decisive, it could be a reflection of technical language, confirming that the South is a territorially defined entity whose population is entitled to exercise, within that territorial definition, the act of self-determination. Finally, the introduction expressly awards 'the right of self-determination' to the South. This is no longer qualified by a requirement that this right be exercised in favour of territorial unity of the Sudan. It is substantively unconditional, although certain procedural modalities are attached.

The Protocol itself consists of a preamble (which does not, in fact, refer to the right to self-determination), three main parts covering agreed principles, the transitional process and structures of government, an agreed text on the state and religion and an agreed text on the right to self-determination for the people of the South. The provisions for government will be reviewed in greater detail later, together with the relevant parts of the Naivasha Protocols. For now, it is sufficient to consider the arrangements relating to self-determination.

Agreed principle 1 lays down once again apparently contradictory aims. Paragraph 1.1 confirms that:

> the unity of the Sudan, based on the free will of its people democratic governance, accountability, equality, respect and justice for all citizens

of the Sudan is and shall be the priority of the parties and that it is possible to redress the grievances of the people of South Sudan and to meet their aspirations within such a framework.

This provision appears to be a reversion to the previous view that self-determination implies, in this case, a preference for territorial unity. However, Paragraph 1.3 clearly states: 'That the people of South Sudan have the right to self-determination, *inter alia*, through a referendum to determine their future status.'

As opposed to previous settlement attempts, there is no doubt left that the South is a self-determination entity in the international legal sense, and that it can exercise the act of self-determination according to the established principal modalities of integration, association or full independence, based on the will of its people. A compromise was found here whereby the GOS accepted the right to self-determination in full, while the SPLA/M agreed to a prolonged interim period, during which self-governance for the South within a united Sudan would be attempted. The SPLA/M also agreed to give this experiment its fullest backing, joining with the North in making continued unity attractive through bona fide cooperation with the Centre in the interim period. To this end, Paragraph 1.10 commits the parties 'to design and implement the peace agreement so as to make the unity of the Sudan an attractive option especially to the people of South Sudan'.

The attractiveness of a common future is to be assured on the basis of a number of principles, including:

- The right of the South to control and govern affairs in their region;
- Full and equal participation in the National Government;
- A shared common heritage and a commitment to work together to establish genuine democracy, diversity, equality and economic and social advancement;
- The sharing of the wealth derived from the exploitation of natural resources;
- The freedom of belief and the absence of distinction based on religion in relation to public office or any other form of discrimination.

The substantive safeguards are to be achieved through a system of governance based on the 'division of powers and the structures and functions of the different organs of government'. This division of powers is to be established through an overall national constitution that will enjoy the status of supreme law. There will be a national government and a process to generate national legislation. This may still be religiously based, but only inasmuch as it addresses areas outside the South. Other regions or states may derogate from such legislation, too.

The Machakos Protocol foresees a pre-interim period of six months to commence upon signature of the definite peace agreement. During this period, a National Constitutional Review Commission is to draft a Legal and Constitutional Framework based on the peace agreement. That framework is to govern the interim period of six years. During this period, a full constitution will be developed. At the end of the six-year period, there will be an internationally monitored referendum for the people of South Sudan to confirm the unity of the Sudan by voting to adopt the system of government established under the peace agreement, or to vote for secession. An Assessment and Evaluation Commission consisting of equal representation of the parties, and up to six international representatives, is to support the improvement of institutions and arrangements created under the agreement, also with a view to making unity attractive.

An interesting additional provision concerns the territorial definition of the self-determination unit. This is composed of the Southern States according to the internal borders in existence upon independence. Hence, the South enjoys its own *uti possidetis* definition. However, a special provision was added in the Protocol on the Resolution of the Abyei Conflict. That territory, defined as the area of the nine Ngok Dinka chiefdoms transferred to Kordofan in 1905, is to enjoy a special status during the interim period. Its residents will be represented in both the Northern and Southern legislatures and the territory will be administered by its own elected local Executive Council, subject to the authority of the national Presidency. When the referendum is held in the South, a separate referendum will be held in Abyei, offering the option to remaining part of the North while retaining the special autonomy foreseen in the Protocol, or integrating with the South.

The Southern Kordofan/Nuba Mountains and Blue Nile States are also to enjoy a special status. According to the protocol on resolving that conflict, quite detailed provisions are established for autonomy and self-governance of both states. However, they do not enjoy a right freely to opt into the North or South, or even to choose independence. Instead, a 'popular consultation' is to be held. That consultation is to confirm approval of the peace agreement, including the special autonomy provisions, by the two respective states. The consultation is to be administered according 'to the will of the people of the two States through their respective democratically elected legislature', after a review process to evaluate the implementation of the peace agreement. There is also the possibility of re-negotiating the autonomy provisions, if the peace agreement is found wanting.

The Machakos Protocol introduces an additional element into the category of interim self-determination settlements. Like the case of Bougainville, there is provision for an interim period followed by a referendum on independence. However, in addition to that sequence, there is a positive commitment of all parties, including the (formerly?) secessionist SPLA/M, to work in good faith towards a confirmation of unity at the point of the referendum.[7] To this end, there is even an internationalised mechanism to support the parties in carrying through on this commitment. On the other hand, and again in sharp contrast to the Bougainville settlement, there is a clearly defined term for the interim period, and the holding of the referendum is not contingent on subjective factors or conditions, such as the achievement of standards of good governance within the entity seeking independence.

State structure

The Machakos protocol is very vague on the state structure, other than confirming that there will be a national government and addressing the reach of religiously-based law. However, in preparation for the achievement of the overall peace agreement, a number of further protocols have been generated throughout 2003 and 2004, filling out the Machakos structure. These consist of:

- The Agreement on Security Arrangements during the Interim Period;
- The Framework Agreement on Wealth Sharing during the Pre-Interim and Interim Period;
- The Protocol on Power-sharing;
- The Protocol on the Resolution of Conflict in southern Kordofan/ Nuba Mountains and Blue Nile States;
- The Protocol on the Resolution of the Abyei Conflict;
- The Nairobi Declaration on the Final Phase of Peace in the Sudan.

These Protocols, and the Machakos Protocol, plus certain cease-fire undertakings, were tied together in the Nairobi Declaration of June 2004 on the Final Phase of Peace in the Sudan. This has been further reinforced in a permanent cease-fire and an implementation plan. With a slight delay, the entire package was approved in January 2005.

The state structure is spelt out in the Protocol on Power-sharing, along with the Protocols on the Kordofan/Nuba Mountains and Blue Nile States and Abyei. The Protocol on Power-sharing commits the parties to decentralisation and empowerment of all levels of government as cardinal principles for the effective and fair administration of the country. The agreement expressly describes the organisation of powers as 'a decentralised system of government with significant devolution of powers, having regard to the National, Southern Sudan, State, and local levels' (Paragraph 1.5.1.1.). The arrangements for Southern Sudan and for the states are expressly designated as 'autonomy' arrangements (Paragraph 1.4.1). However, it would be misleading to describe the Sudan during the interim period as a unitary state arranged according to principles of decentralisation and autonomy. Rather, the principle of decentralisation is a guiding principle that is to apply throughout all of the divisions of the state that are to be established. The essential character of the state structure is determined through these divisions, rather than the fact that each of them will apply principles of decentralised government.

Given that the South has been established as a constitutional self-determination entity (i.e., an entity that enjoys elements of sovereignty in itself), it is not conceptually possible to designate the state as unitary, with decentralisation and autonomy having been granted by the centre through devolution. One may presume that these designations had to be adopted to maintain the view of the GOS that Sudan remains one unitary state, despite the fact that it has been rendered, in effect, into a conditional federacy, or quasi-confederal arrangement.

The overall state can best be described as a complex, asymmetric construction. The arrangement is asymmetric, inasmuch as there is provision for one federal-type entity, the Southern Sudan. That entity is established through its own constitution, its institutions and legislation. This is not matched by a second unit (the North), that would ordinarily also be expected to have its own separate constitution, institutions or legislation.

The system is not only asymmetric, it is also complex. This is due to the fact that the relations of the states in the South and the national layer of governance are mediated through the Southern Sudan entity.[8] Given that the North does not have its own constitutional or institutional identity, the Northern states interact directly with the national government. Complexity arises due to the presumption of continued unity which imposes common principles of governance affecting the states both in the South and in the North, despite this distinction in their status. In addition, there are the special arrangements for the Southern Kordofan/Nuba Mountains and Blue Nile states, and for Abyei. Moreover, the capital city of Khartoum also falls under a special legal regime. The management of this complex relationship is to be determined in the Interim National Constitution and the Southern Constitution, both of which will take some time to develop.

Institutions and power sharing

At the centre, there is provision for a bi-cameral legislature, composed of an Assembly and a Council of States. Representation of the South in both bodies is to be 'equitable'. What is equitable is to be determined according to 'relevant considerations' (Paragraph 2.2.2.2). The setting of modalities for the elections to the Assembly is left to an Electoral Commission that is to be established, along with 'fair electoral laws'. The Council of States is composed of two representatives of each state. One cannot help but be struck by the somewhat open, if not casual, way of addressing these crucial issues of representation, and of the future electoral system, or of putting off decisions in relation to them until some future time.

The first elections are to be held before the expiry of a period of three years, unless, it seems, the parties meet and determine otherwise. One might speculate whether this outcome could perhaps be connected with the structure of the negotiations and the accords. After all, there has been a strictly unipolar representation of the South and the North (or the Centre) respectively. According to the Protocol, this exclusivity is to be maintained until elections are held. Hence, the NCP led by President al Bashir is simply to assume 52 per cent of the seats in the National Assembly, the SPLA/M will assume 28 per cent. Other Northern political forces are to occupy 14 per cent, other Southern political forces receive 6 per cent. It appears that the two principal parties will also exercise some control over the designation of these 'other' political forces (Paragraph 2.2.4).

As in most consociational power-sharing arrangements, a dual veto mechanism exists at the national constitutional level. First, there are qualified voting rules relating to decisions in the Assembly. These are backed up by the requirement of consent from the Council (the upper chamber of the parliament), where parallel qualified voting rules apply. With respect to constitutional changes, 75 per cent of the members of each chamber must approve. Where such amendments would affect the peace agreement, the parties to the agreement must also approve separately before such amendments may even be introduced. Legislation affecting the states requires passage by a two-thirds majority in the Council. Other decisions are taken by simple majority in both houses.

When applied to the South, this means that it can veto constitutional changes through its representation in the Assembly also, at least during the period before the elections, when the SPLA/M is guaranteed 28 per cent membership. With respect to any other decision, there would need to be a finding that the matter at issue affects the states, and then the South would need to muster the relevant quorum of 34 per cent in the Council of States. This provision is therefore somewhat unusual, as it does not give the South its own institutional identity that could affect central legislative decision-making. In this sense, the 'South' does not appear as an entity whose consent is necessary for critical decisions. Instead, it is a certain quorum of states generally.

In terms of executive power-sharing, the identity of the South is more pronounced. There will be a Presidency, composed of a President and two Vice Presidents. Declarations concerning war and states of emergency, and certain appointments and decisions concerning the Assembly must be taken jointly by the President and the first Vice President. Again, for what may well be a prolonged period until elections are held, the current President is assured of retaining that office, to be joined by the SPLA/M Chairman as first Vice President, who is also awarded the post of President of the Government of South Sudan. The role and relevance of the second Vice President is not so clear. However, in general, decisions are to be taken through a 'collegial decision-making process' (Paragraph 2.34). When elections are held, the possibility is open for a candidate from the

South to win the post of President, in which case the first Vice President is to be from the North.

There is to be a government of national unity, accountable to the President and the Assembly. The government consists of the President and the Vice Presidents, and an inclusive Council of Ministers. The posts are to be shared among the two parties, who in turn determine the representation of 'other political forces'.

The Protocol on Power-sharing also provides for the redressing of imbalances in the composition of the civil service. A special programme aimed at improving representation of people from South Sudan to a target of between 20 and 30 per cent is foreseen.

The judiciary exists at the level of the constitutional court with a mandate to uphold the interim national, the South Sudan and the state constitutions and to remove legislation that is incompatible with constitutional provisions. The Court is also the court of appeals in relation to decisions from the South Sudan Constitutional Court on matters of the South Sudan's Constitution and the constitutions of the Southern states. Moreover, it determines disputes relating to exclusive or concurrent competences exercised by the various layers of government. Given the primacy of the interim national constitution, its power to adjudicate disputes between the national level and the South is a notable feature. It is also one of the very few bodies that addresses relations between the states of the North and the national level.

Somewhat oddly, the Protocol on Power-sharing determines that the Constitutional Court shall be independent of the judiciary, and 'shall be answerable to the Presidency' (2.11.3.2.[i]). This may perhaps be an inelegant translation, as a subsequent provision confirms that judges on the court shall perform their functions without political interference (2.11.4.3). The President of the Constitutional Court is appointed jointly by the President and First Vice President, others are appointed by the Presidency upon recommendation by the National Judicial Service Commission subject to approval by a two-thirds majority in the Council of States, to ensure appropriate representativeness. The Court's decisions are final and binding. There also exists a National Supreme Court as principal court of review and cassation in relation to matters arising from national law.

In addition to this institutional establishment at the national level, the Protocol on Power-sharing also addresses the institutions of the South. The South is to give itself a constitution, to be adopted by a Transitional Assembly by a two-thirds majority. The Protocol assigns 70 per cent of seats in the Southern Assembly to the SPLA/M (i.e., a sufficient majority to determine the constitution on its own), with 15 per cent held by the NCP and 15 per cent by others. The first elections are to be held in accordance with the national provisions noted above, rendering their timing somewhat uncertain.

The South Sudan government is composed of a President, a Vice President and a Council of Ministers, posts being assigned prior to elections according to the same formula as applies to the Assembly. There is also provision for a court system.

During the Interim Period, both the North and South retain their armed forces. A merger of both is foreseen if continued unity is the result of the referendum. In order to prepare for the merger, pilot integration programmes will be administered.

The third level of governance concerns the state. These also have legislatures, and executive and judicial institutions. The Protocol on Power-sharing once again assigns representation in the legislature and executives for the period until elections are held. Interestingly, it is required that one governor of a Southern state must be an NCP nominee. The electoral process is to follow nationally established rules to be determined by the National Election Commission. On the other hand, and somewhat unusually, each state can determine the nature of local government according to its own constitution.

Special provision is made for special territories. Abyei has its own structures of autonomous governance, operating directly under the authority of the national Presidency. Detailed provisions are foreseen for the autonomy of the administrative structures of the Kordofan/Nuba Mountains and Blue Nile states.

Layering of competences and the legal order

In many constitutional negotiations, one will find considerable emphasis on the question of original and residual power. The keen contest about such powers is connected with the implications they may have for the character of the overall state (a confederation, a federation, a unitary state that has devolved authority, etc.) and the status of the entities of which the state is composed. In the case of Sudan, the resolution of the underlying self-determination dispute through the referendum pledge has allowed the parties to adopt an open approach. National legislative and executive competence is exclusive where defence, borders, foreign affairs, immigration, currency and exchange, national police and other national services are concerned. The South enjoys exclusive powers to its own constitution, police and security, macro-economic policies, development of financial resources including the raising of public loans, and a whole host of public services. The states, too, are endowed with quite extensive lists of exclusive competences. Given the magnitude of these three lists, considerable overlap even among the exclusive competences appears inevitable. Moreover, there is also a very long annex specifying concurrent powers to be exercised by all three layers of authority. Finally, the Kordofan/Nuba Mountain and Blue Nile states are awarded separate schedules detailing their competences.

Residual powers rest with whichever layer is most closely connected with the issue concerned, although there appears to be a preference for competence to be allocated to the South if the problems at issue are susceptible to Southern Sudan regulation. Disputes are to be decided according to the following principles:

- The need to recognise the sovereignty of the Nation while accommodating the autonomy of Southern Sudan or of the states;
- Whether there is a need for national or Southern Sudan norms and standards;
- The principle of subsidiarity;
- The need to promote the welfare of the people and to protect each person's human rights and fundamental freedoms.

These quite general provisions may not be sufficient to resolve disputes, especially given the rather loose assignment of competences to all three layers. This leads to the suspicion that in practice most competences will rest with the South in relation to its own affairs, and with the North in relation to the Northern states.

In addition to questions of original and residual authority, the issue of supremacy of law arises. Throughout the agreements, it is clear that the peace agreement and the national interim constitution enjoy supremacy, subject, however, to the requirement that freedom of belief is guaranteed and respected. The supremacy of national constitutional law is to be enforced by the Constitutional Court. In the South, the South Sudan constitution also prevails over state constitutions.

With respect to the reach of national law, there is, however, a unique provision in the Machakos Protocol that states:

> 3.2.2 Nationally enacted legislation having effect only in respect of the states outside Southern Sudan shall have as its source of legislation Sharia and the consensus of the people.
>
> 3.2.3 Nationally enacted legislation applicable to the southern States and/or to the Southern Region shall have as its source of legislation popular consensus, the values and customs of the people of Sudan, including their traditions and religious beliefs, having regard to Sudan's diversity.
>
> 3.2.4 Where national legislation is currently in operation or is enacted and its source is religious or customary law, then a state or region, the majority of whose residents do not practice such religion or customs may: (i) Either introduce legislation so as to allow or provide for institutions or practices in that region consistent with their religion or customs, or (ii) Refer the law to the Council of States for it to approve by a two-thirds majority or initiate national legislation which will provide for such necessary alternative institutions as applicable.

It is somewhat odd that these provisions, which are being described in the Machakos Protocol as being subject to further development, are not picked up in the Protocol on Power-sharing. After all, here we find introduced the concept that national legislation can be adopted that applies to the North only, giving it some sort of a disguised identity without consecrating the North a formal unit of the state. Moreover, and crucially, it is clear that the South can exempt itself entirely from Sharia-based law. One has to admire the delicacy with which this result is established. The slight difference in wording between Articles 2.2.2 and 2.2.3 can be interpreted as such an exemption by the South, whereas the al-Bashir government need not exactly admit that it has accepted the revocation of Sharia law from an area where it once applied. Under Islamic conceptions, such an admission might have grave consequences.

In addition to the constitution and national law, human rights are to apply throughout the territory. Internationalised peace agreements will often tend to incorporate into a settlement a whole host of international standards and make them directly applicable in domestic law. The Protocol on Power-sharing reiterates the treaties to which the Sudan is at present a party and requires compliance with these by all levels of government. It is doubtful, however, whether these standards would be directly applicable where they are of a self-executing nature, and whether they are domestically enforceable. Instead, the Protocol establishes its own limited listing of 'rights and freedoms to be enjoyed under Sudanese law, in accordance with the provisions of the treaties referred to'. Only this minimum catalogue, it seems, is directly applicable and perhaps enforceable, although these provisions are at least to be interpreted, one presumes, in the light of treaty obligations in force for the Sudan. Given the limited list of human rights obligations to which the Sudan is subjected, the exhortation in the Protocol that the Sudan 'should endeavour' to ratify other human rights treaties it has signed sounds rather modest (Paragraph 1.6.1).

As has already been noted, the contested issue of religion that was addressed in the Machakos Protocol in terms of legislation does not feature again in the Protocol on Power-sharing. This applies also to the issue of religious rights, as opposed to the issue of legislation based on religious precept that was addressed above. Given the importance of this issue, this is somewhat surprising, and perhaps a result of the inability of the parties to address this issue more fully. The Machakos Protocol contains an Agreed Text on State and Religion. It commits the parties to the granting of the freedom of worship and the absence of discrimination on religious grounds. There is also a mini catalogue of religious rights to be granted by both parties. Moreover, there is provision for personal autonomy in relation to personal and family matters that may be determined by the 'personal laws' (including Sharia or other religious laws, customs, or traditions) of those concerned.

As is stated expressly in the case of the sources of legislation, in relation to religious rights the unspoken assumption would be that Islam remains the underpinning of public life in the North, but that the South is, henceforth, exempted from this. To state this expressly would perhaps not have been politically possible for the GOS. While the South would be removed from Islamic governance, individuals in the South can conduct their personal lives according to Islamic precepts on the basis of religious rights and the personal autonomy that was granted. The position of those wishing to opt out of religiously-based legislation and adjudication in the North is less clear.

In addition, special regulations will be applied to specific territories. For instance, in relation to Khartoum, the North is entitled to legislate, but special consideration is to be given to its multi-cultural and multi-faith population. The implementation of laws through judges or enforcement agencies is also to be sensitive to differing traditions, and non-Muslims are to be exempted from certain forms of punishment. A special commission is to watch over the treatment of non-Muslims in the capital and to ensure that they are not adversely affected by the application of Sharia Law. These special provisions only apply to the capital, which once more raises the question of the position of non-Muslims in other areas of the North.

The no-less-delicate issue of state languages has been addressed in a rather diplomatic way, but with clear results. Arabic is identified as a language that is 'widely spoken in the Sudan'—a rather open compromise formulation, it seems (Paragraph 2.8.2). As a result, Arabic 'as a major language at the national level, and English' are the official working languages of the National Government, of business and languages of instruction for higher education (Paragraph 2.8.3). At the state level, additional languages may be promoted to the status of official languages.

While the settlement leaves a number of substantive issues open, it offers an unusual detail of provision on the issue of resource sharing—a problem most often overlooked in agreements of this kind. Given the special background of the extraction of oil in some of the conflict areas, it is perhaps not surprising that this issue has been considered and resolved. With reference to oil extracted in the South, 50 per cent of net revenue is to go to the North, with the other 50 per cent being assigned to the South. Two per cent shall be allocated to the oil producing state or region in proportion to output produced there.[9]

What is impressive about the Wealth-sharing Protocol is the detail that has been devoted to other fiscal and financial arrangements. Given the fact that the South has been starved of resources in the past, it is perhaps natural that a great deal of attention was paid to the way in which its development can be funded and sustained. The financial provisions are also backed up by monitoring and other bodies that can support actual implementation.

Conclusion

The Sudan settlement is in many ways innovative. It clearly advances the concept of interim self-determination settlements based on autonomy or self-governance. The South is constituted as a self-determination entity, but in the clear expectation that it will in the end opt for continued territorial unity after a clearly defined interim period. While this expectation may not necessarily be shared by all in the South, the SPLA/M has committed itself to a cooperative process of making the settlement work and making continued unity attractive. It will be interesting to see whether it will carry through on this commitment.

One factor that may be conducive to possible success, despite the difficult history of the region, lies in the fact that this peace process has been genuinely owned by the two principal parties. While the international mediators have helped to move the process along, and have offered technical advice in relation to some particularly difficult issue areas, both delegations have had their own highly competent teams of experts and negotiators. What has resulted is a genuine compromise—a compromise that was not externally imposed, but one the parties agreed to accept after having worked through the issues for themselves.

But will this settlement succeed in its purported aim of safeguarding the unity of the Sudan by effectively dividing the country into two entities? In this instance, near complete control of the South by the SPLA/M is matched by the political ambition of that group in the North. Hence, there may be an incentive to perform its role within the overall Sudan, even after self-government for the South has been formalised through implementation of the agreement. The wealth-sharing aspects of the settlement and the role foreseen for representatives from the South in the national government structure may also contribute to a willingness to give unity a chance. Whether such a wish, if it exists, can be translated into a referendum result that opposes independence may be a different matter. This case will certainly furnish an intriguing test for the purported integrative power of autonomy-based settlements.

The settlement is quite detailed in some aspects, such as wealth-sharing, but quite open in others. The complex, asymmetrical format of the future state is a difficult design to implement, and one has to confess that it is as yet only expressed in rather general terms in the Protocols. This is to be filled out through a constitutional drafting process. This process is a very ambitious one, incredibly aiming to generate a Legal and Constitutional Framework Text within six weeks of the presentation of the peace agreement. To this end, a national Constitutional Review Commission is to be formed. The Legal and Constitutional Framework is then adopted as the Interim Constitution by the National Assembly and the SPLA/M National Liberation Council. Strangely, the National Constitutional Review Commission is also meant to prepare model constitutions for the states. This is surprising, given that special requirements would appear to exist for the Southern states alone. Their legislative frameworks will have to comply with the constitution of the South.

The settlement is marked by a number of anomalies that reveal the reluctance of the central government to accept in altogether too visible terms the division of the state into two entities. Rather than developing the Sudan as a confederation of the North and South, it can pretend that the state continues to exist as a unitary, although devolved, state. Hence, Southern Sudan is considered as a 'level of governance' of the Sudan, along with the national government or the states. Accordingly, the South does not have its own identity in the Council of States, for instance. The North has no identity as an entity at all.

This approach does not only reduce the symbolic sacrifice that has to be made by the Centre in terms of granting self-governance to the South. It may also help forestall conflict in the North. Having avoided a sense of the division of the Sudan into two parts, the sense of northern opposition groups of having been left stranded alone in a hostile North, no longer counter-balanced by the groups in the South, is avoided.

Presumably, in actual practice the North will have to overcome its reluctance to conceive itself as an 'entity' in the new constitutional setup and provide for a legislative framework for its own relations with states and local authorities. Given that there is no Assembly for the North, nor any executive structure that is separate from the national Ministries, procedures to facilitate the differentiated functioning of such institutions when addressing the North, and when addressing the national level, will need to be established. Conversely, it is also not clear how the relationship between Southern states and the national level is to be arranged in view of their appurtenance to the 'superior' Southern entity.

The lack of a constitution for the North also raises difficult issues for those populations living there that do not feel represented by the present Khartoum government. Such sentiments do not only extend to Darfur where violent conflict has recently erupted. A number of other areas, some of which boast populations of several million, do not feel accommodated by the settlement that has been obtained. Many of these groups have organised themselves in the National Democratic Alliance, seeking access to the peace process. This access was not granted, given the strictly bipolar nature of the talks. Instead, the SPLA/M has argued that these groups are also represented through its structure. There have also been intensive diplomatic efforts to keep up the level of confidence of the NDA members in the SPLA/M. These contacts will need to be maintained or even enhanced if the next round of conflict after the conclusion of the settlement is to be avoided. The settlement thus far does not appear to offer a great deal to groups outside the South and outside the three states that have achieved separate special autonomy provisions. Hence, the two parties will need to be serious about the inclusion of the 'other' groups in the very intensive constitutional draft process that is now about to begin.

If the Northern dimension is thus far largely unaddressed in terms of state construction and autonomy, one must also note that there is not a great deal of effect of the settlement as far as functional or personal autonomy is concerned. The catalogue of human rights provided in the settlement is slender. Minority rights are left out altogether. The failure to incorporate international standards leaves significant room for a minimalist interpretation of the provisions that are included. And there does not appear to be any significant implementation infrastructure relating to human rights. One may also doubt whether there is significant commitment to invest in the training of governmental officials, law enforcement agencies or courts in relation to this issue.

Of course, this dimension must be considered in the light of the regional standards of practice, and one also has to admit to the particular issue of the religious dimension as concerns the North. In relation to the South, the religious issue has been settled by being silent about it in the agreement. In this way, the North has not been forced to make an impossible concession by giving up on the doctrine of the primacy of Sharia law, while effectively leaving the matter in the hands of the authorities of the South in relation to the areas they control. Northern groups opposing religious governance will remain dissatisfied about addressing the issue in this way. On the other hand, this has principally been a North/South settlement, and it is understandable that the negotiators were unwilling to mortgage that deal with additional problems that appeared to be peripheral to the central conflict.

Another interesting area is the way in which the two political forces in charge of the negotiations have entrenched their own future mandates in the actual agreements, at least for a period of three years, and probably far beyond. While the future of the NCP may be more uncertain, this applies especially to the SPLA/M and its governance in the South. There are pledges to bring in other actors, and involve them in constitutional drafting, in the assembly and in ministerial work. However, it is not clear how this will be done, and how transparent this process will be. After all, this process of broadening governance and of permitting the introduction of checks and balances will be administered by the two main parties themselves.

Other actors may also be doubtful whether they will have a chance to develop a profile for themselves in time for the elections. The principal parties will have been able to demonstrate their competence. There will not have been an opposition, other than members in the parliamentary assembly from other parties that they would have picked themselves. And the principal parties will be in uncontested charge of the electoral process.

The settlement that has been achieved only provides an outline for the interim period. Much will depend on the agreed implementation plan for the settlement that is to be signed along with the whole package of protocols, and even more on the willingness and ability of the actors to fill in the blanks in the agreements in a comparatively short time thereafter. In order to obtain the initial peace agreement, a number of difficult issues have simply been left for further treatment during this upcoming next phase. In particular, there will need to be a realistic and more inclusive constitutional drafting process to ensure that this complex asymmetrical interim design can be made to function. If that endeavour fails, the South will develop its separate structures, cooperating with the North only to the extent necessary (wealth sharing), until full independence is obtained. If, in the meantime, further conflict erupts in the North, the very concept of interim autonomy settlements for self-determination conflicts may be undermined and possibly fail altogether. Yet, such a dim prospect is no foregone conclusion. Thus far, the two main conflict parties have proven themselves capable at the negotiation table and away from it and have remained committed to the deal they reached. They may very well continue to be successful in the politically and constitutionally difficult implementation process ahead, even if independence for the South remains very much on the cards.

Notes

1 The definition of colonial self-determination cases is a very narrow one. It only applies to genuine colonies, the 'people' entitled to exercise the right are those defined by the colonial boundaries, and they may only exercise this right once.
2 A similar arrangement was accepted by the Russian Federation in relation to Chechnya in 1996. However, Russia subsequently unilaterally reneged on the accord.
3 Eastern Timor was a case of secondary colonialism, i.e., an entity forcibly integrated by neighbouring Indonesia at the very point of exercising its act of self-determination. An analogous case awaiting resolution is that of the Western Sahara.
4 A US side letter confirmed that the reference to 'the will of the people' meant a pledge to hold a referendum on independence in Kosovo.
5 Population estimates vary quite considerably, from around 30 million to 38 million.
6 Sudan was formally declared independent on 1 January 1956.
7 In the Bougainville settlement, there is a provision noting that the peace agreement is intended to 'assist in building a new relationship between Bougainville and the nation as a whole' (Paragraph 340a), but no clear commitment by the parties to work in good faith towards a referendum result in favour of continued territorial unity.
8 '1.5.1.3. The linkage between the National Government and the state in the Southern Sudan shall be through the Government of Southern Sudan, subject to paragraph 1.5.1.4. below, and as provided for in the Interim National Constitution and the Southern Sudan Constitution.' Paragraph 1.5.1.4 protects the independent exercise of the powers assigned to the respective layers of governance from encroachment by others and requires cooperation among them.
9 The agreement does not clarify from which half share the additional two per cent is to be funded.

8 Two steps forward, one step back

Indigenous peoples and autonomies in Latin America

Willem Assies[1]

Introduction

The last three decades of the past century have seen a remarkable surge of activism by and on behalf of indigenous peoples in Latin America. States, in turn, have responded by formally abandoning the integrationist and assimilationist policies of indigenismo and have reformed their constitutions to recognize the pluriethnic and multicultural composition of their populations.[2] The region furthermore stands out for the fact that among the 17 countries that ratified ILO Convention 169 (1989) 13 are Latin American.[3] The constitutional reforms and the ratification of ILO Convention 169, one might surmise, provide a legal framework for the emergence of autonomy regimes for indigenous peoples.

The dialectics between the identity politics practiced by indigenous peoples' movements and the politics of recognition that have been adopted by the states have certainly contributed to the dynamism of what has been called the 'indigenous emergence' (Bengoa, 2000). Indigenous peoples' demands and the responses to these demands have become important elements in the ongoing processes of transformation of the Latin American states which, it has been suggested, may point to the emergence of a 'multicultural regional model' (Van Cott, 2000: 265; Sieder, 2002). Indigenous peoples, however, are not the only actor in these transformation processes and the emergence of autonomy regimes is far from a smooth process and in fact is mostly rather conflictive and contested. Nonetheless, the processes of state transformation suggest a significant departure from the nation-state model as it emerged in the nineteenth century and will have profound implications for the concepts of citizenship, democracy, development and human rights predicated upon this model.

This chapter seeks to place indigenous peoples' movements in a broader context and to examine their role in the process of state transformation in order to assess the scope of emerging autonomies and some of their possible implications. First, I will briefly discuss the Latin American context. Then I will examine the emerging legal framework and discuss some aspects of autonomy regimes. In the third section of the chapter I will first provide a general overview of the constitutional reforms that have taken place in Latin America and then examine four cases in which stipulations regarding a formal political autonomy regime were included in the constitution: Panama, Colombia, Ecuador and Nicaragua. The final section offers some reflections on these cases and the process of state transformation in Latin America.

Indigenous peoples and movements in Latin America

Estimates of the indigenous population of Latin America are highly variable. Generally it is assumed that there are between 30 and 40 million indigenous people, corresponding to about 8 to 10 percent of the total population, and that there are some 400 indigenous peoples (Hopenhayn and Bello, 2001: 13–15; Psacharopoulos and Patrinos, 1994: 21–54). In Bolivia, Guatemala and Peru indigenous people constitute the majority of the population. In Ecuador they make up between 30 and 40 percent of the population, in Mexico and Belize between 15 and 20 percent and in the remaining countries they would be less than 6 percent of the total population. A major problem is the friction or mismatch between the ways states classify and count their populations and the ways these populations define themselves. In Mexico, for example, the official number of indigenous groups has been 56 for decades, but the groups and the way they were counted changed from year to year (Levi, 2002: 6–7). On the other hand, according to the 2000 Brazilian census, the number of people identifying themselves as 'Indian' was 701,462; that is twice as much as in the previous 1991 census. Natural growth by itself cannot explain such outcomes, which suggest that an increasing number of people somehow identify themselves as 'Indian' (Brackelaire, 2002: 34). Such numbers, it should be noted moreover, cover a wide range of situations, going from still relatively isolated hunters and gatherers, through settled indigenous peasantries to the rapidly increasing numbers of indigenous peoples living in urban areas.

From the 1960s onward new movements of indigenous peoples have emerged. Various developments contributed to this dynamic and the manner in which these movements framed their discourses. Let me just mention a few:

- The indigenist education policies had the, perhaps paradoxical, effect of contributing to the emergence of a new generation of indigenous intellectuals capable of articulating a discourse that found resonance both with the indigenous people(s) and with sectors of the 'national' society and, perhaps even more importantly, in the transnational arena. In the course of the 1970s a transnational movement emerged that skillfully articulated a 'politics of shame' in this arena;

- New links emerged between rural and urban areas as a consequence of the increased mobility of rural populations;
- The agrarian reforms of the 1950s to 1970s often broke up rural power structures and contributed to the consolidation of holdings of the indigenous peasantries;
- The accelerated occupation of the Amazon region, the 'last frontier,' through policies of colonization and the search for natural resources triggered the concern of ecologist movements and directly affected the hitherto relatively isolated indigenous peoples of the region. An emerging alliance greatly contributed to the 'visibility' of the indigenous peoples of the region and brought new items to the agenda. On the one hand it resulted in a, often highly problematic, convergence of indigenous and ecologist discourses. On the other, it brought a concern with 'territory.' Whereas the indigenous-peasant populations of the Andean highlands and parts of Meso-America had become accustomed to articulate their demands largely in terms of 'land' in the context of state-sponsored agrarian reform policies, those of the Amazon region would formulate their demands in terms of 'territory' and this would infuse indigenous movements' demands with a new dynamic;[4]
- Liberation Theology[5] as well as the emergence of human rights movements in the context of the 'democratic transitions' brought new allies to the indigenous cause. The end of the authoritarian regimes opened further political spaces for indigenous peoples' movements;
- The end of the Cold War meant that the formerly quasi automatic polarization in terms of a class struggle discourse weakened and that campesinos (peasants) could become indios otra vez (Indians again);[6] a process that received further impetus as result of the celebration of diversity, by both neoliberals and postmodernists;
- The celebration of the 'Encounter of two worlds' in 1992[7] rapidly was transformed into a commemoration of '500 years of resistance,' which through the organization of continental encounters contributed to the strengthening of networks and interchanges among indigenous organizations and to an enhanced visibility.

The conjunction of such developments accounts for the emergence of vibrant and varied indigenous movements in the region and their becoming prominent social and political actors. In the course of this process demands have increasingly centered upon autonomy claims in the sense of coupling territorial demands with claims to the recognition of their own ways of doing politics and their own ways of imparting justice. Such claims are partly sustained by ILO Convention 169, which in the course of time has been ratified by a significant number of Latin American countries.

ILO Convention 169, self-determination and autonomy

ILO Convention 169 has become a key element in framing indigenous demands in Latin America and in the struggle for reform of Latin American constitutions. Ratification means that the Convention acquires the status of domestic law.[8] It therefore is worth briefly discussing it. The Convention defines indigenous peoples as

> Peoples in independent countries who are regarded as indigenous on account of their descent from the populations which inhabited the country, or a geographical region to which the country belongs, at the time of conquest or colonization or the establishment of present state boundaries and who, irrespective of their legal status, retain some or all of their own social, economic, cultural and political institutions.

The Convention furthermore states that self-identification is to be regarded as a fundamental criterion for determining the groups to which the Convention applies. Albeit hedged in with qualifiers, the Convention contains stipulations regarding the 'right to retain their own customs and institutions' (art. 8), respect for 'the methods customarily practiced by the peoples concerned for dealing with offences committed by their members' (art. 9) and the recognition of 'the rights of ownership and possession (...) over the lands which they traditionally occupy' (art. 14) and it stipulates that the term 'lands' shall 'include the concept of territories, which covers the total environment of the areas which the people concerned occupy or otherwise use' (art. 13).[9]

A notable feature of the Convention is that it is the only international legal instrument that uses the term 'peoples' in relation to indigenous peoples. This, however, is immediately followed by the stipulation that the 'use of the term 'peoples' in this Convention shall not be construed as having any implications as regards the rights which may attach to the term under international law' (art. 1). Thus, although under the pressure of indigenous delegates who participated in the drafting of the Convention the terms 'populations' and 'minorities' were avoided at the same time indigenous peoples were denied the right of peoples under international law, that is the right to self-determination by virtue of which they 'freely determine their political status and freely pursue their economic, social and cultural development.' Self-determination under international law would include the right to sovereign independence and this met with the objection of state representatives.

In the debates over a UN Declaration on the rights of indigenous Peoples the controversy over terms and the issue of 'self-determination' is ongoing. In such debates the notion of 'internal self-determination' has cropped up.[10] Martínez Cobo (1987: 20) once defined it as meaning that 'a people or group possessing a definite territory may be autonomous in the sense of possessing a separate and distinct administrative structure and judicial system, determined by and intrinsic to that people or group.' Some years later, at the expert meeting on internal self-government in Nuuk, Greenland, Bennagen (1992: 72) outlined five operational features of such self-government:

- control of territory (expressed variously as ancestral domain, ancestral homeland, indigenous territory, etc.) and its natural resources, both surface and subsurface;
- legislative, executive, and judicial bodies, to include corresponding indigenous institutions;
- proper actual representation of the indigenous cultural communities in the various organs of power, not only in the autonomous territorial unit but also in the national Government;
- fiscal autonomy, including the power to raise revenues, a just share of national revenues, and a capable fiscal administration;
- respect, protection, and development of indigenous cultures.

More recently, Hoekema (1996) has sought to further develop the concept of internal political autonomy and self-government – the institutionally guaranteed capacity of a social entity or territory to rule itself within the ambit of sovereignty of a state – and to develop some criteria for the assessment of such an arrangement. In the first place he addresses the aspect of *formal political autonomy* which he defines as a legal regime, whereby (revocable or irrevocable) powers of self-government, including legislative competence, concerning one or more specified areas – within the overall constitutional make-up of the State in question – are conferred on a distinct group of individuals (defined by their ethnic origin and/or language, etc.) or on inhabitants of a specific and distinct territory.[11] Here political autonomy refers to a concept in constitutional law. The addition of a reference to a territorial form of self-government is meant to highlight the fact that self-government can come in several forms. One form is non-territorial, conferring some rights on an indigenous people independent of the place of residence, for example through mechanisms of positive discrimination where an indigenous council has a say in the implementation of such policies. The Saami parliaments in Scandinavia, which have some say in sectoral policies, are an example of such de-linking between self-government and territoriality.[12] The territory-based type of self-government can take two forms. One is what Hoekema calls 'ethnic self-government' in which, we might say, legal pluralism and the diversity of political institutions are institutionalized. The other form relies on the drawing of administrative boundaries in such a way that in practice chances are great that indigenous persons exercise the authority. Such a territory is seen as deserving a special status, although the institutional structure is modeled after established public bodies. This distinction corresponds largely to the distinction between direct and indirect consociation (cf. Assies, 1994).

Such arrangements, Hoekema argues, can be of a federal type or be adopted in a unitary state; a distinction that again converges with the distinction between direct and indirect consociation. In a federal state all constituent parts have a special status and are not subordinated to the central government but to the constitution. A variant is where one or some specific regions constitutionally receive a special status. Within unitary states, by contrast, decentralization would be the mechanism but then the powers delegated to local authorities can be diminished or even (formally) abolished by the central government and/or legislature.

A second level of analysis is that of *effective political autonomy*, which refers to the way in which real decision-making powers are distributed among indigenous incumbents of official positions, as well as (other) indigenous leaders on the one hand, and outside authorities and functionaries on the other. The point of making the distinction between formal and effective political autonomy is that one can come across cases of effective autonomy without much formal autonomy as well as cases of hardly effective formal autonomy.

A third level of analysis is that of *autonomy as the freedom of a social collectivity to choose its own destiny* and concerns the process of being autonomous, the exercise of autonomy itself. This is a socio-cultural criterion to assess if effective political autonomy reflects and promotes a social process of self-determination of the people in question. Does it serve the best interests of the people? Is the people 'really' choosing freely its own destiny? Of course, Hoekema points out, answering such questions is fraught with practical and epistemological problems, but these are questions that have to be posed. What if, for example, effective political autonomy benefits only a tiny elite or promotes the displacement of traditional authorities by younger indigenous people more capable in dealing with the administrative structures and functionaries of the state? Could this not result in more subtle forms of domination than outright oppression through a sort of 'colonization of the mind' and, to put it otherwise, a disempowerment of a people in choosing its own destiny?

Such an approach seems to be useful. One might argue, for example, that until now indigenous communities or peoples have managed to maintain a certain effective autonomy despite efforts by the state to encroach upon it. States now have opted for formal recognition. Does this make autonomy more effective and does it augment the scope for self-determination? This type of question also informs the current debate over 'neoliberal multiculturalism' (Gustafson, 2002; Hale, 2002) in which the recognition of indigenous peoples' rights is embedded in, and restricted by, the policies of decentralization recommended by the multilateral development agencies as part of their post-Washington Consensus 'second generation' structural adjustment policies.

Mechanisms like ILO Convention 169 and constitutional reforms provide the legal framework through which the politics of recognition are operated. They suggest some degree of recognition of territorial claims and claims to recognition of indigenous systems of authority and forms of administering justice. This would occur through the formalization of regimes that outline the competencies, ambit and scope of 'internal autonomy' and its relation to the state.

Constitutional reforms and autonomies

In her overview of Latin American constitutions and indigenous rights Van Cott (2000: 266–268) finds that only in four cases is an autonomy regime included, while in a later article she identifies five cases (Van Cott, 2001). More recently, Mendoza (n.d.: 8) has presented an overview similar to the one drawn up by Van Cott (2000: 266–268). The overview I present in Table 8.1 here is inspired by these overviews but has been revised and updated with the help of the database on indigenous legislation of the Inter-American Development Bank (IADB, 2003).[13] It should be clear that in many cases we confront a situation of what Van Cott (2000) calls a 'rhetorical recognition of multiculturalism.'[14] In my representation the recognition of territorial autonomy in Venezuela has received the benefit of the doubt. The 1999 Venezuelan Constitution includes an article that makes it possible to create a special regime for municipalities with an indigenous population (art. 169). It is not very clear what this eventually may imply. As we shall see, the wording used in constitutions often is deliberately ambivalent[15] and Venezuela's Article 169 is no exception, but read in conjunction with other articles it suggests that formal political autonomy may be granted.[16] Eventually the constitutional provision might, for example, have important effects in the state of Amazonas where nearly half of the population is indigenous and rural municipalities are overwhelmingly indigenous.

We thus find five cases where territorial autonomy is reflected in the constitution: Ecuador, Colombia, Nicaragua, Panama and Venezuela. The Panamanian and Colombian arrangements are examples of 'ethnic autonomy' whereas Nicaragua is a case of indirect consociation, while the case of Ecuador is inconclusive, as is the case of Venezuela. I will discuss the debate that is ongoing in Ecuador, but I will not discuss the Venezuelan case since at this stage hardly anything is known about the terms of debate over the possible implementation of some sort of autonomy regime.

Panama

Panama's first *comarca* was created in the wake of the 1925 Kuna revolt against the attempts at forced assimilation by the Panamanian state (Howe, 1998).[18] A peace treaty was signed under USA supervision,

Table 8.1 Latin American constitutions and indigenous rights

	Venezuela	Ecuador	Colombia	Nicaragua	Peru	Paraguay	Brazil	Mexico	Panama	Guatemala	Bolivia	Argentina	Total
Recognition of collective property of indigenous lands	yes	yes	yes	yes	yes	yes	yes	yes	yes	yes	yes	yes	12
Recognition of multiethnic and pluricultural reality	yes	yes	yes	yes	yes	yes	yes	yes	yes	yes	yes	no	11
Bilingual education	yes	yes	yes	yes	yes	yes	yes	yes	yes	yes	no	yes	11
Recognition of customary law	yes	yes	yes	yes	yes	yes	no	yes	no	no	yes	no	8
Official indigenous languages	yes	yes	yes	yes	yes	yes	no	no	no	no	no	no	6
Consultation for natural resource exploitation	yes	yes	yes	no	no	no	yes	no	no	no	yes	yes	6
Territorial autonomy	yes	yes	yes	yes	no	no	no	no	yes	no	no	no	5
Protection of collective intellectual property rights	yes	yes	no	no	no	no	no	no	no	no	no	no	2
Political participation and representation[17]	yes	no	yes	no	no	no	no	no	no	no	no	no	2
Number of reforms adopted by each state	9	8	8	6	5	5	4	4	4	3	3	3	–

recognizing the autonomy of the Kuna region without much specification. In 1930 a reserve was created which eight years later was transformed into the Comarca de San Blas. It comprises some 50 small islands and a strip of land on Panama's east coast, ending at the Colombian border. Meanwhile, in the wake of the revolt the Kuna undertook a comprehensive, planned reorganization of their social system under the leadership of their traditional authorities. After factional divisions had been overcome, in 1945 this process resulted in the drawing up of an Organic Charter of San Blas, which specified the governmental structure of the local community congresses, stipulated that there would be three principal *caciques* and created a Kuna General Congress.[19] In 1953 a Panamanian law organized the San Blas Comarca (or Kuna Yala),[20] detailed the areas of Kuna autonomy and recognized the political structure as established in the 1945 Organic Charter. The comarca is officially administered by a government-appointed *Intendente* while the Kuna authorities, according to rank, were given the status of 'police inspectors' on the state payroll (*América Indígena*, 1995; Pérez, 1998, Turpana, 1994).

Although this construction has been a source of friction, the Kuna have managed to defend their land and self-government. Kuna autonomy has regularly come under pressure from different sides. Tourism is one of the problems that generated tensions from the 1960s onward. North American tourist ventures were established in the late 1960s with the permission of the Kuna chiefs, but without permission from the General Congress. By 1981 the two resorts were closed after having been attacked and torched by groups of Kuna. Similarly, the Panamanian government has sought to sponsor large-scale projects such as a resort hotel on an artificial island in Kuna territory, which in the late 1970s led to a deep crisis between the government, the Kuna Congress and the *caciques*, who had endorsed feasibility studies without Congress permission. By the mid 1990s the government developed plans to construct a military base in Kuna territory to counter drug trade and armed intrusions from Colombia. As a result of opposition from the Kuna the project finally was shelved. Intrusions by Colombian guerrilla bands, groups of gold-miners and drug-traders constitute further problems, as well as the incursions of mestizo peasants in search of land. The latter problem was countered with the much-praised PEMASKY project, a cooperative effort between the Kuna Congress and environmentalist NGOs to establish a self-managed forest-reserve. The project managed to halt the invasion by peasants and buy out those already established, but failed to achieve its broader aims (Arias and Chapin, 1998; Howe, 2002).

Meanwhile, the Kuna are attempting to strengthen their self-government structures and improve administrative continuity. Also, at least since the early 1980s attempts have been made to update the Kuna Organic Charter and the 1953 enabling legislation, but such attempts have not met with government support (*América Indígena*, 1995; Howe,

2002). Neither has the government been responsive to demands that it ratify ILO Convention 169.

The Comarca Kuna Yala and its mode of governance has stood as a model for the creation of other *comarcas* in Panama, which by 2000 numbered five. Two of them are Kuna *comarcas* (1996, 2000) on the mainland and two others were created for the Emberá-Wounaan (1983) and the Ngöbe-Buglé (1997). One of the problems with introducing this form of self-government for the latter groups is that the governance structure of the Kuna Organic Charter was copied, although it does not fit their modes of social and political organization.

Colombia

Colombia is the other case where we find a direct consociation model of formal political autonomy, which was instituted through the 1991 Constitution.[21] That same year the country ratified ILO Convention 169. Colombia counts over 80 indigenous peoples, which together count a little under 800,000 persons and make up nearly two percent of the total population. Despite this small number indigenous representatives came to play a key role in the constitutional process and Colombia's indigenous peoples gained an important set of rights (Van Cott, 2000). The *resguardos* were recognized as inalienable collective property governed by indigenous *cabildos* (councils) according to the regulations and customary practice of the indigenous communities.

Resguardos, governed by *cabildos*, had first been created under colonial rule. During the nineteenth century attempts were made to extinguish them until, in 1890, the process was temporarily stalled by Law 89, which recognized the existence of the *resguardos* and *cabildos* for the time being. Nevertheless, *resguardos* continued to be divided up[22] and by the 1960s only some 70 still existed. In 1961, encouraged by the Alliance for Progress, an agrarian reform law was passed and a year later the *Instituto Colombiano de Reforma Agraria* (INCORA) was created. In the late 1960s the new institute became more active under the pressure of emerging indigenous and peasant movements that started to implement a land reform of their own through invasions.[23] Beginning in the early 1980s the still existing *resguardos* were consolidated and new ones were created. Besides the *resguardos*, from 1967 onward often very large 'reserves' were formed in the Amazon region, sometimes containing various indigenous peoples. After the promulgation of the 1991 Constitution these 'reserves' were converted into *resguardos* and thus became the collective property of their inhabitants. By the early 1990s some 400 *resguardos* existed and after the promulgation of the new Constitution the number grew to 638 in 2001. By then, the *resguardos* covered some 31 million hectares, about a quarter of the national territory. 85 percent of this total is located in the Amazon region, which houses 9 percent of the total indigenous population, divided into 58 peoples.[24] It is estimated that 87 percent of the indigenous population lives in the *resguardos* (Arango and Sánchez, 2002; Colombia, 1995; Pineda, 2001: 36–37).

The 1991 Constitution not only consolidated the *resguardos* and recognized *cabildos*, but specified a further set of rights. Indigenous authorities have the right to exercise jurisdiction in the *resguardos* according to their own norms and procedures (special jurisdiction) (art. 246), to apply legal norms of land use and population in their territories, to design and implement development plans, to promote public investment, to receive and administer (financial) resources, to conserve natural resources, to coordinate projects of the communities in their territory, to cooperate with the maintenance of public order following the instructions and dispositions of the national government and to represent their territories to the national government (art. 330). Furthermore, it was stipulated that statutory law should determine which *resguardos* will be given a status equal to that of the municipalities and in this way receive a portion of the national income.[25] The share of national income going to municipalities or their equivalents would rise to 22 percent in 2002 (art. 357).

According to another article in the Constitution departments, districts, municipalities and indigenous territories are considered *entidades territoriales* and will be autonomous within the limits set by the Constitution and the law (art. 286). They are entitled to: 1. govern themselves through their own authorities; 2. exercise the competencies that correspond to them; 3. administrate resources and establish taxes necessary to fulfill their functions; 4. partake in national tax-revenues (art. 287).

The Constitution as well envisions the creation of *Entidades Territoriales Indígenas* (ETIs) (art. 329) in the context of a *Ley Orgánica de Ordenamiento Territorial*. The idea was that the ETIs would be something like autonomous indigenous regions and this was strongly advocated by indigenous representatives in the constituent assembly (Cepeda, 2001: 160–170). The proposal, however, met with strong opposition and was only introduced in the constitution at the last minute in very ambiguous terms (Van Cott, 2000: 94–95).

The new constitution also created a special electoral district by which two seats in the national Senate are reserved for indigenous representatives (art. 117).[26]

Colombia's constitutional process responded to the mounting crisis in the country (Van Cott, 2000) and was not only influenced by indigenous delegates and their allies in the constitutional assembly but also by social movements, liberals and neoliberals who, for diverse motives, pushed for decentralization. The recognition of indigenous autonomy therefore should be viewed in this broader context of a decentralization drive and the attempts to end the violent conflicts plaguing the country.

Implementation of the reforms was facilitated by government commitment to the reform agenda, the rulings of the new Constitutional Court that often were in favor of indigenous peoples, and the strength of the indigenous movement and related political parties (Cepeda, 2001; Van Cott, 2000; 2002). Funds started to be disbursed in 1994 and by 1997 the *resguardos* were receiving approximately US$61,000 on average. This also has resulted in difficulties, however. Non-indigenous mayors or departmental governors act as intermediary recipients of the funds and the *resguardos* have to present an investment plan. In some cases these have not been duly transferred to the *resguardos* (Arango and Sánchez, 2002; Van Cott, 2002: 50–51).[27] Within the *resguardos* themselves the administrative capacity is unequal. The start of the transfers was accompanied by a series of seminars, workshops etc., which made one indigenous leader remark that 'nowadays, one needs a lot of time to be an Indian' (Padilla, 1995: 147). Such accommodation to administrative norms of the state perhaps is not simply bad in and of itself but, as Padilla (1995) argues, it has its drawbacks in that it tends to increase the possibilities for state intervention in the internal affairs of indigenous peoples and in requiring them to act according to state norms in the management of budgets, projects and development plans. Traditional knowledge and authority figures tend to be set aside and younger people, or even NGOs, assume the management of indigenous affairs (Padilla, 1996). Such 'normalization' diminishes the possibilities for freely choosing their own destiny.

The delegation of administrative affairs to the *resguardos* is based on the assumption that their self-government is organized according to the *cabildo*-model that has emerged in the Andes region since colonial times. This, however, is not always the case and, particularly in the Amazon region, this has created problems. Another case is that of the Wayúu who do not have a centralized political organization. The availability of funding triggered a genuine regional crisis when some Wayúu groups were qualified and others excluded (Pineda, 2001: 50).

This form of autonomy, in the context of state decentralization, thus may come as a mixed blessing. On the other hand, while the Gaviria government showed some commitment to the indigenous cause, since 1994 the hopes generated by the new constitution have been dashed. In the context of neoliberal policies and in response to the growing fiscal and political crisis the Colombian governments have sought to implement mega-projects for natural resource exploitation (oil, minerals, hydroelectricity, African palm) that often affect indigenous peoples. By the late 1990s the requirements for granting licences for natural resource exploitation on indigenous territories were relaxed and the government sought to condition the granting of *resguardo* lands to the prior approval of production projects based on 'strategic alliances' with the private sector. Agroindustrial projects have become key to the Plan Colombia. Such policies and above all the escalation of armed conflict threaten the very existence of the indigenous peoples of Colombia (Jackson, 2002).

On the other hand, as noted, the 1991 Constitution foresees the creation of a new type of territorial entity, the ETI, albeit in very ambiguous terms. Some efforts to define such ETIs were made with the support of the PNUD and in cooperation with the ONIC but soon the process stalled. By 2001, however, the government had launched a new initiative to formulate a *Ley Orgánica de Ordenamiento Territorial* (LOOT). This initiative plays on the ambiguity of the constitution. Whereas the ONIC would argue that Article 286 implies the automatic recognition of *resguardos* as indigenous territorial entities and that Article 329 provides for the creation of regions comprising several *resguardos* or perhaps some sort of multiethnic regions, the government project argues that the two articles should be related, with nefarious implications for the status of the *resguardos* because it introduces population size (>3,000 inhabitants) or surface (>80,000 hectares) as criteria for the recognition of territorial entities of whatever type.[28] Only 74 *resguardos* comply with one or both of these criteria. They house nearly 70 percent of the people living in *resguardos* and represent some 85 percent of the total area covered by *resguardos*. 40 percent of the indigenous population of the country, that is including those not living in *resguardos*, would be barred from the possibility to live in an *Entidad Territorial Indígena* (ETI) (Arango and Sánchez, 2002). This is what might be called a 'bitter harvest' of indigenous participation in the confection of the 1991 constitution and the subsequent neoliberal and increasingly right-wing implementation of this constitution.

Ecuador

Ecuador's indigenous peoples began creating new organizations in the 1960s and in 1986 formed the umbrella organization *Confederación de Nacionalidades Indígenas del Ecuador* (CONAIE), one of the strongest indigenous organizations in Latin America.[29] In 1990 a *Levantamiento General* made the indigenous cause a national concern and was followed by various other large mobilizations throughout the decade. In 1994 the organization launched its political platform in which it demanded a new constitution (CONAIE, 1994). CONAIE played a key role in the ousting of President Abdalá Bucaram in 1997 and, through the related Pachakutik political party, successfully pressured for the convocation of a constituent assembly that produced a new Constitution in June 1998 (Espinosa, 2000; Macdonald, 2002; Van Cott, 2002). ILO Convention 169 was ratified that same year.

To pressure for the convocation of a Constituent Assembly CONAIE and other social movements organized a 'People's Assembly' of their own to develop a proposal for a new constitution. The assembly started its work on October 12, Columbus Day, and by mid December, just before the official Constituent Assembly began to meet, the People's Assembly approved a *Proyecto de Constitución del Estado Plurinacional de Ecuador* (CONAIE, 1998). In early January this project was officially presented in the National Constituent Assembly.

As a result of such pressure and the presence of Pachakutik delegates in the official assembly the new constitution came to include some of the viewpoints of the indigenous movement. In its first article it declares the Ecuadorian state to be pluricultural and multiethnic. It also is the first Latin American constitution that includes the Quechua moral principles *ama quilla, ama lulla, ama shua* (don't be lazy, don't lie, don't steal) (art. 97). The idea of a multinational state advocated by CONAIE, however, was only vaguely reflected in an article, which speaks of 'indigenous peoples, who define themselves as nationalities' (art. 83). The next article stipulates a series of collective rights of indigenous and Afro-Ecuadorian peoples (art. 84) and the chapter on the territorial organization of the state and decentralization introduces the possibility of creating ethnically defined territorial circumscriptions (art. 224).

Despite the multinational rhetoric of CONAIE and its allies and despite the fact that the proposal of the People's Assembly spoke of the 'territories of the indigenous nationalities' and of 'territories of the black comarcas,' very little of all this was concretely reflected in the new constitution except for the mention of the 'territorial circumscriptions' to be created by law. Overall, however, the new constitution is more concerned with decentralization and hardly modifies the territorial organization of the state.

This can be attributed to various factors. For most political actors in Ecuador the theme of decentralization was secondary and was mostly promoted by the multilateral banking agencies. In 1997 a law was adopted according to which by 2000 15 percent of the national budget was to be assigned to the 'sectional governments.'[30] As far as the autonomy theme is present, it is mostly related to Guayaquil regionalist demands for autonomy for the Guayas Province motivated by the wish not to share taxes generated there with the other provinces. This may be one reason for the indigenous movement not to play out the autonomy theme.[31] Although there is quite some debate over decentralization and a reordering of the country's administrative structure there is hardly any consensus, and in the end the Constituent Assembly left the existing structure of provinces, cantons and *parroquias* (parishes) untouched. It only attempted a somewhat more specific definition of competencies, but they remain vague and ill defined (León, 1998).

On the other hand, there is no consensus within the indigenous movement and a variety of proposals to implement 'territorial circumscriptions' is in circulation. The lack of consensus is related to rivalries within and between movements and to different views of a possible autonomy regime.[32] Proposals that go in the direction of democratization and multiethnicity vie with proposals that are based on a monoethnic vision.[33] Neither is it clear whether the circumscriptions should coincide with one of the existing levels of the administrative structure or constitute a new level with distinct functions (Trujillo, 2000; Van Cott, 2002). This is further complicated by regional differences. While in some regions, especially the Amazon region, indigenous peoples occupy continuous territories, the situation is much more complex in the highlands.[34] While debate is ongoing the Pachakutik party has made important electoral gains, both on the national and the sub-national level. In 2000 it won the elections for prefects in 5 provinces as well as 27 municipalities giving rise to attempts to create alternative forms of local government without modifying the institutional structure of the provinces and cantons. In this context the tendency seems to be to assimilate the indigenous territorial circumscriptions to the local community level and the *juntas parroquiales*.[35]

Meanwhile, the trajectory of the indigenous movement has been marked by the January 2000 uprising, which ended the Mahuad government and briefly brought CONAIE leader Antonio Vargas to the presidency. New protests against the neoliberal policies of the Noboa government took place in February 2001 and in the 2002 elections Lucio Gutiérrez, the colonel who had led the lower-rank military in the ousting of Mahuad, was elected to the presidency with strong support from the indigenous population. The initial honeymoon soon was over, however, and by April 2003 the indigenous movement started to pressure its representatives within the new government to withdraw if no clear break was made with IMF policies and free trade area initiatives. A few months later the alliance with Gutiérrez broke down.

Nicaragua

Nicaragua's Atlantic coast region, which comprises about half of the country's surface, has had a history that sets it apart from the rest of the country. Whereas the west of the country was occupied by Spanish colonial forces on the less accessible Atlantic coast the indigenous population forged alliances with pirates from various European countries and in 1687 the British crowned a Miskito 'king' whereby the region became a British protectorate. That ended in 1860 when, after rivalries with the USA, the British signed a treaty by which the region was returned to Nicaragua. A border conflict with Honduras in 1894 spurred the military incorporation of the region and brought an end to the Miskito 'kingdom.' By the mid nineteenth century the Moravian Church established itself in the region and became a principal structure of governance. The regional economy was largely dominated by US interests that exploited wood and minerals and established banana plantations (Standard Fruit).

The autonomy regime for the region is the outcome of the conflict with the Sandinista revolutionary government that replaced the Somoza dictatorship in 1979. Although relations with the Sandinistas initially seemed promising they soon deteriorated. The introduction of Spanish language alphabetization in a region where indigenous languages and English predominated was one issue; attempts to incorporate the region and its natural resources to the benefit of the revolutionary nation was another. Suspicions about local separatism led the Sandinistas to arrest local indigenous leaders and tensions were exacerbated by the 1982 Sandinista decision to evacuate Miskito villages in the border region with Honduras, which had become a center of *contra* attacks and alliance-making with the indigenous leadership, sponsored by the Reagan administration.[36] In response the Sandinista government changed its attitude and started negotiating an autonomy statute for the region in the context of a pacification strategy (Scherrer, 1994).

The changes in the constitution and the autonomy statute were achieved in 1987.[37] Initial high-level negotiations between the government and one of the indigenous organizations broke off five months after the cease-fire in 1985. Both the Sandinistas and the leadership of the organization had their reasons for not continuing these negotiations. The Sandinista then initiated a broad consultation process with the local population, which although skeptical was willing to accept what the government had to offer (Hale, 1996). The outcomes of the process were approved during a mass meeting in April 1987.[38] The autonomy statute created two 45+ seat[39] autonomous regional councils to govern the autonomous regions of the north Atlantic coast (RAAN) and the south Atlantic coast (RAAS), to be elected by popular vote. The councils, in turn, elect a governing board and a coordinator (*gobernador*). Each of the indigenous peoples in the regions, four and six in RAAN and RAAS respectively, should have at least one representative on the governing board to assure representation of the smaller groups.[40] Candidates can either be presented by political parties or by *grupos de suscripción popular* (popular lists), which was meant to allow for the formation and participation of regional political organizations. The regions, in turn, are subdivided into municipalities. The statute furthermore incorporates a series of economic, cultural, juridical and ecological rights.[41] The statute is only a first step and should be complemented by further regulatory legislation.

The autonomy granted by the statute is rather relative. The regional councils do not have a budget of their own but present a proposal to the central government. They may initiate social, cultural and economic projects, but only on the basis of regional taxes to be established conforming to state laws and the promotion of regional market integration. For other development programs they participate in design or execution or administrate programs in coordination with state agencies. The regions share in the benefits deriving from natural resource exploitation, but the share they receive is not specified. And although mention is made of 'communal authorities' this does not go beyond a token recognition of indigenous authorities or political institutions (Acosta, 1996; Cunningham, 1998; Scherrer, 1994).

Implementation of the autonomy regime only slowly got under way due to the difficult circumstances in the region and factional struggles among indigenous organizations, some siding with the Sandinistas and others with the opposition. For their part, the Sandinistas had an interest in postponing elections for the councils and implementing development projects and social services in the meantime to garner sympathy among the population. The elections were only held in 1990 and then coincided with the national elections in which the Sandinistas were defeated by the *Unión Nacional Opositora* (UNO) coalition. None of the parties in the new government coalition had any sympathy for the autonomy statute. Moreover, at the regional level, one of the leaders of the autonomy movement, Brooklyn Rivera, had at the last moment declared support for the UNO in return for promises to gain a cabinet post. Rivera became minister of a new government agency, the *Instituto Nicaragüense de Desarrollo de las Regiones Autónomos* (INDERA). INDERA was not only assigned a budget beside which the budget allocated to the regional councils paled but it also was given decision powers over natural resources in the autonomous regions which turned their autonomy into a scam. The effective implementation of an autonomy regime under new governments of a neoliberal, and paradoxically[42] centralizing, orientation thus was prone to generate a series of conflicts and crises.

The first years after the 1990 election of regional councils were characterized by strong polarization. In the RAAS the UNO majority rejected any cooperation with the nearly equally strong Sandinista delegation. Although in subsequent elections, held every four years, *grupos de subscripción popular* gained some influence national level parties continued to dominate regional politics. A crisis in the RAAN council, which failed to meet throughout May 1999 to May 2000, reflected national level rivalries and was finally resolved through a pact between the Sandinistas and the *Partido Liberal Constitucional* (PLC). Similarly, conflicts between the councils and the coordinators reflected national level loyalties. Such political polarization often virtually paralyzed the regional councils and led traditional authorities, Councils of Elders, to call for solutions. Thus, paradoxically, the non-recognition of traditional authorities enhanced their respectability.

Despite such problems the regional councils did not altogether fail to function and in 1993 they proposed regulatory legislation for the 1987 autonomy statute. In 1998 a new proposal was presented as a citizen's initiative, supported by 12,000 signatures, but national governments have until now lacked the political will to consider the proposal. The absence of regulation translates into problems of institutionalization and accountability of the autonomous governance structure. It also is reflected in the relations between the regional structures and the central government, which became more conflictive under the Alemán government (1997–2001) that sought to recentralize power in the executive (Cunningham, 1998; Díaz-Polanco, 1999; MIN/CALPI, 2000; Ortega, 1996).

Natural resource management, in particular, is an area of conflict. One of the best-known cases is that of the community of Awas Tingni, which saw its lands invaded by the Korean lumbering enterprise SOLCARSA. A concession had been granted by the Ministry of the Environment and Natural Resources (MARENA) with the support of the governing board of the RAAN. Although the Supreme Court of Justice decided in 1997 that the concession was illegal, MARENA pressured the RAAN regional council into endorsing it. In the face of the laxity of the justice system, to which it appealed on various occasions, the Awas Tingni community appealed to the Inter-American Commission for Human Rights. In an unprecedented decision in 2001 the Commission ruled in favor of the community and ordered the Nicaraguan government to delimit and title community lands (Acosta, 2000). To date the government has failed to do so.[43] Nonetheless, by the end of 2002 a law on demarcation and titling of communal lands was approved and is expected to have some beneficial effects in the long run.

Conclusion

The last decades of the past century have seen important changes in the relation between indigenous peoples and the Latin American states. Formally, at least, the multicultural and pluriethnic composition of the populations has been recognized, but as Stavenhagen (2002:34) has put it, after these promising beginnings 'the going will be rough from now on.' The foregoing discussion confirms this view. In this chapter I focused on four cases of formal political autonomy regimes in Latin America. It should be noted, however, that there are other types of legislation that purport to enable indigenous self-determination. The 1994 Bolivian Law of Popular Participation is a case in point. However, although this law opened up some space for indigenous participation in local government it is essentially a decentralization measure in the context of neoliberal 'second generation' reform policies (Albó, 2002; Calla, 2000). Another example might be the Mexican state of Oaxaca, which in 1995 recognized the right of indigenous communities to elect their authorities according to customary practice. On the other hand, we might mention the self-styled effective autonomy of the Zapatista communities and the *Regiones Autónomas Pluriétnicas* in Chiapas, which are inspired by the Nicaraguan model (Díaz-Polanco, 1997; Lopez y Rivas, 1995; Mattiace, Hernández and Rus, 2002).

Let us try to summarize some of the main points that emerge from the foregoing discussion in the light of the theoretical framework developed in the first part of this chapter, looking at the formal aspect, the scope of effective political autonomy and autonomy as empowerment or the freedom of a population to choose its own destiny (Table 8.2).

The comparison presented here is, of course, extremely crude, but nevertheless suggestive. In Panama we find an autonomy regime that has taken form since the 1920s, in the case of the Kuna, and which has

Table 8.2 Comparison of autonomy regimes in Latin America

	Panama	Colombia	Ecuador	Nicaragua
De jure				
Level of autonomy	Regional	Local, ETIs not implemented	Local, status of territorial circumscriptions unclear	Regional
Type of autonomy	Direct consociation	Direct consociation	Indirect consociation	Indirect consociation
De facto				
Control of territory	High	Declining	Moderate	Low, but perhaps increasing moderately
Institutional	High	Formally high	Not formal, but in practice	Low
Representation	Through established party system	Electoral district and own parties at national and municipal level	Through own political party and representation in government agencies	Through established parties but also through regional 'popular lists'
Fiscal autonomy	Somewhat	Formally recognized but declining	Municipal level 'alternative' government	Low, largely depending on paltry allocations
Respect	Moderate	Declining on the part of the state	Moderate	Low
Empowerment	Reasonable, probably increasing	Tenuous in a context of violence	Increasing	Low and disputed

allowed them to exercise a relatively high degree of what Bonfil Batalla (1981) has called 'cultural control.' Bonfil Batalla's scheme (Table 8.3) is helpful in framing the issues at hand.

The framework proposed by Bonfil Batalla can be combined with Barth's (1969) perspective on interethnic relations, which was subsequently taken up by Nagel and Snipp (1993) in their discussion of 'ethnic reorganization,' which includes forms of social, economic, political and cultural reorganization. Such frameworks highlight the dynamics of intercultural interaction and the degree of control over cultural change, or 'agency,' exercised by the 'subaltern' population. If we look at the cases under study from this perspective it becomes clear that the Kuna have achieved a relatively high degree of cultural control, blending autonomous culture with appropriated elements in a process of comprehensive reorganization of their social and political system led by their traditional authorities. Currently they are pushing for further internal reform and a clarification of their relation to the Panamanian state, a process that affects the framing of issues for the other indigenous peoples in the country who, more recently, saw their autonomy condoned.

If we look at the formal aspects of the four cases presented here we should first of all note the difference in scale. In Panama and Nicaragua we find regional level autonomy, in the first case monoethnic and in the second case pluriethnic. In Colombia we have an intermediary situation in the sense that some *resguardos* are quite large, comprise several communities and sometimes are pluriethnic. The promise held out by the ETI formula however did not materialize and, as we saw, may actually be turned against *resguardo* autonomy. In the case of Ecuador the status of indigenous territorial circumscriptions remains undefined, but we have noted that, particularly in the Andes region, they tend to be assimilated to the lowest level of the institutional state structure. It would rather be a matter of labeling specific *parroquias* 'indigenous.'

To be sure, each of these cases should be considered against the background of the specific national context. That might explain, for example, why in Ecuador regional autonomy is not a big issue in the Andean context and working through the existing institutional structure of municipal government seems to be a viable option. Moreover, the indigenous

Table 8.3 'Cultural control'

Cultural elements	Decisions	
	Own	*Alien*
Own	Autonomous culture	Alienated culture
Alien	Appropriated culture	Imposed culture

Source: Bonfil Batalla, 1981: 50.

movement is strong at the national level and heavily engaged in national politics and in the implementation of policies through CODENPE, where it is strongly represented on the governing board. The engagement in national politics also means that popular demands and demands for democratization are balanced with specific ethnic demands. The issue of the scale of autonomy, however, is not altogether irrelevant. Díaz-Polanco (1997: 27–31) talks of the 'myth of the invincible community' to argue in favor of regional autonomy. The community, he argues, is not as invincible as some would claim but rather is a last line of resistance. Creating an additional level of supra-community administrative organization would contribute to strengthening the local level and thus contribute to effective autonomy; hence his defense of regional autonomy schemes.

Looking at the question of effective autonomy we can combine the notion with Bennagen's operational features of self-government. Probably we should say that the Kuna have succeeded in defending a rather high level of effective autonomy while at the same time establishing a pragmatic, though not tension-free, working relationship with the Panamanian state. Above all they have managed to ward off state-imposed projects for natural resource exploitation and tourism development. They also largely control their internal structures of governance and the way they adapt them to changing circumstances. They have some capacity to raise local taxes and to demand compensation for certain uses of their territory (e.g. telephone or electricity cables). By contrast, natural resource use is a highly contested issue in Nicaragua where the autonomy regime is weakly institutionalized and poorly respected by the national governments. Some advances can be signaled (e.g. local universities) and political and interethnic polarization has been held in check (Cunningham, 1998). Nonetheless, the political infighting and the consequent virtual paralysis of the autonomous councils is resulting in a decreasing interest among the local population, which is reflected in the abstention rates in regional elections, which went from 22 percent in 1990 to 63 percent in 2002, though it should be noted that abstention is significantly higher among the mestizos than among the indigenous population. The difficulties in substantiating autonomy and the increasingly tense relations with the national government have led the Miskito Council of Elders to adopt a radical stance advocating the creation of an independent state (Marshall and Gurr, 2003: 58).

In Colombia and Ecuador issues of natural resource use also are prominent. In both cases consultation procedures have been introduced. How sound such procedures are is controversial. In the case of the U'wa in Colombia a ruling by the Constitutional Court in favor of the U'wa, who rejected oil exploration in their territory, was overruled by the Council of State in 1997. As noted, since 1994 Colombian governments have sought to reverse and reduce the advances made possible by the 1991 Constitution and their policies may be characterized as a case of 'neoliberal multiculturalism' and token recognition of the rights of indigenous peoples. While in nearly all cases the exploitation of subsoil resources is a source of conflict, the overlap of conservation areas and national parks with indigenous territories is another source of friction and dispute over the management of surface resources.

With regard to natural resource use and previous consultation the 'colonization of the mind' theme has recently been taken up by Ramírez (2002), in a, in my opinion, somewhat perverse way, in relation to oil exploitation in Colombia. She argues that in such consultations local leaderships and traditional authorities tend to be displaced by new ' "indigenous elites" – state sponsored leaders' – and that regional and national level leaders overruled the decisions made by local traditional authorities. A local organization had negotiated a US$ 25,000 'major integral development plan'[44] with an oil company in exchange for allowing exploitation. This was vetoed after the intervention of a national-level ONIC leader. It is not the place here to go into the details of the case, but rather to point to Wray's (2000) discussion of the logic of previous consultation in Ecuador. She shows how oil companies seek to present segmented information that does not reveal the full potential impact and how they seek to come to agreements with different groups, playing them off against each other. In such circumstances one cannot be too sure that the outcome is in the best interest of a local community and the intervention of a higher level organization may well be desirable. That is to say that somewhat colonized minds may be required to see the dangers of negotiating with powerful interested parties. The improvement of previous consultation procedures is an ongoing and controversial process and a strengthening of the parties that negotiate from a disadvantaged position is badly needed to assure that they have more effective control over their destiny.

The recognition of indigenous institutions is related to the formal features of the autonomy regime, whether it follows a direct or indirect consociation model. The situation on the ground can be highly complex, however. While in Panama and Colombia a direct consociation model has been adopted formally, we also have noted that the Kuna charter with its Congress model and the *cabildo* form of government have provided models that have been applied to situations where other forms of indigenous organization exist. On the other hand, in Ecuador indigenous forms of organization coexist and interact with municipal organization, while in Nicaragua the relation between indigenous institutions and the regional and national government is fraught with tension and conflict. While we can say that much, it should be noted that it is difficult to generalize because situations vary by region, particularly in the cases of Ecuador and Colombia where the differences between the Andean highlands and the Amazonian lowlands with their distinct modes of indigenous organization should be taken into account. Furthermore, regarding the Colombian case we have noted that the possibilities for effective self-government tend to be undermined by new legislation and the freedom of peoples to choose their own destiny is increasingly hedged in by the attempts to incorporate the *resguardos* into the formal administrative structure of the state and its supervisors. Although more funding has been reaching the *resguardos* and has contributed to the improvement of some conditions it tends to come at the price of an imposed administrative culture, particularly in the Amazon region. The escalation of violence further reduces the scope for effective self-government and the pursuit of a self-chosen destiny.

As to political involvement and representation in state structures Iturralde (1997) has pointed to the dynamic of indigenous political organization and argues that the articulation of a political platform tends to involve a maximization and juridization of demands and that this creates tensions with the local organizations characterized by more immediate production and welfare oriented concerns. More generally, the process of political organization is fraught with paradoxes and presents the indigenous movements with a series of challenges. It is beyond the scope of this article to fully discuss such issues, but let me briefly enumerate some. For one thing, there is the relationship between leadership and bases. This involves the process of class differentiation among indigenous peoples. The emergence of the new movements was related to the emergence of something like a native middle class, which certainly is being empowered through the dialectics between identity politics and the politics of recognition. At the same time this affected organizational structures and created tensions between traditional authority structures and emerging leaderships of new organizations. In his classic essay, Barth (1969: 35) had already observed that in situations of conflict the opposed parties tend to become structurally similar and differentiated only by a few clear criteria. One paradox here seems to be that while this creates tensions between traditional authority structures and emerging organizational structures it also spurs 'strategic essentializing' and a renewed emphasis on 'tradition' which, formally at least, might empower traditional authorities.[45] The tension between the Kuna Congress and their traditional authorities illustrates the complexity of the issue and it refers back to my discussion of the dynamics of previous consultation. The Kuna Congress repeatedly disavowed decisions made by the traditional authorities and this highlights the issue of internal democracy of the indigenous movements, or more precisely what the Zapatistas call *mandar obedeciendo*. In the case of the Kuna Congress we might say that on some occasions the voice of those whose minds were a bit more 'colonialized' strengthened self-determination.

These considerations bring us back to Hoekema's (1996) thoughts on empowerment. Does the recognition of indigenous rights really enfranchise a 'people' or does it only benefit a small elite? Again, it is difficult to generalize. As has been noted, the emergence of the new indigenous movements was related to processes of internal differentiation among indigenous peoples and to the rise of a new generation of indigenous intellectuals. At the same time the formation of the new movements imply processes of ethnic reorganization. Such processes are not tension-free and often involve a questioning of traditional power structures and the emergence of new power groups. How this actually works out can only be assessed on a case by case basis. Quite probably the difficulties in institutionalizing the Nicaraguan autonomy regime are related to interethnic and intraethnic friction, fuelled by the state and the party system. On the other hand, in the other three cases more solid forms of organization seem to balance or check such tensions, often through the introduction of elements of democracy, as is the case in the reorganization of Kuna governance and the establishment of the congress system. The involvement with 'wider society' and in the struggle for democracy and respect for human rights furthermore influences the processes of ethnic reorganization and it is in such a context that one can speak of 'reflexive identity politics' (Eriksen, 2001: 45). Such reflexivity leads to a questioning of certain features of indigenous cultures and issues like the position of indigenous women, human rights or the relation between ethnicity and class[46] are a matter of debate within indigenous movements.

Finally, one important feature of autonomy is that it is not about isolation but rather about the conditions for participation (Assies, van der Haar and Hoekema, 2000: 301). As noted, Colombia has reserved two seats in the senate for indigenous representatives. In that country indigenous political parties do reasonably well on the national level due to the sympathy vote of the urban electorate and actually three more indigenous senators have been elected while on the local level indigenous people have been elected mayor and into municipal councils (Arango and Sánchez, 2002). In Ecuador the Pachakutik party has become a strong political player. In Nicaragua and Panama indigenous representation is channeled through the established party system and we have noted the problems this can create in the case of Nicaragua. One challenge for such political involvement is to go beyond formulating national proposals for indigenous issues and to come up with indigenous proposals for national problems (Iturralde, 1997). Another, related, challenge is not to get trapped in the juridization of discourse. The framing of demands in terms of self-determination and the rights of peoples in quasi-international relations terminology may be helpful but it also has its limitations. One of these limitations is that the autonomy discourse makes it difficult to address the structural concerns that determine the role of indigenous peoples, such as overall fiscal, agrarian, transport, housing, educational and other economic and social policies (Plant, 2000: 42). In particular, the autonomy discourse, with its oftentimes rural bias, does not address the concerns of the increasing number of indigenous people living in urban areas. Such issues, as well as the question of the construction of pluriethnic regions, suggest that while autonomy and self-determination may be important, they should be embedded in a broader process of democratization, both formal and substantive, that empowers people to challenge 'neoliberal multiculturalism' as well as neoliberalism as such.

Notes

1 This chapter is a revised version of a paper delivered at the Second International Conference on Regional Autonomy of Ethnic Minorities, 12–17 June 2003, Uppsala University, Sweden & Åland, Finland. I thank Donna Lee Van Cott, André Hoekema, René Kuppe, Ana Irene Méndez, Joris van de Sandt and Diana Vinding for their helpful comments on earlier drafts and/or supplying me with additional material for writing this article.

2 Guatemala (1985), Brazil (1988), Nicaragua (1987, 1995), Colombia (1991), Mexico (1992, 2001), Paraguay (1992), Peru (1993), Argentina (1994), Bolivia (1994), Panama (1997), Ecuador (1998) and Venezuela (1999). Chile adopted special legislation in 1993.

3 ILO Convention 169 was ratified by Mexico (1990), Norway (1990), Colombia (1991), Bolivia (1991), Costa Rica (1993), Paraguay (1993), Peru (1994), Honduras (1995), Denmark (1996), Guatemala (1996), the Netherlands (1998), Fiji (1998), Ecuador (1998), Argentina (2000), Venezuela (2002), the Dominican Republic (2002) and Brazil (2002).

4 This reflects one of the, very gross, distinctions often made between the peoples of the highland regions and Meso-America and those of the Amazon region. The former often have extensively been involved in market relations and in forms of peasant trade unionism, either promoted by left-wing organizations or by developmentist states. The latter often are not sedentary, have not been involved in market relations on the same scale and have had little experience with peasant unionism. Their emergence and new visibility dates from the 1970s.

5 Liberation Theology is a current within the Catholic Church that emerged after the Second Vatican Council (1962–1965), which opened the way for dialogue with Marxism and dependency theory. In the late 1960s the Latin American Church officially adopted a 'preferential option for the poor.' Liberation Theology was extremely important in the opposition against authoritarian rule in a country like Brazil and the rights of indigenous peoples figured prominently on the agenda. One should also remember that the ground for the Chiapas rebellion in Mexico was partly prepared by Liberation Theology inspired missionary labor.

6 This, however, should not lead us to reduce the issue to ethnic identity and deny that class or other dimensions play a role. It is rather the intersection between different aspects such as ethnic identity, class, gender, religion, etc. that should be taken into account. The notion of 'being Indian again' is taken from Vázquez (1992).

7 Christopher Columbus 'discovered' the Americas in 1492. To celebrate the event Ibero-American diplomacy invented the lavishly-funded 'encounter,' which was an occasion for indigenous peoples and their allies to drum up (often literally) support for counter-manifestations and international networking.

8 This depends on the national constitutional systems of the respective states, and the way they address the incorporation or transformation of international obligations into domestic law. A recasting of the convention through legislation into domestic law may be required.

9 The Inter-American Development Bank (IADB) (2003) database allows for an assessment of congruence of national legislation with ILO Convention 169, which takes into account 36 key criteria.

10 For a discussion see Assies (1994). 'Internal self-determination' is something that stops short of secession but its scope and depth are ill defined as well as the way it relates to the state and to representation and participation in decision-making processes.

11 This definition slightly adapts an earlier definition by L. A. Rehof, one of the participants in the Nuuk meeting. The difference resides in the addition of 'or on inhabitants of a specific and distinct territory.'

12 It is important to note that such parliaments arose in the context of rather solid 'Welfare States' and that territoriality perhaps is an emerging issue related to a way of life (reindeer herding). In the Latin American context territoriality still is a central rhetoric issue, despite the fact that indigenous people are often highly deterritorialized as a result of temporary labor migration or definitive migration to urban areas where they may claim autonomous neighborhoods. The question of how to deal with such issues is pending in Latin America. Indigenous movement representatives, even if they have lived in urban areas for most of their lives, tend to adopt a romantic view of 'rural life' (interview with Nina Pacari, Quito, March 21, 2001). Rethinking such visions may be one of the main challenges for Latin American indigenous movements and political parties in times ahead.

13 This does not mean that I always follow the IADB classification. According to that classification, for example, the Bolivian Constitution declares the country plurilingual but, curiously for a country with a majority indigenous population, it does not say anything about the official use of indigenous languages. Similarly, the IADB index suggests that Mexico grant indigenous peoples legal status (*personalidad jurídica*) and regional autonomy, which is definitely not the case. The Mexican Constitution, reformed in 2001, speaks of indigenous communities as 'entities of public interest' and can be considered as a example of ambiguity. For Latin American legislation see also the compilation by González Guerra (1999).

14 The IADB (2003) database provides some insight into the actual impact of constitutional stipulations on primary and secondary legislation and on jurisprudence. The database uses 142 variables to compare national legislation and jurisprudence yielding an indigenous legislation index and a country ranking different from the one presented here. The difference partly reflects the greater sophistication of the IADB index but it also is suggestive of the problems of classification and comparison.

15 For an analysis of the wording used in Latin American constitutions see Méndez (2002). The ambivalence in wording makes it difficult to present a definitive overview of the rights 'granted' in the different constitutions. Panama's Constitution speaks of 'promoting' bilingual alphabetization and Mexico 'favors' bilingual and intercultural education. What words mean in practice depends on ongoing struggles over their interpretation.

16 Van Cott (2001) is more optimistic in this respect than Kuppe (2003), who highlights the ambiguities in Venezuela's constitution.

17 Institution of an 'indigenous circumscription' granting participation in the national congress.

18 The comarca has its antecedents going back to the times before Panama was separated from Colombia in 1903 to create the Canal.

19 Kuna governance is based on village meetings of a political-religious character. Each village has its principal *cacique* or *saila*, versed in Kuna lore. At the village

meetings he chants from a hammock in a sacral language and is interpreted by the *argar*. They are assisted by *sualibedis*, a sort of police who maintain order during the meetings and call the population to attend them. The General Congress meets at least twice a year and is made up of *sailas* and a variety of other delegates and invitees. Besides the General Congress, which is the highest political-administrative organism, there is a General Congress of Kuna Culture, which is of a more religious nature and which elects the three principal *caciques* (Saila Dummagan) who then are ratified by the General Congress and represent the Kuna in relation to the Panamanian state.

20 Only in 1998, after long-standing pressure from the Kuna, was the name changed to comarca Kuna Yala. Out of a total of 58,000 Kuna in Panama some 32,000 live in Kuna Yala (Howe, 2002).

21 After attempts by the executive to introduce a reform of the constitution had failed the student movement started a campaign in favor of a Constituent Assembly and a plebiscite was held alongside the 1990 presidential elections. The movement in favor of a reform was partly triggered by drug-trade related violence.

22 Between 1910 and 1918, resistance in the Cauca region was organized by the Quitín Lame movement, called after its leader, who between 1914 and 1916 led the movement in an armed rebellion.

23 In 1970, a government-sponsored *Asociación Nacional de Usuarios Campesinos* (ANUC) was formed, from which an independent shadow-ANUC soon split off and began land-invasions. A year later indigenous people in turn split off from this organization and formed the *Consejo Regional Indígena del Cauca* (CRIC) from which a nation-wide organization *Organización Nacional Indígena de Colombia* (ONIC) emerged in 1980. At the same time another movement emerged that became known as the *Movimiento de Autoridades Indígenas de Colombia* (MAIC), which criticized the CRIC leadership for its conceptualizations of territory and indigenous identity (Findji, 1992).

24 This is important to note since it also suggests that the creation of *resguardos* has not resolved problems of land concentration in other regions, particularly in the Andes region (Arango and Sánchez, 2002). The creation of *resguardos* largely relied on the transfer of state lands and much less on redistribution.

25 This stipulation was eliminated in 2001.

26 An arrangement only matched by Venezuela's 1999 Constitution. For a discussion of political participation of indigenous people through party structures, whether linked to the indigenous movement or not, see Arango and Sánchez (2002). The success of such participation depends to a large measure on the support of non-indigenous voters in the large cities.

27 Law 60 from 1993, which regulated the transfer of funds to the *resguardos*, was replaced by a new Law 715 in 2001. Both laws expressly stipulate the areas in which transfer funds should be invested (Arango and Sánchez, 2002).

28 By 2001 the government had dropped an earlier proposal (DNP-UDT, 1999) according to which all *resguardos* would be given a status equal to municipalities and receive funding on that basis.

29 CONAIE was formed out of the *Confederación de Nacionalidades Indígenas de la Amazonía Ecuatoriana* (CONFENIAE) and the Andean *Ecuador Runacunapac Riccharimui* (ECUARUNARI) and in 1997 was joined by the *Coordinadora de Organizaciones Indígenas de la Costa Ecuatoriana* (COINCE). Besides CONAIE exist two rival organizations, the *Federación Ecuatoriana de Indígenas Evangélicos* (FEINE) and the *Federación Nacional de Organizaciones Campesinos, Indígenas y Negros* (FENOCIN). Ecuador counts 12 indigenous 'nationalities' and one of them, the Quichua, who are the most numerous, is in turn subdivided in a dozen 'peoples.' Since each of these peoples is represented in the CONAIE, and in

relations with government agencies in this manner the Quichua balance their numerical majority against the other smaller nationalities.

30 'Sectional governments' are the 22 provinces and the 215 cantons (municipalities). Within the municipalities there are *parroquias* (parishes). According to the constitution the provinces and cantons enjoy full autonomy.

31 Interview with Antonio Vargas, CONAIE President, Quito, March 21, 2001.

32 Such rivalries are also related to competition over power shares in the *Consejo de Desarrollo de las Nacionalidades y Pueblos del Ecuador* (CODENPE), a semi-government agency responsible for a broad range of policies concerning indigenous peoples that was established in 1998, replacing earlier agencies (Van Cott, 2002).

33 Interview with Miguel Lluco, General Coordinator of the Movimiento Pachakutik, Quito, March 20, 2001. In this interview Lluco clearly expresses his doubts about the territorial circumscriptions and asserts that they might be a mechanism of self-isolation. On the other hand he stresses participation in elections and points out that the new constitution introduced the elections for *juntas parroquiales* which were first held in 2000.

34 Interview with Nina Pacari, national deputy for the Pachaktik movement, Quito, March 21, 2001. In this interview Pacari furthermore argues that the theme of territorial circumscriptions still requires debate and points to the issue of the rights of non-indigenous minorities within such circumscriptions. Whereas she argues that in the Amazonian context larger regions might be feasible in the Andes context, the *juntas parroquiales* might want to denominate themselves *circumscripciones territoriales indígenas*. She attributes the lack of progress in the discussion over the circumscriptions to the priority accorded to the confection of a Law on the Indigenous Nationalities and Peoples, which basically would regulate their relations to state agencies with CONAIE as an intermediary instance.

Where territories are concerned it should be noted that some territories have been granted in the 1990s in the Amazon region but that this has occurred in an ad hoc manner and without an adequate legal or institutional framework. In the Andes individual titling took place in the context of the agrarian reform legislation of the 1960s and 1970s (Plant and Hvalkof, 2002).

35 On the other hand, the movement of Afro-Ecuadorians has developed a proposal for territorial circumscriptions according to which regional territorial councils (of the *palenque*) should be created, which unite various local communities.

36 *Yapti Tasba Masraka nanih asla taranka* (Unity of Children of the Land, YATAMA) emerged in 1987 as an umbrella organization bringing together three existing organizations. For an account of the complexities of local politics and of factionalisms and realignments see Scherrer (1994).

37 In 1995 the constitution was modified. Although initially an attempt was made to reverse the autonomy stipulations of the 1987 constitution, this was impeded by a coalition among indigenous peoples and Sandinista representatives (Díaz-Polanco, 1999).

38 At the time ILO Convention 169 was not yet available as a frame of reference and, significantly, the post-Sandinista governments have not been inclined to ratify it (MIN/CALPI, 2000). In the negotiations over the autonomy statute the Sandinista leadership rejected the ethnic autonomy proposals forwarded by the Miskito leadership and proposed to create multiethnic regions with limited and vaguely defined competencies. For an account of the episode see Hale (1996).

39 To the 45 members of the council the national deputies chosen in the region

are added. Thus the RAAN council effectively counts 48 members and the RAAS council 47.

40 In 1995, the population of the RAAN is estimated at 186,354 inhabitants; 42 percent mestizos, 40 percent Miskitos, 10 percent Creoles and 8 percent (Mayagnas) Sumos. The RAAS population would be 123,930; 54.8 percent mestizos, 29 percent Creoles, 12.1 percent Miskitos, 1.7 percent Garífunas, 0.7 percent Ramas and 0.2 percent (Mayagnas) Sumos (Acosta, 1996: 11).

41 For an overview of relevant legislation see MIN/CALPI (2000).

42 In their pacification efforts the Sandinistas had given up part of their centralist orientation, which was mostly about nationalism and access to the resources of the Atlantic region. Authority over resources is the main issue at stake for the neoliberal administrations, although they should be ideologically inclined to enhance decentralization and local management.

43 In 1998 the government presented a project for the regulation of indigenous community property in the region, which was related to a project for a biodiversity reserve (BOSAWAS) to be financed by the World Bank. The local population had not been consulted at all and rejected the plans and began to draw up its own law for demarcation of community lands (MIN/CALPI, 2000).

44 Ramírez mentions 'guaranteed employment, construction of schools, and financing training workshops that were not in accordance with the agenda of the national indigenous movement' (centered on land) and some pages later mentions the sum of US$ 25,000 (Ramírez, 2002: 150, 156).

45 For an incisive intervention in the debate see Zúñiga (2000). Without denying that there are important questions involved I suspect that the recent buzz over 'strategic essentializing' and 'performance' is very much part of a backlash discourse which relies on disqualifying the 'other' by strategically calling his or her 'authenticity' into question by reducing it to some sort of opportunistic rational choice strategizing while denying that they may be capable of reflecting upon themselves, their aims and cultural values. To put things in their proper perspective we rather need to study 'reflexive identity politics' (Eriksen, 2001).

46 See, for example, Bastos and Camus (2003) and Warren (1998).

References

Acosta, María Luisa (1996) *Los derechos de las comunidades y pueblos indígenas de la Costa Atlántica en la Constitución política de Nicaragua y La implementación de autonomía en las Regiones Autónomas de la Costa Atlántica de Nicaragua,* Nicaragua: Agencia Canadiense para el Desarrollo Internacional.

—— (2000) 'The State and Indigenous Lands in the Autonomous Regions of Nicaragua: The Case of the Mayagna Community of Awas Tingni,' in Assies, W., G. van der Haar and A. Hoekema (eds.) *The Challenge of Diversity; Indigenous Peoples and Reform of the State in Latin America,* Amsterdam: Thela Thesis, 261–274.

Albó, X. (2002) 'Bolivia: From Indian and Campesino Leaders to Councillors and Parliamentary Deputies,' in Sieder, R. (ed.) *Multiculturalism in Latin America; Indigenous Rights, Diversity and Democracy,* Basingstoke: Palgrave, Macmillan, 74–102.

América Indígena (1995), Vol. LV, no. 4 (Special Issue on Panama).

Arango, R. and E. Sánchez (2002) *Los pueblos indígenas en el umbral del nuevo milenio,* Bogotá: Departamento Nacional de Planeación (available on-line: www.dnp.gov. co/01_CONT/DES_TERR/DIV_ET.HTM#8).

Arias, M. and M. Chapin (1998) 'Panamá: El proyecto de estudio para el manejo de las áreas silvestres de Kuna Yala (PEMASKY),' in IWGIA *Derechos Indígenas y conservación de la naturaleza; Asuntos relativos a la gestión,* Copenhagen: IWGIA (Document no. 23), 247–292.

Assies, W. (1994) 'Self-Determination and the "New Partnership"; The Politics of Indigenous Peoples and States,' in Assies, W. and A. J. Hoekema (eds) *Indigenous Peoples' Experiences with Self-Government,* Copenhagen, Amsterdam: IWGIA and University of Amsterdam (IWGIA Document no. 76), 31–71.

Assies, W., G. van der Haar and A. Hoekema (eds) (2000) *The Challenge of Diversity; Indigenous Peoples and Reform of the State in Latin America,* Amsterdam: Thela Thesis.

Barth, F. (ed.) (1969) *Ethnic Groups and Boundaries; The Social Organization of Cultural Difference,* Bergen-Oslo, London: Universitets Forlaget, George Allen and Unwin.

Bastos, S. and M. Camus (2003) *Entre el mecapal y el cielo: Desarrollo del movimiento maya en Guatemala,* Guatemala: FLACSO.

Bengoa, J. (2000) *La emergencia indígena en América Latina,* México D.F., Santiago: Fondo de Cultura Económica.

Bennagen, P. L. (1992) 'Fiscal and Administrative Relations between Indigenous Governments and States,' paper presented at the Meeting of Experts, Nuuk, Greenland, 24–28 September 1991 (E/CN. 4/1992/42/Add. 1).

Bonfil Batalla, G. (1981) 'Lo propio y lo ajeno: una aproximación al problema de control cultural,' *Revista Mexicana de Ciencias Políticas y Sociales,* no. 103: 183–191.

Brackelaire, V. (2002) *Balance y perspectivas de la cooperación con los pueblos indígenas en América Latina,* La Paz: Fondo Indígena, Praia.

Calla, R. (2000) 'Indigenous Peoples, the Law of Popular Participation and Changes in Government: Bolivia, 1994–1998,' in Assies, W., G. van der Haar and A. Hoekema (eds) *The Challenge of Diversity; Indigenous Peoples and Reform of the State in Latin America,* Amsterdam: Thela Thesis, 77–94.

Cepeda Espinosa, M. J. (2001) 'El Estado multicultural en Colombia; Potencialidades y limitaciones de la transformación constitucional,' in Cepeda Espinosa, M. J. and T. Fleiner (eds) *Multiethnic Nations in Developing Countries,* Bâle, Genève, Munich: Helbing and Lichtenhahn (Institut de Fédéralisme Fribourg Suisse), 75–316.

Colombia (1995) 'Programa de apoyo y fortalecimento étnico de los pueblos indígenas de Colombia, 1995–1998,' *Anuario Indigenista,* Vol. XXXIV: 155–182.

CONAIE (1994) 'Proyecto político,' *Anuario Indigenista,* Vol. XXXIII: 203–244.

—— (1998) *Proyecto de Constitución del Estado Plurinacional del Ecuador,* Quito: CONAIE.

Cunningham, M. (1998) 'La autonomía regional multiétnica en la Costa Atlántica de Nicaragua,' in Bartolomé, M. A. and A. M. Barabas (coord.) *Autonomías étnicas y Estados nacionales,* Mexico D.F.: CONACULTA, INAH, 275–303.

Díaz-Polanco, H. (1997) *La rebelión zapatista y la autonomía,* Mexico D.F.: Siglo XXI.

—— (1999) 'Los desafíos de la autonomía en Nicaragua (entrevista con Myrna Cunningham),' *Desacatos,* no. 1: 37–55.

DNP-UDT (1999) *El desarrollo constitucional del proyecto de Ley Orgánica de Ordenamiento Territorial y su articulación con el Plan Nacional de Desarrollo 'Cambio para construir la paz,'* Bogotá: Departamento Nacional de Planeación.

Eriksen, T. H. (2001) 'Ethnic Identity, National Identity, and Intergroup Conflict,' in Ashmore, R. D., L. Jussim and D. Wilder (eds) *Social Identity, Intergroup Conflict, and Conflict Reduction*, Oxford, New York: Oxford University Press, 42–68.

Espinosa, M. F. (2000) 'Ethnic Politics and State Reform in Ecuador,' in Assies, W., G. van der Haar and A. Hoekema (eds) *The Challenge of Diversity; Indigenous Peoples and Reform of the State in Latin America*, Amsterdam: Thela Thesis, 47–56.

Findji, M. T. (1992) 'From Resistance to Social Movement: The Indigenous Authorities Movement in Colombia,' in Escobar, A. and S. E. Alvarez (eds) *The Making of Social Movements in Latin America; Identity, Strategy, And Democracy*, Boulder CO, San Francisco, CA, Oxford: Westview Press, 112–133.

González Guerra, G. (1999) *Derechos de los pueblos indígenas; Legislación en América Latina*, Mexico D.F.: Comisión Nacional de Derechos Humanos.

Gustafson, B. (2002) 'Paradoxes of Liberal Indigenism: Indigenous Movements, State Processes, and Intercultural Reform in Bolivia,' in Maybury-Lewis, D. (ed.) *The Politics of Ethnicity: Indigenous Peoples in Latin American States*, Cambridge MA, London: Harvard University Press, 267–306.

Hale, C. (1996) 'Entre la militancia indígena y la conciencia multiétnica: Los desafíos de la Autonomía en la Costa Atlántica de Nicaragua,' in Varese, S. (coord.) *Pueblos indios soberanía y globalismo*, Quito: Abya-Yala, 485–524.

Hale, Charles (2002) 'Does Multiculturalism Menace? Governance, Cultural Rights and the Politics of Identity in Guatemala,' *Journal of Latin American Studies*, no. 34: 485–524.

Hoekema, A. J. (1996) 'Autonomy and Self-Government, a Fundamental Debate,' Amsterdam: University of Amsterdam, Department of Sociology and Anthropology of Law (Internal memo, Project 'Images of Self Rule').

Hopenhayn, M. and A. Bello (2001) *Discriminación étnico-racial y xenofobia en América Latina y el Caribe*, Santiago: CEPAL (Serie: Políticas Sociales 47).

Howe, James (1998) *A people who would not kneel; Panama, the United States, and the San Blas Kuna*, Washington and London: Smithsonian Institution Press.

—— (2002) 'The Kuna of Panama: Continuing Threats to Land and Autonomy,' in Maybury-Lewis, D. (ed.) *The Politics of Ethnicity: Indigenous Peoples in Latin American States*, Cambridge MA, London: Harvard University Press, 81–106.

IADB (2003) *Índice de Legislación Indígena*, www.iadb.org/sds/ind/site_3152_e.htm (consulted August 2, 2003).

Iturralde Guerrero, D. A. (1997) 'Demandas indígenas y reforma legal: retos y paradojas,' *Alteridades*, Vol. 7, no. 14: 81–98.

Jackson, J. (2002) 'Caught in the Crossfire: Colombia's Indigenous Peoples during the 1990s,' in Maybury-Lewis, D. (ed.) *The Politics of Ethnicity: Indigenous Peoples in Latin American States*, Cambridge MA, London: Harvard University Press, 107–133.

Kuppe, R. (2003) 'Reflections on the Rights of Indigenous Peoples in the New Venezuelan Constitution and the Establishment of a Participatory, Pluricultural and Multiethnic Society,' *Law and Anthropology*, Vol. 12: 52–75.

León Trujillo, J. (1998) 'Una descentralización a contracorriente, el caso del Ecuador,' in Chiriboga Zambrano, G. and R. Quintero López (eds.) *Alcances y limitaciones de la reforma política en el Ecuador*, Quito: Friedrich Ebert Stiftung, ILDIS, Proyecto Latinoamericano para Medios de Comunicación, Escuela de Sociología y Ciencias Políticas de la Universidad Central del Ecuador, AAJ, 175–199.

Levi, J. M. (2002) 'A New Dawn or a Cycle Restored? Regional Dynamics and Cultural Politics in Indigenous Mexico, 1978–2001,' in Maybury-Lewis, D. (ed.) *The Politics of Ethnicity: Indigenous Peoples in Latin American States*, Cambridge MA, London: Harvard University Press, 3–49.

López y Rivas, G. (1995) *Nación y pueblos indios en el neoliberalismo*, Mexico D.F.: Plaza y Valdés, UIA.

Macdonald Jr., T. (2002) 'Ecuador's Indian Movement: Pawn in a Short Game or Agent in State Configuration?' in Maybury-Lewis, D. (ed.) *The Politics of Ethnicity: Indigenous Peoples in Latin American States*, Cambridge MA, London: Harvard University Press, 169–198.

Marshall, M. G. and T. Gurr (2003) *Peace and Conflict 2003; A Global Survey of Armed Conflicts, Self-Determination Movements, and Democracy*, Maryland: University of Maryland, CIDCM.

Martínez Cobo, J. R. (1987) *Study of the Problem of Discrimination against Indigenous Populations, Volume V, Conclusions, Proposals and Recommendations*, New York: United Nations (E/CN.4/Sub.2/1986/7/Add.4; Sales No. E.86.XIV.3).

Mattiace, S. L., R. A. Hernández and J. Rus (eds.) (2002) *Tierra, libertad y autonomía: impactos regionales del zapatismo en Chiapas*, Mexico, Copenhagen: CIESAS, IWGIA.

Méndez, A. I. (2002) 'Los derechos de las naciones indígenas en las constituciones de los países latinoamericanos,' ponencia presentada en el *Tercer Congreso Europeo de Latinoamericanistas en Europa*, Amsterdam, 2–6 July.

Mendoza, C. (n.d.) 'Indigenous Struggles for Political Recognition and Participation in Guatemala: Long Walk to Democratic Consolidation' (unpublished research paper).

MIN/CALPI (2000) *Diagnóstico de la legislación nacional sobre los pueblos indígenas de Nicaragua y exposición de motivos de la presentación de Convenio 169 como anteproyecto de ley ante la Asamblea Nacional de la República de Nicaragua*, Nicaragua: Movimiento Indígena de Nicaragua (MIN) and Centro de Asistencia Legal a Pueblos Indígenas (CALPI).

Nagel, J. and C. M. Snipp (1993) 'Ethnic reorganization: American Indian social, economic, political, and cultural strategies for survival,' *Ethnic and Racial Studies*, Vol. 16, no. 2: 203–235.

Ortega Hegg, M. (1996) 'Autonomía regional y neoliberalismo en Nicaragua,' in González Casanova, P. and M. Roitman Rosemann (coord.) *Democracia y Estado multiétnico en América Latina*, Mexico D.F.: CIICH/UNAM, La Jornada, 201–221.

Padilla, G. (1995) 'What Encompasses Goodness, the Law and the Indigenous People of Colombia,' in The Woodrow Wilson Center *Ethnic Conflict and Governance in Comparative Perspective* (Latin American Program Working Paper Series, no. 215), Washington: The Woodrow Wilson Center: 139–153.

—— (1996) 'Derecho mayor indígena y derecho constitucional; comentarios en torno a sus confluencias y conflictos' in Varese, S. (coord.) *Pueblos indios, soberanía y globalismo*, Quito: Abya-Yala.

Pérez Archibold, J. (1998) 'Autonomía kuna y Estado panameño,' in Bartolomé, M. A. and A. M. Barabas (coord.) *Autonomías étnicas y Estados nacionales*, Mexico D.F.: CONACULTA, INAH, 243–274.

Pineda, R. (2001) 'Colombia y el reto de la construcción de la multiculturalidad en un escenario de conflicto,' in Cepeda Espinosa, M. J. and T. Fleiner (eds) *Multiethnic Nations in Developing Countries*, Bâle, Genève, Munich: Helbing and Lichtenhahn (Institut de Fédéralisme Fribourg Suisse), 1–74.

Plant, R. (2000) 'Indigenous rights and Latin American Multiculturalism: Lessons from the Guatemalan Peace Process,' in Assies, W., G. van der Haar and A. Hoekema (eds) *The Challenge of Diversity; Indigenous Peoples and Reform of the State in Latin America*, Amsterdam: Thela Thesis, 23–43.

Plant, R. and S. Hvalkov (2002) *Titulación de tierras y pueblos indígenas*, Washington: Banco Interamericano de Desarrollo.

Psacharopoulos, G. and H. A. Patrinos (eds) (1994) *Indigenous People and Poverty in Latin America; An Empirical Analysis*, Washington: The World Bank.

Ramírez, María Clemencia (2002) 'The Politics of Identity and Cultural Difference in the Colombia Amazon: Claiming Indigenous Rights in the Putumayo Region,' in Maybury-Lewis, D. (ed.) *The Politics of Ethnicity: Indigenous Peoples in Latin American States*, Cambridge MA, London: Harvard University Press, 135–166.

Scherrer, C. P. (1994) 'Regional Autonomy in Eastern Nicaragua; Four Years of Self-Government experience in Yapti Tasba,' in Assies, W. and A. J. Hoekema (eds) *Indigenous Peoples' Experiences with Self-Government*, Copenhagen, Amsterdam: IWGIA and University of Amsterdam (IWGIA Document no. 76), 109–148.

Sieder, R. (ed.) (2002) *Multiculturalism in Latin America; Indigenous Rights, Diversity and Democracy*, Basingstoke: Palgrave, MacMillan.

Stavenhagen, R. (2002) 'Indigenous Peoples and the State in Latin America: An Ongoing Debate' in Sieder, R. (ed.) *Multiculturalism in Latin America; Indigenous Rights, Diversity and Democracy*, Basingstoke: Palgrave, MacMillan, 24–44.

Trujillo, J. C. (2000) 'Los derechos colectivos de los pueblos indígenas del Ecuador: Conceptos generales,' in Bernal, A. M. (comp.) *De la exclusión a la participación: Pueblos indígenas y sus derechos colectivos en el Ecuador*, Quito: Abya Yala, 7–34.

Turpana, A., (1994) 'The Duel Nation of the San Blas Comarca: Between Government and Self-Government,' in Assies, W. and A. J. Hoekema (eds) *Indigenous Peoples' Experiences with Self-Government*, Copenhagen, Amsterdam: IWGIA and University of Amsterdam (IWGIA Document no. 76), 149–156.

Van Cott, D. L. (2000) *The Friendly Liquidation of the Past; The Politics of Diversity in Latin America*, Pittsburgh: The University of Pittsburgh Press.

—— (2001) 'Explaining Ethnic Autonomy Regimes in Latin America,' *Studies in Comparative International Development*, Vol. 35, no. 4: 30–58.

—— (2002) 'Constitutional Reform in the Andes: Redefining Indigenous-State Relations,' in Sieder, R. (ed.) *Multiculturalism in Latin America; Indigenous Rights, Diversity and Democracy*, Basingstoke: Palgrave, Macmillan, 45–73.

Vázquez León, L. (1992) *Ser indio otra vez: La purepechización de los tarrascos serranos*, México: CONACULTA.

Warren, K. B. (1998) *Indigenous Movements and their Critics: Pan-Maya Activism in Guatemala*, Princeton: Princeton University Press.

Wray, N. (2000) *Pueblos indígenas Amazónicos y actividad petrolera en el Ecuador; Conflictos, estrategias e impactos*, Quito: IBIS, Oxfam.

Zuñiga, Gerardo (2000) 'La dimensión discursiva de las luchas étnicas, Acerca de un artículo de María Teresa Sierra,' *Alteridades*, Vol. 10, no. 19, 55–67.

9 From centralized authoritarianism to decentralized democracy

Regional autonomy and the state in Indonesia

Mark Turner

Introduction

Systems of government in countries which have large populations or territories are generally characterized by significant degrees of decentralization. They often take the form of federal systems, such as in India, the USA or Brazil, but can even be negotiated orders such as in China. Indonesia is a large country both in terms of population and area. There are more than 210 million inhabitants distributed across 6000 islands in an archipelago which stretches for 5000 kilometres from east to west and 1770 from north to south. There are also over 300 different ethnic groups. Such statistics suggest that some form of political decentralization would be an appropriate mode of government for Indonesia. However, since 1945, despite debate and legislation on decentralization through regional autonomy (*otonomi daerah*), centralization has been the dominant theme.

While national political elites have made constitutional provisions and passed laws introducing and shaping regional autonomy they have paradoxically, in practice, continued to favour central control. They have emphasized the 'unity component of the national motto—'unity in diversity'.

This preference for centralization was rudely overturned in 1999 when the interim government of President Habibie enacted Law 22 on Regional Governance and Law 25 on the Financial Balance Between Central and Regional Government. These two laws represented a major disjunction with past practice as they devolved considerable powers and functions to democratically elected regional governments across Indonesia. Furthermore, there was to be no delay in implementing the laws despite their lack of detail and occasional ambiguity. Laws 22/99 and 25/99 marked a major transformation of the Indonesian state that was both radical and rapid. They have ushered in an ambitious experiment in decentralized governance in one of the world's most populous countries.

This chapter traces the history of regional autonomy in Indonesia. It demonstrates how the concept of autonomy can be defined and operationalized in strikingly different ways over time and place within one country thus confirming Potier's (2001: 54) observation that autonomy 'escapes definition because it is impossible to concretize its scope'. The chapter also explores other important issues of regional autonomy in Indonesia. These include the role of external participation, the relationship between ethnicity and territorial autonomy, and the variable institutional structures which are used in autonomy experiments.

Centralization and regional autonomy

In the Elucidation of the Indonesian Constitution of 1945 it was stated that Indonesia was a unitary state which would be divided into autonomous democratic or administrative regions. Furthermore, when determining the government structures of regions account would be taken of their particular histories. These provisions indicated from the outset of the Republic the struggle that would take place between the centripetal forces of centralization evident in the dominant coalitions of successive national elites and the centrifugal forces emanating from local elites in the regions of Indonesia.

Law 1 of 1945 established three types of autonomous region but as in colonial times regional autonomy was restricted to a narrow range of functions referred to as 'household affairs' while regional heads were centrally appointed (Mokhsen 2003). A federal system of government was then agreed under the terms of independence but quickly abandoned for a unitary state by a national political elite which saw national unity as a prime objective. They were conscious of presiding over a country assembled by a colonial power and comprised of disparate peoples. 'Imagining the nation' and disseminating that vision became a preoccupation of the nation's founding leaders. The challenge, as Anderson (1991) observes, was to make people in Sumatra, who were physically and ethnically close to Malaysians across the narrow Straits of Malacca, categorize themselves as Indonesians alongside Ambonese several thousand kilometres to the east with whom they shared neither ethnicity, language nor religion. Emanating from the centre was a constant and often successful propagation of a 'vision of Indonesia as a diversity of cultural streams brought together into the one great unity' (Legge 1972: 342).

The elite's fear that things could fall apart was confirmed by uprisings in Sumatra, Sulawesi, the Moluccas and Kalimantan during the 1950s. This led to intensification of efforts to assert and maintain the unity of the state. Thus, while legislation was undertaken to provide regional autonomy (and there were some ardent advocates in parliament) implementation saw consistent attempts to impose central control over regional affairs. The rebellions provided the national political elite with ample evidence of the possibility of state fragmentation and confirmed their belief in the need for central regulation of regional affairs.

More than two decades of deliberations and legislation over the distribution of power within the Indonesian state culminated in the chaos of President Sukarno's 'guided democracy' in the late 1960s. Stability was re-established under the authoritarian rule of the New Order regime headed by President Suharto. During the first few years of the New Order there were discussions of political devolution and drafting of legislation which indicated that a substantial range of powers would be transferred to regional governments. But as the new regime and its political party, Golkar, consolidated their hold on the state a more centralist philosophy attained dominance in policy-making circles. This was expressed in Law 5 of 1974 on regional government, not so much in the law's contents, but in its implementation.

Law 5/74 was used by the New Order regime to design and legitimate a framework for subnational government which was strongly centralist despite the use of the terminology of autonomy. It was based on three guiding principles: decentralization *(azas decentralisasi)*, deconcentration or administrative decentralization *(azas dekonsentrasi)* and co-administration *(azas tugas pembantuan)*. The law appeared to grant some measure of political decentralization but in practice it provided a foundation for limited deconcentration coupled with strong central supervision and control. The principle of decentralization was interpreted as 'delegation' rather than as the devolution of political authority (Rohdewohld 1995). It took 18 years for the government to produce the regulation listing the functions that were to be devolved to regional governments. In the meantime, other regulations had been introduced to strengthen the role of the centre in determining the organization and conduct of subnational administration and politics.

Administrative control was exerted by strong central ministries, while political control over weak local assemblies was maintained by the government party, Golkar. The military's presence in all subnational regions gave further impetus for local officials to comply with central wishes. The autonomous governments of the subnational regions were seen as the implementers of central government tasks. The all-encompassing system of central planning set up by the New Order required such compliance. Policy formulation remained firmly with the centre as did control of finances. Analysts of New Order 'regional autonomy' noted the limited nature of decentralization. Rohdewohld (1995: 87) described it as 'a rather incremental and slow process'; Devas (1997) saw it as 'elusive'; Gerritsen and Situmorang (1999: 51) characterized the system as one in which 'regional government was obliged to follow a national line'; Turner and Podger (2003) believed that 'regional aspirations were largely unexpressed and discouraged'; while Mokhsen (2003: 168) has argued that the government 'never really intended to promote regional autonomy'. Even when the government attempted to portray itself as a promoter of regional autonomy the results did not match the rhetoric. Thus, in the

1990s, a donor-funded project to promote greater regional autonomy failed to make any significant impact on established patterns of decision-making in the state (Devas 1997; Mokhsen 2003).

Over the period 1945–99, the national political elite in Indonesia appeared to have fulfilled their ambition to consolidate the nation and entrench the notion of the unitary state. Their 'imagined nation' had become a reality. Dissent was suppressed and regional sentiments kept under control. It was, however, felt necessary to maintain the discourse of regional autonomy which had commenced prior to 1945 and still had its advocates. However, the bounds of the discourse were tightly prescribed by central government, which simultaneously maintained the fiction that regional autonomy actually existed. The entire country was certainly divided into territorial divisions which were called autonomous regions, all of which had the same institutional and political structure. But Indonesian autonomy meant both compliance to the centre and standardization, characteristics absent from accepted definitions of territorial autonomy. The centre determined the nature of regional autonomy and did not hold to Daftary's (2000: 5) assertion that autonomy means that powers devolved to the autonomous entity 'may not be revoked without consulting with the autonomous entity'. Political mobilization along ethnic lines was strongly discouraged or violently suppressed. In three cases—Aceh, East Timor and West Papua—there were secessionist movements based on perceptions of ethnic difference but in each case the central state primarily relied on a military solution. The Indonesian government considered ethnicity to be a sensitive matter, a possible threat to national unity, and did not even collect statistics on ethnic groups in the census (Suryadinata *et al.* 2003).

The mechanics of a paradox—centralized autonomy

As we have seen, the New Order government of President Suharto succeeded in creating a paradox—a system of autonomous regional governments which in practice was highly centralized. This raises the question of how institutions can be built which are ostensibly devoted to one purpose—regional autonomy—when in actual fact they promote the opposite—central control. This section examines this question by showing how the New Order government created institutions, structures and processes which ensured central control over so-called autonomous regions.

According to Law 5/74 the territorial divisions of the Indonesian state were the province *(propinsi)*, the district *(kabupaten and kotamadya)*, and the sub-district *(kecamatan)*. Responsibility for the administration of functions such as agriculture, education, health and public works was allocated to the province and district. Also in these sub-national territories were organizations which supported the service delivery agencies. At both provincial and district levels there were two types of service delivery agencies. The 'autonomous' regional governments presided over offices known as *dinas* while the offices of central government agencies operating at the sub-national level were known as *kanwil* at provincial level and *kandep* at district level.

The principal support agency in both province and district was the Sekretariat Wilayah Daerah *(Setwilda)* which provided 'technical and administrative services to all regional agencies and personnel and to all *kanwils* and branches of central government agencies present in the region' (Galbraith 1989 as quoted by Rohdewohld 1995: 61–62). Running this powerful secretariat was a career civil servant, known as the *sekwilda*. He combined the role of secretary to the autonomous regional government with that of secretary to the deconcentrated *wilayah* administration. There were elected assemblies *(Dewan Perwakilan Rakyat Daerah—DPRD)* in all provinces and districts but they were dominated by the government party, Golkar, and acted more as deliberative than as decision-making bodies (Turner 2001). The three parties which were permitted to contest elections were nationwide organizations devoid of links to ethnicity.

The most important figure in sub-national government was the head of region *(kepala daerah)*. Like the secretary, the head of region straddled both the autonomous regional government and the deconcentrated agencies of central government. Indeed, the head of region relied on the service of the secretariat and other coordinating bodies such as the regional planning body. However, the *kepala daerah* was responsible only to the President who appointed him. The DPRD merely suggested candidates for the post but could not demand accountability from the head of region.

Presiding over the complex structure of sub-national government was the Ministry of Home Affairs *(Departemen Dalam Negri—DDN)*, 'a national ministry with a local agenda' (Morfit 1986). This vast bureaucracy managed appointments to leading positions in the regions, gave directives about the conduct of subnational government and controlled the approval process for regulations issued by regional governments. While Rohdewohld (1995: 72) describes the DDN as having 'a strong coordinating role' it might equally be identified as a leading instrument of central control over sub-national territories.

The New Order system of central-local relations, while claiming to be about regional autonomy and the decentralization of authority to regions, fell far short of this image in practice. The provincial and regional governments, as represented by the DPRDs and *dinas*, were officially delineated as 'autonomous regions', but they were anything but autonomous. Central ministries in Jakarta determined policy, issued instructions and handed down regulations. The leading officials in the regions were selected by the centre to whom they owed allegiance. They supervised on Jakarta's behalf. Accountability was unidirectional—upwards—and was 'obscured from public view' (Turner 2001: 72). Democratic elections were controlled and dominated by the government party, Golkar, while military structures ran parallel to administrative ones adding emphasis to the dominant themes of hierarchy and control. Dependency rather than autonomy best characterizes the overall system. Even the efficiency of the system has to be called into question. The complex mix of regional government agencies and deconcentrated central agencies resulted in overlapping responsibilities and duplication of functions while a legal framework covering central-local financial arrangements was lacking. There was no difficulty in spotting bureaucratic dysfunction.

Crisis and change

Crisis opens up policy space, which allows or even encourages decision-makers to take bold initiatives which are impossible when relative stability prevails (Grindle and Thomas 1991). In 1997–98, Indonesia and the authoritarian regime of President Suharto were in crisis. After three decades of political stability, economic growth and steady improvement in welfare indicators the country was suddenly plunged into economic crisis while emboldened students brought pro-democracy demonstrations into public view. There was discontent in some provinces which were keen to wrest more power from the centre. The IMF was called in to bail out the economy and save the regime. Survival was becoming precarious for President Suharto and one of his last desperate attempts to remain in office was the creation of the Coordinating Ministry for Development Supervision and Administrative Reform. This, he thought, would demonstrate his commitment to reform. One of the new ministry's tasks was the preparation of a revised Law 5/74. Decentralization was back on central stage.

Suharto was reappointed President by his faithful Golkar supporters in the People's Consultative Assembly (MPR) in March 1998 but increased opposition on the streets and the loss of key backers elsewhere led to Suharto's resignation on 21 May 1998. The Vice-President, Habibie, assumed the presidency until democratic elections could be held in November. Despite being in an interim position Habibie embarked on an ambitious legislative program which became known as 'the rush to law'. One of his targets was decentralization. The Coordinating Minister for Development Supervision and Administrative Reform, a survivor from the Suharto cabinet, immediately produced a paper advocating devolution of power to the regions, especially the districts (Turner and Podger 2003). He was also anxious to improve the financial position of the regions and recommended that a long-awaited law on fiscal balance should be drafted. Action in the executive was complemented by the granting of a political mandate to pursue decentralization from the People's Consultative Assembly *(Majelis Permusyarawatan Rakyat*—MPR) where the regional representatives were now flexing newly found political muscle.

Responsibility for drafting Law 22/99 on regional governance and Law 25/99 on fiscal balance was left to small teams of professionals known for their support of decentralization, drawn both from inside the Ministries of Home Affairs and Finance and from outside. This hand-picked policy elite 'utilised the opening of policy space to promote benefits they saw to be in the public interest' (Turner and Podger 2003: 19). Consultation with the regions or with other stakeholders was minimal. Those who were going to be most affected by the laws did not participate in the policy process. However, time was of the essence. There was a determination by the government and MPR that there should be radical changes in central-local relations and that they should be as fast as possible. This would be both a demonstration of good governance and responsiveness to regional aspirations. Some may also have looked into the future and correctly hypothesized that a newly elected national assembly *(Dewan Perwakilan Rakyat—*DPR) comprised of multiple parties and shifting coalitions would be an arena with strong potential for gridlock. Radical legislation would have little chance of enactment in such conditions. Thus, the urgent task was to get a law approved immediately. Any problems could be ironed out later. The logic of the Habibie government was that opportunities for major change must be taken before incrementalism is restored as the dominant characteristic of the policy process. There may also have been self-interest on the part of Golkar—to portray itself as the promoter of decentralization and then, as the most numerous party in regional assemblies, to consolidate its hold on political power at the regional level.

The rapid and exclusive policy-making process meant that there was little time to consider issues in depth and to canvas opinion about the contents of the laws. The laws are modest documents of 20–40 pages each, a stark contrast to the several hundred pages in the neighbouring Philippines' *Local Government Code 1991.* Two issues emerge from this. Firstly, there was an inevitable failure to anticipate the full implications of what was being proposed as there was insufficient time for such analysis. Also, the perspectives of other stakeholders were not taken into account. Secondly, many items were not fully delineated. Law 22/99 has numerous instances where it is stated that a particular matter will be determined in a regulation. Thus, the law required a massive regulatory program, one which is as yet unfinished.

The basic elements of Laws 22/99 and 25/99

Law 22 was formally authorized in May 1999. It appears to have been driven by the imperative for democratization following 30 years of authoritarian rule. The most important statement of purpose appears in the preamble where it is 'deemed to be necessary to emphasize more the principles of democracy, community participation, equitable distribution and justice, as well as to take into account the Regions' potential and diversity'. But there are also mentions of the need to uphold unity in the face of the country's diversity, and reminders that Indonesia is a unitary state, a matter of great importance for all regimes since independence. Law 22/99 lacks any managerial and economic arguments for decentralization.

The first major change introduced by Law 22/99 is the removal of the regional hierarchy in which provinces supervised the districts. These 'autonomous regions' comprised of regencies *(kabupaten)* and cities *(kota,* formerly *kotamadya)* interact directly with central government. The province retains its status as an autonomous region but is stripped of many functions as well as its supervising authority. It is also an administrative region as in the past and although the provincial governor is democratically elected he/she is seen to represent central government. The major duties of the province are to undertake tasks which the districts are currently unable to perform.

Law 22/99 devolves a large number of functions to the control of the autonomous regions of regency and city. The list includes public works, health, education and culture, agriculture, communication, industry and trade, capital investment, environment, land, cooperatives, 'manpower affairs' and the management of national resources. The central government retains authority relating to national policy-making such as foreign affairs, defence and security, the judiciary, religion and monetary and fiscal policy. But almost all activities that can be classified as service delivery have been devolved to the districts.

The increased functional responsibility and relative autonomy of the regions means that every Regional People's Representative Assembly *(Dewan Perwakilan Rakyat Daerah*—DPRD) has become extremely important in terms of decision-making on matters which are of importance to local populations. In the past, they simply toed the line set by Jakarta. Now they are empowered to set policy for the regions and to demand accountability from the executive. Members of the DPRD are elected democratically from authorized political parties. In New Order times there were only 3 parties, while in the 1999 elections there were 48, although each party must still have nationwide representation. This minimizes the chances of ethnically based parties emerging. The DPRD elects the head and deputy head of region and chooses the local representatives to the People's Consultative Assembly (MPR), the highest state assembly. Members of the DPRD cooperate with the head of region in determining and enacting legislation and budgets. They also monitor the implementation of them as well as the actions of the head of region. He/she is now primarily accountable to the DPRD rather than to the provincial governor and central agencies in Jakarta. However, there is still an obligation for the head of region to report to central government. Finally, the DPRD is supposed to be the prime institution for facilitating democratization, but the law is somewhat sketchy on how this is to be achieved.

The head of region leads 'the organization of regional governance' (Art. 44/1) and remains a powerful figure in regional governance although the new accountability to the DPRD should act as a democratic check on executive power. The head of region is the chief executive and presides over a large bureaucracy. The dual structure of bureaucracy which featured both national (*kandeps* and *kanwils*) and local government (*dinas*) offices has been simplified. They have been amalgamated to form 'one integrated structure of regional executive government' (Turner and Podger 2003: 25). Law 22/99 leaves the design of this structure to each region. It also provides for the devolution of a broad range of personnel functions including 'the authority to conduct appointments, transfer, dismissal, stipulation of pension, salary, allowance, welfare as well as education and training' (Art. 76).

Districts can contain large populations. For example, on Java the regencies each house approximately one million people. Thus, there are levels of government below the district. Principal among these is the sub-district (*kecamatan*). Law 22/99 identifies it as an administrative territory under the direction of the district with officials appointed by the district executive. There is no formal representative body at the sub-district level. However, at the lower level of village *(desa)* the law provides for a directly elected village head and village representative board. Various aspects of rural governance are assigned to the village officials as is the income to perform them. There is no provision in the law for an urban equivalent to the *desa* system of governance.

Law 22/99 re-establishes the Regional Autonomy Advisory Board (*Dewan Pertimbangan Otonomi Daerah*—DPOD) to oversee the regional autonomy process. This high-level body involves the ministers of finance and home affairs, other ministers and members of regional associations. The formal inclusion of the latter category of members provided the necessary imperative for creating a variety of new representative bodies such as for the heads of regencies or city legislative leaders. The DPOD reports to the president but is not empowered to issue instructions to government agencies.

Financial matters are mentioned in passing in Law 22/99, but are the focus of Law 25/99. The major mechanisms for transferring resources to the regions under the New Order have been abolished. These were the *Subsidi Daerah Otonomi* (SDO) for paying public servants and routine expenditures and the *Inpres* grants which funded development projects and ensured central control over development planning. In their place is a general allocation grant (*Dana Alokasi Umum*—DAU) which is to be a minimum of 25 per cent of domestic revenue. The law awards 90 per cent of the DAU for the districts and 10 per cent for the provinces. A formula is used to determine the amounts for specific territories in each category.

The financial matter which marked the most significant break from past practice was the introduction of revenue sharing between central and regional governments. Previously all resource revenues accrued to central government, a practice resented by resource-rich regions. Under Law 25/99 there is revenue-sharing involving land and building tax, land acquisition, forestry, fisheries, mining and oil and gas. A special allocation grant (*Dana Alokasi Khusus*—DAK) has also been created by the law, its purpose being to finance special initiatives in the regions. Regions also have greater opportunities for securing loans while provisions for financial accountability to both the regional assembly and central government are delineated in the law. However, there is a certain vagueness in the legislation about the supervisory role and authority of central government. Law 22/99 makes a brief mention of central government's responsibility to supervise and guide regions (Art. 112–114) including the Minister for Home Affairs' power to veto any regional regulation or instruction which does not comply with higher legislation or the 'common good'.

Several lessons can be learned from the regional autonomy legislation in Indonesia. Firstly, when devolving functions to sub-national territories it is highly desirable to match these functions with finance. Unfortunately, in the Indonesian case this did not happen. Laws 22/99 and 25/99 were drafted separately with little coordination between the two responsible ministries. Secondly, where autonomy laws are brief and require a substantial regulatory program it is essential that clear guidelines are given for this program. The advantage of brief laws is that they can be drafted relatively quickly and, if popular like Laws 22/99 and 25/99, can provide support and legitimacy to government. However, with numerous matters unresolved stakeholders can be left confused and potentially antagonistic if implementing regulations are not produced in an orderly, predictable and comprehensible manner. Thirdly, when basic legislation leaves many matters to be determined in regulations there may be an opportunity for central governments to regain control over ostensibly autonomous territories (World Bank 2000). Finally, where radical decentralization laws are enacted, especially if they are brief, huge implementation problems should be expected. Some issues may be anticipated but many others will arise only as implementation proceeds. The situation will be exacerbated if there has been little participation by stakeholders. They view the legislation from different perspectives and thus identify implementation issues which a small group of autonomous drafters will overlook.

Implementing regional autonomy

There were many sceptics in Indonesia and elsewhere who regarded the implementation schedule for the regional autonomy program as too ambitious—too much, too fast. The most pessimistic saw chaos spreading across the archipelago and a disintegrating state. Even the supporters of regional autonomy were anxious about the scale and pace of change. However, on 1 January 2001, only 19 months after the legislation had been enacted, full implementation commenced. There were no fanfares or celebrations. It was merely a quiet day marking a revolution in the organization of the state. The business of government continued without any obvious disruption. The newly empowered DPRDs took up their new responsibilities with enthusiasm and the heads of region began to turn their attention from Jakarta to the local elected assembly. The central bureaucracy managed the enormous task of processing the documentation to transfer 2.44 million public servants from central agencies to the new regional governments. There were 1.6 million personnel, mostly teachers, from the Ministry of National Education alone and over a quarter of a million from the Ministry of Health. More than 20,000 facilities were transferred from central governments to regional governments. Inventories of equipment and other assets were also drawn up and passed on to the regions although many items were reportedly missing or unlisted.

Management of the initial transition was an undoubted success. This derived from five factors. Firstly, small groups of central government public servants worked with a strong commitment to meet the implementation schedule. Secondly, their exertions were complemented by foreign technical assistance in various areas of key ministries. Thirdly, the routine nature of massive tasks such as the transfer of personnel and assets suited the mechanistic bureaucracies of central government. Fourthly, regional governments and their constituent populations were committed to decentralization. Regional officials, especially in the DPRDs, were keen to take control of their own destinies. Finally, the multilateral financial agencies supported decentralization as a strategy for good governance. They provided funds and maintained pressure on the Indonesian government to comply with the ambitious implementation schedule. However, there were no kin-states or kin-groups abroad which exerted influence on the design or implementation processes. The assistance extended for the implementation of regional autonomy was for a design that was authentically Indonesian.

After the transition to regional autonomy came the much more difficult stage of making the new system work to produce the anticipated democratic and welfare gains. There have been some encouraging signs. The first Indonesia Rapid Decentralization Appraisal (IRDA) reported that 'after one year, local governments in most regions surveyed are coping well with the additional responsibilities that have been thrust upon them' (Asia Foundation 2002: 2). The report pointed to such things as the increased popular participation in developing transparency and public accountability, the emergence of citizens' fora, the creation of conditions for innovation and the enhanced participation of local media and civil society. The second IRDA reported that regional governments were 'generally maintaining pre-existing services' and in some cases were 'developing new initiatives' (Asia Foundation 2003: 11).

But regional autonomy is by no means all good news. There are many problems which could jeopardize efforts to achieve good governance and welfare improvement through democratic decentralization. Firstly, the regulatory program required for regional autonomy remains incomplete. The second IRDA emphasizes 'the need for a coherent regulatory framework encompassing national laws, ministerial decrees, implementing regulations, as well as legislation concerning forestry, mining, fisheries, civil service and other specific sectors' (Asia Foundation 2003: 4). Some regulations have proved to be inadequate, such as Government Regulation 110/2000 on regional finances, and have been withdrawn (Turner and Podger 2003). Even Laws 22/99 and 25/99 have been found to be wanting and efforts are being made to revise the legislation. One draft was withdrawn from circulation in 2002 while another was also criticized on its first presentation.

There has also been concern about the arrangements for and conduct of local politics. The emergence of 'money politics' is of particular concern. This term refers to practices such as payments to DPRD members by contractors for favourable decisions or by candidates for executive appointments to secure their election by the DPRD. Concerns have been aired in the media about 'money politics' (e.g., *Jakarta Post* 29 August 2001 and 9 November 2001). It has been described as 'a worrying trend, that if allowed to persist, will signal to the population that democratic politics is merely about internal struggles between local elites' (Turner and Podger 2003: 71). One review of regional autonomy concluded that 'the voice of the people is not yet being effectively channeled through its representatives' (Usman 2001: 16).

Also under scrutiny is the election of the head and deputy head of region by the DPRD rather than the population at large. According to World Bank (2000) research popular election of the chief executive is more likely to promote good governance as those elected will have widespread legitimacy and a mandate from the community. They also have a greater chance of being elected on the basis of proposed policies and past performance. However, in some developing countries such as the Philippines personality politics can override such rational choice. A further political issue is the election of DPRD members and heads of regions at different times. The former are elected simultaneously nationwide, but the heads of region are chosen according to an electoral schedule which differs between regions. One problem arising from this arrangement is that DPRDs are often working with heads of region they did not select. Strained relations have been reported between the regional legislators and chief executives potentially leading to problems of efficiency and effectiveness in the running of government.

Accountability is a major theme of Laws 22/99 and 25/99. The lack of it is identified as a leading problem of government in Indonesia. In a 2001 survey over 75 per cent of respondents pointed to corruption as the country's leading problem (PGRI 2001). All social classes recorded similar opinions. Central government agencies appeared near the bottom of the list of organizations ranked according to their perceived integrity. Subnational government institutions were clustered in the middle. The worry is that the levels of corruption attributed to central government agencies now seep down to the regional level. Theoretically this should not happen as local populations and their elected representatives are now empowered to demand the accountability of local officials. However, both officials and population are often unfamiliar with the tools for democratic accountability, while there have been delays in transforming a declared need for new forms of accountability into action. The post-Suharto growth of civil society has been encouraging as regards the promotion of accountability but considerably more needs to be done if local-level accountability regimes are to be established and enforced.

Another potentially worrying trend is the creation of new regions. Since 1999, 4 provinces and 106 districts and cities have been created by the national assembly (*Far Eastern Economic Review* 29 May 2003). Other applications for regional status are being considered but as only five have been rejected so far we can expect the trend to smaller sub-national territories to continue. One positive reading of the situation would be that it reflects the capacity to transform local aspirations into reality and is therefore evidence of the success of democratization. This view suggests that the opportunity to form new autonomous regions reflects the flexibility of the new system to accommodate the wishes of ethnic groups to form their own regions and so determine their own developmental paths. An alternative interpretation is that local elites have been seeking power and wealth through the delineation of new regions. They are seen to be opening up new opportunities for political office. In 2004, there was a general election and each district was entitled to one representative. Each new region must also have its own elected assembly, a head of region and a budget decided by them. There may also be the potential for raising finances through revenue-sharing arrangements although critics argue that some of the new regions are not sustainable. They do not make economic or administrative sense. Furthermore, the triumph of one ethnic group in establishing a new autonomous region will reconfigure the ethnic map and potentially create new minorities who might feel aggrieved or marginalized.

Enhanced inequity is a further danger of regional autonomy. Several factors indicate this possibility. Firstly, revenue-sharing arrangements for natural resources result in the creation of some regions which are rich and others, possibly even neighbours, which have no such income and are typically poor. Budgetary constraints mean that topping up the income of poor regions through the special allocation fund is simply not feasible. There are insufficient resources in the national treasury. Secondly, after the transfer of assets and personnel to regions from the centre it was noted by some analysts that there were considerable inequalities in the distribution of these resources between regions. The situation was described as 'giving cause for serious concern' (Turner and Podger 2003: 104). In a decentralized Indonesia the mechanisms to make more equitable distribution of personnel and assets are not immediately obvious and pre-existing patterns may become entrenched. They are already contributing to the fact that 'deep fiscal inequalities exist between regions' (CGI 2001, 4.4). Regions with the highest general allocations have also been receiving the largest amounts from revenue-sharing arrangements. According to financial plans for 2002 the richest district was to receive more than 50 times the amount per capita in income than the poorest district (Turner and Podger (2003: 143). Efforts to move towards more equitable funding arrangements are meeting opposition from the better resourced regions.

While theory tells us that decentralization should lead to improvements in public sector management empirical reality reveals a somewhat different story in developing countries (Smith 1985; Crook and Manor 1998; Turner 1999; Wunsch 2001). In Indonesia, regional governments embraced and acted quickly on the need to restructure their administrative organizations by amalgamating offices from the dual structure to make one unified administrative organization in each region. However, this is only one aspect of restructuring. There are concerns that other actions to reform administration have not occurred or are at best happening very slowly and varying considerably between regions. The administrative structures, work processes and organizational cultures established and embedded at subnational level during the New Order regime are bureaucratic in the sociological sense of the word (Beetham 1987). Decentralization is supposed to introduce into public sector management qualities such as responsiveness, rapid action, participation, sensitivity to local needs and improved coordination. However, embedded patterns of bureaucratic behaviour do not disappear overnight and anecdotal evidence suggests that there may be resistance to changes towards more flexible, accountable and responsive organizational forms. While grand schemes of organizational re-engineering are to be avoided because of the severe disruption they entail, there should be concern that much-needed incremental changes to management are not necessarily happening. The situation could be exacerbated by the failure to introduce significant public management reforms in central government. This is a familiar omission in decentralization experiments where attention is primarily directed at sub-national government and the initial transition phase of decentralization. Officials overlook the fact that the central agencies need to be reinvented and reoriented to ensure that the new system of central-local relations works. In Indonesia this central transformation is yet to be achieved.

Autonomy and secession

A leading feature of regional autonomy in Indonesia is that it attempts to be all-encompassing. That is, the central government legislated a standardized template for the conduct of regional affairs and central-local relations for the whole nation. All Indonesians and all territory are incorporated into autonomous regions. It is not a matter of selecting territories or particular ethnic configurations for special treatment as autonomous regions. This omnibus approach means that there can be profound differences between autonomous regions in their ethnic make-up. For example, some regions on Java may be ethnically indistinguishable from neighbouring regions. By contrast, in many regions outside of Java there is a mixture of ethnic groups. In some circumstances, such as in Kalimantan, there can be clear divisions between the original Dyak population and migrants from Madura, and bloody conflicts can result. Elsewhere there may be accommodation between different ethnic groups. The general point is that the same institutional arrangements are being used to cover quite different ethnic situations.

In three instances the designers of regional autonomy decided that the standard template was inadequate and that region-specific arrangements had to be instituted. These would apply to the provinces of East Timor, Aceh and West Papua. Each had a history of opposition to Indonesian or central rule, each had an insurgency demanding secession, and each had ethnic groups which identified themselves as different from the major ethnic groups across Indonesia.

East Timor was a Portuguese colony occupying half of one island in the eastern part of the Indonesian archipelago. Portuguese attempts to decolonize in 1974 precipitated a civil war in East Timor between those favouring independence and those seeking integration with Indonesia. Portugal withdrew from its colony and Indonesian forces invaded in 1975, and the government of Indonesia formally annexed East Timor as its twenty-seventh province. Continued conflict and famine led to the deaths of up to 200,000 people out of a population of approximately 700,000. The independence-seeking Falintil continued 'a low-grade insurgency' (Freedom House 2000). Commencing in 1982 successive Secretaries-General of the UN held regular talks with Indonesia to resolve the status of the territory (UN 2004). In 1998, the Indonesian government proposed special, but still limited, autonomy arrangements within the context of the Indonesian state. This eventually led to agreements between Indonesia and Portugal, and to the Secretary-General of the UN being granted authority by Indonesia to conduct 'popular consultation' to determine whether the proposed 'special autonomy' was acceptable to the majority of the population. The proposal was overwhelmingly rejected (78.5 per cent to 21.5 per cent) and pro-Indonesian elements backed by members of the Indonesian security forces embarked on a campaign of violence and destruction across the territory. An Australian-led multinational force was dispatched to Indonesia in September 1999 and quickly restored order. The United Nations Transitional Administration in East Timor (UNTAET) was established to administer the country until full independence on 20 May 2002.

Pressure for secession has been associated with the government's push for regional autonomy. The opening of political space and democratization following the collapse of the New Order have facilitated the growth of secessionist sentiments and activities in the provinces at either extreme of the country—Papua and Aceh. Neither of the secessionist movements is new but they have certainly been reinvigorated and pose significant threats to the important constitutional principle of unity. The hope of the lawmakers was that troubles would subside in Papua and Aceh by granting these provinces special autonomy arrangements. This was a major miscalculation.

The province of Aceh at the northernmost tip of Sumatra has 'a long history of cultural separateness and resistance to colonial intrusion' (May 1990: 34). The Dutch colonists only managed to secure the surrender of the Sultan of Aceh in 1903 after 30 years of struggle, and even then the province was awarded 'a substantial degree of autonomy' (ibid.) The early years of the republic witnessed rebellion in Aceh aimed at establishing some form of territorial autonomy. The rebellion ended in 1961 although discontent about perceived Javanese colonialism and the plundering of Acehnese wealth surfaced from time to time (Kell 1995). In 1989, 100 Libyan-trained guerrillas returned to Aceh with the objective of revitalizing the rebellion. They succeeded in provoking an appalling backlash from the Indonesian military with over 1000 Acehnese killed in the first 3 years of military operations (Human Rights Watch 2001). The resignation of President Suharto and the collapse of authoritarian rule raised hopes in Aceh that justice would be done concerning the human rights abuses of the previous decade. This did not occur and violence continued between the military and the Free Aceh Movement (*Gerakan Aceh Merdeka*—GAM). This lack of government accountability led to GAM considerably widening its support base 'building on the increasing anger of a disaffected populace' (ibid.: 10). A shadow administration organized by GAM spread across much of Aceh and involved the reinstitution of some traditional forms of governance. A referendum was suggested by the President and then withdrawn while the violence continued to worsen. A truce was negotiated in November 2002 on the back of promises by President Megawati Sukarnoputri to give more control over local revenues to the provincial government (*Far Eastern Economic Review* 9 October 2003). But few benefits were seen by the Achenese population and clashes continued between GAM and the Indonesian military. In June 2003, the Indonesian government decided on a military solution and sent in a force of 50,000 troops and police accompanied by considerable military hardware to eradicate the guerrilla army of GAM (*Far Eastern Economic Review* 5 June 2003). According to the International Crisis Group (2003), this aggression has 'completely undermined' the notion of special autonomy for Aceh. Furthermore, accusation of corruption and official misuse of Aceh's resources continue to jeopardize further talks on a special autonomy arrangement within Indonesia.

West Papua lies at the eastern end of Indonesia and comprises half of the island of New Guinea. It was not originally incorporated into the Indonesian state but was included in 1969 after a UN-sponsored 'Act of Free Choice' which has been described as 'a managed public consultation (*musjawarah*) among Indonesian-appointed delegates rather than a popular vote and it took place amid widespread reports of repression and intimidation' (May 1990: 40). Before this act, opposition to Indonesian rule in West Papua had already coalesced around the Free Papua Movement (*Organisisi Papua Merdeka*—OPM) which, in 1971, announced the territory's independence. For the next three decades, the ill-equipped and numerically small OPM was never more than an irritation to Indonesian authorities but its diplomatic efforts attracted some sympathy from overseas. The opening of democratic space following the departure of President Suharto raised expectations among OPM supporters and a wider Melanesian public that their grievances could be addressed.

The most influential Papuan body has been the Presidium of the Papuan Council which speaks on behalf of the broad Papuan Congress and wages a 'largely peaceful independence campaign' (International Crisis Group 2002). Although the independence movement's platform is based on rejection of the legitimacy of Indonesia's annexation of Papua in 1969, current antipathy to Indonesia focuses on the exploitation of natural resources such as timber and conflict arising over differences between indigenous and government interpretations of land ownership and rights.

The Indonesian government's solution to West Papua was to pass Law 45 of 1999 making special autonomy arrangements in the territory. These included the creation of two new provinces, three new districts and one new city. This was perceived by West Papuan interest groups as an attempt to divide and rule especially as there had been no community consultation prior to framing the legislation. The government returned to the drawing board and came up with a new law in 2001 (Law 21). This maintains West Papua as a single province and in addition to the elected legislature has the novel element of an upper house comprised of cultural representatives to protect 'Papuan natives' rights'. However, Law 21 has not yet become effective as the necessary secondary regulations needed to make the new system work have not been put in place. The institutions to enact such regulations have likewise not been put in place.

Each of the special cases of East Timor, Aceh and West Papua have involved political mobilization on an ethnic basis. West Papua and East

Timor are particularly interesting as they have involved the creation of a new overarching ethnicity which encompasses a number of distinct ethnic groups. The Papuan identity is claimed by the original Melanesian inhabitants of the West Papuan province, who can be separated into approximately 250 language groups. In East Timor it was the twelve ethnic groups which lay inside the colonial boundaries of the territory. Common grievances drew these different ethnic groups under the one banner. For Aceh, the commonality of interest was easier to spread among a single ethnic group in a territory which had a long-established self-awareness and history of opposition to external rule.

The grievances of the ethnic groups have been similar. They all feel that they have been exploited by outsiders and that they are not getting the full benefits of the resources which are in their territories. All three territories have rich natural resource bases. The use of military force has exacerbated the situation leading to numerous serious complaints about human rights violations. Where there is an obvious difference is in the case of East Timor. It succeeded in gaining independence, a development which is most unlikely for both West Papua and Aceh. The explanation appears to rest on two matters: the place of East Timor in the nationalist vision of Indonesia and the intervention of outside agencies. The nationalist vision corresponded to the colonial map and so overlooked East Timor, possibly rendering both its acquisition and loss of less significance to Indonesia than Aceh and West Papua, which have always been parts of the idea of Indonesia. The lengthy involvement of the UN was also of considerable importance and paved the way for subsequent Australian-led intervention under UN auspices.

It has proved impossible for Aceh and West Papua to secure UN involvement although there have been efforts by Papuan nationalists to encourage the UN to revisit the so-called 'Act of Free Choice' of 1969. None of the three cases has secured the assistance of a kin-state or significant kin-group elsewhere. For East Timor and Aceh there are no such entities. For West Papua, the neighbouring country of Papua New Guinea is similarly populated by diverse Melanesian societies but has not provided support for the separatist movement. Indonesia's colleagues in the Association of South East Asian Nations (ASEAN) have been similarly non-interventionist, adhering faithfully to their policy of non-involvement in members' domestic affairs. Norway has brokered peace talks on Aceh but the overall picture is one of the Indonesian government assiduously avoiding outside external participation in determining the future of both Aceh and West Papua. The Jakarta policy is to allow special autonomy provisions for both regions but to keep them firmly inside the unitary state. The government has no intention of repeating its policy miscalculations on East Timor.

Conclusion

A prominent feature of Indonesia's post-colonial political history has been the search for a balance between two conflicting imperatives—to decentralize power to autonomous regions while maintaining the integrity of the unitary state. The former imperative reflects demands for self-determination from ethnically diverse territories across a vast archipelago. The latter derives from the national elite's project to construct and disseminate an Indonesian identity to combat the threat of state fragmentation along regional lines. Between 1945 and 1999, the dominant theme was the perceived need to consolidate the unitary state. This resulted in policies of centralization which after a shaky start came to fruition under the authoritarian regime of President Suharto. But even then allowances were made for autonomy by creating autonomous regions across the entire Indonesian territory. However, these so-called autonomous regions did not conform to most, if not all, definitions of what an autonomous territory should be. They were dependent on and compliant with the centre. They were also not conceptualized in ethnic terms. Ethnicity was perceived as a potentially destabilizing concept which needed to be nullified as a basis for political mobilization.

The economic crisis of 1997 and the attendant democracy movement marked a major change in central-local relations in Indonesia. Policy space was opened up and the opportunity taken to introduce a radical initiative for regional autonomy. All regions in Indonesia were given extensive new functions and finance while power was invested in democratically local assemblies. Despite the ascendance of centrifugal forces the architects of regional autonomy and subsequent governments have still been keen to maintain the integrity of the unitary state. Thus, the autonomy laws were designed by small groups of centrally appointed officials. The ensuing program for writing the numerous implementing regulations has been undertaken by central government ministries. The major transfers of functions and finance were to districts not provinces, the latter being seen as having greater potential for exerting pressure on central government even to the extent of seceding. The failure to resolve claims for self-determination in the provinces of Aceh and West Papua is seen as confirmation of the validity of this strategy. Finally, the new democratic party system is designed to avoid the emergence of ethnically based parties by insisting that nationwide coverage is a compulsory requirement for registration of a political party—and there are no independent candidates in Indonesian elections.

External actors have generally played only minor support roles in relation to regional autonomy in Indonesia. The design of central-local relations has been an exclusively domestic matter. There have been no kin-states or external kin-groups involved at any stage. ASEAN neighbours have not interfered while multilateral and bilateral aid agencies have put resources into the implementation rather than the design of regional autonomy. The case of East Timor provides a stark contrast as it was external involvement by the UN that led to secession from the Republic. The secessionist movements in Aceh and West Papua have failed to mobilize such external assistance and the central government of Indonesia has been adamant that these conflicts are entirely domestic affairs.

The approach to regional autonomy in Indonesia favours standardization, a bureaucratic solution to democratic and regional pressure for power and resources. The legislation applies across the whole country to all territories with the exception of special legislation for autonomous regions in West Papua and Aceh. Structures of regional government have been in part regulated or advised from the centre although there is now, unlike in the past, room to manoeuvre and express regional preferences in organizational design. As everywhere and everybody in Indonesia are incorporated into an autonomous region the question arises as to what is so special about them. For example, how do they differ from the decentralized local government units (LGUs) in the neighbouring Philippines? The Philippine LGUs have devolved powers, functions and finance along the lines of Indonesia but not quite so extensive. The Philippines LGUs elect local assemblies and chief executives. The Philippines is also ethnically diverse. But the Philippines reserves the term 'autonomous region' to only two territories which are special cases demanding special measures. By contrast Indonesia has always employed the term 'regional autonomy' (otonomi daerah) to describe any decentralization of power and authority to subnational territories. The question that now arises is whether the latest and most radical experiment with regional autonomy will provide the flexibility and opportunity for diversity to be expressed in regional governance arrangements. Embedded models of bureaucracy have so far entailed little deviation from past organizational practice but the new regional autonomy is still in its early stages, a work in progress.

References

Anderson, B. (1991) *Imagined Communities.* Verso: London.
Asia Foundation (2002) *Indonesia Rapid Decentralization Appraisal (IRDA), First Report.* Asia Foundation: Jakarta.
—— (2003) *Indonesia Rapid Decentralization Appraisal (IRDA), Second Report.* Asia Foundation: Jakarta.
Beetham, D. (1987) *Bureaucracy.* Open University Press: Milton Keynes.
CGI (Consultative Group in Indonesia) (2001) *The Imperative for Reform.* World Bank: Jakarta (Report Number 23093-IND).
Crook, R. and Manor, J. (1998) *Democracy and Decentralisation in South Asia and West Africa: Participation, Accountability and Performance.* Cambridge University Press: Cambridge.
Daftary, F. (2000) *Insular Autonomy: A Framework for Conflict Settlement. A Comparative Study of Corsica and the Åland Islands.* European Centre for Minority Issues: Flensburg.

Devas, N. (1997) 'Indonesia: what do we mean by decentralization?', *Public Administration and Development*, 17(3): 351–368.

Gerritsen, R. and Situmorang, S. (1999) 'Beyond integration? The need to decentralize central-regional/local relations in Indonesia', in M. Turner (ed.) *Central-local Relations in Asia Pacific: Convergence or Divergence?* Macmillan and St Martin's Press: London and New York, 48–70.

Freedom House (2000) 'East Timor: political rights and civil liberties'. Accessed 11 November 2003, http://www.freedomhouse.org.

Grindle, M. and Thomas, J. (1991) *Public Choices and Policy Change.* Johns Hopkins University Press: Baltimore.

Human Rights Watch (2001) 'Indonesia: the war in Aceh', *Human Rights Watch*, 13(4): 2–41.

International Crisis Group (2002) 'Indonesia: resources and conflict in Papua'. Accessed 28 August 2003, http://www.intl-crisis-group.org/projects/showreport.cfm? reportid=774.

Kell, T. (1995) *The Roots of Achenese Rebellion 1989–92.* Cornell Modern Indonesia Project: Ithaca.

Legge, J. (1972) *Sukarno: A Political Biography.* Penguin: Harmondsworth.

May, R. (1990) 'Ethnic separatism in Southeast Asia', *Pacific Viewpoint*, 31(2): 28–59.

Mokhsen, N. (2003) *Decentralization in Indonesia.* Unpublished PhD dissertation, Australian National University.

Morfit, M. (1986) 'Strengthening the capacities of local government: policies and constraints', in C. MacAndrews (ed.) *Central Government and Local Development in Indonesia.* Oxford University Press: Singapore, 56–76.

Partnership for Governance Reform in Indonesia (PGRI) (2001) *A National Survey of Corruption in Indonesia: Executive Summary.* PGRI: Jakarta.

Potier, T. (2001) *Conflict in Nagorno-Karabakh, Abkhazia and South Ossetia: A Legal Appraisal.* Kluwer International Law: The Hague.

Rohdewohld, R. (1995) *Public Administration in Indonesia.* Montech: Melbourne.

Smith, B. (1985) *Decentralisation: the Territorial Dimension of the State.* George Allen and Unwin: London.

Suryadinata, L., Arifin, E. N. and Ananta, A. (2003) *Indonesia's Population: Ethnicity and Religion in a Changing Political Landscape.* Institute of Southeast Asian Studies: Singapore.

Turner, M. (ed.) (1999) *Central-local Relations in Asia Pacific: Convergence or Divergence?* Macmillan and St Martin's Press: London and New York.

—— (2001) 'Implementing Laws 22 and 25: the challenge of decentralization in Indonesia', Asian Review of Public Administration, 13(1): 69–82.

Turner, M. and Podger, O. with Sumardjono, M. and Tirthayasa, W. (2003) *Decentralisation in Indonesia: Redesigning the State.* Asia Pacific Press: Canberra.

UN (2004) 'East Timor—UNMINSET—Background', http://www.un.org/Depts/dpke/missions/unminset, accessed 17 November 2004.

Usman, S. (2001) *Indonesia's Decentralization Policy: Initial Experiences and Emerging Problems.* SMERU Working Paper, Jakarta.

World Bank (2000) *World Development Report 1999/2000.* Oxford University Press: New York.

Wunsch, J. (2001) 'Decentralization, local governance and "recentralization" in Africa', *Public Administration and Development*, 21(4): 277–288.

10 'Masters of their homelands'

Revisiting the regional ethnic autonomy system in China in light of local institutional developments

Erik Friberg[1]

The practice of regional autonomy not only ensures the rights of the ethnic minorities to exercise autonomy as masters of their homelands, but also upholds the unification of the state.

PRC National Minority White Paper, 1999[2]

Introduction

Approximately 110 million persons, counting for 8.4 per cent of the total population, belong to the 55 officially recognised 'national minorities' in the People's Republic of China (National Bureau of Statistics PRC 2001).[3] Considering that the vast number of the minorities, estimated to number 150 million by 2010, cover more than 60 per cent of the Chinese territory, scholars argue that China in general has experienced considerable success in dealing with the relations between the national minorities and the majority Han ethnic group (Ghai 2000: 92; Zhu and Yu 2000: 41; Mackerras 1998: 42). This does not mean that unrest and serious challenges to the Beijing authority in the form of self-determination claims do not exist and continue, beyond the more commonly known situations in Tibet, Xinjiang and Inner Mongolia. Historical conflicts forming part of collective memory include the bloody suppression of the Miao and Hui uprisings in the eighteenth and nineteenth centuries; the uprisings of mainly the Yi and Yao in the 1950s and 1960s; the dismantling of the autonomous areas with significant losses of territory to neighbouring non-autonomous provinces and other events during the Cultural Revolution; and the ethnic conflict involving the Utsat Muslim minority on Hainan Island (Heberer 2000: 5; Kaup 2000: 111; Pang 1998: 142–162). Applying this volume's editors' definition of a 'self-determination conflict' ('a self-defined segment of an existing state's population, inhabiting solely or with others a specific territory, seeks to increase the level of, and resources for, self-governance') demands from ethnic leaders in various areas aiming at increased self-governance and improvements of the existing autonomy system would also be included.

While not based on ethnicity, the establishment and developments of Hong Kong and Macao as Special Administrative Regions provides an alternative institutional 'autonomy arrangement' in China, and have inspired leaders from several western and north-western provinces to press Beijing for 'Hong Kong style' autonomy.[4] The re-unification of Taiwan remains an uncertain process. The Special Economic Zones set up during the 1980s in the coastal areas were given law-making powers in 1996, and have been argued to hold more 'autonomy' than the minority areas and to hold the greatest share of decentralised power in China (Saich 2001: 142).[5] These different arrangements demonstrate that China applies central-local relations asymmetrically, while being a 'unitary' state governed by the principle of 'democratic centralism', thus subordinate to the State Council and in effect putting the power in the hands of the Chinese Communist Party (CCP) leaders or some higher level responsible to the centre (Ghai 2000: 77).[6]

Surveys indicate that a rather large percentage of people in China expect growing ethnic conflicts in the near future (Heberer 2000: 4). The ethnically related disputes during the past 20 years have mainly been related to economic disparities, dissatisfaction over cultural policies, ethnically related discrimination, internal migration patterns and religious disputes rather than 'external' self-determination claims aiming at outright separation from the Chinese State. Heberer identifies various sources of conflict, including continued and uneven distribution of economic development between non-Han and Han regions, and observes the growing influence of religion and traditional culture as an indication of rising ethnicity (Heberer 2000: 1–19). Under these circumstances, it could be counterproductive for the PRC government to overplay Chinese nationalism appealing largely to the Han history and nation, since this may cause resentment among minority nationalities (Zhao 2000: 15). A future of ethnic warfare cannot be excluded if chauvinistic, centralising Han rulers are incapable of meeting the self-governance demands of regional and ethnic communities (Friedman 1995: 61).

Has the Chinese ethnic autonomy system been successful in meeting existing ethnic self-governance demands? The legal foundation of the ethnic autonomy system in China is provided by the 1982 Constitution and the enabling act, the 1984 Law on Regional Ethnic Autonomy (LREA). By the end of 1998, 5 autonomous regions, 20 autonomous prefectures and 120 autonomous counties had been established exercising these regional ethnic autonomy powers (Information Office PRC 1999, chapter III). This chapter will focus on the design and implementation of the existing regionally based ethnic autonomy system, mainly from a legal perspective, in light of the transformation of local organs of self-government, in particular the increasing role of the 'legislative' local People's Congresses and electoral experiments enabling enhanced downward accountability. These institutional developments at local levels, coupled with expectations that the 2001 amendment of the LREA would address existing uncertainties connected with the granted autonomous powers, merit a re-visit of the Chinese regional ethnic autonomy system. Several scholars completely reject the Chinese autonomy model as being negated by the absolutist existence of the Communist Party and the application of the Leninist principle of democratic centralism (Ghai 2000: 96; Hannum 1996: 426; Heintze 1998: 15). These assertions may be becoming too categorical, while it is clear that the Chinese autonomy system remains distant from 'genuine' autonomy arrangements, as referred to in international academic discourse. Institutional constraints continue to make the actual differences in the scope of local self-government between autonomous and non-autonomous areas highly questionable. However, this chapter will argue that trends of increasing bottom-up accountability and strengthened institutional power within local People's Congresses can encourage emerging local agencies to put real contents in the autonomy provisions and exercise the powers of ethnic local self-governance within the Chinese State.

The history of Chinese policies on regional ethnic autonomy

During the Republican period one purpose of officially recognising minorities was to win the loyalty of the different ethnic groups in order to unite with the Han Chinese in the struggle against foreign intervention and domination. Ethnic classification was conducted in the 1950s and 1960s taking subjective criteria into account to some extent, while mainly based on Stalin's definition of ethnicity: a group sharing a common territory, economy, language and culture.[7] There were 400 ethnic groups claiming recognition, which in the end was reduced to 55 officially recognised 'national minorities', resulting in remaining contestations (Heberer 1989: 30–39).

The assumption that children do not lose their born ethnicity when cultural convergence takes place leads to the ironic situation that ethnic fusion is legally impossible, although perhaps culturally desired by the state (Shih 2002: 253). While appearing to aim at 'integration' rather than outright either 'pluralism' or 'assimilation', Chinese minority policies remain part of a 'civilising project'. This is visible in the statutory language of preserving the 'fine' traditions of national minorities and steadily 'raising' the cultural levels among national cultures, i.e. measured by the yardstick of the Han Chinese civilisation. Various preferential policies aim at reversing the traditional Chinese pattern of marginalisation and subordination of non-Han nationalities and constructing a minority elite whose loyalty is deemed essential to political stability, particularly in the strategic border areas. Far-reaching special measures are in place for issues including family planning, university admissions and access to public service.

While the extent of the actual implementation of these measures of positive discrimination is contested, it may be indicative that millions of citizens previously classified as Han changed their status to minority during the 1980s and 1990s partly in order to benefit from these preferential policies (Sautman 1999: 286).

The Communist Party adopted Leninist ethnic policies in 1931 and the Jiangxi Soviet constitution included a minority right to secession, which was altered to promises of minority autonomy within a unitary framework in 1938. This remained Mao Zedong's policy after gaining control over mainland China and the founding of the PRC in 1949. The ethnic groups were downgraded from 'nations' – guaranteed autonomous republics – to 'nationalities', entitling them at best an autonomous region (Ghai 2000: 80). The 1949 Common Program of the Chinese People's Political Consultative Conference set out regional ethnic autonomy as the basic policy on nationalities and an important component of the political system of China. As within all states, China has over time experimented in its central-local relations with alternating periods of decentralising and centralising trends. During the 20th century the trend was clearly centralisation until the 'open door policy' with economic liberalisation brought decentralising trends from the end of the 1970s. Similarly, the autonomy system in China has varied in scope and extent over time. In 1947 the first autonomous region under communist rule was established, the Inner Mongolia Autonomous Region. During the 1950s regional national autonomy was gradually implemented throughout the country to better integrate the minorities into the Chinese nation (Zhu and Yu 2000: 50). Autonomy provisions appeared in the first 1954 PRC Constitution, although severely circumscribed by lacking enabling legislation and leaving complete central control to arbitrarily dissolve the limited autonomy granted (Sautman 1999: 288; Heberer 1989: 41–42).[8] This formal autonomy was abolished during the Cultural Revolution years and then re-established in the 1978 Constitution, while provisions enabling financial autonomy for minority areas remained absent (Sautman 1999: 288). This aspect was added in the currently-in-force 1982 Constitution. Heberer exemplifies the repeated policy alterations on minority autonomy with the rise and fall of the Li and Miao Autonomous Prefecture in Hainan. This autonomy arrangement was established in the early 1950s, dissolved in 1958 and then restored in 1962. In 1966, following the abolishment of all autonomous arrangements during the Cultural Revolution, the autonomous prefecture was again dissolved, later to be restored in the 1970s before ultimately being abolished in 1988 (Heberer 2000: 11).[9]

Currently, autonomous areas include: autonomous regions where persons belonging to one ethnic minority group live in concentrated communities (such as the Xinjiang Uygur Autonomous Region); autonomous prefectures with two ethnic minorities (such as the Miao and Dong Autonomous Prefecture); and autonomous counties with several ethnic minorities (such as the Shuangjiang Lahu, Va and Blang Autonomous County in Yunnan province). Autonomous areas have also been established within larger autonomous areas when different ethnic minorities live in compact communities (such as the Oroqen, Exenki and Duar autonomous banners within the Inner Mongolia Autonomous Region and the Mengcun Hui Autonomous County). As demonstrated above, an autonomous area places the regional title in front of the ethnic title. This may seem reasonable considering that not all inhabitants in the area belong to the ethnic group(s) holding autonomy. In fact, as Zhou observes, the ethnic minority population of most autonomous areas are not even the local majority population, which indicates that ethnic autonomy in itself is not 'majoritarian democratic', and is possibly more 'regional' than 'ethnic'.[10]

Regional ethnic autonomy design: contents and discontents

The preamble of the 1982 Constitution stresses the unitary, multinational nature of the Chinese State and opposes the dual threats of great-Han chauvinism and local national chauvinism. The main constitutional provisions concerning autonomy state that regional autonomy should be practised by minorities living in compact communities to preserve and reform their own ways and customs, make the local minority language the official language of the autonomy arrangement, allow for local security forces and reserve key positions for national minority cadres (1982 Constitution, Arts 4(3), 113–114, 122–123). The organs of local autonomous self-government are granted power to 'enact regulations on the exercise of autonomy and other separate regulations in the light of the political, economic and cultural characteristics of the nationality or nationalities in the areas concerned' (1982 Constitution, Art. 116). The 1984 Law on Regional Ethnic Autonomy (LREA) was adopted to implement the constitutional provisions related to ethnic autonomy while further strengthening the structure of autonomous regimes by giving more economic and cultural rights to minorities (Zhu and Yu 2000: 54). There exists some joint central/autonomous authority concerning issues of common concern, such as policing and mineral extraction (Sautman 1999: 294).

The 2001 amendment to the 1984 LREA was reported by Xinhua News Agency to focus on 'the economic system and the support and help that State organs at higher levels offer to localities under ethnic autonomy', and to 'accelerate economic development and social progress in localities under ethnic autonomy and gradually narrow the gap between these localities and developed areas' (as reported by Tibet Information Network 2001). Revisions did not, however, address the crucial issues of the demarcated scope of autonomous powers granted or procedures for settling disputes concerning the boundaries of exercising these autonomous powers. The most important revision was probably the indication of acceptance of the principle that areas supplying natural resources should receive compensation for their exploitation (Loper 2002: 25). The status of the regional ethnic autonomy system has also been, at least semantically, upgraded from being an 'important' to a 'basic' political system of the State (UN CERD 2001:2). The focus of amendments on economic matters is in line with the policy launched in 1999 of 'Reviving the West', which relies on state infrastructure investment combined with political persuasion of the more developed provinces to shift investment to interior provinces (Saich 2001: 151).[13] This focus on economics and central transfers can, in fact, provide for increased direct central involvement in the economic development of autonomous areas.

While the Chinese concept of 'autonomy' can be argued to mainly refer to administrative matters rather than legislation, concepts become blurred since the distinction between the two has traditionally been unclear. However, in the wake of market-economic reforms, China has moved towards becoming a country ruled by law, with an increased role of enacted laws at central and sub-central levels, although continued 'vagueness' in the drafting continues to leave wide discretion for executive implementation. The following analysis is nevertheless focused on the exercise of 'legislative' powers as demonstrating the current scope of autonomy in China and identifying the institutional challenges connected.

Legislative autonomy

Between the three power centres existing at each administrative level – the party committee, the local (executive) People's government and the local (legislative) People's Congress (LPC) – the latter formally holds the superior power in the 1982 Constitution as constituting the 'highest organ of state power'. Nevertheless, in effect LPCs have traditionally been (and remain) the least influential. Since local governments and LPCs are state organs designed to implement party policy and thus complement each other and co-operate, legislative-executive relations in China have been argued to be a division of labour, rather than a division of powers (Cho 2002: 729).

The autonomous LPCs in China are distinguished from regular LPCs in two ways. Firstly, the former is granted independent law-making power to alter superior legislation to local conditions and to enact separate legislation on the exercise of autonomy (LREA, Arts 19–20; Legislation Law Art. 66). Whereas legislative authority in non-autonomous areas halt at provincial level, these powers apply to LPCs down to prefecture and county level in autonomous areas. Provisions enabling autonomous LPCs to modify national policies and laws in line with local customs is reaffirmed in various national laws, including the 1980 Marriage Law, the 1985 Succession Law and the 1991 Adoption Law. However, no judicial autonomy exists in ethnic autonomy areas (Chao 1994: 104). Secondly, rules apply to increase the number of minority deputies and ensure adequate representation. For example, one or more of the leadership positions in the People's Congress Standing Committee in an autonomous area is guaranteed to be assigned to a minority (LREA, Arts 16 and 19–20).

Article 5 of the LREA provides at least two fundamental problematic issues concerning the exercise of legislative powers from a legal point of view. Article 5 provides the duty for autonomous governments to uphold the 'unity' of the PRC and guarantee that the Constitution and 'other laws' are observed and implemented. Firstly, the central authorities can therefore declare any legislative action from an autonomous area as contrary to 'national unity' and render it null and void. This also applies to the provisions in Article 7 which state that the organs of self-government shall 'place the interests of the State as a whole above anything else'. Secondly, continued uncertainty exists as to whether the phrase 'other laws' means 'any' laws. What is then the normative hierarchy between a 'general' law enacted by the central legislature vis-à-vis a local 'specialised' law enacted by the autonomous area legislature? While it is naturally reasonable to demand that autonomous areas abide by the Constitution, where is the line drawn and who draws this line? Phan questions whether a better approach would be to list what 'other laws' or categories of laws the autonomous governments are expected to uphold and enforce (Phan 1996: 96). Otherwise the difference to non-autonomous legislatures decreases significantly, since LPCs in non-autonomous areas are similarly prohibited to enact legislation conflicting to the Constitution and 'other laws'. However, these regular LPCs are in addition prohibited to contravene 'policies, decrees, and administrative orders of the state' (Chao 1994: 111; Article 27 of the Local Organic Law). Stearns argues that the 2000 Legislation Law made 'limited inroads into the dark' by stipulating that when autonomous legislatures modify national law and regulations, this must not violate the 'central principles' of the central legislation (Stearns 2001: 8). The problem is however that the provisions fail to clarify the procedure for deciding whether such a 'central principle' is violated. Continued ambiguity concerning granting genuine autonomy powers can be seen in the vague legal language used in the LREA. The concepts of 'national unity' and 'primacy of national law' therefore constrain the powers granted to organs of ethnic self-government and enable arbitrary interventions from the centre.

The lack of dispute mechanisms

The vague legal language of the enabling act could be mitigated by dispute mechanisms, where questions concerning the relation of central-autonomous powers could be consistently and impartially adjudicated by a judicial organ. However, there is a continued lack of such dispute

resolution mechanisms (cf. Ghai 2000: 85). The protection from perceived and actual vertical and horizontal arbitrary interference therefore
remains a considerable challenge to the regional ethnic autonomy system
in China. Instead of legal venues to deliver clarifications on these questions, the decisions end up being taken within the non-legal arena of
bureaucratic discretion. Stearns provides the example of the People's
Congress of Xishuangbanna Dai Autonomous Prefecture in the Yunnan
province, which sought to pass a regulation allowing marriage at an age
lower than stipulated under national law. This was rejected by the provincial authorities for unclear reasons. Since the law neither provides guidance for when the provincial perception of local interests overrides the
autonomous entity's own determination of local interest, nor provides
dispute mechanisms where this intervention from above can be challenged, the narrow scope of autonomy powers granted to self-governing
organs becomes limited or non-existent (Stearns 2001: 9).

Ladder of approval procedures

With unclear statutory language and the absence of adequate dispute resolution mechanisms, the ladder of approval procedures provides an additional layer restricting autonomous discretion. The 1984 LREA reiterates
that autonomy areas shall be under the 'unified state leadership' and governed by the principle of democratic centralism (LREA, preface, Art. 3 and
15). When exercising the autonomy power to enact separate legislation
these considerations surface, since the laws have to go through ladders of
approval and pass the scrutiny of the immediately higher administrative
level. The exercise of law-making power by a provincial level autonomous
People's Congress must be approved by the Standing Committee of the
National People's Congress, and the Standing Committee of the provincial
People's Congress must approve the legislative actions by autonomous prefecture and county (LREA, Art. 19–20 and Legislation Law Art. 65). Also,
all legislative acts of autonomous areas are to be submitted to the Standing
Committee of the National People's Congress for registration. In addition
to these vertical ladders of approval, horizontal ladders exist with respect to
same-level party structures. These combined approval procedures provide a
'nearly fail-proof checking system' (Phan 1996: 95). Even if the provincial
standing committees did allow an undesirable local legislation or modification to become law, the centre can block the law when it is reported to the
committee for the record. A law passed by lower level LPCs are sometimes
so extensively revised at provincial level that their original meaning is lost
(Chao 1994: 105). As an example, the Guangxi Zhuang Autonomous
Region has submitted 14 drafts since 1984 of the Guangxi Autonomy Regulation to the State Council for consideration. All of these drafts have been
returned for revision, leaving the region without a working document
clearly defining its relationship with the centre (Kaup 2000: 117).

Stearns provides an example of the consequences of unclear legal hierarchies and procedures between local autonomous power and powerful administrative interests involving persons of the Ewenki minority in Inner Mongolia. An Ewenki banner LPC attempted to use its law-making power to redesignate, as collectively owned grassland, a large tract of land formally administered by the forestry department. Interests opposing this LPC action argued that such a separate autonomous regulation would contradict the National Forestry Law, thus violating the requirements of autonomous law-making to observe national law. Stearns argues that given continued disagreement concerning the hierarchy of legal instruments in Chinese law, it was open to the LPC to argue the validity of their use of autonomy power under LREA (passed by the National People's Congress plenary, NPC) over provisions of the National Forestry Law (passed by the National People's Congress Standing Committee, NPCSC). In the absence of judicial review, such a strategy could also have served the purpose of contributing to clarification of the relationship between law passed by NPC and law passed by NPCSC. Since it was predictable that the Forestry Ministry would defeat the intended regulation in the approvals procedures, the banner altered the regulation and adopted vague legal language, which Stearns observes to be an example of the weakness in autonomous law making (this paragraph builds on Stearns 2001: 11–12).

It has been argued that the LREA does not command sufficient respect among central government departments and that central policies often conflict with this law (Chao 1994: 116). For example, although Article 14 of the LREA grants consultative rights to autonomous governments before boundary changes, this stipulation is often ignored (ibid.). The continued uncertainty, coupled with low awareness, of the legal hierarchy in China makes the nexus of approval procedures indirectly determine the outcome of the scope of self-government, leaving the lower autonomous levels in a weak position.

Administrative and financial autonomy

In addition to legislative rights, the autonomy provisions grant the autonomous organs of local self-government increased administrative and economic functions. Fiscal decentralisation during the 1980s and 1990s has made several economic rights specified under the 1984 LREA apply throughout the country, with general local latitude in determining the expenditure of money allocated to the area by the state, and allow larger exemptions from taxation than under state law (cf. 1992 Constitution Article 117, LREA Articles 33 and 35). Sautman distinguishes between the 'dependency' result of LREA Article 33 providing subsidies and Article 35 displaying 'self-reliance' by permitting autonomies to lower their taxes to improve the investment climate, and thus partially compensate for the greater state investment along the coastal areas (Sautman 1998: 104). Institutional constraints include continued reluctance among some governmental departments at provincial and state level to effectively devolve economically related powers to autonomous areas. Protective policies for trade in autonomous areas have been disrupted following reforms that removed the economic system from the centrally planned economy (Zhu and Yu 2000: 55). Autonomous regions generally face rising deficits coupled with decreasing financial transfers from the central government, the latter since the centre's disposable funds for re-distribution among provinces has declined (Saich 2001: 149–155). It is expected that some preferential policies autonomous regions currently enjoy will be restricted through China's membership in the World Trade Organisation. Minority leaders in autonomous areas appear to seek the combination of enhanced autonomy and a centre with strong redistributive powers.

The administrative mandate also includes the right to elect and recall local officials and to conduct formal nomination procedures for the LPC presidium (Chao 1994: 114). Article 20 enables the autonomous governments to cease implementation of any objectionable policy given prior approval from the state organ at the higher level. Discretion remains concerning family planning measures with exceptions made for the one-child policy. Urban minority couples may often have two children and rural minorities more than two children (Sautman 1999: 294). Phan argues that it is only in some, mostly administrative and 'soft', issues that 'true' autonomy is granted to autonomous areas, including powers over education, cultural development, health care and environmental protection – 'less politicised issues which the party-state can do without' (Phan 1996: 99). Phan further observes that while the 'leadership and assistance' provided by the centre, in the form of sending staff and experts to the autonomous areas, are intended to help the generally underdeveloped autonomous areas in the western regions of the PRC, this is reminiscent of the 'Trojan Horse', giving the state the necessary pretext to relocate Han Chinese into the geopolitical strategic areas (ibid.: 100).

Local institutions: the rise of Local People's Congresses

The vertical and horizontal lines of authority within the institutional landscape of China governed by the Leninist principle of 'democratic centralism' provide multiple challenges for genuine autonomous arrangements aiming to provide enhanced ethnic self-rule. It is, for example, unclear whether a provincial party organ is a representative of the centre or a representative of the province in questions concerning central-provincial relations.[14] Overall, there has been a growth of provincial power relative to China's central government in the reform era (Fitzgerald 2002: 25). Political and administrative leadership in the 1990s appears to have become more localist, with rising eagerness of localities to strive for their own interests (Goodman 2000: 159–183). The implementation of decentralised powers varies foreseeably between and also within provinces. While most provinces have gained discretionary powers, it can be noted that central control has been argued to have increased in Guangtong and Sichuan provinces (Mori 2002: 5). With the dynamics of transition to the market offering far more opportunities for corruption than previously, the centre has increasingly been looking for mechanisms to control sub-central power structures, as described below (Fabre 2002: 553). Overall, however, the legal and policy framework is still top-down and centralised with key policymaking and relevant implementation resources still controlled by the central government.

The political reforms following the economic reforms since the late 1970s have given the 'legislative' LPCs increased political importance (Saich 2001: 142). LPC leaders have increased their power and re-vitalised the People's Congresses as an institutional actor by weaving institutional linkages and exploiting the subordination to the party and executive in order to gain acceptance (Xia 2000: 187). LPCs have recently become more independent-minded and created their separate space in the political power structure by the move from applying exclusively 'co-operative' strategies towards increasingly employing 'confrontational' strategies towards local governments (Cho 2002: 724; Xia 2000: 186–188). In particular, the provincial legislatures have started a new round of political reform in developing the right to check the executive administration and to some extent the party itself (Chao 2003: 3). Increased LPC rejection of party-sponsored candidates has forced the party to pay more attention to screening candidates. Elected officials have increasingly become more attentive to public opinion while remaining accountable to the deputies, and in this way indirectly accountable to the local people (Xia 2000: 190–192).

However, since these increased powers have mainly related to supervisory mechanisms of the local government and to questions of personnel selection, it still remains unlikely that the LPCs would initiate legislative action without support, let alone contravene the opinions of the more powerful local governments and party committees. Party groups formed in the LPC Standing Committees in practice lead the work of the legislature and are directly subordinated to Party committees, and thus are expected to follow party line (Cho 2002: 727). The LPCs risk becoming the institutional vehicle for the Party to indirectly carry out supervision of local government (ibid.: 740). In practice, local government organisations including LPCs have always been controlled by the local Party committees, which Chao argues 'use the LPCs to carry out and legitimise their decisions' (Chao 1994: 116). These developments have nevertheless provided LPCs with some limited political space, enough to decide and handle some of their own matters without the Party's prior approval, at least in issues of limited importance (Cho 2002: 728).

The institutional developments of the LPCs are not happening at the expense of Party authority. On the contrary, by endorsing these changes it is argued that the Party has benefited accordingly in authority, although increasingly leaving day-to-day decisions to the government and legislature (Chao 2003: 21–22). Some scholars argue that the Party is decentralising its control over law-making and imply an erosion of Party control over legislative organs (Tanner 1994: 384–388). Others argue, on the contrary, that Party influence has in fact increased. Stearns also finds that an enhanced Party involvement contributes to the perception by LPC workers that LPCs are gaining in institutional importance, citing interviewees stating that 'the party would not bother with an unimportant institution' (Stearns 2001: 20). Nevertheless, the LPCs can be argued to be competing with the Party for one of the most valuable power resources, local people's loyalty and mandate (Xia 2000: 212).

Legislative capacity

Similarly to the national level, the legislative initiatives and main drafting at sub-central levels often takes place in the government and upon initiative by, or merely after gaining acceptance from, the Party. These clearcut boundaries are, however, rapidly changing. An amendment of the Organic Law of the Local People's Congresses and the Local People's Governments in 1979 decided that People's Congresses should establish Standing Committees (Zhu 1999: 28–46). The LPCs are stipulated to hold sessions at least once a year, and sessions last merely about two weeks. While the LPCs are not in session, the LPC Standing Committees hold the legislative mandate. Due to the limited sessions of LPCs, the LPC Standing Committees in fact handle most legislation (Chao 1994: 103). LPC Standing Committees also have the power to discuss and decide 'major issues' according to Article 8 of the Local Organic Law, including the power to approve major policy decisions taken by governments at the same level and hold, similarly to non-autonomous areas, supervisory powers to rescind government decisions and orders which contravene the Constitution, laws or administrative regulations (ibid.: 114–115). The Party can bypass the LPCs by exerting influence on the less numerous Standing Committee members and even encourage them to revoke decisions previously taken by the LPC plenary session (Shih 1999: 242). A second 'suborgan' within the LPCs becoming increasingly authoritative and efficient is the 'chairman's group' (Chao 2003: 15). The 'chairman's group' holds significant power by setting the agenda, and constitutes the core of the People's Congress power. Members include the Standing Committee, the Director, the Vice-Directors and the Secretary General. Local governments, LPC Standing Committee members or 'chairman's group' meetings generally propose the bills which then are handled by the LPC Standing Committees.

Ad hoc or permanent 'special committees' with the right to draft legis-lative proposals, and to examine legislative drafts originating elsewhere, have emerged as the core of the central legislature. With enhanced capac-ity building and resources trickled downward in the administrative struc-tures, the specialised committees can be expected to evolve in the LPCs as a third influential 'sub-organ'. While currently on average 5.4 'special committees' exist at provincial level, lower level People's Congresses hardly have any such committees (Chao 2003: 24). At the county LPCs, however, 'working committees' under the Standing Committee are expanding, often reflecting the bureaucratic developments at the provin-cial level. The structural independence of a 'special committee' at the provincial level is theoretically greater than that of a 'working committee' at the county level, although members of the latter in fact take on major responsibilities in drafting groups reworking drafts several times before submitting them to the Standing Committee.[15] In comparison with the local government, LPCs continue to suffer from being under-resourced, and their financial dependency on the local governments discourages them from resolutely supervising governments (Cho 2002: 730). Besides being subordinate in financial and practical resources, most LPC deputies are not able to compete with the local government in terms of functional capacity (Shih 1999: 243). Traditionally those deputies posted for posi-tions in the People's Congresses were cadres approaching retirement, although this has changed significantly in recent years (Stearns 2001: 15). Although most LPC deputies reportedly perceive their election as an honour, the lack of proper incentives for unpaid LPC deputies often makes them feel unconnected to the legislative work (cf. Shih 1999: 237–239). Within this limited political space of changed legislative-executive relations since the early 1990s, LPCs have nevertheless dared to dismiss leading officials when carrying out supervision, revealing that LPCs can use 'confrontational' strategies and have evolved as possible institutional vehicles capable to bring change (Cho 2002: 731).

Before turning to the question of minority representation, it can be concluded that those positions holding the limited yet autonomous powers granted to autonomous LPCs are a narrow elite within the People's Congress 'Standing Committee and members of the 'chairman's group'. Making creative use of autonomous legislative powers is more likely to originate from here than from the LPC plenary with its infre-quent sessions and deputies with low-level incentives.

Ethnic representation in the organs of local self-government

The crucial question arises whether the leaders of the ethnic groups within the autonomous areas *in fact* can exercise the existing, yet limited, independent law- and decision-making powers provided for the autonomous organs of local self-government. The LREA stipulates that local autonomous governments are to be led by ethnic leaders. However, the minority group bearing autonomy powers in a locality may not necessarily constitute the local majority population. Mechanisms exist to ensure minorities at least proportional representation, and the rules generally provide numerical over-representation (1995 Election Law Chapter IV). In the Tibet Autonomous Region, over 80 per cent of all members of the various organs of state power and close to 100 per cent of county and township heads are Tibetans (Sautman and Eng 2001: 49, 55–56). The top government post in an autonomous area and either the chair or one vice-chair of all local People's Congresses are positions to be held by a person of the ethnic minority, although the Party secretary at provincial and often at prefecture levels are more likely to be Han Chinese (Yee 2003: 449). If different ethnic minorities form the population, each ethnic group is guaranteed at least one deputy, even if the ethnic group is not numerous in the area. Article 16 of the Electoral Law provides that minorities constituting more than 30 per cent of the total population in an area do not benefit from preferential policies. A minority counting for less than 15 per cent of the area population is guaranteed proportionally more deputies than other more numerous minorities, although they cannot count for more than twice their 'proportional' number. Groups between 15 and 30 per cent get gradually adjusted proportions of deputy positions (1995 Election Law Art. 18(2)).

Party control over deputies

Under the banner of achieving representativity, the CCP intervenes in the selection process by handling the nomination procedures (Shih 1999: 177–198). Taking a county as an example, the three local power bodies – Party, government and People's Congress – are elected in different ways. The Party secretary is appointed by the immediately higher level Party committee. The head and deputy heads of the county government are elected by county People's Congress deputies, who in their turn have been directly elected by the county residents (Li 2002: 706). Direct elections of the local 'legislative' LPCs are thus held up to county level. Deputies to autonomous districts, regions, and provinces, however, are elected 'indirectly' by these lower-level legislative bodies, following nominations by the incumbent Standing Committee of the People's Congress at the relevant higher level. While recent interesting developments have taken place concerning nominations, with elements of self-nomination and non-conditionality of party membership, the Party remains in overall control.

This Party control over nomination procedures makes it unlikely that minority representatives holding views far from the mainstream Party line on minority policy will emerge. Also, even if dedicated minority deputies wish to promote their ethnic constituencies, indirectly they may be prevented from becoming vocal by not wanting to be perceived as 'small nationalist chauvinists', punishable by dismissal or worse (Kaup 2002: 883).[16] A minority deputy, even in an autonomous area, could therefore need to retreat into speaking on behalf of his or her territory. It has also been argued that many current non-Han leaders' general appeal in the eyes of their ethnic fellows may have declined, since they no longer necessarily work within their ethnic groups before taking on leadership positions, and thus become less effective if they are to fulfil the task of facilitating reconciliation between minority groups and Han Chinese (Zang 1998: 127). Preferential policies in general mainly benefit the ethnic elites, who tend to be the culturally most assimilated members of the minority in question, and often little represent the interests of their ethnic fellows in the mountainous regions. These tendencies have lead to intra-ethnic conflicts, as seen with radical Uygurs in southern Xinjiang targeting Uygur cadres working for the state much more often than Han cadres (Shih 2002: 254). Stearns implies that delegates from ethnic minorities may in fact be more beholden to the Party than to their constituents (Stearns 2001: 17).

Thus, the actual degree of minorities' representation and the influence they have on the exercise of the, anyway limited, autonomous powers granted is difficult to assess because of the different layers of control and institutional constraints that exist in the system. However, it should be noted that the long-term direction appears to be geared towards increasingly competitive elections (Shih 1999: 249). The implementation of direct village elections, which also has been cautiously experimented with at township level in a few areas in Sichuan province, could be forthcoming at higher levels of the 'executive' government structures as well, at least to include county heads.[17] Former Premier Zhu Rongji was quoted at a news conference in March 2000 as saying that he would like to see direct elections extended to higher levels as soon as possible (Li 1999: 705). The extension of direct elections to higher than village level is nevertheless widely contested, with opponents including the former CCP General Secretary Jiang Zemin (ibid.). The Central Committee issued a document in July 2001 stating that direct election of township heads is out of line with constitutional provisions and the Organic Law of Local People's Congresses and Local Governments (ibid.: 704). It is probably unlikely that any bold moves along these lines will originate from minority areas, particularly where the politicisation of ethnicity has gone far, as in Tibet and Xinjiang, although this electoral innovation could spread from positive practices in Han Chinese areas. The normal work tasks – such as collecting taxes – of county-type levels are often unpopular. In a situation of increased downward accountability, this leaves these lowest lower-level deputies increasingly concerned about popular support. Even if upwards accountability remains relatively stronger, deputies may become increasingly attentive to local calls for using the legal framework of autonomy to alter and supplement central law and policy to suit local conditions.

County level autonomous organs of local self-government could become the administrative level where autonomy powers are exercised by directly elected ethnic deputies in LPCs and local government. Thus, the county level appears to be the administrative level holding the strongest potential for supporting enhanced elements of ethnic local self-government under the LREA.

Party control over personnel management

The 'key representatives' of ethnic minorities are often not the elected minority deputies in the local People's Congress and local governments but minority persons in other positions, such as the staff of these two organs and particularly the local party forming part of China's governing cadres. The state policy of enhancing the percentage of minority staff can be displayed by the 20 per cent increase in Tibetan state employees between 1980 and 1997, when numbers reached 74.8 per cent. However, there do not appear to be any internal rules requiring minority representation and participation in Party organs, and the 6.1 per cent of minority Party members as of 1999 is lower than their share of the population (Xinhua 28 June 1999; Sautman 1998: 94). In 2000, nearly one third of the chairmen of the provincial People's Councils were also secretaries of the Party committees (Chao 2003: 21). Recently a central directive was passed demanding that all local Party secretaries concurrently serve as LPC directors, which now is commonly the case (ibid.: 12). Locally elected autonomous leaders are in most cases Party members (Sautman 1999: 294). The 1993 Regulation on the Administration of Ethnic Townships stipulates that governments in autonomous areas are to be staffed 'as fully as possible' by minorities and to use minority languages (ibid.: 295). Minority cadres in China increased from less than 3 per cent in 1980 to more than 7 per cent in 1996 (Sautman 1998: 116). In the 1980s personnel authority was largely given to the provinces, although the centre continues to directly appoint numerous key positions. Relocation of provincial cadres and governors in the late 1990s has taken place to weaken the provincial identity of the cadres as well as to restore the centre's authority over appointments and dismissals (Mori 2002: 6). Also, the Party re-centralised control by taking back the nomenklatura authority of the important bureau level which it had handed to the Ministry of Personnel in 1988, a measure that weakened the Ministry of Personnel in cadre management.[18] Although over-representation of minority deputies in political structures is common, key positions in autonomous areas are covered by the nomenclature (Ghai 2000: 85). The Party's former exclusive right to personnel management is, however, now also being challenged by People's Congresses in the name of legislative oversight (Chao 2003: 23). Some provincial LPCs have rejected Party nominees for state leadership in an attempt to express local discontent over the centre's personnel appointments and remind the Party to respect the opinions of LPCs concerning personnel affairs (Cho 2002: 724).

Towards 'genuine' ethnic autonomy through local institutional developments?

International comparisons of past autonomy arrangements within socialist states provide quite a negative picture, with autonomy merely used as a tool of control for the majority ethnic group in general, and the Communist Party in particular. Autonomous ethnic areas in socialist settings have often, in practice, held less autonomy than the non-autonomous areas. Are the respective priorities for Beijing and some ethnic minority leaders to maintain party control on the one hand, while enhancing ethnic local self-government on the other, simultaneously met in the current Chinese autonomy system? Writings often tend to dismiss the Chinese autonomy system because of the negative role of the Communist Party and the 'near impossibility of securing genuine autonomy in a communist system', arguing for the necessary link between genuine autonomy and substantive democracy (Ghai 2000: 96). Can international concepts of 'genuine' autonomy exist in a socialist state structure?

In Hannum's definition of what constitutes 'genuine autonomy', a fully autonomous territory possesses most of the following characteristics: (1) a locally elected legislative body with some independent legislative authority; (2) a locally selected chief executive with responsibility for the administration and enforcement of state as well as local laws; (3) an independent local judiciary with full responsibility for interpreting local laws; and (4) areas of joint concern subject to power-sharing arrangements between autonomous and central governments (Hannum 1996: 467–468). The purpose of comparing the Chinese model with this set of 'standards' is not to bluntly criticise the Chinese model, which does, however, provide a framework to re-visit the Chinese autonomy system. With regard to the first characteristic, regional ethnic autonomies down to county level in China do elect a legislature, directly and locally at county level, and indirectly for autonomous legislatures above county level. There exists some limited legislative authority to be exercised by the increasingly important LPCs. This authority can, however, hardly be referred to as being exercised 'independently', due to the ladders of approval procedures and party structures running parallel to the state structures, with these two decision-making structures not being equally devolved. The limited authority granted remains ambiguous and the 2001 revision of the 1984 LREA did not replace political language with clear legal language. Concerning the second characteristic, the chief executive is not locally selected, although trends indicate direct local elections spreading from village level and experiments at township level could reach at least county level. Challenges of achieving adequate representation in electing legislatures and chief executives, beyond formal statistics, remain due to the nomination procedures, although developments such as increased self-nomination should be noted. As to the third characteristic, there exists no local judicial autonomy in China. On the contrary, the lack of dispute resolution mechanisms concerning the exercise of autonomy remains a crucial obstruction to independent and consistent adjudication restraining arbitrary intervention from the centre and local oversteps of granted autonomy powers. Finally, there are a few areas of joint concern identified with joint authority on paper, without however being subject to any power-sharing arrangement in any formal or informal way.

To be or not to be autonomous – an irrelevant question?

Like all other local governments, autonomous governments are 'bridges and key points to link the state leadership and the masses'. Considering that merely 15 per cent of central laws are 'faithfully' implemented, it also appears as if non-autonomous areas de facto can modify central policy and laws to fit local circumstances, or choose not to implement them (Chao 2003: 16). People's Congresses in non-autonomous provinces, at least in practice, hold strikingly similar 'autonomy' powers to those in 'autonomous provinces', by power granted to promulgate local legislation so long as it does not conflict with the objectives of national legislation, and can flesh out the details of national legislation (Saich 2001: 149).[19] Dissatisfaction with the degree of ethnic autonomy has surfaced among minority leaders, grumbling about the 'half-legislative' powers granted to regional ethnic autonomous areas (Sautman 1999: 296). Arguments go that the autonomy powers granted to minority areas are in fact less than in the non-autonomous areas, in particular when compared to the coastal Special Economic Zones. Despite the legal framework, ethnic autonomy appears to hold little more than the kind of 'autonomy', or local discretion, that all local administrations enjoy in China (Shih 2002: 251). The fact that there are numerous cases where lower-tier administrative levels within higher-level autonomous areas that do not strive to establish their own local ethnic autonomy indirectly indicates that they are not bothered by the exercise of autonomy powers 'above' (ibid.: 255).

Autonomy regulations do not resolve self-determination conflicts if not built around viable institutions. The lack of an independent judicial mechanism that could define the boundaries of autonomy powers prob-ably represents the most fundamental missing component that could distinguish autonomy powers from general local discretion. This shortcoming also affects the establishment and dissolution of regional ethnic autonomy arrangements. Autonomy arrangements should not be revoked without consulting, or even requiring the consent of, the autonomous entity. The dissolution of the Hainan autonomy and the non-establishment of the Qinghai province autonomous region despite 97 per cent of the territory constituting Tibetan autonomous prefectures, indicate that the legal terms of autonomy are negated when it suits the central government (Sautman 1999: 296).

Concerning multi-ethnic autonomies, Shih argues that since multi-ethnicity cannot effectively represent any specific ethnicity, it can be better to dissolve them and give way to lower-level single-ethnic arrangements (Shih 2003: 7). Kaup observes that the central government has played regional and ethnic politics in Zhuang areas off against each other in a manner that limits both, while purportedly promoting each (Kaup 2002: 864–866). Superimposing territorial loyalties on ethnic loyalties is intended to assure that ethnic-nationalism will not grow beyond the state's control. The division between Zhuang, on the provincial boundary of Yunnan, and Guangxi has created such regional loyalties, which divide ethnic unity and weaken prospects for greater pan-Zhuang activism (ibid.: 884). This implies that the autonomy granted is regional rather than ethnic, although the Zhuang may constitute an exceptional case as being a less politicised ethnic minority than many others, and as demanding greater inclusion in the Chinese state rather than exclusion from it (Kaup 2000: 180).

Application to date of the Chinese autonomy system

As stated by the editors in the introductory chapter, autonomy can only be a sustainable solution to self-determination conflicts when there is room for compromises short of secession, where the territorial claim of the self-determination movement is internal rather than external. Can the degree of 'success' of the Chinese autonomy model be simultaneously measured from two different perspectives: (1) whether it promotes minority rights and autonomy as a bottom-up mechanism enabling enhanced modes of local self-government, and (2) from its contribution towards maintaining and strengthening 'national unity' as a top-down device with the duty of officials to implement autonomy for ethnic areas under their jurisdiction? From the 'state' perspective, regional ethnic autonomy has proven successful in territorial zero-sum games, consolidating the sovereign borders of China. The 1959 Tibetan uprising remains the most serious ethnic movement to date aimed at disintegration of a part of the Chinese State. From the 'minority' perspective, conflicting views have been presented concerning the extent that regulations on the exercise of autonomy have been enacted. Also, providing mere statistics of the numbers of enacted laws and regulations under autonomy powers obviously tells us little about the quality of their contents. Official figures note that by the end of 1998, 126 regulations on the exercise of autonomy and 209 separate regulations had been enacted by the autonomous areas (Information Office PRC 1999: Chapter III). However, some scholars state that by 1998 no separate autonomous regulation had been adopted anywhere in China (Zhu and

Yu 2000: 56). Official PRC figures from May 2003 note that in Xinjiang the region's Autonomous People's Congress had 'enacted 199 local laws and 71 statutory resolutions and decisions, approved 31 local laws and 3 separate regulations formulated by local people's congresses and 173 administrative rules and regulations formulated by the government of the autonomous region' (PRC Foreign Ministry 2003). Stearns argues that due to the lack of implementing regulations from the State Council on the LREA, the five autonomous LPCs at provincial level have not dared to use their power to promulgate regulations on the exercise of autonomy (Stearns 2001: 8). Various autonomous areas appear to have enacted provisions altering the application of central laws, for example the 1980 Marriage Law. Some autonomous areas have in this way reduced the marriageable age and Xinjiang and Inner Mongolia autonomous areas provide that family planning is not mandatory for national minorities (Phan 1996: 103). Phan concedes that minority areas are accorded 'true autonomy' as to 'soft issues', including education, family planning, culture, environment, sports, health care and science and technology (Phan 1996: 99). Sautman argues that within the institutional and financial constraints, minorities in rural areas generally do govern their townships and have, in some places, made educational, health and economic advances due in part to preferential policies (Sautman 1999: 296). In all, however, legally based local adjustments of central law remain limited. This indicates a continued uncertainty as to the actual powers granted. Shih identifies an example of practice leading beyond the 'teleology of the state' within the Muslim County of Dachang in Xinjiang in that the county, while displaying loyalty to the state, has established direct exchange relationships with Islamic states.[20] Other examples of cross-border institutions can be seen in the Yunnan province. The Yunnan provincial government encourages local governments at prefecture and county levels to co-operate with neighbouring Vietnam, Laos and Myanmar, for example in some environmental issues.[21] Along these lines there exist localised border-trading zones, inter-provincial networks co-ordinating the south-west's approach towards Beijing and direct provincial participation of the Yunnan province in an international Asian Development Bank organised international forum of states sharing an interest in the Mekong River.[22]

Conclusion

China takes great pride in its regional ethnic autonomy system providing the minorities within its borders the 'right to mastery'. International observers on the other hand may too categorically have rejected the autonomy system as nothing but an instrument ensuring central and Party control. China's ethnic minorities benefit from a constitutionally protected legal framework for regional ethnic autonomy, although the institutional landscape where these provisions are to be implemented provide multiple challenges under the provisions of 'unity' and the governing principle of 'democratic centralism'. The 2001 amendments to the 1984 LREA did not resolve the ambiguity at the centre over the extent of powers devolved to the regional ethnic autonomies. The result of generally unclear powers granted to the organs of local ethnic self-government combined with the lack of adequate dispute mechanisms deny safeguards from arbitrary interventions by the centre as well as an objective assessment of whether autonomous powers have been excessively applied. Further, horizontal and vertical approval procedures hinder the effective exercise of the limited autonomous powers granted.

Another revision of the autonomy regulations is not likely to occur in the immediate future. Therefore, developments are more likely to take place based on autonomy practice and attempts to operationalise the existing autonomy provisions through institutional transformations. 'Genuine' autonomy does not merely come with the institutional design, but with the actual practice of autonomy, an 'enabled autonomy'. Currently, there are in effect limited differences between the local self-rule enjoyed in regional ethnic autonomous compared to regional non-autonomous areas. To the extent that 'autonomy' in fact exists in minority areas, it is thereby 'regional' or 'economic' rather than 'ethnic'. Nevertheless, some recent institutional reformations point in directions favourable to enabling the statutory autonomy provisions to be applied in the future. Territorial autonomous arrangements do not exist in a vacuum, but evolve with other changes caused by public administration reform and transition in the general central-local relations. China moving towards being ruled by law has released legislative powers that can be exercised for local autonomous legislative action. The increased role of the LPCs affects two crucial layers of autonomous powers, the legislative agenda and the selection of deputies and personnel. As rural populations are beginning to take the experiments of village elections seriously, these elections may provoke similar reforms at the next administrative levels, township and county. While these two institutional developments have been initiated for purposes including combating local corruption and legitimising Party control through inspecting local governments, these transformations hold value for the potential developments of the existing regional ethnic autonomy system in China. The administrative level of county can in the near future harbour organs of ethnic self-government with independent law-making authority exercised by deputies more genuinely representing the population of the locality in question. Local agency will assume an increased space for local ethnic cadres to make bolder moves in using the autonomous powers.

The centre will only tolerate enhanced ethnic autonomy as long as it is demonstrated that implementing national policy and laws flexibly contributes to national unity. Shih calls this contribution to national unity a

'China moment', outside of which local communities in general can develop their own agenda (Shih 2002). As long as this 'contribution' to (or at least not contravention of) national unity is forthcoming, the centre will increasingly see no problem with diverging local practices, for example in linguistic promotion and possibly even religious education. Ethnic minorities in China will in this case need to demonstrate that they form part of 'Chineseness' before their local minority leaders can practice autonomy, thus they must have a conception of minority membership of the Chinese national community while claiming their cultural distinctiveness. The fact that members of some minorities increasingly argue their claims based on autonomy provisions, in conjunction with these institutional developments, suggests that the discourse of autonomy has taken on a life of its own (McCarthy 2000: 109).

The CCP will in this way be granting an ambiguous 'margin of appreciation' to the LPCs, which may be 'wide' on questions regarded as less significant, but 'narrow' on more sensitive issues. The margin will be fluid and determined by the conditions of the localities, including the courage and capacity among minority leaders to, if necessary, contravene the official Party line. This emerging 'margin' could be available for deputies and cadres increasingly attentive to local concerns, thus enabling enhanced modes of local self-governance. Those local governments, which concurrently fulfil financial and other responsibilities as mandated by their superiors, can with 'illegal monies' pursue particular interests, including those at odds with the interest of the centre (Wedeman 2000: 491). In this context, the differences between inland and coastal areas come into play again, with the more prosperous provinces better equipped to elaborate on particular interests in comparison with most minority areas in Western China, which have experienced diminished central transfers and find little room for supplementary local funding.

Would these possible de facto developments add up to the elements of 'genuine' autonomy in China and, more importantly, satisfy the various ethnic claims for enhanced local self-governance? The observed developments are not necessarily specific to autonomous areas, de facto discretion can be expected to increase also in non-autonomous areas and the 'margin' can be expected to be even 'wider' in areas where no ethnic component triggers fears of separatist tendencies. On the other hand, the legal framework for regional ethnic autonomies provides enhanced legally protected powers if operationalised. Whether the Chinese autonomy system will approach standards of 'genuine autonomy' depends on whether PRC leaders grasp the concerns of its national minorities and consider it 'safe' to expand their autonomy rights in light of external pressures on the country's political system and territorial integrity. Sustained economic disparities and unequal development between regions and ethnic groups coupled with exploitation of local resources in minority areas could lead to increased politicisation of ethnicity and territory beyond the situations in Tibet, Xinjiang and Inner Mongolia. This can lead various ethnic minorities to increasingly question whether the Chinese autonomy system indeed enables them to become 'masters of their homelands'. Positive state practice elsewhere of innovative combinations of territorial and non-territorial autonomy arrangements as means of meeting minority demands short of secession is more likely to persuade the Chinese government than solely pointing to international standards. This could demonstrate to the Chinese leadership that effectively enabling minorities local self-rule *promotes* rather than *challenges* national 'unity'. Sautman argues that displaying trust in minorities by appointing more minority party secretaries, expanding the scope of ethnic autonomy and forming coalition governments in some minority areas are concrete measures which best can reduce separatist sentiments (Sautman 1999: 300–301). A modest experiment would be to enable autonomous People's Congresses to enact local legislation that potentially conflicts with national law without first having to secure prior approval from higher authorities, while remaining subject to higher judicial adjudication if complaints arise from the centre. Further, party structures would need to be equally as devolved as the parallel state structures to enable genuine local self-rule.

Scholars in Beijing think-tanks have advocated a legal institutionalisation of greater power sharing between the centre and the minority areas (as reported by Lam 1997: 17). The ethnic conflicts in China appear to be increasingly 'internal' in scope, which validates the potential of territorial (possibly combined with non-territorial) autonomous arrangements as a sustainable solution in the Chinese context. The Chinese autonomy model could meet many self-government demands if the centre has the courage and the leadership to resolve the institutional challenges currently hindering ethnic localities to put into effect the autonomy provisions.

Notes

1 Erik Friberg (LL.M. Lund University, E.MA. Padua/Strasbourg) is Research Assistant at the Fletcher School of International Law and Diplomacy. The author wishes in particular to thank Professor Florence Benoît-Rohmer for providing the institutional support enabling this research at Université Robert Schuman, Strasbourg, France. Also, the valuable comments by Jonas Grimheden, Chih-yu Shih, Lisa Stearns, Amy West and the editors of this volume on an earlier version are greatly appreciated.
2 Information Office of the State Council of the People's Republic of China, *National Minority Policy and its Practice in China*, 1999, Chapter III.
3 In this chapter the terms 'national minority', 'ethnic minority' and 'minority group' will be used interchangeably.
4 The juridical basis for the Basic Laws of Hong Kong and Macau is found in Art. 31 of the 1982 Constitution authorising the National People's Congress to establish Special Administrative Regions. Chan provides an account of the contrast between Hong Kong's and Macau's return to PRC with the former's

'widespread crisis of confidence' and the latter's 'sense of acceptance' (Chan 2003: 493–518; see also Xu and Wilson 2000: 1–38).

5 The Special Economic Zones (SEZ) were established to receive foreign technology and to be reform laboratories. The locations include Shenzhen, Zhuhai and Shantou in Guangdong, Hainan province, Xiamen in Fujian province and the Pudong area in Shanghai. The Guangdong SEZs are for example granted power to make local laws subject to a four-month period of review by the legislature (Saich 2001: 142).

6 Zhu provides an overview of the developments of the principle of democratic centralism in the PRC (Zhu 1999: 28–29).

7 The classification procedure has been argued to have imposed identities and lumped different groups together, using a large measure of arbitrariness to suit political convenience. Ghai exemplifies this with the 'improbable recognition of the Hui' (Ghai 2000: 81; see also Gladney 1996: 96–97). Tapp provides a more conciliatory view (Tapp 2002: 63–84). Kaup argues that the Zhuang as a nationality was artificially created, imposed – against partial resistance – to better integrate them administratively into the Chinese state (Kaup 2000: 78–80).

8 Article 70 (1) of the 1954 Constitution stipulated that 'The organs of self-government of all autonomous regions, autonomous chou, and autonomous counties exercise autonomy within the limits of the authority prescribed by the Constitution and the law'.

9 Curiously, the official reason submitted for abolishing the Autonomous Prefecture was that full territorial control was required to be held by the Hainan provincial government in order for economical progress. Li cadres argue, however, that the dismantling of the Autonomous Prefecture was part of a 'mainlander conspiracy' to exploit their rich natural resources. In any case, it should be noted that several minority counties with a majority of Li and Miao communities were re-designated autonomous counties (cf. Pang 1998: 157–158; Feng and Goodman 1997: 68).

10 Y. Zhou, 'Probing into the Road of Combining China's "Regional Autonomy" and "Ethnic Autonomy"', in *Proceedings of International Workshop on Regional Autonomy of Ethnic Minorities*, Beijing, 2001 (as referred to by Shih 2002: 255).

11 This rejection can partly be derived from policies in the former Soviet Union, where cultural autonomy was considered as counter-revolutionary because it promoted bourgeois nationalism and hindered class solidarity of the proletariat. Any attempt to divide the various nations in a single state permanently in cultural and educational matters was regarded as 'reactionary' (Cf. Brünner and Küpper 2002: 21). While this rejection of non-territorial autonomy thus has been explained with ideological reasons, Eide argues that it was for 'purely tactical reasons' that Lenin and Stalin preferred territorial autonomy, which was considered to obtain the broadest possible revolutionary support among the different nationalities (Eide 1998: 270–271).

12 However, it should be noted that for example land issues, often the most crucial issue for indigenous peoples and minority groups, cannot be effectively addressed solely through non-territorial autonomy arrangements, since land issues are linked to the administrative structures of a state.

13 Becquelin raises several questions about the 'Reviving the West' policy's 'top-down, one-size-fits-all, central state imposed approach to development'. He argues that the campaign is 'actually a revamped state-project aimed at increasing extraction of resources and speeding up colonisation of minority areas' (Becquelin 2002: 10).

14 While the first party secretary of a province may be regarded primarily as an

agent of central control, the picture is more nuanced for the provincial leadership as a whole, which increasingly is recognised for its mediating role between the centre and local constituencies (Saich 2001: 147–148).

15 Stearns provided this information in a personal communication, 18 August 2003. She observes the development of 'working groups' at county level to be one of the signs of institutionalisation of LPCs at the county level.

16 Sautman observes, however, that it seems as if minority politicians can press for measures to benefit minorities without committing the delict of 'local nationalism' (Sautman 1998: 99).

17 This was argued by Du Runsheng, former Director of the Policy Research Institute of the Central Party Committee (see Li 2002: 705; see also Derichs and Heberer 2002: 153). For an account of direct village elections describing the sudden support by the Party and the state for village self-government, see Lin *et al.* (2001: 3–23) Cheng discusses the politics behind the direct elections at township levels in Sichuan province in the late 1990s (Cheng 2001: 104–135).

18 The 'nomenklatura system' of party-sanctioned appointment of leading personnel is a key opportunity for the centre to exert political control over the localities (see Brødsgaard 2002: 361).

19 The Constitution and Organic Law enables local People's Congresses to decide on the 'vital issues' in areas such as economics, education, science, culture, civil affairs and minorities. Chao observes that it has been suggested in academic circles in China that 'vital issues' be further divided into 'issues with overall implications' and 'issues with limited implications'. It is suggested that party involvement should step aside and merely 'provide leadership by guidance' in questions concerning the latter category, which includes minority protection and educational reforms (see Chao 2003: 21).

20 Shih explains this as the historical result of the 'state's diplomatic strategy to win recognition from Arab countries in Beijing's tug of war with Taipei' (Shih 2002: 255).

21 This includes joint assessments of acid precipitation in the Red Valley, a joint inventory of biodiversity in border areas of the Mekong watershed, co-operative forest management and farmer-to-farmer exchanges (see Ting 2003: 53).

22 It should be noted though that while the province of Yunnan is populated by various ethnic minorities with different sub-provincial autonomy arrangements, it is not an autonomous area at the provincial level.

References

BBC News (2004), 'China's minority fears', 4 November 2004 at http://news.bbc.co.uk/go/pr/fr/-/1/hi/world/asia-pacific/3982537 (accessed 20 November 2004).

Becquelin, N. (2002), 'Who benefits? Regional disparities and the campaign to "develop the west"', *China Rights Forum*, 3: 10–15, 27.

Brødsgaard, K. E. (2002), 'Institutional Reform and the Bianzhi System in China', *The China Quarterly*, 170: 361–386.

Brünner, G. and Küpper, H. (2002), 'European Options of Autonomy: A Typology of Autonomy Models of Minority Self-Governance', in K. Gal (ed.) *Minority Governance in Europe*, Hungary: Open Society Institute, 11–36.

Chao, C. (1994), 'The Procedure for Local Legislation in Mainland China and Legislation in National Autonomous Areas', *Issues and Studies*, vol. 30, 9: 95–116.

—— (2003) 'The National People's Congress Oversight Power and the Role of the CCP', *Copenhagen Journal of Asian Studies*, no. 17, 6–30.

Cheng, J. (2001), 'Direct Elections of Town and Township Heads in China: The Dapeng and Buyun Experiments', *China Information*, vol. XV, 1: 104–135.

Cho, Y. N. (2002), 'From "Rubber Stamps" to "Iron Stamps": The Emergence of Chinese Local People's Congresses as Supervisory Powerhouses', *The China Quarterly*, 171: 724–740.

Derichs, C. and Heberer, T. (2002), 'Asian Crisis and Political Change', *European Journal of East Asian Studies*, vol. 1, 2: 147–176.

Eide, A. (1998), 'Cultural Autonomy: Concept, Content, History and Role in the World Order', in M. Suksi (ed.) *Autonomy: Application and Implications*, The Hague: Kluwer, 251–276.

Fabre, G. (2002), 'Decentralisation, Corruption and Criminalisation: China in Comparative Perspective', *China Report*, vol. 38, 4: 547–569.

Feng, C., and Goodman, D. (1997), 'Hainan: Communal politics and the struggle for identity', in D. Goodman (ed.) *China's provinces in reform: Class, community and political culture*, New York and London: Routledge, 53–87.

Fitzgerald, J. (ed.) (2002), *Rethinking China's Provinces*, London: Routledge.

Friedman, E. (1995), *National Identity and Democratic Prospects in Socialist China*, New York: ME Sharpe.

Ghai, Y. (2000), 'Autonomy Regimes in China: Coping with Ethnic and Economic Diversity', in Y. Ghai (ed.) *Autonomy and Ethnicity: Negotiating Claims in Multi-ethnic States*, Cambridge: Cambridge University Press, 77–98.

Gladney, Dru C. (1996), *Muslim Chinese: Ethnic Nationalism in the Peoples Republic*, Cambridge: Harvard University Press.

Goodman, D. (2000), 'The Localism of Local Leadership Cadres in Reform Shanxi', *Journal of Contemporary China*, vol. 9, 24: 159–183.

Hannum, H. (1996), *Autonomy, Sovereignty, and Self-Determination. The Accommodation of Conflicting Rights*, Philadelphia: University of Pennsylvania Press.

Heberer, T. (1989), *China & Its National Minorities: Autonomy or Assimilation?*, New York: ME Sharpe.

—— (2000), 'Some Considerations on China's Minorities in the 21st Century: Conflict or Conciliation?', *Duisburg Working Papers on East Asian Studies*, no. 31, 1–25.

Heintze, H.-J. (1998), 'On the Legal Understanding of Autonomy', in M. Suksi (ed.) *Autonomy: Applications and Implications*, The Hague: Kluwer, 7–32.

Information Office of the State Council of the People's Republic of China (1999), *National Minority Policy and its Practice in China*.

Kaup, K. (2000), *Creating the Zhuang: Ethnic Politics in China*, London: Lynne Rienner.

—— (2002), 'Regionalism versus Ethnicnationalism in the People's Republic of China', *The China Quarterly*, 172: 863–884.

Lam, W. (1997), 'Ethnic Tension Bares State's Failure in Regionalism Issue', *South China Morning Post*, 19 March, 17.

Li, L. (2002), 'The Politics of Introducing Direct Township Elections in China', *The China Quarterly*, 171: 704–723.

Liu, Y., The Carter Center and Georgia Perimeter College (eds) (2001), 'Chinese Law and Governance', vol. 34, no. 6, Nov/Dec, 3–23.

Loper, K. (2002), 'Self-determination, a key to the solution of the Tibet problem', *China Rights Forum*, 3: 20–27.

Mackerras, C. (1998), 'Han-Muslim and Intra-Muslim Social Relations in

Northwestern China', in W. Safran (ed.) *Nationalism and Ethnoregional Identities in China*, London: Frank Cass, 28–46.

McCarthy, S. (2000), 'Ethno-Religious Mobilisation and Citizenship Discourse in the People's Republic of China', *Asian Ethnicity*, vol. 1, 2: 107–116.

Mori, K. (2002), 'Integrative and Disruptive Forces in Contemporary China', paper presented at the Japan-India Seminar on Contemporary China, Delhi University, March.

Pang, K-F. (1998), 'Unforgiven and Remembered: The Impact of Ethnic Conflicts in Everyday Muslim-Han Social Relations on Hainan Island', in W. Safran (ed.) *Nationalism and Ethnoregional Identities in China*, London, Frank Cass, 142–162.

People's Republic of China Foreign Ministry (2003), 'History and Development of Xinjiang (Part 8)', 27 May, as seen on www.china-embassy.org/eng/49698.html (visited 5 August 2003).

Phan, B. G. (1996), 'How Autonomous Are the National Autonomous Areas of the PRC? An Analysis of Documents and Cases', *Issues and Studies*, vol. 32, 7: 83–108.

Saich, T. (2001), *Governance and Politics of China*, New York: Palgrave.

Sautman, B. (1998), 'Preferential Policies for Ethnic Minorities in China: The Case of Xinjiang', in W. Safran (ed.) *Nationalism and Ethnoregional Identities in China*, London: Frank Cass, 86–118.

—— (1999), 'Ethnic Law and Minority Rights in China: Progress and Constraints', *Law & Policy*, vol. 21, 3: 283–314.

Sautman, B. and Eng, I. (2001), *Tibet: Development for Whom?*, China Information, vol. XV, 2: 20–74.

Shih, C. (1999), *Collective Democracy: Political and Legal Reform in China*, Hong Kong: Chinese University Press.

—— (2002), 'The Teleology of State in China's Regional Ethnic Autonomy', *Asian Ethnicity*, vol. 3, 2: 249–256.

—— (2003), '3 + 1 + 1 = 1: Disempowerment in Longsheng Multiple Ethnic Autonomous County', paper presented at the Preparatory Symposium for the Second International Conference on Regional Autonomy of Ethnic Minorities, Uppsala, June.

Stearns, L. (2001), 'Chinese Autonomous People's Congresses: Conditions of Law-Making under the National Regional Autonomy Law', paper presented at the RWI Conference on Legal and Political Reforms in the PRC, Lund, Sweden, June.

Tanner, M. S. (1994), 'The Erosion of Communist Party Control over Lawmaking in China', *China Quarterly*, 138: 381–403.

Tapp, N. (2002), 'In Defence of the Archaic: A Reconsideration of the 1950s Ethnic Classification Project in China', *Asian Ethnicity*, vol. 3, 1: 63–84.

Tibet Information Network (2001), 'National autonomy law revised to support Western Development Strategy', 13 March, as read on www.tibetinfo.net/news-updates/nu130301.htm (visited 5 August, 2003).

Ting, Z. (2003), 'A Perspective on China's Yunnan Province', in The Regional Environmental Forum for Mainland Southeast Asia (eds) *Advancing Environmental Governance: Perspectives from the Regional Environmental Forum for Mainland Southeast Asia*, 49–55 (www.ref-msea.org/aeg.pdf).

UN Committee on the Elimination of Racial Discrimination (CERD) (2001), 'Summary Record of the 1468th meeting', 31 July, UN Doc. CERD/C/SR.1468.

Wang, L. (1998), *Sky Burial: The Fate of Tibet*, Hong Kong: Mirror Books.

Wedeman, A. (2000), 'Budgets, Extra Budgets, and Small Treasuries: Illegal Monies and Local Automony in China', *Journal of Contemporary China*, 489–511.

Xia, M. (2000), 'Political Contestation and the Emergence of the Provincial People's Congresses as Power Players in Chinese Politics: a network explanation', *Journal of Contemporary China*, vol. 9, 24: 185–214.

Xinhua News Agency (1999), 'Chinese Communist Party has 61 Million Members', 28 June, Item no. 0628208.

Xu, X. and Wilson, G. D. (2000), 'The Hong Kong Special Administrative Region as a Model of Regional External Autonomy', *Case Western Reserve Journal of International Law*, vol. 32, 1: 1–38.

Yee, H., (2003), 'Ethnic Relations in Xinjiang: a survey of Uygur-Han relations in Urumqi', *Journal of Contemporary China*, vol. 12, 36: 431–452.

Zang, X. (1998), 'Ethnic Representation in the Current Chinese Leadership', *The China Quarterly*, 153: 107–127.

Zhao, S. (2000), 'Chinese Nationalism and Its International Orientations', *Political Science Quarterly*, vol. 115, 1: 1–34.

Zhu, G. (1999), 'Constitutional Law and State Structure', in G. G. Wang and J. Mo (eds) *Chinese Law*, The Hague: Kluwer, 23–61.

Zhu, G. and Yu, L. (2000), 'Regional Minority Autonomy in the PRC: A Preliminary Appraisal from a Historic Perspective', *International Journal on Minority and Group Rights*, 7: 39–57.

11 Recent trends in autonomy and state construction

Marc Weller and Stefan Wolff

This book started out with a paradox: autonomy is increasingly proposed as the principal remedy for the resolution of self-determination conflicts, while it had previously been seen as a first step towards secession and the disintegration of the state. By the beginning of the 1990s, this position had fundamentally changed and autonomy came to be presented as the only effective guarantee for the maintenance of the territorial unity of states threatened by ethnic strife. Academics and practitioners alike asserted that the apparent disintegrative mechanism of autonomy—of institutionalised separation within the state—would serve to integrate and stabilise states otherwise prone to severe and violent conflict.

This view was advanced with particular vigour by the crisis managers of Western Europe when suddenly faced with violent secessionist conflicts in the region of the former Yugoslavia, in the Caucasus, and in Moldova. Where the original state could not be reconstructed, as was the case in the Socialist Federal Republic of Yugoslavia, the successor states would at least need to be stabilised through extensive provisions of self-governance for ethnically defined territories within them. Where the degree of separation had not yet evolved to a stage that demanded international acceptance, settlements were being sought on the basis of models of self-governance ranging from autonomy to full federalisation. Georgia, Moldova, and the Federal Republic of Yugoslavia are cases in point.

Even where ethno-territorial conflicts where addressed through self-governance, success has remained elusive. The Dayton peace settlement, generating a complex mix of entities—a federated ensemble of cantons, a centralised republic, municipalities, and districts with special status (Brčko) all under a loose common roof—remains fragile, even a decade after its conclusion. While conflict has not recurred and while there has been remarkable progress in reconciliation, the units within Bosnia and Herzegovina have not shown a natural tendency towards further integration, although some tenuous progress is being made. In Kosovo, self-governance (the term autonomy cannot be used, as it would prove inflammatory to the majority population) is perceived as a delaying tactic by the international community towards what the local majority perceives to be inevitable independence. Furthermore, in Croatia, autonomy for areas inhabited, or formerly inhabited, by ethnic Serbs has not come about in any real sense. Only in Macedonia can a precarious stabilisation be observed. The latter is a case where territorial autonomy was avoided as part of a settlement; rather it was applied in a slyly disguised form of 'enhanced local self-governance'.

Set against this apparently disheartening experience with autonomy to address self-determination conflicts in Eastern Europe, it appeared appropriate to test the application of autonomy models in other regions of the world. We have reviewed the experiences of Western Europe, Africa, Asia, and Latin America. In the cases we have considered, autonomy settlements were generally adopted before a cataclysmic self-determination conflict could take hold. Of course, in a number of instances, a prolonged insurgency had taken place, in Northern Ireland, in some Latin American states, in Sudan, and in Indonesia. As long-lasting as these conflicts may have been, they did not reach the intensity of the experiences of the Balkans or the Caucasus. Where there have been intense and unrequited self-determination conflicts, as in Papua and Aceh, the attempted autonomy settlement has, in fact, failed thus far.

The prospects for the successful establishment of autonomy arrangements in instances of frozen conflict, such as in Azerbaijan and Georgia are more difficult to assess. While we have not addressed such conflicts in particular in this volume, autonomy settlements, in many such cases, would be a way to formalise and regularise a de facto status quo and defuse otherwise volatile situations. The difficulty that needs to be overcome, however, is one of a lack of credible leadership rather than institutional design. As long as conflict parties maintain maximum demands, if only in rhetoric rather than action, and feel that any settlement would discredit them and undermine their control over their own constituencies, establishing territorial autonomy regimes with far-reaching competencies is unlikely to be an agreeable option. This is all the more the case in conflict situations in which the interests of neighbouring states and regional powers are directly affected, as they limit the room for manoeuvre that the local conflict parties have available to reach a settlement.

However, even experiences at the very sharpest end of engagement with violent and/or frozen self-determination conflicts may not offer as grim a picture in relation to the utility of autonomy-based settlements as one would perceive. Given the depth of conflict in Bosnia and Herzegovina, a decade appears not to be a terribly long time for a new state identity to take root. Moreover, the Dayton solution has been an exercise in conflict termination, rather than an example of rational state design. It is not surprising that it has not offered a viable constitutional settlement that can remain without mid-term modification. As Bosnia and Herzegovina develops institutionally, economically, and socially, however, it appears inevitable that strong elements of both territorial and non-territorial autonomy will continue to feature in its constitution.

Similarly, the experience of Kosovo is not as damning an indictment of self-governance as it may at first seem. After all, the issue of territorial status was deliberately left unaddressed and very few would have expected that the experience of provisional self-governance under international tutelage would have hardened into an acceptance of autonomy as the definite solution. The significant remaining instability is not necessarily attributable to the application of an autonomy settlement, however. Thus far, it has been attributable to the inability to agree to a settlement for the territory.

Neither is it entirely accurate to describe autonomy in Croatia as a failure, given that in reality no autonomy settlement was ever achieved. In Macedonia, on the other hand, the moderate, stealthily established autonomy settlement has a chance of success, despite the sensitive nature of the issue of 'decentralisation' that has led to public riots the very week this conclusion is being finalised. In between these two poles lie the partially-suspended, but inconclusive, Northern Ireland settlement and the questionable degree of implementation in the case of autonomy in Aceh, the negotiation process of the latter having been disrupted by military action.

Hence, the verdict on autonomy as a means of addressing conflict and post-conflict situations may not be as negative and clear cut as it appears at first sight. Apart from the areas noted above, in similarly long-standing and/or violent self-determination conflicts, more recent settlements have opted for self-governance solutions, at least in the interim, for example in Southern Sudan and Papua New Guinea/Bougainville.

What transpires from those cases that have experienced long-standing and/or intense violence and in which there seems to be no bargaining space in which the demands of the conflict parties could be accommodated simultaneously is that autonomy remains a viable and desirable institutional arrangement even if (initially) only for an interim period. The cases of Sudan and Kosovo, and, with some qualifications, Northern Ireland fall into this category, as does the settlement between Bougainville and Papua New Guinea. In all these cases the conflict parties, often with significant 'encouragement' from the organised international community, decided to postpone a final decision on the issue of self-determination for a more or less clearly defined period of time. This is a relatively novel mechanism, although it has precedents in earlier inter-state territorial disputes decided by referendum after an interim period of international administration, such as in the case of the Franco-German dispute over the Saarland after each of the two World Wars. The idea behind an interim period is simple: the conflict parties lay down their arms, agree on the issues they can agree, and postpone a settlement of those on which they cannot reach agreement to the future. If nothing else, such a 'solution' brings peace to a war-torn region, albeit not necessarily a guarantee for its sustainability. As the relevant case studies in this volume, as well as evidence from other relevant cases, seem to indicate, another key rationale behind such interim settlements is the hope, on the part of central governments and the organised international community, that whatever institutional arrangement is adopted will prove attractive enough to sway the people to vote for its continuation in a subsequent referendum rather than for independence. So far, there is little evidence that this strategy will indeed succeed, but there is likewise no evidence for its failure. On the contrary, our cases show a certain degree of stabilisation and normalisation after the conclusion of such interim settlements—without a doubt, an immeasurable improvement compared to continuation of violent conflict in the absence of such settlements.

What about autonomy when applied to disputes over self-determination before they have turned violent, or before low-level violence has turned into full-blown ethnic warfare? Here, the examples reviewed in this book offer a number of important insights. First, autonomy remains the prevalent mode of dispute settlement. Given space constraints, only a number of cases could be considered in this volume. The experiences of Mali and neighbouring states in relation to the Tuareq, or other examples further south on the African continent, had to be left out of this analysis, for instance. Second, it is clear, however, that in virtually all constitutional settlements to self-determination conflicts, autonomy plays a significant role. Third, while non-territorial forms of autonomy remain the exception, this may lead to a sense of exclusion during processes of political change on the part of ethnic populations living outside the territory slated for autonomy. Moreover, this is also the case for those not living in compact settlements, because they cannot enjoy the benefits of enhanced self-governance as long as autonomy is applied almost exclusively as a territorial conflict settlement mechanism.

This study has also drawn attention to the often neglected issue of minorities within autonomies. The most pronounced case seen here is that of the Crimean Tatars, whose identity was not substantially recognised in the Crimean autonomy that appears to have benefited the majority Russian population for the most part. In a number of other instances, however, the dominant group within the overall state may find itself a local minority within a newly autonomous territory; an issue often left unaddressed. A particular variation of this problem occurs where indigenous peoples obtain territorial autonomy. This is often coupled with the adoption of forms of governance that are particular to the indigenous population concerned, where application of these norms can create unintended negative consequences.

When reviewing what appear to be successful autonomy solutions in circumstances other than an immediate post-conflict environment, a number of additional issues surface. First, there is the way in which the settlements were generated. It appears particularly important to ensure that autonomies are not mere acts of unilateral devolution of public powers; Rather the process of establishing them must be based on a genuine constitutional consensus. Ordinarily, one would expect negotiations with the representatives of populations or territories seeking autonomy to be followed by formal acts of approval through legal representative bodies and the national parliament.

Second, there needs to be an implementation plan incorporated into any settlement. In a number of instances settlements have become extremely difficult, if not impossible, to implement due to delays and procrastination. As the example of Indonesia confirms, implementation, even if pursued in good faith by all sides, can be a very technical, large and long-lasting undertaking. Implementation of a settlement plan must be accompanied by sufficient preparation, resources, and mechanisms of implementation monitoring and implementation support.

Third, there is the issue of the degree of completeness of the functions and powers of self-governance. Clearly, sufficient competences must be transferred alongside devolved responsibilities to make autonomy meaningful. This transfer should be established at the level of constitutional law, and be coupled with an institutional establishment that encompasses legislative, executive and judicial capacities.

These transferred capacities should be unambiguously assigned and it should be clear where residual authority rests from the outset. Most commonly, governments of autonomous territories hold powers in the areas of economic development, the provision of social services, education, culture, and language. In some cases, they are also able to limit immigration to their territory (both of the cross-border and internal varieties) and, in others, to impose specific conditions before migrants can exercise the full range of political and civil liberties, including the right to vote. In a number of cases, autonomous territories have been able to devise their own constitutions, achieving greater manoeuvrability in terms of institutional design, including the structure of government, the nature of the regional electoral system, and so forth. Particularly complex problems arise where the control of natural resources is concerned. This difficulty is not only restricted to indigenous peoples, who can claim a particular entitlement to an area of land and the riches it may bear. Wealth sharing between governed and self-governing groups has, therefore, been explored as an area of regulation in settlements more recently. Generally, a territorially autonomous regime must have resources at its disposal. In a number of instances, institutions of self-governance have been left with significant tasks, but few financial and fiscal means to realise them. Sustainable autonomy settlements will include a reasonable balance between the right to raise revenue locally, and the need to obtain additional funding from the centre.

'Substantive autonomy'—the unique bargaining space between full independence and direct central rule that leaves both conflict parties better off than the status quo—can be defined in many ways. A list of competences that fits one case, or even a set of cases, may be wholly unsuitable for another. Regardless of how many competences are transferred and where residual authority rests, two aspects of autonomy regimes will always be relevant: the overall constitutional framework of the state in question will remain applicable and the governments of autonomous territories will have to adhere to certain standards of good governance to be politically and 'technically' viable institutions.

Steps must be taken to ensure that the institutions of self-governance are indeed representative of those on whose behalf the autonomy was adopted in the first place. The quality of governance is an important concern in this context. However, comprehensive minority representation is not enough. Some of the examples reviewed here show that autonomy can lead to unaccountable governance, even if it is fully representative on the basis of ethnicity. Corruption and undemocratic practices can take hold at times. These problems are particularly pronounced where no checks and balances exist within the established system of self-governance, including independent courts.

Where autonomy is measured according to units of self-governance, the issue of relations with other elements of the state arises. A number of cases reviewed here indicate that genuine autonomy cannot be practiced where the decisions adopted, in pursuit of self-governance and within the competence that has been transferred, are subject to routine review at superior levels of governance. Instead, it is clear that an independent judicial mechanism must exist to address clashes of authority, or conflicts about the lawful exercise of authority.

Of course, territorial autonomy solutions can be varied indeed. Even within the confines of this book we have noted simple asymmetrical designs, where one autonomous unit is generated within an otherwise unitary state. At the other extreme, there can exist numerous, significant, and different levels of self-government, symmetrical or asymmetrical, and based on ethnic criteria, or on pre-existing administrative boundaries, or both at the same time. While such complexity may only be considered necessary in very large and ethnically heterogeneous states, even in situations which are far less complex from this perspective, the institutional design of autonomy regimes has become increasingly complex nonetheless, involving power-sharing institutions, minority rights systems, and a host of other mechanisms aimed at providing stability not only to the overall state but also to the autonomous territory and its inhabitants. Regional consociations are probably the most advanced examples of such complex institutional designs, and as such they offer important insights into the consequences of such complexity. Institutional multiplication is, on the one hand, a cost issue and can therefore be easily dismissed as prohibitive. Institutional multiplication also raises issues of competency assignment, coordination and arbitration, and could therefore cause institutional paralysis and potential collapse. However, these caveats only turn into self-fulfilling prophecies when there is no serious commitment to implementation among political leaders and their followers, that is, when the settlement was not negotiated in good faith in the first place.

Many self-determination conflicts are highly complex situations in which simple 'solutions' are unlikely to provide long-term stability. In the same way that many ethnically diverse societies cannot simply get by with majoritarian democracy, ethnically diverse autonomous territories are equally unlikely to succeed using this strategy. Responsible and responsive government means to recognise diversity and accommodate it—be it through consociational structures or integrative techniques of powersharing. Obviously, ethnic minorities that have just 'won' autonomy from a central government may resent the fact that they will have to share power with other ethnic groups, including members of the majority of the overall state. Yet the dual character of autonomy—providing devolved government to the entire resident population within a given territory irrespective of ethnicity and also increasing the level of self-governance for a particular ethnic group within this territory—may demand the sharing of power for an autonomy regime to function well and be stable in the long term. In such cases, complex institutional designs can provide the necessary safeguards for all ethnic groups involved and make territorial autonomy desirable for the entire population of the territory in question.

The complexity of autonomy designs, however, does not only extend to the autonomous entity as such. It often also involves special arrangements between the central government and the government of the autonomous territory addressing representation of interests at the centre. This is particularly the case in situations where a wide range of powers have been transferred to the autonomous entity, which may be affected by agreements that the central government concludes with third parties or by legislation applicable to other parts of the state. Permanent consultation mechanisms, cooptation of leaders from the autonomous territory into central government bodies, judicial arbitration, and formal consociational structures are just some of the many design options available to regulate the relations between autonomous and central government. One further lesson that our case studies imply, therefore, is that an autonomy regime will only contribute to resolving or preventing self-determination conflicts if it is applied within the context of an overall institutional design that provides stability within the autonomous entity as well as in the relations between autonomous and central government.

This book has also noted the benefits of the prospect of a dimension of regional integration as a stabilising factor. Perhaps too much has been made of the lure of EU membership as a tool of stabilisation in relation to South Eastern Europe. However, it is undeniable that this prospect has played a very significant role in attempting to move some of the Yugoslav successor states from a post-conflict footing (or a pre-conflict footing in relation to a new round of hostilities) to one of increased stability. It should be noted, however, that this process tends to be based on the benefits of regional harmonisation of legal standards and governmental practices.

Regional integration may also offer a solution in cases where political and ethnic boundaries are incongruent and where claims to self-determination generate demands ranging from better opportunities for cross-border cooperation between members of the same ethnic group to re-drawing existing international boundaries to forge new states including all the members of a particular ethnic group.

Where autonomy and regional integration meet, new problems may arise. In Europe, for example, the claims for recognition of the special status of historically established autonomies do not appear to have been fully answered by the EU, while the Nordic Council has been able to establish arrangements that take account of such special status territories in its member states. Again, this only underlines the fact that institutional design is an open-ended and infinitely flexible process that can accommodate all kinds of 'special needs', provided that the political will exists to see them through to a comprehensive solution.

So what about our paradox? We have tried to resolve it in this conclusion, but we also have to be realistic about our degree of success, as the evidence from the case studies presented in this book is mixed. Autonomy does not have an unambiguous track record of either success or failure. If we are more specific in our case selection, we are able to discern some factors that facilitate success—early, generous and genuine application—and those that are more likely to end in failure—application after bloody civil wars, as a delaying tactic, or without sufficient elite and popular consent. In other words, where autonomy is merely applied as a means of (temporary) conflict termination, it is unlikely to address the causes that gave rise to the conflict in the first place. By the same token, if autonomy is merely meant to separate conflict groups, integration and stabilisation of fragmented states and societies are unlikely, if not impossible, to follow.

On the other hand, autonomy can make a significant contribution to the stabilisation of conflict-prone states, preventing their violent disintegration. As a conflict settlement mechanism, this is exactly what autonomy is meant to achieve: it does not generate peace in itself, but provides space for a transition to peace.

The most important contribution that this volume has to offer to the theory and practice of conflict resolution is this: autonomy can only serve in the stabilisation of states facing self-determination conflicts if it is part of a well-balanced approach that draws on elements of consociational techniques, moderated by integrative policies, and tempered by a wider regional outlook. Where such a comprehensive settlement is achieved, any possible alternatives will become less attractive and autonomy regimes will indeed be mechanisms of stabilisation and integration. This is not to make a tautological argument along the lines of 'autonomy only succeeds in the absence of viable alternatives'. Rather, the point is that in situations where there is no alternative to the preservation of an existing state's territorial integrity, carefully designed autonomy and self-governance regimes can provide the institutional structures that offer sufficient space to non-dominant groups to experience genuine self-governance, while simultaneously making dominant groups less insecure about the future existence of the overall state. In other words, introducing genuine and generous autonomy and self-governance structures can mean the difference between prolonged and violent ethnic conflict and peaceful interethnic coexistence.

Index

272 *Index*

Lightning Source UK Ltd.
Milton Keynes UK

176097UK00001B/25/P

9 780415 339865